Carl-Ludwig Holtfrerich

The German Inflation 1914–1923

Carl-Ludwig Holtfrerich

The German Inflation 1914–1923

Causes and Effects in International Perspective

Translated by Theo Balderston

Walter de Gruyter · Berlin · New York 1986

Dr. Carl-Ludwig Holtfrerich
Professor at the Freie Universität Berlin
John-F.-Kennedy-Institut für Nordamerikastudien

Dr. Theo Balderston
University of Manchester
Department of History

Library of Congress Cataloging in Publication Data

Holtfrerich, Carl-Ludwig:
The German inflation, 1914–1923.
Translation of: Die deutsche Inflation 1914–1923.
Bibliography: p.
Includes indexes.
1. Inflation (Finance)–Germany–History. I. Title.
HG999.H7313 1986 332.4′1′0943 86-11567
ISBN 0-89925-206-0 (U.S.)

CIP-Kurztitelaufnahme der Deutschen Bibliothek

Holtfrerich, Carl-Ludwig:
The German inflation 1914–1923 : causes and effects in internat. perspective / Carl-Ludwig Holtfrerich. Transl. by Theo Balderston. – Berlin ; New York : de Gruyter, 1986.
Einheitssacht.: Die deutsche Inflation 1914–1923 <engl.>
ISBN 3-11-009714-1

 – Typesetting and Printing: Tutte Druckerei GmbH, Salzweg-Passau. Binding: D. Mikolai, Berlin. – Cover Design: K. Lothar Hildebrand, Berlin. – Printed in Germany

Table of Contents

List of Tables

List of Diagrams

List of Abbreviations and Conventions

Bd. Bde.	*Band, Bände* (i.e. volume, volumes)
bn.	billion, used in this work to signify one thousand millions
Heft, Hefte	issue, issues (as of a periodical)
Nr.	*Nummer* (i.e. number)
trillion	used in this work to signify one million millions
ff.	at least the two following pages (also volumes or years)

Acknowledgments

From among the many who have assisted, enriched and made possible the research for this book I have space here to mention only a few persons and institutions who deserve particular thanks. The Free University of Berlin, where I was in post while the research was being done, provided generous research facilities and assisted my archival trips financially. Colleagues in the *Arbeitsbereich Wirtschafts- und Sozialgeschichte* (Dept. of Economic and Social History) stimulated my thinking on many points and kept alive the quantum of resolution that persistence in a large study project always needs. I must mention particularly Prof. Drs. W. Fischer and Dr. H. Kiesewetter, whose desk for many years was adjacent to mine. Prof. Dr. D. Lorenz of Berlin and Prof. G. D. Feldman of Berkeley read the manuscript before it went to print and made numerous useful suggestions for its improvement.

A one-year trip to the U. S. A. in 1975/6, spent at the Center for European Studies, Cambridge, Mass., and in various U. S. archives, proved especially fruitful: the trip was made possible by a J. F. Kennedy Fellowship from Harvard University. Among my American colleagues there I am above all indebted to Prof. Stephen A. Schuker. In numerous conversations and discussions he shared with me his rich understanding of the period and eased my path to the source material by his virtually inexhaustible knowledge of the archives. The *Deutsche Forschungsgemeinschaft* generously supported my periods of research in European archives. In the final stages of preparation the enthusiastic cooperation of secretarial colleagues of the *Arbeitsbereich*, particularly Frau H. Siesslack, deserves especial gratitude.

As against the German original of the book (1980) I have incorporated some of the more recent literature into the English version. Some references to standard textbooks in English were added. I have also made minor corrections and additions.

I am indebted to *Internationes*, Bonn, for providing the funds for the English translation. Dr. Theo Balderston of the University of Manchester who translated the book deserves a special note of my gratitude, not only for breaking the language barrier, but for doing so with a complete understanding of my arguments.

Berlin-Dahlem, April 1985 *Carl-Ludwig Holtfrerich*

Introduction

The Current State of Research

Three standard works, namely, those by Frank D. Graham,[1] Costantino Bresciani-Turroni,[2] and Karsten Laursen and Jørgen Pedersen,[3] reflect the character of existing research on the course, causes and consequences of the German inflation of 1914–1923. They have the following in common:

(1) They were all written by non-Germans, were published outside Germany and have not been translated into German. Despite the extraordinary importance of the inflation in German history, and the long shadow it has cast over subsequent events, the literature generated by German economic historians about the period is, to date, rather slight.

(2) They all confine their attention to the period following the First World War, without due regard to the fact that the origins of the postwar inflation lay in the financial policy of the Reich during the War itself.

(3) They were all written by economists with primarily theoretical interests.

(4) Historical and archival source material that could provide information concerning the intentions of contemporary makers of economic policy, and the process of decision-making, was either not consulted by these authors, or was not then available for them to consult.

The differences between the three works relate above all to the theories underlying their explanations of the postwar inflationary process. Graham and Bresciani-Turroni employed theories which were already being debated during the inflation itself. Graham inclined towards the so-called "balance of payments theory", regarding a factor external to Germany, the reparations demands made by the victorious powers, as a major cause of the external depreciation of the mark, in turn causing the internal price inflation. Bresciani-Turroni, on the other hand, favored a "quantity theory" explanation of both

---

1 Frank D. Graham: *Exchange, Prices and Production in Hyper-Inflation: Germany, 1920–1923* (New York, 1930, reprinted 1967).

2 Costantino Bresciani-Turroni: *The Economics of Inflation. A Study of Currency Depreciation in Post-War Germany* (London, 1937, reprinted 1968). First published in Italian, 1931. Bresciani-Turroni had eyewitness experience of the inflation and as an official of the Reparations Commission had access to unpublished sources of information.

3 Karsten Laursen und Jørgen Pedersen: *The German Inflation 1918–1923* (Amsterdam, 1964).

the internal and the external currency depreciation, and hence regarded domestic economic policy as the chief cause of the inflation.[4] Writing after the so-called "Keynesian Revolution", Laursen and Pedersen invoked a wages-led "cost push" hypothesis to explain the rise of prices in Germany between 1918 and 1923, and in the tradition of Keynes they cast the money supply in a rather passive, accommodating role. Both Graham and Laursen/Pedersen emphasized the positive effects of the inflation upon growth and employment, as having contributed to the social pacification of the Weimar Republic in its early stages.[5] Bresciani-Turroni, on the other hand, stressed the distortions in the economic structure induced by the frantic "flight into real values" and the hectic investment activity of the inflation period, distortions that came fully to light only in the form of structural unemployment and the need for wide-scale rationalization after the stabilization.[6] Laursen and Pedersen argued that the inflation not only enlarged the national income available for distribution but also, through its tendency to promote full employment, caused that income to be more equally distributed than it would have been under policies orientated towards currency stability, such as those which in other countries were precipitating the depression of 1920–1921.[7] Against this Bresciani-Turroni maintained that the great German inflation effected a "revolution of the social classes" during which inequality actually increased. A few who knew how to concentrate the nation's wealth in their hands benefited whilst millions were reduced to poverty.[8]

These markedly contradictory assessments of the causes and the consequences of the German inflation after the Great War reflect not only the

[4] D.H. Robertson, the well known British monetary economist, who otherwise admired Bresciani-Turroni's study, believed the chief weakness of its argument to lie in the fact that the author placed the responsibility for the inflation entirely on the shoulders of the German politicians. Bresciani-Turroni did not "deal as they deserve with those victorious Powers whose blind rapacity helped to impose on the leaders of the young Republic a task so manifestly beyond their strength. I for one feel... that in this single but important respect his book lacks balance." D.H. Robertson, "C. Bresciani-Turroni: The Economics of Inflation...", review article in *Economica*, 5 (1938), p. 234.

[5] In his contribution, "Die Rolle der Staatsfinanzen für den Inflationsprozess", in Deutsche Bundesbank (ed.): *Währung und Wirtschaft in Deutschland 1876–1975* (Frankfurt/M., 1976) Heinz Haller goes so far as to judge, "The survival of parliamentary democracy was, I repeat, the great positive consequence of the inflation" (p. 152).

[6] C. Bresciani-Turroni: *Economics of Inflation*, pp. 403–404, 195ff.

[7] K. Laursen and J. Pedersen: *German Inflation*, pp. 120–123.

[8] C. Bresciani-Turroni: *Economics of Inflation*, p. 404. In his foreword to this book Lionel Robbins even advanced the subsequently popularized thesis: "Hitler is the foster-child of the inflation" (p. 5).

differing theoretical starting points of their authors but also the inadequate state of empirical research into the economic and social processes of the inflation period. Existing compilations of historical statistics for the German economy generally leave gaps for the years 1914–23.[9] The historian Gerald Feldman has summarily designated the inflation "a historical desert with few oases,"[10] and has called upon historical research to move beyond explanation simply in terms of economic theory towards treatment of the political causes and consequences.[11] The economic historian Knut Borchardt has likewise warned against treating the 1914–1923 inflation simply as a "mechanical breakdown in the capitalist economy." "On the contrary, it is primarily a political phenomenon," one which it is possible to judge only after taking into account "what alternative prescriptions lay to hand."[12] Peter-Christian Witt has also urged that the purely economistic manner of viewing the inflationary events of 1914–1923 be abandoned, and that the discussion of monetary policy be restored "to its proper context, that of the totality of the decision-

---

[9] Cp. Walther G. Hoffmann *et al.*: *Das Wachstum der deutschen Wirtschaft seit der Mitte des 19. Jahrhunderts* (Berlin, 1965). Statistisches Bundesamt, *Bevölkerung und Wirtschaft 1872–1972* (Stuttgart, 1972), pp. 87 ff.

[10] Gerald D. Feldman: " Gegenwärtiger Forschungsstand und künftige Forschungsprobleme zur deutschen Inflation", in Otto Büsch and Gerald D. Feldman (eds.): *Historische Prozesse der deutschen Inflation 1914 bis 1924. Ein Tagungsbericht* (Berlin, 1978), p. 3.

[11] *Ibid.*, pp. 10, 18. Feldman himself is the distinguished author of several comprehensive studies of the interplay of political forces during the inflation years. Cp. his books: *Army, Industry, and Labor in Germany, 1914–1918* (Princeton, 1966), *Iron and Steel in the German Inflation, 1916–1923* (Princeton, 1977), and, with Heidrun Homburg: *Industrie und Inflation. Studien und Dokumente zur Politik der deutschen Unternehmer 1916–1923* (Hamburg, 1977). See also the results of a five-year interdisciplinary and international research project, "Inflation and Reconstruction in Germany and Europe, 1914–1924", initiated by G. D. Feldman, C.-L. Holtfrerich, G. A. Ritter and P.-C. Witt and financed by the Stiftung Volkswagenwerk, Hannover, from 1978 to 1983. G. D. Feldman, C.-L. Holtfrerich, G. A. Ritter and P.-C. Witt (eds.): *The German Inflation Reconsidered. A Preliminary Balance* (Berlin, 1982), and *The Experience of Inflation. International and Comparative Studies* (Berlin, 1984). Further collections of essays and monographs with results of the research project will be forthcoming.
On the political aspects of inflation and stabilization, see the wide ranging and exhaustive study by Charles S. Maier: *Recasting Bourgeois Europe. Stabilization in France, Germany and Italy in the Decade after World War I* (Princeton, 1975). The following study also deals with the political dimension, but molds it into a crude conspiracy theory: Agnete von Specht, *Politische und wirtschaftliche Hintergründe der deutschen Inflation 1918–1923* (Frankfurt/M., 1982).

[12] Knut Borchardt: "Die Erfahrung mit Inflationen in Deutschland", in J. Schlemmer (ed.): *Enteignung durch Inflation? Fragen der Geldwertstabilität* (Munich, 1972), p. 17. The political dimension of inflation, especially the political representation of economic interests, has recently attracted increasing attention from economists. Cp. the collection of essays in Fred Hirsch and John H. Goldthorpe (eds.): *The Political Economy of Inflation* (London, 1978).

making process in the realm of financial politics," in order that the underlying political decisions may be adequately analyzed.[13]

Objectives of the Present Study

The aims of the present work may be deduced from the above. It is intended as a contribution towards filling out the inadequate historiographical picture of the German inflation in certain specialist areas. But it is not simply intended as this: in addition to the specialist research it aims to provide a more general overview of the actual phenomenon of the inflation, its causes and its consequences. Taking into account the criticisms of the existing standard works that have been discussed above, and the more recently formulated research desiderata, I have considered it especially important to place emphasis on four areas: firstly, to incorporate consideration of the war years in which the inflationary financial policy had its origin; secondly, to move beyond narrowly economic explanations of the inflationary developments and take into account the foreign and domestic political factors which helped to shape the economic changes; thirdly, to make some contribution toward closing the gaps in our statistical knowledge of the German inflation; and fourthly and not least, to examine the inflationary developments in Germany in their international context and from a comparative international perspective.

Consideration of the international 'dimension' is essential for the very reason that monetary and related economic developments within Germany did not occur in isolation from the world outside. Because Germany was one of the world's major industrial economies, the effects of her inflationary policies were felt abroad, and influenced the path taken by the world economy. Conversely, political decisions and the course of economic events abroad affected the course of economic (and political) change in Germany; at the very least they helped to place limits upon the range of feasible options open to German economic policy. Other countries' policies towards Germany on the reparations issue, foreign trade and foreign lending provide clear examples of this. But even the more specifically internal decisions of major foreign states, as they sought to implement monetary and fiscal policy and control the domestic

[13] Peter-Christian Witt: "Finanzpolitik und sozialer Wandel in Krieg und Inflation 1918–1924", in H. Mommsen, D. Petzina, B. Weisbrod (eds.): *Industrielles System und politische Entwicklung in der Weimarer Republik* (Düsseldorf, 1974), p. 397.

trade cycle, also had repercussions on the economic parameters of the course of events within Germany.

Furthermore, there are logical grounds for asserting that international comparisons form an indispensable part of this study. Such comparisons serve as a means of separating out from the mass of causal relationships which, even in the economic sphere alone, weave in and out of the historical process, those factors and those effects which are to be related specifically to the inflation itself. Many of the economic, social and political problems that surfaced in the postwar world were common to countries undergoing quite different currency experiences: such similarities can even be discerned between polar cases, such as Britain, where deflation ruled after 1919, and Germany, with her inflation. Problems of reconstruction and reconversion of the economy from wartime to peacetime production emerged after the Armistice in every country which had been directly or indirectly involved in the war economy, and policies with a variety of implications for currency stability were employed to solve them. Franz Eulenburg, in his pioneer study of the social effects of the inflation, warned long ago of the danger of constructing "complex chains of causal connections which trace every alteration of the social structure back to the single factor" of the currency and its manipulation. The question should rather be "How much of the final outcome is to be attributed to the currency alone and how much to the other causes?"[14] Eulenburg was skeptical of the value of international comparison as a means of solving this problem, however, "since conditions generally differ so much, as for example, between Britain and Germany."[15] However, it seems to me that international comparisons (along with intertemporal ones) offer the only practical method of avoiding sheer arbitrariness in identifying the causes and effects of the inflation. It goes without saying that in dealing with so multifaceted a historical process as inflation it is not always possible to proceed in a strictly systematic fashion, still less to confine oneself to the tools of econometric analysis. Instead when developments abroad offer interesting and relevant contrasts with or parallels to developments in Germany, they will be drawn on illustratively and descriptively as a means of elucidating the German developments and of confirming the explanation offered for them. This seems the best course of action, the more so since a systematic comparison of the inflationary developments following the First World War already exists in the outstanding League

---

[14] Franz Eulenburg: "Die sozialen Wirkungen der Währungsverhältnisse", in *Jahrbücher für Nationalökonomie und Statistik,* 122 (1924), p. 749.

[15] *Ibid.*

of Nations study by Ragnar Nurkse,[16] and we possess Phillip Cagan's econometric comparison of the experience of hyperinflation in seven twentieth century economies.[17]

The investigation that follows is arranged in three parts. Part One offers a statistical account of the German inflation. Following today's definition of inflation, it charts the process of continuously rising prices, and of the currency's persistent loss of external and internal purchasing power; it also charts the process of monetary expansion itself – which was more central to the original and contemporary usage of the word.[18] This part of the book is dominated by discussion of the statistical problems encountered in measuring inflationary phenomena, and will be of interest mainly to economists. Readers who are more interested in the inflation's political aspects and its consequences may safely commence their reading with Part Two.

The subject of this second part is the causation of the inflation. It deals with the economic factors which initiated, influenced and constrained the history of inflation; behind these with the underlying political determinants. In particular it examines the financial policies of the Reich during and after the war, and the effect of the Reparations problem on the rate of inflation; it investigates the credit policies of the Reichsbank and the political constraints under which that institution acted. It explores the constraints upon real supply which contributed from that side to the "inflationary gap" on the goods market and lastly it deals with the problem of "confidence in the currency" – i.e. in the stability of its future purchasing power – and the impact of this politically sensitive variable upon short run variations in the course of inflation.

Part Three deals with the effects of the inflation – especially on growth and employment and hence, on the size and the distribution of national income. It also examines the way in which the German inflation stimulated economic activity in other countries, particularly during the world slump of 1920–21, and shows that the postwar inflation effected a redistribution of wealth from the rest of the world to Germany on a scale scarcely less than that associated with the German capital imports of the second half of the 1920s: this inter-

[16] Ragnar Nurkse: *The Course and Control of Inflation. A Review of Monetary Experience in Europe after World War I* (Geneva, 1946).

[17] Phillip Cagan: "The Monetary Dynamics of Hyperinflation", in M. Friedman (ed.): *Studies in the Quantity Theory of Money* (Chicago, 1956), pp. 25–117.

[18] On the evolving connotations of the word compare Kurt Singer: "Inflation", in the *Handwörterbuch der Staatswissenschaften*, vol. 5 (Jena, 1923), pp. 444–445; also Friedrich Bendixen: *Das Inflationsproblem* (Stuttgart, 1917), pp. 11–13, and Fritz Neumark: *Begriff und Wesen der Inflation* (Jena, 1922), pp. 11 ff.

national redistributive effect is critical to any overall assessment of the inflationary process.

The book ends with a survey of the ultimately inevitable stabilization measures and of the revaluation legislation which attempted to correct retrospectively some distributional consequences of the inflation.

In this work I have sought to avoid one-sided theoretical interpretations, and to take into account in my discussion as broad a spectrum as possible of causes and consequences. The reader is thus given the opportunity of picking out and evaluating those causes and consequences which seem of most importance to him, as judged by his particular scale of preferences. Ultimately, judgments about the desirability or otherwise of the various effects of the inflation are value judgments, and have in turn implications for the reader's assessment of the various theoretical accounts of the inflation's causes. If for example the short run effects of inflation on growth and employment score high in his scale of values, so high as to outweigh the perhaps negatively assessed allocative or distributional effects, then he is likely to prefer theoretical interpretations such as Laursen and Pedersen's. On the one hand, they emphasize the beneficial effects of the inflationary process. On the other hand, they see this process rather as the outcome of the conjuncture of circumstances than as the product of an evil intention, rather as the result of "a lack of policy" than of deliberate strategy.[19] This viewpoint obviously serves to excuse the contemporary policy makers for the less favored effects of inflation.

Those, in contrast, who judge the inflation to have been an avoidable evil will then have to relate the costs of combating it to the benefits of stabilization, and this too involves them in value judgments. This class of reader will tend to prefer theoretical interpretations in which the cost appears tolerable relative to the benefit. Suppose for example that there is theoretical support both for the proposition that inflation can be combated by measures to improve the balance of payments (e.g. mobilizing long-term foreign loans) and for the proposition that it can be combated by reductions in public expenditure; suppose further that the costs of the former measures are thought tolerable in relation to the benefits of stabilization, but the social implications of the latter are thought too high a price to pay: – then such readers will naturally be drawn, following Graham, to the 'balance of payments' theory of the inflation. Strict 'quantity theory' interpretations such as Bresciani-Turroni's will, lastly, be preferred by those in whose eyes the social benefits outweigh the social costs of stabilization through cuts in the budget, even considering the precarious internal and external political conditions that followed the First World War.

---

[19] K. Laursen and J. Pedersen: *German Inflation*, p. 123.

That this was evidently the value judgment of those responsible for Great Britain's financial and monetary policy after the war is revealed by her early decision in favor of deflation; not without cause has the quantity theory sometimes been designated the "English" theory.[20]

Thus inflation can be viewed as the final "output" of a political, social and economic "production process", and, like the production volume of a manufacturing plant, as the result of a variety of "inputs". The determination of the rate of inflation is then analogous to the problem of controlling the rate at which a machine produces. Different methods of control are possible – for example varying the power supply, or – with the power supply unchanged – merely adjusting the rate of feed from the previous stage of production. While both methods achieve the same ends, the decision between them will depend on the costs associated with each. But – to return to the inflation – since in the sphere of social relations there exists no objective measure of cost and benefit, the process of deciding between theories of inflation and their associated policy prescriptions can never be simply one of checking their formal adequacy, logical consistency and empirical relevance; subjective valuations must inevitably play a large part as well.

[20] C. Bresciani-Turroni: *Economics of Inflation,* p. 46.

Part One
Statistical Measures and their Problems

Chapter 1
Classifying Inflations

Inflations may be classified by the causes ascribed to them, and designated for example, "cost push", "demand pull" or "imported" inflation.[1] Alternatively they may be classified by the form they take, and described as "open" or "suppressed". Whether "open" or "suppressed", all major inflations necessarily imply the existence of excess demand on the goods market: other names for this are an "inflationary gap" or "goods gap". The dynamics producing this gap always arise in practice from the demand side. Theoretically the gap could originate from the supply side – through, for example, the disturbing effects of war on real output. But the necessary supply-side precondition for continuously rising prices (assuming aggregate monetary demand to be constant) would be the continuous contraction of production, and although wars do precipitate large discrete reductions in output these do not in practice become cumulative. Thus in all cases of historical significance inflation has been associated with an increase of aggregate demand at current prices that outstrips the growth of aggregate real supply and is related to a continuous expansion of the money supply. This is what the word "inflation" originally signified: a "blowing out" of the money supply and of aggregate monetary demand.

What distinguishes an *open* inflation, in empirical terms, is the evidence of prices rising continuously over a considerable period.[2] In such a case the rising

---

[1] A convenient classification is provided by Otmar Issing: *Einführung in die Geldtheorie* (Munich, 3rd edn. 1977). Amongst English introductions to the theory of inflation are: John S. Flemming: *Inflation* (Oxford, 1976), and James A. Trevithick and Charles Mulvey: *The Economics of Inflation* (London, 1975).

[2] Artur Woll: *Allgemeine Volkswirtschaftslehre* (Munich, 5th edn. 1976), p. 369. Some writers include so-called "profit inflation" (or, "relative inflation") in the "open" inflation category, even though under certain circumstances this may be associated with price stability: for example, other things being equal, when the rate of wage increase is less than the rate of productivity increase. In this case the trend followed by costs diverges from that followed by selling prices, to the benefit of profit margins. Cp. Herbert Giersch: "Inflation: Die 'Gewinninflation'", *Handwörterbuch der Sozialwissenschaften* (Stuttgart, 13 vol. 1956–1968), vol. 5 (1956), p. 282. In the interests of clarity I leave such cases, which cannot be ascribed to a widening gap between monetary demand and real supply, out of consideration. Short term cyclical increases in the price level, insofar as they are counterbalanced in the short or medium term by corresponding falls in the price level, are likewise not regarded as inflationary phenomena.

prices will of themselves tend to close the inflationary gap. On the one hand they will tend to absorb the excess demand and on the other to attract additional supplies on to the market. However the power of this tendency will be contingent upon the state of market expectations about future price change. If the transactors on the goods market expect a fall in the price level, or even just a deceleration in the rate of price increase, the tendency just described will operate so much the more powerfully: moderate price rises and moderate increases in real supply will prove sufficient to close the "goods gap". But if the market expects the upwards price "push" to accelerate, then the initial price rise will trigger off still greater increases in monetary demand ("flight into real values") and still greater contraction of the real supply reaching the goods market. Excess demand and the inflationary dynamic will intensify.

Under "open" inflation the measurement of changes in the price level is obviously of central significance, and a variety of indicators has been used to do this, depending on the precise purpose of the investigation. Among these are the implicit GNP deflator, the wholesale and retail price indexes. The external parity of the currency, too, has frequently been employed as a measure not only of the currency's international but also of its domestic purchasing power.[3] Today the cost-of-living index would usually be considered the most appropriate index[4] because the achievement of long term cost-of-living stability has become a principal aim of present day economic policy (the whole population being consumers, instability in the cost of living affects everybody). Once the rate of price change has been measured, 'open' inflations can be classified more finely according to their severity: creeping inflation (up to 10% p.a.), "cantering" (10%–50% p.a.), galloping (above 50% p.a.) and hyperinflation (above 50% per month).

When the state intervenes to exert direct influence on prices which were previously determined freely by market forces, we are dealing with "suppressed" inflation. The state may do this for example to prevent shortages of basic foodstuffs from causing their prices to rise; however the same principle is at work when private sector monopolists do not raise prices unless they can refer to increased production costs or parallel cost-of-living rises as public justification for their action.[5] What distinguishes "suppressed" inflation is the

---

[3] Especially in cases where other indicators are not available as for example in the bullion controversy in early 19th century England. Cp. Frank W. Fetter: *The Development of British Monetary Orthodoxy 1797–1875* (Cambridge, Mass. 1965), pp. 27–28.

[4] On the history of the definition and method of measuring inflation, see Harald Scherf: "Inflation", *Handwörterbuch der Wirtschaftswissenschaften* (Stuttgart, 10 vols. 1977–83), vol. 4 (1978), p. 159.

[5] H. Giersch: "Inflation", p. 285. Behavior of this sort was displayed to some extent by iron and

existence of "official" prices which are below market-clearing equilibrium prices. The consequence is a "goods gap" which suppliers experience as lengthening order books, abnormal delivery delays, queues and vanishing stocks of saleable finished goods, and which buyers experience as unintended accumulation of monetary assets. This accumulation of monetary assets is sometimes referred to as the "monetary overhang" and is observable in the increased ratio of cash balances to income – in other words as a reduction in the velocity of circulation.[6] "Suppressed inflation" is the same thing as "cash balance inflation" and may be present even when no price increases are observable. This may be illustrated by a simple application of Irving Fisher's so-called "equation of exchange":

$$M \cdot \frac{1}{k} = Y_r \cdot P \qquad \text{where } \frac{1}{k} = V$$

M = the stock of money; V = the income velocity of circulation; k = the observed proportion between cash balances and money national income; Y_r = real national income; P = the price level.
Expressing this in terms of rates of change, we have:

$$\dot{M} - \dot{k} = \dot{Y}_r + \dot{P}$$

where the dot over the variable denotes rate of change.
In this notation pure price inflation is present where

$$\dot{k} = O; \qquad \text{and hence} \qquad \dot{P} = \dot{M} - \dot{Y}_r > O$$

Pure cash balance inflation is present where

$$\dot{P} = O; \qquad \text{and hence} \qquad \dot{k} = \dot{M} - \dot{Y}_r > O$$

and finally mixed price and cash balance inflation is present where

$$\dot{P}, \dot{k} > O$$

Suppressed inflation usually originates with the imposition of maximum prices. In the early stages these do not need to be reinforced by controls of the sales volumes (e. g. rationing or the enforcement of quotas). However once

steel industrialists during 1919/20. Cp. Gerald D. Feldman: *Iron and Steel in the German Inflation 1916–23* (Princeton, 1977), pp. 88 ff.

6 H. Jörg Thieme: "Inflation in westlichen Marktwirtschaften und östlichen Planwirtschaften", *List Forum*, 9 (1977/78), p. 293.

the "goods gap" has widened to the extent that the demand for commodities can no longer be satisfied, even by substitute products, and monetary overhang in buyers' hands has reached such proportions that they seek all means to reduce it, quantitative controls on demand become unavoidable. A variety of systems – for example the distribution of ration cards to consumers or the assigning of consumers to specific retailers – are used to displace the price system as the allocative mechanism in the goods market. Money remains the formal unit of account, but loses much of its function as a means of exchange. As administrative controls intensify in particular markets, and as the spread of supply scarcities causes an increasing number of previously uncontrolled markets to be brought within their orbit, the "market economy" itself becomes transformed into a "centrally administered economy". This transformation is not without cost. Incentives become distorted and this distorts the structure of production; producers are induced to skimp the quality of controlled goods and services and to work the more basic commodities up into luxuries which may be sold on the remaining uncontrolled markets. Hoarding increases. Bottlenecks in production and distribution are reflected in the mushrooming of queues. A costly administrative apparatus develops to manage and police the system. The emergence of black markets (illegal money transactions in controlled goods) and grey markets (illegal barter of controlled goods) signalizes the onset of advanced stages of suppressed inflation.

Whereas, then, a continuously rising price level is evidence of an "open" inflation, a "suppressed" inflation may be detected from the behavior of the following variables.

1. The length of delivery periods.
2. The relationship between the price of controlled and uncontrolled commodities.
3. The relationship between official and black market prices for controlled commodities.
4. The level and rate of increase of savings deposits – both absolutely and in relation to other variables such as retail turnover.
5. Change in the velocity of circulation of money, as evidence of "monetary overhang".

Chapter 2
Price and Purchasing Power Movements

2.1. Exchange Rates and Wholesale Prices

When contemporaries sought evidence about the rate of price inflation the indicators they chiefly relied on were those pertaining to movements of the external exchange rate and of wholesale and retail prices. The first obviously measured changes in the mark's international purchasing power, the second and third measured changes in its domestic purchasing power. Retail price statistics had been relatively undeveloped in Germany before the First World War.[1] With the coming of war and inflation however, and the increasing institutionalization of wage bargaining, demands increased from employers and workers alike for reliable measures of the purchasing power of the working-class household, to be used as a basis for negotiating collective wage agreements. This forced government statistical offices to improve the retail price statistics they could supply, with the result that the inflation period became formative in the development of German cost-of-living statistics. Because of its importance this development is discussed separately in section 2.2.

Movements in wholesale prices had been investigated by the Imperial Statistical Office (after 1918, Reich Statistical Office) since 1879; but all that had been done was to record and publish separately the prices of about forty commodities.[2] This primitive approach was only beginning to be improved by the end of our period: a proper weighting scheme was officially adopted in 1921 (and used to recalculate the pre-1921 values retrospectively). Not until after 1923 however was the range of commodities used for compiling the index enlarged to conform to present-day standards.[3] The wholesale price index reacted more sharply than the indexes of retail prices to changes in market conditions – especially after the end of the war. This was because the prices entering the retail indexes – particularly foodstuffs prices – were still strictly controlled, whereas at the wholesale stage prices were freer. In ad-

[1] Cp. Statistisches Bundesamt: *Bevölkerung und Wirtschaft...*, p. 28.

[2] *Ibid.*

[3] 400 commodities in 1926; in subsequent years up to 1000.

dition, domestic wholesale prices were also more sensitive than retail prices to change in world market conditions.

However the most sensitive index of changes – actual and anticipated – in a currency's purchasing power is its price in the foreign currency markets. This index reflects primarily changes in international purchasing power and operates provided that exchange rates are flexible and subject to only limited official intervention. This was largely true of the mark and other leading currencies in the early postwar years. Today it is customary to use a trade-weighted index of foreign currency quotations, as expressed in the domestic currency, to measure the domestic currency's changing international value. In the period we are considering the international depreciation of the mark was measured simply by its dollar exchange rate. There are a number of reasons why in those days the dollar rate was the accepted yardstick of movements of floating currencies. The dollar had been more continuously on the gold standard than any other currency, convertibility having been suspended only for the brief period when the U. S. A. was actually at war (1917–1919). Moreover the U. S. A. had emerged from the war as the world's predominant power economically and financially, and international currency reserves were increasingly held in dollars rather than in sterling.[4]

Table 1 compares the monthly movements of the German wholesale price index with those of the dollar rate on the Berlin foreign exchange market over the entire period 1914–1923. Both are expressed to base 1913 = 1. A striking feature of the comparison during the war years is the way in which the rise in the dollar rate lagged behind the rise in the wholesale price index. In this the effects of exchange controls on international transactions may be seen: the purpose of these controls was to prevent a visible decline in the international value of the mark.[5]

This exchange control policy reflected real economic priorities. The problem during the war years was not primarily one of gaining overseas markets; the state's insatiable demands for war matériel eliminated all "overproduction" problems. Rather it was one of securing the imports essential to the war effort at the best (i. e. lowest) possible prices. Priorities changed after the war

[4] William Adams Brown: *The International Gold Standard Reinterpreted 1914–34* (New York, 2 vols. 1940), vol. 1, pp. 146ff.

[5] Robert Liefmann: *Die Geldvermehrung im Weltkriege und die Beseitigung ihrer Folgen* (Berlin, 1918), esp. chapter 7, "Die Regelung des Devisen- und ausländischen Effektenverkehrs im Weltkriege", pp. 123–139. H. Kleine-Natrop: *Devisenpolitik in Deutschland vor dem Kriege und in der Kriegs- und Nachkriegszeit* (Berlin, 1922), pp. 12ff. Recently, R. Kühne: *Die Devisenzwangswirtschaft im Deutschen Reich während der Jahre 1916 bis 1926. Eine währungspolitische Reminiszenz* (Frankfurt/M., 1970).

Table 1. Comparative movements of the German wholesale price index and the dollar/mark exchange rate 1914–23 (1913 = 1) (E = exchange rate index; W = wholesale price index)

Month	1914 E	1914 W	1915 E	1915 W	1916 E	1916 W	1917 E	1917 W	1918 E	1918 W
January	1.002	0.96	1.10	1.26	1.27	1.50	1.38	1.56	1.24	2.04
February	1.001	0.96	1.12	1.33	1.28	1.51	1.40	1.58	1.26	1.98
March	1.000	0.96	1.15	1.39	1.32	1.48	1.39	1.59	1.24	1.98
April	0.999	0.95	1.16	1.42	1.30	1.49	1.54	1.63	1.22	2.04
May	0.999	0.97	1.15	1.39	1.24	1.51	1.56	1.63	1.22	2.03
June	0.998	0.99	1.16	1.39	1.26	1.52	1.69	1.65	1.28	2.09
July	0.999	0.99	1.17	1.50	1.31	1.61	1.70	1.72	1.38	2.08
August	0.998	1.09	1.17	1.46	1.33	1.59	1.70	2.03	1.45	2.35
September	0.997	1.11	1.16	1.45	1.37	1.54	1.72	1.99	1.57	2.30
October	1.043	1.18	1.16	1.47	1.36	1.53	1.74	2.01	1.57	2.34
November	1.097	1.23	1.18	1.47	1.38	1.51	1.65	2.03	1.77	2.34
December	1.072	1.25	1.23	1.48	1.36	1.51	1.35	2.03	1.97	2.45
Annual Average	1.017	1.05	1.16	1.42	1.32	1.52	1.57	1.79	1.43	2.17

Month	1919 E	1919 W	1920 E	1920 W	1921 E	1921 W	1922 E	1922 W	1923 E	1923 W
January	1.95	2.62	15.43	12.56	15.46	14.39	45.69	36.65	4281	2783
February	2.17	2.70	23.60	16.85	14.60	13.76	49.51	41.03	6650	5585
March	2.48	2.74	19.97	17.09	14.87	13.38	67.70	54.33	5048	4888
April	3.00	2.86	14.20	15.67	15.13	13.26	69.32	63.55	5826	5212
May	3.06	2.97	11.07	15.08	14.83	13.08	69.11	64.58	11355	8170
June	3.34	3.08	9.32	13.82	16.51	13.66	75.62	70.30	26202	19385
July	3.59	3.39	9.40	13.67	18.26	14.28	117.49	100.59	84186	74787
August	4.48	4.22	11.37	14.50	20.07	19.17	270.26	192.0	1100632	944041
									in mill.	in mill.
September	5.73	4.93	13.81	14.98	24.98	20.67	349.18	287.0	23.5	23.9
									in bn.	in bn.
October	6.39	5.62	16.23	14.66	35.76	24.60	757.73	566.0	6.0	7.1
November	9.12	6.78	18.39	15.09	62.64	34.16	1711.08	1154	522	725.7
December	11.14	8.03	17.38	14.40	45.72	34.87	1807.83	1475	1000	1261.6
Annual Average	4.70	4.15	15.01	14.86	24.91	19.11	449.21	341.82		

Source: Statistisches Reichsamt: *Zahlen zur Geldentwertung in Deutschland 1914 bis 1923* (Berlin, 1925), pp. 6, 16, 17.

was over. Domestic productive capacity could now be fully utilized only if more could be sold abroad; the securing of imports on the other hand became both less difficult and less costly once the allied blockade had been lifted in the summer of 1919 and the world economy had begun to slide into recession in 1920. These altered priorities were, not surprisingly, reflected in the relaxation of exchange controls: the centralized handling of all foreign currency transactions at the Reichsbank – required by the Foreign Exchange Decree of early 1917 – was suspended on September 11, 1919.[6] The official justification for the suspension of controls was that the so-called "hole in the west" (i. e. the unsupervised borders between France and Germany resulting from the cession of Alsace-Lorraine and the occupation of parts of western Germany) rendered them unworkable. The real grounds of the suspension are rather to be deduced from the statement of H. Kleine-Natrop when he wrote "Underlying German currency policy [sc. 'after the war'] was one basic and enduring principle, that as far as it lay in our power, circumstances and events were to be manipulated in the economic interests of our country."[7] Kleine-Natrop was a Reichsbank civil servant and so must have had inside knowledge of the matter.

After the lifting of currency controls the wartime relationship between exchange rates and wholesale price movements became reversed (see Table 1). Domestic forces – chiefly the financing of the budget deficits – continued to fuel inflation, but now the rise in the dollar rate outstripped the rise in the domestic wholesale price index.[8] Most of the commodities whose prices were used to calculate the wholesale price index were internationally tradable. It is tempting therefore to deduce changes in Germany's international competitivity directly from the relative rates of change of this index and of the dollar rate (e. g. a more rapid rise in the former than the latter signifying a deterioration in competitivity). This however is too simple. International competitivity is strictly speaking a function not of prices as such but of unit costs: hence changes in competitivity are the result of differential changes in productivity and other elements in cost. Even ignoring this refinement however two points must be considered.

Firstly, in making a simple bilateral comparison of German and U. S. competitivity the movement of U. S. wholesale prices must also be taken into

---

[6] H. Kleine-Natrop: *Devisenpolitik...* p. 27.

[7] *Ibid.* On the regulation of German foreign trade see Günther Haberland: *Elf Jahre staatlicher Regelung der Ein- und Ausfuhr. Eine systematische Darstellung der deutschen Außenhandelsregelung in den Jahren 1914–1925* (Leipzig, *1927*).

[8] With the exception of a few months in mid-1920, when the world recession was starting abroad.

account. The gold convertibility of the dollar signified only the constancy of the dollar's power to purchase gold, not of its power to purchase commodities in general. Wholesale prices had also risen in the U. S. A. between 1913 and 1920 – even if not as rapidly as in Germany[9] – and despite a decline thereafter, they remained above the 1913 level. Thus a simple comparison of the rates of increase of the dollar/mark exchange rate and the German wholesale price index understates the improvement of German competitivity vis-à-vis the U. S. economy. This point is depicted in Diagram 1.

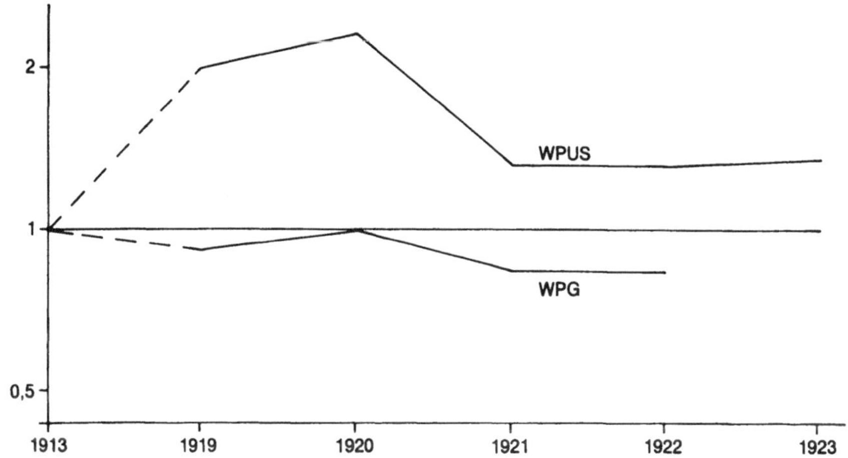

Diagram 1. Movements of German (WPG) and United States (WPUS) wholesale prices in U.S. dollars 1913–23 (Annual averages, 1913 = 1, semi-logarithmic scale)
Source: WPG Table 1; WPUS Ben J. Wattenberg: *Statistical History*..., p. 200.

In this diagram the "WPG" line represents the German wholesale price level expressed in dollars and to base 1913 = 1. It was obtained by dividing the official German wholesale price index by the current mark/dollar exchange rate after both had been converted to base 1913 = 1 (as in Table 1). From the diagram we can see that throughout the postwar inflation period the dollar equivalent of the German wholesale price index remained below its 1913 level. However the true change in German competitivity vis-à-vis the U. S. economy is more accurately measured by comparing the "WPG" line with the change in the United States' own wholesale price level since 1913 (the

[9] Ben J. Wattenberg: *The Statistical History of the United States. From Colonial Times to the Present* (New York, 1976), p. 200.

"WPUS" line); the vertical distance between the two representing Germany's competitive advantage relative to 1913.

Secondly, movements of the mark's exchange rate against the dollar are not representative of movements of its international value against all currencies. In particular its movements against other European inconvertible currencies were quite different. Diagram 2 shows the exchange rates of various currencies against the dollar. Throughout the 1919–22 period the mark/dollar exchange rate showed greater short term variability than the others;[10] nevertheless up to the middle of 1921 it followed a trend similar to the rest – even to the sterling/dollar rate. From then on – really, from the London Ultimatum of May 1921 – the trend of the mark/dollar exchange rate became sharply differentiated from the trends of other currencies' dollar rates. Up to this date the exchange movements of the mark had been shaped by the problems of coping with postwar reconstruction common to all the belligerents, whereas after May 1921 the politics of Reparations came to dominate German currency movements, causing them to follow a distinctive path.

The greater part of Germany's trade was with Europe. Since the depreciation of the mark against other European currencies was smaller than against the dollar, it follows that a trade-weighted index of the mark's international value against a "basket" of currencies will show a smaller depreciation than the simple dollar exchange rate. Such a trade-weighted index is shown in the first two columns of Table 2. The weights for combining the separate mark exchange rates against individual currencies into the index were the aggregated imports originating from, plus exports destined for, the corresponding country, expressed as a percentage of total German commodity imports plus exports, using in all cases the averages of the values for the two years 1920 and 1923. Exchange rates against the fourteen currencies possessing weights, thus calculated, in excess of 1 % were included in the basket, one version of which also included the dollar rate.[11] Following the method currently used by the Deutsche Bundesbank[12] I used the geometric mean to calculate my trade-

[10] Convenient and comprehensive tabulations of the exchange rates of all major currencies against the dollar are to be found in: Board of Governors of the Federal Reserve System: *Banking and Monetary Statistics* (Washington, D.C., 1943), pp. 662–82; also in John P. Young: *European Currency and Finance* (Washington, D.C., 1925).

[11] The shares came out as follows (in percentages); Hungary 1.000, Spain 1.545, Norway 2.120, Belgium 2.365, Austria 2.950, Italy 3.220, Sweden 3.550, Denmark 3.730, Poland 3.855, Czechoslovakia 3.950, Switzerland 4.530, France 5.250, Netherlands 9.950, Great Britain 10.110, U. S. A. 19.130. These added up to 77.2 % of German external trade (58.1 % excl. the U. S. A.).

[12] "Zur Berechnung des gewogenen Außenwerts der D-Mark", *Monatsberichte der Deutschen Bundesbank*, vol. 31, no. 4 (April 1979), pp. 22–25.

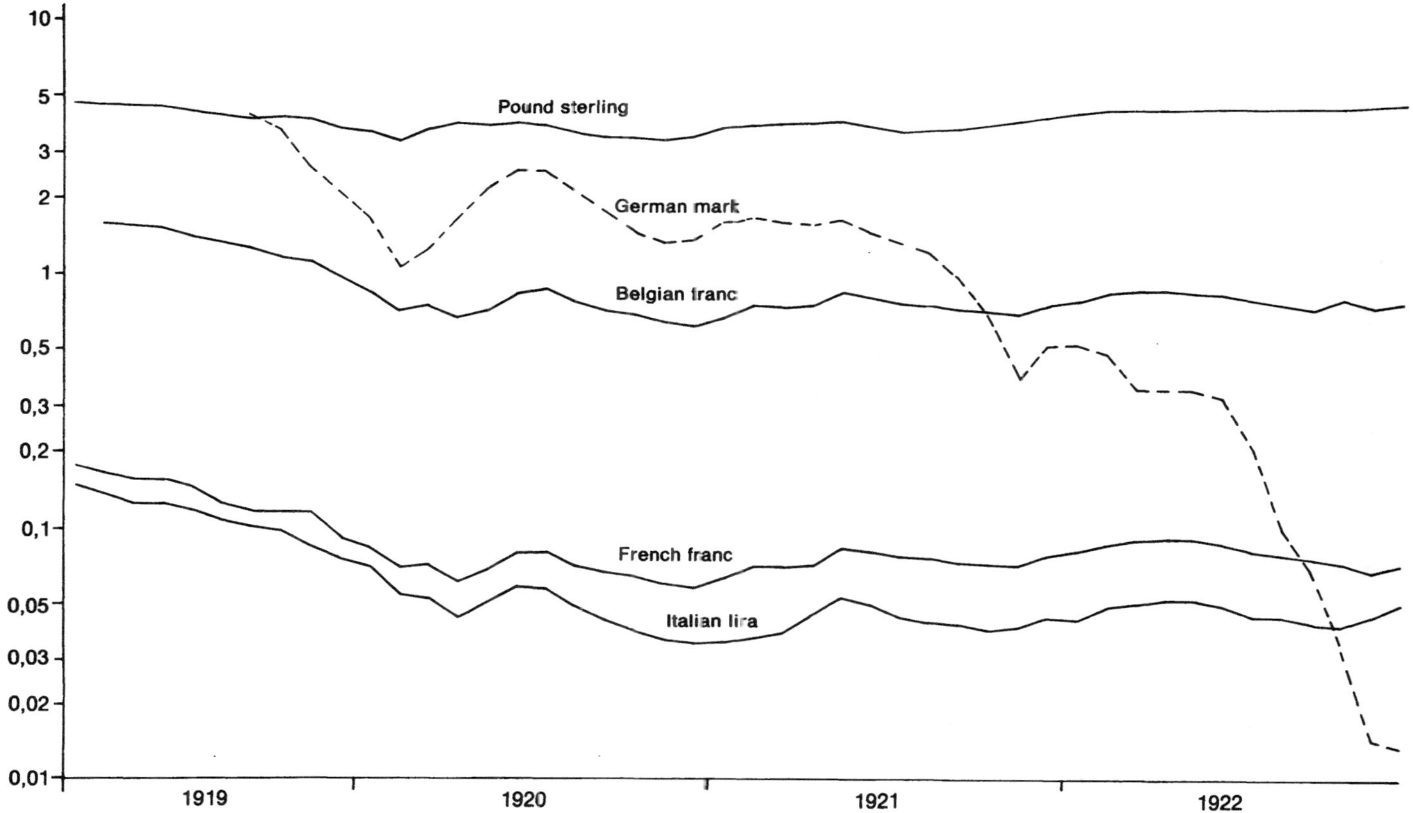

Diagram 2. Movements of average monthly prices of selected European currencies in U. S. dollars 1919–22 (semi-logarithmic scale)
Source: Board of Governors...: *Banking and Monetary Statistics* (Washington, D.C., 1943), pp. 663–681.

weighted index, having first reduced the prices of the several foreign currencies in marks to individual indexes with base 1913 = 1. In symbols:

$$T = a_1^{w_1} \cdot a_2^{w_2} \cdot \ldots \cdot a_n^{w_n}; \ \Sigma w_i = 1$$

where T is the required trade-weighted index, a_1 to a_n are the indexes of the mark prices of the several foreign currencies to base 1913 = 1, and w_1 to w_n are the weights expressed as a proportion of the aggregate weights of the fourteen or fifteen currencies in the "basket". The first column of Table 2 reproduces the monthly values of such an index when calculated against the fourteen European currencies only; the second column shows its value when calculated against these currencies plus the dollar.

A comparison of the movement of this trade-weighted index with the movement of the simple mark/dollar exchange rate recorded in Table 1 reveals at a glance how much more moderate the depreciation of the trade-weighted index was. In January 1920 for example the price of the U.S. dollar on the Berlin foreign exchange market was 15.4 times its 1913 price; the trade-weighted index of the mark prices of the fourteen European currencies was only 5.69 times its 1913 base, or 7.78 times when the index is expanded to include the dollar rate. The difference grew after the onset of hyperinflation in the summer of 1922: in December 1922 for example the dollar index reached 1808, the trade-weighted index excluding the dollar only 362.3, including the dollar only 539.4.

Our study of German competitivity with abroad must now be amended to take account of this more comprehensive measure of the exchange rate. If we relate the movements of the trade-weighted index to domestic wholesale price movements we discover a converse relationship to that between the simple mark/dollar rate and domestic wholesale prices. In January 1920 for example the German wholesale price index stood at 12.6 times its 1913 level, but the trade-weighted index of exchange rates to the same base had reached only 5.69 excluding the U.S.A., 7.78 including it. In December 1922 the wholesale price index had reached 1475, the trade-weighted indexes 362.3 or 539.4 respectively.

However it would be just as erroneous to deduce a deterioration of Germany's competitivity with abroad from this relationship as it was for contemporaries to deduce its improvement from the fact that the dollar rate rose more rapidly than domestic wholesale prices. Price developments abroad also have to be taken into account. I have therefore collected the *wholesale price indexes* for the same fourteen European countries (and the U.S.) to base 1913 = 1, and calculated their trade-weighted geometric average, both excluding and including the U.S.A., for the same period and using the same weights and formula as for the exchange rates. From the two indexes thus derived and from the German wholesale price index I formed the ratio WPG/WPA – where WPG is the German wholesale price index and WPA is the trade-weighted index of wholesale prices abroad. If the undeflated trade-weighted index of the mark's international value is then divided by this ratio, a measure of the change in the trade-weighted real external value of the mark, relative to 1913, is obtained. This is the measure shown in the third and fourth columns of Table 2, the third excluding, the fourth including consideration of the U. S. A. It is from these measures that conclusions may be drawn about changes in Germany's international competitivity: when the index exceeds

Table 2. Indexes of the undeflated and real trade-weighted value of the mark against foreign currencies 1920–23*. 1913 = 1

	Undeflated trade-weighted value of the mark against		Trade-weighted real value of the mark against	
	14 European currencies	14 European currencies and US dollar	14 European currencies	14 European currencies and US dollar
	1	2	3	4
1920				
J	5.69	7.28	2.24	2.36
F	7.86	10.32	2.40	2.57
M	7.05	9.12	2.18	2.29
A	5.19	6.66	1.82	1.89
M	4.10	5.25	1.49	1.56
J	3.68	4.63	1.43	1.47
J	3.63	4.60	1.46	1.50
A	3.89	5.07	1.50	1.57
S	4.40	5.84	1.68	1.76
O	4.92	6.61	1.93	2.01
N	5.15	7.06	1.98	2.06
D	4.80	6.61	1.88	1.93
1921				
J	4.45	6.06	1.68	1.70
F	4.37	5.90	1.66	1.64
M	4.51	6.06	1.70	1.68
A	4.76	6.33	1.74	1.71
M	4.79	6.34	1.73	1.69
J	4.90	6.62	1.69	1.67
J	4.98	6.87	1.65	1.67
A	5.28	7.35	1.33	1.35
S	6.19	8.74	1.49	1.52
O	8.68	12.3	1.75	1.80
N	15.4	21.8	2.26	2.31
D	12.0	16.7	1.75	1.75

Table 2. (continued)

	1	2	3	4
1922				
J	11.5	16.2	1.59	1.60
F	12.7	17.8	1.57	1.58
M	16.7	23.6	1.57	1.59
A	17.4	24.5	1.40	1.42
M	17.1	24.2	1.38	1.40
J	17.8	25.5	1.38	1.40
J	25.3	37.1	1.41	1.47
A	57.2	84.0	1.69	1.81
S	72.8	107.3	1.53	1.58
O	152.4	226.7	1.66	1.72
N	335.1	501.8	1.78	1.91
D	362.3	539.4	1.57	1.62
1923				
J	805.8	1218	1.93	2.01
F	1221	1857	1.54	1.59
M	918.1	1400	1.37	1.41
A	1054	1609	1.49	1.53
M	2014	3090	1.81	1.86
J	4389	6831	1.71	1.77
J	13470	21204	1.41	1.45
	in mill.	in mill.		
A	0.167	0.266	1.44	1.48
S	3.538	5.656	1.24	1.28
O	787	1303	1.025	1.067
	in bn.	in bn.		
N	66.0	110.1	0.915	0.936
D	119.5	202.2	1.011	1.036

* The indexes represent the prices in marks (undeflated and real) of the two 'baskets' of foreign currencies.

Sources: The data used to compute the above indexes were derived from the following sources: Shares in German foreign trade: *Statistisches Jahrbuch für das Deutsche Reich*, vol. 42 (1921/22), Berlin 1922, pp. 224–5; *ibid.*, vol. 44 (1924/5), Berlin 1925, pp. 175-6.
Exchange rates: Stat. Reichsamt: *Zahlen zur Geldentwertung*... pp. 12–15.
Wholesale prices: John P. Young: *European Currency and Finance* (Washington, D.C., 1925); International Conference of Economic Services (eds.): *International Abstracts of Economic Statistics* (London, 1934). The few unobtainable wholesale price data were inter- or extrapolated with the help of, e.g., the retail price index.
Method of calculation: cp. "Zur Berechnung des gewogenen Außenwerts der D-Mark", in *Monatsberichte der Deutschen Bundesbank*, vol. 31, no. 4 (April 1979), pp. 22-5; also the explanations in the text.

unity the German competitive position has improved by comparison with 1913, i.e. the increase in the mark price of foreign currencies exceeds the increase in the ratio of German to foreign wholesale prices. When the index is less than unity, the German competitive position is poorer than in 1913.

With this in mind we can interpret the third and fourth columns of Table 2. Our indicators show that throughout the period from January 1920 to October 1923 the German competitive position relative to abroad was uniformly more favorable than it had been before the war. The short term dynamics of this competitive relationship should also be noted. It can be seen that in periods of accelerating mark depreciation – such as the months following August 1921 or June 1922 – German competitive advantage showed an enlargement. Conversely in periods when the mark exchange rate appreciated – such as the months following February 1920 – Germany's competitive advantage diminished. The reasons for this are to be found in the laggardly adjustment of domestic price movements to changes on the foreign exchange market.

2.2. The Cost of Living

Index number problems

A variety of cost of living indexes was calculated during the inflation. Before attempting an evaluation of them some more general remarks should be made about the "index number problem" and its bearing upon the performance of cost-of-living indexes in times of rising prices.[1]

Essentially the problem of an index number arises because it attempts to measure a complex statistical change by a simple ratio. On the one hand the prices of the different commodities entering the "cost of living" (to take the

[1] On the "index number problem", cp. Paul Flaskämper: "Indexzahlen", in *Handwörterbuch der Sozialwissenschaften* (Stuttgart, 13 vols., 1956–1968), vol. 5 (1956), pp. 191–195. More recently, Oskar Anderson: "Indexzahlen", in *Handwörterbuch der Wirtschaftswissenschaften* (Stuttgart, 10 vols., 1977–83), vol. 4 (1978), pp. 98–108. More comprehensive and still standard works on the subject are: Gottfried Haberler: *Der Sinn der Indexzahlen* (Tübingen, 1927), and Irving Fisher: *The Making of Index Numbers. A Study of their Variety, Tests and Reliability* (Boston, 1922). See also R. G. D. Allen: *Index Numbers in Theory and Practice* (London, 1975). Specifically on the German inflation, see Costantino Bresciani-Turroni: "The Movement of Wages in Germany during the Depreciation of the Mark and after Stabilization", *Journal of the Royal Statistical Society*, 92 (1929), pp. 374–403.

example that concerns us) do not change uniformly; on the other the proportions in which these commodities are purchased are not constant. The proportion of total household expenditure devoted to each commodity changes, both as a result of influences on the demand side, such as changes in money income and tastes, and of influences on the supply side such as changes in costs of production that affect the relative price structure. These demand and supply side influences plus the appearance of new consumer goods on the market cause the range of commodities purchased by households to change. The quality of individual commodities also changes over time so that to some extent price changes reflect quality changes.

Changes in the actual cost of living are the product of both these types of change – in the prices themselves and in the quantities of goods consumed. To isolate the effects on the cost of living of change in the former variable – prices – it is logically necessary to keep the other variable – commodity composition of consumption – constant; that is, to calculate the change in the money value of a fixed "basket of goods". It is usually easier to ensure the "fixity" of the quantities of each commodity in the basket than of the quality of each commodity over time. The "basket" weights the changing prices of the separate commodities according to their proportionate representation within it: if the representation of goods whose prices are rising rapidly is increased relative to that of goods whose prices are not, the rate of increase of the overall index will accelerate. The composition of the "basket" is usually intended to reflect the actual pattern of consumption either at the start, or at the end, of the period to which the index refers: if the former, it is a "Laspeyres" index, if the latter a "Paasche" index. "Laspeyres" and "Paasche" indexes will yield different estimates of cost-of-living change during a given period: the difference is largely determined by what are called the "income effect" and the "substitution effect".

To begin with the "income effect". A general rise in real income over a given period will cause an increase in the consumption of luxury goods and services relative to the consumption of more basic commodities. If the prices of the former are rising more rapidly than the prices of the latter then (given the rise in real income) the "Paasche" index, reflecting end-of-period consumption patterns, will yield a higher estimate of the rate of cost-of-living increase than the "Laspeyres" index. If conversely the real income level and thus the relative consumption of luxury goods are falling during the period then (given the difference in price developments of luxury and basic goods) it is the "Laspeyres" index – reflecting start-of-period consumption patterns – that will yield the higher estimate.

The "substitution effect" comes into play as changes in the price structure induce changes in the pattern of consumption over the period. As the price structure changes, the tendency is that the consumption of those goods which have become relatively cheaper (i. e. whose prices have risen more slowly than others) increases at the expense of the consumption of goods becoming relatively dearer. Thus the former goods will be more strongly represented in the "Paasche" basket of goods, the latter in the "Laspeyres", and the substitution effect will always tend to cause the "Laspeyres" estimate of price change to exceed the "Paasche" estimate.

While we have illustrated the index number problem with reference to baskets of goods reflecting start-of-period or end-of-period consumption patterns, the remarks made apply equally when indexes based on baskets reflecting the consumption pattern at any point within the period are used to estimate cost-of-living change over periods with different real income levels or price structures.

It follows from these remarks that the more abrupt the changes in real income and price structure during a period, the less precisely the actual rate of cost-of-living change can be measured and the greater the variation between the estimates of this which different indexes yield. The years 1914–23 in Germany were just such a period: war, defeat, blockade and foreign protectionism, production bottlenecks caused by strikes, state controls on the economy, and extreme inflation conspired to cause dramatic shifts both in real income[2] and in the price structure, so that the problems we have been discussing are seen as if through a magnifying glass. This explains the divergences between the price indexes for the period and all the difficulties encountered in trying to reach exact conclusions about real income levels – about the relationship between the prewar and the wartime/postwar real incomes of wage earners, for example.

Assuming however that real household income during and immediately after the war was lower than it had been before 1914 and that inflation and other factors effected considerable changes in the price structure, then (given the price controls on basic goods) our discussion in this section implies that cost-of-living indexes based on baskets reflecting prewar consumption patterns must yield higher estimates of the rate of the cost-of-living increase than indexes based on baskets reflecting wartime or postwar consumption patterns.

---

[2] Cp. chapter 8, pp. 221 ff. *infra*.

Various cost-of-living indexes

How then were the actual cost-of-living indexes of the inflation period constructed and how reliable are the estimates of real income change which may be obtained with their aid?

The various cost-of-living indexes calculated during the period fall basically into three types: what distinguishes them is the method of selecting the "basket of goods".

The first type are the cost-of-living statistics produced under the aegis of the Reich Statistical Office. They were based on information collected on a nationwide scale, first published in December 1919, and then published regularly from February 1920. The basket of goods on which they were based represented only a limited range of household necessities, namely foodstuffs, domestic heating and lighting, accomodation and clothes. The selection of actual commodities corresponded to the restricted consumption possibilities of the early postwar years.

Secondly there were a variety of regional indexes such as those computed by Kuczynski and Silbergleit for Berlin and by Sköllin for Hamburg. The dietary theories of physiologists played a larger part in the formulation of the baskets of goods underlying these indexes, as did distinctive regional patterns of consumption.

Lastly there is the index of foodstuffs prices pioneered by I. Jastrow and carried on by R. Calwer. This utilized a basket of goods based on the daily foodstuffs ration of a prewar German marine. Moritz Elsas broadened the basis of this index to reflect the price movements of other consumer requirements as well, by including clothing, accommodation, heating and lighting and 'miscellaneous' expenditures.

The cost of living statistics of the Reich Statistical Office

Of available cost-of-living statistics the most comprehensive are those of the Reich Statistical Office. Based on surveys carried out in numerous communities of varying population size, they were computed at frequent intervals – at first monthly, from 1922 twice-monthly, from March 1923 weekly and then, in the final stages of the inflation, even twice weekly. The statistics were published in two forms. Firstly a "dearness statistic" (*Teuerungszahl*) represented the value in current marks of the given quantities of all items in the Reich Statistical Office's "basket of goods". Secondly, a cost-of-living index expressed the same value as a ratio of the average value of the basket in 1913/14.

Individual "dearness statistics" and cost-of-living indexes were published for all communities involved in the survey, and a cost-of-living index was also computed for the Reich as a whole.[3] This last is the index shown in Table 4. The Reich Statistical Office described its own procedure in the following terms:

"The cost-of-living statistics are based on surveys conducted in 560 local authority districts, 497 of which comprise all towns with more than ten thousand inhabitants. In each of the towns the required price information is obtained on a pre-determined date, verified as accurate by representatives of the employers and the workers, entered into the return and dispatched to the central statistical office of the state in which the town is situated. The state statistical office checks the returns and calculates the actual 'dearness statistic' for each survey district; these are then forwarded to the Reich Statistical Office. In addition, a so-called express service has been set up whereby price information collected in seventy-one local authority districts on one day in the first half and one day in the second half of each month is processed in the Reich Statistical Office itself to yield a nationwide cost-of-living index which is immediately communicated to the press and published in the periodical *Wirtschaft und Statistik*. The seventy-one districts are so selected as to include large cities, medium and small towns, some of a more industrial, others of a more rural character, from every part of the Reich. Repeated checks have confirmed that, when averaged over the seventy-one districts, the estimates of price change yielded by this method are representative for all German towns with populations in excess of ten thousand."[4]

The basket of goods that underlay both the local and the national cost-of-living statistics in this scheme was supposed to reflect the expenditure of a family of five (two adults and three children aged eighteen months, seven and twelve years respectively) on food, accommodation, heating and lighting and, from April 1922, clothing. It reflected postwar consumption patterns, and while it did not cover all household expenditure – home furnishings, transport, hygiene and personal requirements, educational and recreational outlays were omitted – it did account for 87 % of the expenditures detailed by the household surveys of 1907.[5]

---

[3] See e.g. Statistisches Reichsamt: "Teuerungsstatistik und Reichsindexziffer", in *Vierteljahrshefte zur Statistik des Deutschen Reichs*, 32 (1923), pp. 34–41.

[4] *Ibid.*, p. 33. For an assessment of the methods of the Reich cost-of-living statistics see Johannes Frenkel: "Zur Preisentwicklung der Nachkriegszeit", *Zeitschrift des Preussischen Statistischen Landesamts, 61 (1925), pp. 196–199.*

[5] Statistisches Reichsamt: "Die Reform der Reichsindexziffer für die Lebenshaltungskosten",

Table 3 shows the foodstuffs and their quantities which, with a few modifications in the course of time, were included in the Reich Statistical Office's basket of goods during the early postwar period. The remaining categories of expenditure were represented as follows. Depending on the district, the outlay on heating was represented by the cost of one hundred and fifty kilograms of hard coal or two hundred and fifty kilograms of lignite or two hundred kilograms of lignite briquettes or one hundred and fifty kilograms of coke or three hundred kilograms of peat plus three hundred kilograms of firewood or forty cubic meters of cooking gas. Outlay on lighting was represented by the cost of fifteen cubic meters of lighting gas or five kwh electricity; the cost of accommodation entered the basket as the rent for a dwelling with two rooms plus kitchen. Expenditure on clothing was included as one thirteenth of the assumed annual expenditure (because the "dearness statistic" referred to a four-week period) of a family of five: one men's and one boys' suit, one girls' dress and two women's skirts and blouses, six changes each of men's and women's underwear, six pairs of men's socks, six pairs of women's stockings, one pair each of men's and women's boots, two pairs of children's boots, and the cost of eight boot repairs (men's, soling and heeling).[6]

The early postwar family could obtain these goods from three types of sources, each with its own particular price level. Firstly there were the controlled markets for rationed goods such as bread, certain vegetables, fats, meat, sugar and milk. These markets were governed by official maximum price regulations, but the process of decontrol was reducing the range of goods obtainable in this manner, especially up until the autumn of 1921. Then secondly there were the uncontrolled markets where prices were governed by supply and demand. Thirdly there was the black market in rationed goods. The price surveys took account of price movements in this market; to this extent the black market received official recognition.[7]

The total cost of purchasing foodstuffs of the kinds and in the quantities prescribed in the basket (Table 3) was uniformly determined in each survey district and for each four-week period as follows. The first step was to ascertain the quantities currently available in each district to a family of five at official prices. If this ration fell short of the quantity prescribed in the basket it was assumed that the shortfall could be purchased on the uncontrolled or on the black market. The rations were then valued at official maximum, or actual

---

Wirtschaft und Statistik, 5 (1925) pp. 159–173. This offers a concise account of the history of the index's origins and of changes in its method of calculation.

[6] Statistisches Reichsamt: "Teuerungsstatistik und Reichsindexziffer", p. 33.

[7] Cp. pp. 87ff. *infra*.

Table 3. Foodstuffs in the basket of goods underlying the Reich Statistical Office's cost of living index 1920–25

Foodstuff	Quantity	Calorific Value	Protein Content
Rye bread	47000 g	94000	1645 g
Wheaten bread	–	–	–
Rye flour	4000 g	12240	130 g
Wheat flour	–	–	–
Pearl barley	1833 g	5499	119 g
Wheaten semolina	1833 g	5499	156 g
Rolled oats	1833 g	6599	229 g
Rice	1833 g	5866	115 g
Peas	1833 g	5316	284 g
Beans	1833 g	5224	312 g
Potatoes	70000 g	45500	945 g
Green vegetables	15000 g	2750	125 g
Boiling beef	2500 g	3000	380 g
Belly pork	500 g	1810	75 g
Mutton	–	–	–
Fat bacon (German)	1500 g	11700	41 g
Liver sausage	–	–	–
Butter (German)	–	–	–
Margarine	250 g	17100	9 g
Pork lard (foreign)	2250 g	20700	0 g
Cottage cheese	1750 g	2923	613 g
Cheese	–	–	–
Shellfish	1500 g	225	53 g
Salt herring	1000 g	1085	91 g
Dried fruit	3000 g	5300	0 g
Sugar	3500 g	13650	0 g
Eggs	10	750	65 g
Milk (full cream)	28 ltr	15589	895 g
Bean coffee	–	–	–
Substitute coffee	–	–	–
Cocoa	–	–	–
Table salt	–	–	–
Total		282325	6282 g

Source: Statistisches Reichsamt: "Die Reform der Reichsindexziffer ...", p. 161.

market, prices, whichever were lower, and the shortfall at black market prices. Commodities not subject to price regulation were valued at free market prices.[8]

[8] On the method of calculation, cp. the official directives in: Statistisches Reichsamt, "Die Teuerungsstatistik im Reich", *Vierteljahrshefte zur Statistik des Deutschen Reichs*, 29 (1920), Heft 3, pp. 65–84; also Heft 1, pp. 24^{+}–29^{+}. See too the lucid account in *Die Teuerung in Hamburg. Untersuchungen über die Lebenshaltung der hamburgischen Bevölkerung nach dem Kriege*, *Statistische Mitteilungen über den hamburgischen Staat*, No. 12 (Hamburg, 1921), esp. pp. 13ff.

The "dearness statistic", thus calculated for each of the districts in the survey, was intended "to offer a measure of the effects of the unstable economic conditions upon the cost of living in the various localities of Germany."[9] The statistics did indeed vary considerably from place to place. In part however these variations are attributable, given the method of computation just described, to differences between the rationing scales employed in different districts, and hence reflect "the differing degrees of generosity and farsightedness displayed by different local authorities in their food supply policies."[10] The Reich Statistical Office emphasized in any case that the "dearness statistic" could not be regarded as a measure of the cost of subsistence to a family of five, because certain essential items of consumption were not included in the basket. "The chief utility of the 'dearness statistic', as already expressly emphasized, lies most definitely in the information it conveys about the *movement* of living costs."[11] In 1921 the Hamburg State Statistical Office went so far as to remark that "so many deficiencies and errors attach to the 'dearness statistics' [of the Reich] as to render them incapable of serving as yardsticks of comparison [of the cost of living] between different places. Nevertheless, provided the problems we have stressed are borne in mind, they do make possible intertemporal comparisons within one and the same district."[12]

The Reich averages for the cost of living, reduced to 1913/14 = 1, are reproduced in Table 4 for the period February 1920 until December 1923.

The effectiveness of rent control in holding down the cost of accomodation, and hence retarding the rate of increase of the entire index, is immediately recognizable. The general pace of increase of clothing prices exceeded that of foodstuffs, as of the index as a whole, and to this extent exerted an upward pressure upon it. This observation does not hold good for relative price movements in all periods however. The cost of clothing was practically constant between February 1920 and May 1921, reflecting the stable trend of German wholesale prices and of the mark/dollar exchange rate during that period. Foodstuffs prices continued to rise however (by forty percent), especially during the rest of 1920; heating and lighting costs rose significantly throughout this period (by one hundred and fifty percent).

The explanation of these divergent price trends lies in the distinction between markets which were wholly uncontrolled, and markets which in this

[9] Statistisches Reichsamt: "Die Teuerungsstatistik im Reich", *Vierteljahrshefte zur Statistik des Deutschen Reichs*, 29 (1920), Heft 3, p. 65.

[10] *Ibid.*

[11] *Ibid.*

[12] *Teuerung in Hamburg...*, pp. 18–19.

Table 4. Index of the cost of living in Germany, February 1920–December 1923 (1913/14 = 1)

Month	Aggregate Index	Food	Heating and Lighting	Clothing	Accommod-ation	Cost of living excluding Clothing	Cost of living excluding Accommod-ation
					1920		
February	8.47	9.48	5.01	17.99	1.67	7.00	10.56
March	9.56	11.01	7.08	18.56	1.71	8.17	11.97
April	10.42	12.29	8.79	18.58	1.75	9.16	13.08
May	11.02	13.22	8.83	19.25	1.76	9.75	13.86
June	10.83	12.80	9.20	19.25	1.78	9.53	13.61
July	10.65	12.52	9.38	19.07	1.79	9.35	13.37
August	10.23	11.70	9.68	19.04	1.83	8.87	12.81
September	10.15	11.66	9.46	18.83	1.84	8.81	12.70
October	10.71	12.60	9.71	18.87	1.87	9.45	13.42
November	11.18	13.43	9.74	18.89	1.88	9.99	14.04
December	11.58	14.27	8.86	18.77	1.91	10.47	14.55
					1921		
January	11.79	14.23	11.75	18.85	1.95	10.70	14.81
February	11.47	13.62	11.96	18.85	1.98	10.33	14.38
March	11.38	13.52	12.15	18.51	1.98	10.28	14.26
April	11.27	13.34	12.67	18.07	2.03	10.22	14.11
May	11.20	13.20	12.81	18.07	2.03	10.14	14.01
June	11.67	13.70	12.81	19.38	2.09	10.48	14.61
July	12.50	14.91	12.79	20.66	2.09	11.74	15.69
August	13.33	15.89	13.04	22.46	2.10	11.92	16.78
September	13.74	16.14	13.47	24.23	2.11	12.12	17.31
October	15.04	17.57	14.10	27.74	2.18	13.08	18.99
November	17.75	21.89	14.84	29.47	2.21	15.94	22.52
December	19.28	23.57	19.99	31.07	2.25	17.46	24.51
					1922		
January	20.41	24.63	20.94	34.40	2.36	18.25	25.36
February	24.49	30.20	23.85	40.04	2.40	22.09	30.83
March	28.97	36.02	29.65	45.68	2.50	26.39	36.95
April	34.36	43.56	34.97	48.29	2.87	31.75	44.13
May	38.03	46.80	44.11	56.88	3.00	34.62	48.89
June	41.47	51.19	48.22	65.19	3.13	37.79	53.36
July	53.92	68.36	59.39	80.16	3.43	49.90	69.58
August	77.65	97.46	77.16	125.71	4.03	70.29	100.49
September	133.19	154.17	161.12	260.00	4.17	113.76	173.21
October	220.66	266.23	251.72	386.64	7.95	195.04	285.95
November	446.10	549.82	508.30	741.62	11.33	400.47	579.53
December	685.06	807.02	1038.91	1161.13	16.52	611.56	890.23
					1923		
January	1120.27	1366.06	1611.73	1681.73	37.57	1033.59	1452.55
February	2643	3183	4071	4164	58	2408	3436
March	2854	3315	5529	4323	113	2627	3695
April	2954	3500	5514	4182	181	2764	3805
May	3816	4620	5785	5724	216	3521	4920
June	7650	9347	10378	11995	301	6979	9961
July	37651	46510	36904	66488	714	33300	48986
August	586045	670485	890539	1089571	4932	508631	764389
	in mill.	in mill.	in mill.	in mill.	in mill.	in mill.	in mill.
September	15.0	17.3	23.3	26.5	0.3	13.2	19.5
October	3657	4301	5715	6160	54	3265	4763
	in bn.	in bn.	in bn.	in bn.	in bn.	in bn.	in bn.
November	657	862	834	816	22	633	852
December	1247	1512	1765	1662	218	1182	1562

Source: Stat. Reichsamt: Zahlen zur Geldentwertung ... p. 33. Estimates for 1914–19 derived from Calwer's index of food prices may be obtained from the same source, p. 40. See also Gerhard Bry: *Wages in Germany 1871–1945* (Princeton, 1960), pp. 440–443.

period were in the process of being decontrolled. Clothing belonged to the former category. Prices on this market were determined exclusively by market conditions and during this period the international depression, coupled with the stable tendency of the mark exchange rate, meant that clothing price increases could not be made to "stick"; the same was true of the markets for other manufactures. Falling international commodity prices, furthermore, lessened the pressure on costs. Foodstuffs prices, on the other hand, as also the prices of heating and lighting, were subject to state and particularly to local authority control: foodstuffs were subject to the maximum price regulations already mentioned, heating and lighting to the pricing policies of public utilities owned to a large extent by local authorities. Prices in these sectors were what we today would term "administered" prices, and were only partly subject to market considerations. For the other part they represented the outcome of political decisions about the distribution of the burden of rising production costs between the producer, the state and the consumer: in other words about the distribution of real income. Thus the principal reason for the rising prices of foodstuffs, heating and lighting between February 1920 and May 1921 was the political process of decontrol – the dismantling of what contemporaries called the "compulsion and subsidy economy" (*Zwangs- und Subventionswirtschaft*). Industry, agriculture and independent small businessmen had been demanding decontrol since the end of the war, and the last quarter of 1920 in particular was a period when great progress was being made in this direction at the retail level, decontrol having already been carried through at the producer and wholesale stages.[13] Whereas at the beginning of 1920 the only uncontrolled foodstuffs in the Reich Statistical Office's basket of goods had been rolled oats, eggs and herring, by the beginning of 1921 the only controlled items it contained were bread, flour, sugar and milk.[14] October 1920 saw a particularly marked shift in the basket's balance between low-priced controlled commodities and what could be purchased only on the higher-priced free markets: in that month potatoes, fats and meat were decontrolled. The consequent rise in the overall cost of living can be clearly seen in Table 5.

We must now investigate the implications of the fact, already stated, that the basket of goods on which the Reich Statistical Office's cost-of-living statistics depended, did not include all necessities of subsistence, let alone all components of a conventional standard of living. Would a widening of the range of goods and services included in the basket have tended to raise the index or to depress it?

---

[13] Gerald D. Feldman: *Iron and Steel in the German Inflation* (Princeton, 1977), pp. 160ff.
[14] "Teuerung in Hamburg...", p. 18.

Table 5. The cost of food for a family of five (husband, wife, three children) in Hamburg, January – December 1920

Month	Cost in pfennigs (= 0.01 marks)		
	absolute	%	percentage change against previous month
	of official rations		
January	20809	39.16	
February	29211	48.79	+ 40.38
March	28645	38.03	– 1.94
April	41088	52.50	+ 43.44
May	50461	75.40	+ 22.81
June	46928	66.56	– 7.00
July	52477	74.62	+ 11.82
August	51121	70.55	– 2.58
September	46577	80.52	– 8.89
October	28452	36.50	– 38.91
November	32492	37.16	+ 12.43
December	33692	34.32	+ 3.56
	of additional quantities purchased on uncontrolled markets		
January	32330	60.84	
February	30665	51.21	– 5.15
March	46685	61.97	+ 52.24
April	37175	47.50	– 0.37
May	16460	24.60	– 55.72
June	23580	33.44	+ 43.26
July	17850	25.38	– 24.30
August	21340	29.45	+ 19.55
September	11270	19.48	– 47.19
October	49494	63.50	+339.17
November	54940	62.84	+ 9.91
December	64470	65.68	+ 14.78

Source: "Teuerung in Hamburg ...", p. 27.

Two major elements in essential expenditure not represented in the basket were traditionally supplied and heavily subsidized in Germany by the states or local authorities. These were education and recreation, and transportation. These sectors therefore resembled the controlled sections of the foodstuffs market and the housing, heating and lighting sectors, in that administrative decision-making subject to political influences supplemented market forces in the determination of the relevant prices. The increase in fees for higher education, for example, lagged far behind the general rate of price increase in the same way as the rents for dwellings did (cp. Tables 6 and 4). Passenger fares on the national railways behaved similarly (Table 7). These lagging prices find their counterparts in the rising numbers of high school and university students during 1919–23 compared with numbers before the war,[15] as well as in the swelling numbers of people using the railways, and of person-kilometers traveled. Fares charged by local authority transport undertakings increased only slightly faster than fares on the national railway system (see Table 7); the rate of increase was still well below that of the foodstuffs component of the cost-of-living index, let alone of its uncontrolled components such as clothing (cp. Tables 7 and 4).

Against this must be set the fact that other items of essential household expenditure not represented in the Reich Statistical Office's basket probably exhibited faster than average rates of price increase. Among these are household furnishings, soaps and purchases relating to personal cleanliness: being

Table 6. Fees at Prussian state higher education institutions 1909–23 (Marks per annum)

			Index 140 marks = 1
1. April	1909		
to			
1. Oct.	1919	130–150 M	1
to			
1. Oct.	1920	200–220 M	1.50
to			
1. Oct.	1922	500 M	3.57
to			
1. Jan.	1923	1500 M	10.7
to			
1. April	1923	4000 M	28.6
to			
1. July	1923	20000 M	142.9
to			
30. Sept.	1923	100000 M	714.3
October	1923	8000000 M	

Source: Zentralblatt für die gesamte Unterrichtsverwaltung in Preussen, relevant volumes, *passim*.

[15] As was pointed out long ago by Franz Eulenburg: "Die sozialen Wirkungen der Währungsverhältnisse", *Jahrbücher für Nationalökonomie und Statistik*, 122 (1924), pp. 776–779. The number of students in secondary schools in Germany increased from 11.4 in 1911 to 17.3 in 1921 per 1000 inhabitants, that of university students from 2.8 in 1913 to 6.4 in 1922 per 10000 inhabitants. Both ratios fell after the inflation, the latter one to a minimum of 3.0 in 1934. Peter Flora: *Indikatoren der Modernisierung. Ein historisches Datenhandbuch* (Opladen, 1975), p. 125.

Table 7. Price indexes for 3rd class railroad fares per km and for streetcar fares in Berlin, 1913–23 (1913/14 = 1)

	Railroads	Berlin streetcars
1913/14	1	1
1. Jan. 1918	1	1
1. July 1918	1.23	1.5
1. Jan. 1919	1.23	1.5
1. July 1919	1.60	2.0
1. Jan. 1920	2.41	3.0
1. July 1920	4.81	7.0
1. Jan. 1921	4.81	8.0
1. July 1921	6.50	10.0
1. Jan. 1922	8.45	15.0
1. July 1922	14.79	40.0
1. Jan. 1923	200.00	500.0
1. July 1923	5000.00	10000.0

Sources: Railroads: *Zahlen zur Geldentwertung* ..., p. 36.
Streetcars: Robert R. Kuczynski: *Postwar Labor Conditions in Germany* (Washington, D.C., 1925), p. 52.

mainly manufactures they were, like clothing, not subject to price controls. Thus the effect of including some necessities omitted from the official basket would be to depress the index, while the effect of including others would be to raise it. The net effect might conceivably be small, but neither this, nor the direction of the effect of adding further necessities can be definitely predicted on either logical or empirical grounds.

We can be more definite however in our judgment of the effect upon the index of adding items which, though not necessities, nevertheless had entered the consumption even of lower-income groups before the war and which continued to form part of the consumption of middle-income groups during and after it. A basket of goods constructed on these lines would include a larger proportion of protein-based foods, an enhanced variety of general foodstuffs and larger quantities of some already included – thus raising the basket's overall calorific value. Luxuries such as alcoholic beverages and tobacco products would have to be admitted as well. These additional commodities would however be obtainable only at prices higher on average (relative to 1913) than those of commodities actually included in the official basket. Where the commodities in question were uncontrolled, this conclusion follows from the fact that prices on uncontrolled markets generally rose more rapidly than prices on controlled ones. Where the postulated enhancement of the basket involved increasing the quantities of rationed and controlled commodities, the additional quantities could be obtained only on the black market at very high prices. Thus any enrichment of the basket of goods to reflect a standard of consumption significantly above the subsistence minimum, that is, to reflect something approaching prewar consumption standards, would necessarily have translated into higher estimates of the cost of living.[16] Empirical support for this conclusion is provided by the calculations of the Hamburg State Statistical Office which employed simultaneously a variety of baskets of goods.

Regional cost of living indexes

The "most complete attempts to grapple with the problems of selecting representative households and baskets of goods for the measurement of cost-of-living change" were those of the Hamburg State Statistical Office.[17] This office calculated alternative cost-of-living statistics on the basis of four different baskets of goods.

(1) The first basket contained foodstuffs selected on the basis of scientific nutritional theory. The first stage was to estimate the normal consumption of foodstuffs by a family of five, not – as in the Reich Statistical Office's method – by itemizing commodities or groups of commodities to be included in the basket but, by estimating each family member's daily calorific requirement, and within this total, the proportionate distribution between proteins, fats and carbohydrates. The specifications were as follows:[18]

	proteins g.	fats g.	carbohydrates g.	total calories
man	100	60	500	3000
woman	80	48	400	2400
child (12 years)	75	45	375	2250
child (7 years)	50	30	250	1500
child ($1^1/_2$ years)	30	18	150	900

[16] On this, compare the argumentation of Wilhelm Morgenroth in his article "Indexziffern", *Handwörterbuch der Staatswissenschaften* (Jena 8 vols., 1921–7), vol. 5 (1923), p. 404.

[17] *Ibid.* Cost of living statistics adapted to local conditions were also produced by the municipal statistical offices in Hanover, Nuremberg, Kiel, Leipzig and Erfurt as well as by the statistical wage bureaux in Breslau und Flensburg. Cp. Rudolf Meerwarth: "Über die Bedeutung der Teuerungsziffern", *Schmollers Jahrbuch*, 45 (1921), p. 754.

[18] *Teuerung in Hamburg...*, p. 25.

From this table family foodstuffs requirements for a four-week period were derived. It was then assumed that these requirements would be satisfied in the following manner. The family was first of all credited with the quantities of controlled foodstuffs available as rations: the local surveys in connection with the Reich's 'dearness statistic' provided the necessary price information. When the nutritional and calorific values of these rations did not reach the levels prescribed in the above table, the shortfalls were presumed to have been purchased on other markets at the cheapest price per calorie (not per weight as in the Reich's statistics) at which food of like nutritional composition (in terms of proteins, fats and carbohydrates) could be obtained. The possibilities of substitution afforded by this principle of construction were thus much greater than those present in the Reich's index and meant that a given level of nutrition could be achieved more cheaply on the basis of this first "Hamburg" basket.

(2) The construction of the second "basket" followed that underlying the Reich's cost-of-living statistics.

(3) The third basket of goods was adapted to local patterns of consumption in Hamburg. While it represented a "restricted" pattern of consumption appropriate to postwar conditions, it was not as meager as the Reich's basket.

(4) The fourth basket represented an "unrestricted" version of (3), and was based on the evidence of the Hamburg expenditure surveys of 1907.

It is possible to make a comparison of the long term rates of increase of the indexes based on baskets (2) and (4), but not of those based on (1) and (3), as the latter have not been computed for the prewar period. The Reich's "dearness statistic" for Hamburg – i.e. basket (2) – showed an increase between July 1914 and July 1920 of 1170%. The index calculated on the fourth basket, and derived from the expenditure surveys of one hundred and seventy-nine Hamburg households in 1907 shows an increase over the same period of 1483%.[19] Thus the conclusion, that indexes based on baskets containing higher proportions of "non-necessities" will exhibit higher rates of increase, is verified.

Some regional indexes pertaining to Berlin may be briefly described. Robert Kuczynski's index was designed to reflect, more comprehensively than the Reich's own statistics, the costs of all items of essential expenditure appropriate to the more restricted postwar pattern of consumption.[20] Essential food-

[19] *Ibid.*, pp. 34–35.

[20] Robert R. Kuczynski (ed.): *Finanzpolitische Korrespondenz* (Berlin, 1920 ff.); idem, *Postwar Labor Conditions in Germany* (Washington, D.C., 1925), pp. 9–61. Kuczynski was director of the statistical office of the municipality of Schöneberg bei Berlin during the inflation.

stuffs were calculated on a physiological basis as in the first Hamburg index, but taking account of calorific values only and not also of nutritional values. Accommodation, heating and lighting, and clothing were also represented in the basket as they were in the Reich Statistical Office's. Other items of essential expenditure, such as household furnishings, cost of transport, hygienic and educational expenditures, plus the "pay as you earn" deductions under wage tax (introduced in July 1920), were incorporated by adding a simple surcharge of twenty percent plus the current standard wage-tax rate to the current value of all other items in the basket.

This last procedure cannot of course affect the rate of change of the index; it affects only the absolute value of the outlay represented by the basket of goods. It reflects Kuczynski's particular concern to compare the movements of the actual cost of a household's sheer subsistence with contemporaneous changes in its money income. Kuczynski's calculations may well therefore help to answer the question whether workers' incomes were sufficient at different points during the inflation to keep them above the "poverty line", as he defines it; but they can contribute no more to the question of the relationship between workers' postwar and prewar real incomes than can the computations of the Reich Statistical Office, which are similar in all respects except the surcharge.

Table 8. Weekly cost of minimum subsistence for a family of four in Berlin according to R. R. Kuczynski; 1920–23 compared with 1913/14

Period	Food marks	Accom-modation marks	Heating, Lighting marks	Clothing marks	Miscel-laneous marks	Aggregate in marks	as index
Aug. 1913 to July 1914	9.8	5.5	1.9	5.9	5.8	28.8	1
1920							
Jan.	86	8	12	70	44	220	7.7
Feb.	100	8	13	82	51	254	8.8
March	125	8	20	105	64	322	11.2
April	157	9	22	112	75	375	13.0
May	163	9	22	98	73	365	12.7
June	128	9	22	84	61	304	10.6
July	135	9	22	77	81	324	11.3
Aug.	131	9	21	70	77	308	10.7
Sept.	123	9	22	70	75	299	10.4
Oct.	138	9	22	70	79	318	11.0
Nov.	136	9	22	70	79	316	11.0
Dec.	144	9	22	70	82	327	11.3

Table 8. (continued)

Period	Food	Accom- modation	Heating, Lighting	Clothing	Miscel- laneous	Aggregate in	as
	marks	marks	marks	marks	marks	marks	index
1921							
Jan.	139	9	22	70	80	320	11.1
Feb.	133	9	23	70	78	313	10.9
March	129	9	23	63	74	298	10.3
April	121	9	23	63	65	281	9.8
May	122	9	25	63	66	285	9.9
June	142	9	25	63	72	311	10.8
July	151	10	25	63	75	324	11.2
Aug.	156	10	25	70	78	339	11.8
Sept.	162	10	26	70	81	349	12.1
Oct.	176	10	27	84	89	386	13.4
Nov.	222	10	31	128	118	509	17.7
Dec.	249	10	41	128	129	557	19.3
1922							
Jan.	257	11	43	128	109	548	19.0
Feb.	299	11	52	140	125	627	21.8
March	351	11	62	198	167	789	27.4
April	417	14	74	210	200	915	31.8
May	444	14	86	233	218	995	34.5
June	466	14	96	350	269	1 195	41.5
July	700	14	114	518	417	1 763	61.2
Aug.	1 091	16	154	1 015	682	2 958	102.7
Sept.	1 726	16	380	1 477	1 115	4 714	163.7
Oct.	2 820	32	530	2 306	1 820	7 508	260.7
Nov.	5 934	72	1 079	5 149	4 037	16 271	565.0
Dec.	8 154	193	2 084	8 361	6 202	24 994	867.9
1923							
Jan.	13 098	300	3 467	11 725	8 577	37 167	1 290.5
Feb.	32 376	300	7 667	22 478	18 218	81 039	2 813.8
March	31 957	660	11 425	15 108	15 971	75 121	2 608.4
April	32 198	660	10 346	15 672	15 896	74 772	2 596.3
May	45 312	1 010	10 818	37 372	27 409	121 921	4 233.4
June	98 579	1 045	22 287	73 889	56 782	252 582	8 770.2
July	391 458	2 400	85 329	260 750	207 182	947 119	32 886.1
Aug.	6 307 538	9 800	1 775 761	4 783 333	4 120 458	16 996 890	590 170
	in mill.		in mill.	in mill.	in mill.	in mill.	in mill.
Sept.	162.2	360 000	49.2	110.7	104.8	427.3	14.8
	in mill.	in mill.	in mill.	in mill.	in mill.	in mill.	in mill.
Oct.	51 561.3	24.6	9 838.4	49 605.6	33 309	144 338.9	5 011.8
	in bn.	in bn.	in bn.	in bn.	in bn.	in bn.	in bn.
Nov.	9 354.3	38.3	1 650.9	5 016.7	4 015.0	20 075.2	697.1

Source: Robert R. Kuczynski: *Postwar Labor Conditions* ..., p. 66.

Kuczynski's estimates of the costs of subsistence relate only to greater Berlin. They are calculated for three types of household: the single male, the childless couple and the couple with two children. Table 8 reproduces his index for this last type. Another cost-of-living index for the Berlin region was calculated by H. Silbergleit, director of the Berlin City Statistical Office.[21] It covered only the cost of foodstuffs however and was calculated on the same physiological principles as the Hamburg index.

Calwer's index of foodstuffs prices

This is the only index that provides monthly estimates of the cost of living both for the war years and for the entire postwar period up to the end of 1922.[22] Calculated according to the method first employed by Ignaz Jastrow in 1898,[23] it was based on a basket of goods selected to represent the weekly foodstuffs requirements of a prewar German marine. This was supposed to reflect the nutritional requirements of the average adult. The composition of the ration was as shown at the top of p. 43.[24]
Calwer's actual basket of goods tripled the quantities shown in this table to represent the weekly foodstuffs consumption of a married couple (one "Jastrow" ration each) plus two children (half a ration each). He published monthly estimates of the cost of purchasing such a basket of goods in about two hundred localities in Germany. After 1914 he valued the controlled commodities in his basket entirely at the maximum prices currently in force; only uncontrolled goods were valued at market prices and thus black market prices were disregarded. Calwer also produced a Reich average cost-of-living statistic by averaging the results for the separate localities.

---

21 Cp. Statistisches Amt der Stadt Berlin (ed.): *Die Kosten des Ernährungsbedarfs. Monatliche Ermittlungen*, Berlin, vol. 1 ff. (1920 ff.).

22 Richard Calwer: *Monatliche Übersichten über Lebensmittelpreise*, Berlin, vol. 1 ff., 1911 ff. Indexes of the cost of food for the war years alone are provided by Peter Quante: "Lohnpolitik und Lohnentwicklung im Kriege", *Zeitschrift des Preussischen Statistischen Landesamts*, 59 (1919), p. 366; also Adolf Günther: *Die gesunkene Kaufkraft des Lohnes und ihre Wiederherstellung. Teil II: Kriegslöhne und -preise und ihr Einfluß auf Kaufkraft und Lebenskosten. Schriften der Gesellschaft für Soziale Reform, Bd. 66* (Jena, 1919).

23 Cp. Jastrow's periodical: *Der Arbeitsmarkt*, 2 (1898), cited in Hildegard Heuer: "Die Entwicklung der Metallarbeiterreallöhne auf den Kieler Werften in der Zeit vom 1.4.1920 bis 30.10.1923 "(Dissertation, Kiel, 1929), p. 19.

24 H. Heuer: "Entwicklung der Metallarbeiterlöhne...", p. 20. Cp. also R. Meerwarth: "Über die Bedeutung der Teuerungsziffern", pp. 742 ff.

Foodstuff	Quantity	Calorific value
beef	800 g	1784
pork	750 g	1710
mutton	800 g	1680
rice	150 g	495
beans	300 g	954
peas	300 g	813
wheat flour	500 g	1675
prunes	200 g	400
potatoes	3000 g	2640
sugar	340 g	1329
bread	5250 g	11138
butter	455 g	3463
vinegar	0.11 l	–
salt	106 g	–
coffee	105 g	–
tea	21 g	–
Total		28126 calories per week =4018 calories per day

Calwer's procedures may be criticized on the following counts:
(1) His basket of goods is probably unrepresentative of the foodstuffs consumption of the average family – even in the prewar period. It is much too generous: a daily average calorific intake of over four thousand calories may be appropriate to the adult male engaged in heavy manual labour – among

Table 9. Index of the average level of foodstuffs prices in two hundred German cities 1913–22, compiled by Richard Calwer (1913 = 1)

	1913	1914	1915	1916	1917	1918	1919	1920	1921	1922
January	1.01	0.99	1.15	1.61	2.09	2.20	2.48	5.08	14.85	21.36
February	1.01	0.98	1.23	1.69	2.11	2.20	2.53	5.75	13.99	26.24
March	1.01	0.98	1.28	1.88	2.13	2.22	2.62	6.52	13.86	39.95
April	1.00	0.96	1.34	2.02	2.13	2.22	2.71	7.38	13.67	49.59
May	0.99	0.96	1.42	2.03	2.12	2.23	2.87	8.74	13.74	42.53
June	0.99	0.96	1.45	2.05	2.14	2.24	3.06	9.03	13.68	49.87
July	1.01	0.98	1.48	2.08	2.15	2.26	3.20	9.82	13.97	64.32
August	1.01	1.03	1.52	2.08	2.13	2.31	3.32	10.17	15.41	94.18
Sept.	1.00	1.02	1.55	2.08	2.12	2.37	3.72	10.66	15.55	151.92
October	1.00	1.05	1.63	2.08	2.13	2.40	3.92	12.93	16.28	250.31
November	1.00	1.08	1.51	2.06	2.16	2.43	4.23	13.89	18.44	509.00
December	0.99	1.12	1.53	2.07	2.18	2.45	4.46	14.39	20.02	747.42
Average	1.00	1.01	1.43	1.98	2.13	2.29	3.26	9.53	15.29	...

Source: Richard Calwer: *Monatliche Übersichten über Lebensmittelpreise*, Berlin, 1913ff., as cited in Gerhard Bry: *Wages in Germany 1871–1945* (Princeton, 1960), pp. 440–445.

whom the marine may be counted – but not to the average man or woman in the population as a whole. He probably exaggerated the adult male daily calorific intake by about one-third, the female by about two-thirds, and allowed far in excess of the quantity of foodstuffs contained in the nutritionally based indexes of the Hamburg State Statistical Office, of Kuczynski or of Silbergleit. Even so, the over-generous construction of the basket does not affect the reliability of the index as much as the defect in his method of valuing its contents.

(2) Calwer's principle of valuing the entire quantities of controlled foodstuffs at official maximum prices severely circumscribes its power to track cost-of-living change. The rationed allocations of these commodities were far smaller than the quantities prescribed in his basket, and especially in the years 1916–20 by no means supplied even essential family requirements, so that as we have seen shortfalls had to be made good by purchase either of alternative foods available on the free market or of the same foods illicitly on the black market. Calwer took no account of the higher and often more rapidly increasing prices on these markets as long as official prices were to hand. As a result the decontrol of commodities has a very sharp and immediate effect on his index, accounting for its steep rise in 1920. The same fact also explains why the level of Calwer's index (relative to 1913) is below the level of the Reich Statistical Office's index between February and the last months of 1920 (cp. Tables 4 and 9). Only thereafter do we observe the more generous allocation of foodstuffs in Calwer's basket to be reflected in the higher levels of his cost-of-living index – as the comparison of the various Hamburg indexes would lead us to expect (cp. pp. 38–39). The assessment of the Hamburg State Statistical Office may therefore be fully accepted: "Calwer's index does not lend itself to the measurement of the rate of price increase, at least during the period of price control, unless at the same time one takes into account the movement of black market prices. Not until a free market had been restored in foodstuffs, and every commodity was sold at a single price again, does Calwer's index reliably reflect the rising price level."[25]

Elsas[26] broadened the basis of Calwer's index by adding the categories clothing, accommodation, heating and lighting, and 'miscellaneous' to his basket. Since the original foodstuffs categories still accounted for sixty percent of the value of the enlarged basket however, it is still open to all the objections voiced against Calwer's own calculations.

---

[25] *Teuerung in Hamburg...*, p. 38.

[26] Moritz Elsas: *Der Stand der Kosten der Lebenshaltung. Indexziffern zur Förderung gleitender Entlohnung* (Frankfurt/M., 1920). Elsas was the director of the Frankfurt municipal statistical office.

Chapter 3
Changes in the Money Supply and Liquidity

3.1. Some Theoretical Considerations

Modern definitions should be employed as far as possible to isolate the money supply whose changes we seek to measure. In general we define as "money" those claims, held upon the banking system by the non-bank sector, which function as means of payment.[1] M_1, the narrowest definition of the money supply, includes cash (coins, banknotes and the like) held by the private non-bank sector, plus the same sector's deposits on current account (checking account) with the banking system. Cash balances held by public authorities are excluded. M_2, a somewhat broader definition, includes in addition the private non-bank sector's time deposits with the banking system up to a limit of four years' notice of withdrawal, on the grounds that these can be relatively easily mobilized for use as means of payment. Finally the money supply definition M_3 adds to the categories included in M_2 the savings deposits of the private non-bank sector, on the grounds that these too can be mobilized at short notice as means of payment. Foreign deposits with domestic banks are however not counted as part of the money supply.

A related, more fundamental concept is the "monetary base" (high powered money, primary money). This is defined as "the stock of central bank money in the possession of the so-called private sector of the economy."[2] It consists of cash in circulation plus the deposits of both the banking system and the private non-bank sector at the central bank. The characteristic that distinguishes the monetary base from the money supply under all its definitions is the fact that the former is entirely determined by central bank policy. Changes in the monetary base are considered to be in turn the principal, but not the only, determinants of changes in the money supply. Among the other factors

---

[1] Dieter Duwendag *et al.*: *Geldtheorie and Geldpolitik* (Cologne, 1974), p. 34. Otmar Issing: *Einführung in die Geldtheorie* (Munich, 3rd edn. 1977), p. 6. Amongst English introductions to monetary theory and policy, see Andrew D. Bain: *The Control of the Money Supply* (Harmondsworth, 3rd edn. 1980), and W. T. Newlyn: *The Theory of Money* (Oxford, 2nd edn. 1971).

[2] D. Duwendag *et al.*: *Geldtheorie*... p. 47.

influencing the money supply are the decisions of banking institutions about the proportions in which they employ their cash balances as advances to clients and as cash reserves, and the decisions of the general public about the proportions in which they hold their money balances as cash, and as deposits in sight, time and savings accounts.[3]

Another concept besides "money supply" and "monetary base" that plays an important part in monetary theory and policy is "liquidity". "The liquid assets of the banks form the most important magnitude in monetary analysis. They influence the ease or tightness of banks' lending policies and hence the rate of growth of bank deposits. They determine the climate of opinion on the money and securities markets and hence interest rates."[4] The relationship between the liquid assets of the banking system and the process of credit creation – the process by which the banks influence the rate of monetary expansion – is as follows. Credit creation by banks and other credit institutions can occur only on the basis of the legal tender in which ultimately they are required to discharge their debts: i. e. central bank money. For this reason they take the precaution of maintaining reserves in actual or potential central bank money. These are the banks' "liquid reserves" or "liquid balances" and their level is usually expressed as a percentage of bank liabilities – "the liquidity ratio". Actual central bank money consists of cash plus non-interest bearing deposits at the central bank, withdrawable on demand. Potential central bank money consists of assets readily realizable as actual central bank money. In Germany this included money lent at call ("daily money") or at short notice ("monthly money") in the Berlin money market, plus holdings of bank acceptances and such commercial bills of exchange as were rediscountable at the Reichsbank, plus those stock-market securities which the Reichsbank would accept as collateral ("*lombardfähig*") in granting a loan. In a system of fixed exchange rates banks' short term investments in foreign money markets would be added to this list.[5] Banks and other credit institutions prefer to hold their liquid balances in the form of potential rather than actual central bank money: the former earns interest whereas the latter does not. A simplified version of a bank's liquid reserves and their structure may be set out as follows:

---

[3] *Ibid.*, p. 110.

[4] Claus Köhler: *Geldwirtschaft, Bd. 1: Geldversorgung und Kreditpolitik* (Berlin, 2nd edn. 1977), p. 81.

[5] *Ibid.*, p. 95.

Credit Institutions

	Assets	Liabilities
	α	Deposits from the non-bank sector
	β	
L = LS	γ	
	δ	
	Advances to (non-bank) clients	

"The liquid reserves L are the difference between the banking system's deposits from, and its advances to, the non-banking sector, and they reflect the amount of central bank money available to the system. The liquidity structure LS shows the asset composition of these reserves. Four asset types may be distinguished: α) central bank money, β) domestic money market assets, γ) foreign money market assets, given the existence of fixed exchange rates, δ) stock market securities eligible as collateral for short term central bank credits."[6]

Other things being equal, the higher the banking system's liquid reserves or, in relation to its deposit liabilities, the higher its liquidity ratio, the greater the space for the system to exert an autonomous influence on the rate of credit- and money creation. And therefore the higher the banking system's liquidity ratio, the weaker the central bank's power to compel the banking system, by reduction of the monetary base, to restrict its advances, and hence the weaker the power of the central bank to reduce the size or retard the growth of the money supply as a whole. This is because a banking system possessing a high liquidity ratio to start with has space to permit the restrictive action of the central bank to reduce that ratio without its falling to a dangerously low level.

The banking system may suffer loss of central bank money also through the actions of its customers, as these withdraw deposits or transfer sums deposited with it to accounts at the central bank. In this case the banks' liquid reserves and liquidity ratios are reduced, and the reduction occurs in one of three ways. Either the banks' holdings of central bank money are allowed to fall, or they sell money market securities such as bank acceptances to the central bank, or they borrow from the central bank against the collateral of first class stock-market securities. A fourth possibility exists only under fixed exchange rates: that they sell foreign exchange balances to the central bank.[7]

In taking this kind of action, credit institutions may find their liquidity ratios reduced to dangerously low levels, rendering the banking system liable

---

[6] *Ibid.*, p. 96.

[7] *Ibid.*, p. 99.

to collapse. The history of financial crises illustrates abundantly the depressive consequences for the wider economy of such a collapse.[8]

Even where the money supply is expanding such a liquidity crisis could, in extreme cases, affect the banks. Where exogenous pressures on real supply (wage pressure, raw material shortages in the world economy) raise prices and costs and intensify the demand for bank credit, and where at the same time the non-bank sector decides to hold more money as cash and less as bank deposits or foreigners withdraw deposits with domestic banks, bank liquidity ratios will fall.

Summing up, we may say that changes in the banks' liquidity ratios serve as important indicators of the money creating *potential*, present in the commercial banking system, which would be capable of being mobilized independently of central bank action upon the monetary base and even against that action. When this power of independent operation is high (i.e. the liquidity ratio is high) observed changes in the size of the money supply are being determined less from the supply side than from the demand side. Changes in bank liquidity ratios – whether caused by the action of the central bank, or of private depositors and borrowers – also however signalize when bank liquidity is falling into the danger zone where central bank intervention as "lender of last resort" might be required to prevent the collapse of the system. In an inflationary economy the duty of so intervening might cause central bank action to have an accelerating effect on the growth of the money supply. Where for example the government can compel the central bank to finance its inflationary fiscal policy, falling confidence in the currency may induce a run on the banks and "flight into real values". The central bank remains obligated to stop this run from precipitating a commercial banking collapse with its repercussions on the entire economy, and may be able to do so only by accelerating the expansion of the monetary base.

---

[8] Charles P. Kindleberger: *Manias, Panics and Crashes. A History of Financial Crises* (New York, 1978).

3.2. Empirical Evidence

The money supply

Table 10 summarizes the year-to-year changes in the various components of the money supply between 1913 and 1923. Monthly data are available for some of the components, and these are brought together in Table 11. Data on other components, namely deposits at savings and joint stock credit banks, are available at bimonthly intervals for part of the period. These are derived from the published bimonthly bank balance sheets which public demands for improved bank publicity had brought into existence before the war, beginning voluntarily with the Berlin great banks in 1909, and extending to almost all joint stock credit banks in 1910 once the government had decreed otherwise to prohibit stock market quotation of their shares.[9] Published according to a uniform scheme in the *Reichsanzeiger,*[10] these bimonthly balances were available for eighty-six banks in 1912 and one hundred by 1914, accounting in total for about eighty percent of the aggregate balances of all joint stock credit banks.[11] Publication ceased on July 30th,1914 with the bimonthly balance for the end of June; thereafter these interim balances served only for the information of the Reichsbank and, as war-related personnel shortages increased, the detail diminished which they were required to contain. The last bimonthly balance sheets were communicated to the Reichsbank in 1920.[12] I discovered the bimonthly data pertaining to the period October 1914 – April 1920 in a memorandum which the Reichsbank sent to the government of the Reich on June 28th, 1920 as a background paper for the forthcoming Spa conference. They are now published for the first time in Table 11. Unfortunately the source recorded only four of the five bimonthly balances for each year – for the ends of February, April, August and October. The year-end data are to be found in the annual balance sheets but the figures for June 30th are missing.

---

[9] Karl Nordhoff: "Die Massnahmen der Reichsbank zur Verbesserung der Publizität, Liquidität und Solidarität der Banken", in *Untersuchung des Bankwesens 1933* (Berlin, 1933), Teil I, Band 2, pp. 246–247. Cp. also Luise Schaeffer: "Die Zweimonatsbilanzen der Grossbanken", *Zeitschrift für handelswissenschaftliche Forschung*, 13 (1919), pp. 102–123.

[10] Kurt Wagner: *Stationen deutscher Bankgeschichte. 75 Jahre Bankenverband* (Cologne, 1976), p. 17.

[11] K. Nordhoff: "Massnahmen der Reichsbank ...", p. 247.

[12] *Die Reichsbank 1901–1925* (Berlin, n.d.), Pt. I, p. 33.

Table 10. Components of the money supply and the monetary base. Annual data 1910–23. Mill. marks

	Cash in circulation (excl. balances at banks of issue)							Deposits at banks of issue		
	Coins		*Banknotes*		*Government notes*		*Total*	*Reichsbank*		
End of year	Gold	Other	Reichsbank	Other⁺	Reichs-kassenscheine	Darlehns-kassenscheine		Public sector*		Private sector**
	1	2	3	4	5	6	7	8		9
1910	2939	805	2061	138	68	–	6011	157		554
1911	2930	832	2232	142	89	–	6225	157		553
1912	2984	891	2496	142	104	–	6617	158		588
1913	2755	928	2574	147	148	–	6552	181		612
1914	.	2841	5046	134	236	446	8703	(392)	1757	(1365)
1915	.	1690	6918	143	327	972	10050	(526)	2359	(1833)
1916	.	877	8055	158	352	2873	12315	(1018)	4564	(3546)
1917	.	212	11468	163	350	6265	18458	(1795)	8050	(6255)
1918	.	170	22188	283	356	10109	33106	2927		10353
1919	.	108	35698	257	328	13692	50083	3704		13368
1920	.	241	68805	233	316	11975	81570	(4979)	22327	(17348)
1921	.	466	113640	334	198	8275	122913	7592		25314
1922	.	.	1280095	1470	213	12970	1294748	153191		377335
1923	.	.	$497 \cdot 10^{12}$	$0.078 \cdot 10^{12}$	.			$303 \cdot 10^{12}$		$245 \cdot 10^{12}$

Source: Deutsche Bundesbank: *Deutsches Geld- und Bankwesen in Zahlen 1876–1975* (Frankfurt, 1976), pp. 14, 16, 37–38.

⁺ i.e. the four private banks of issue.

* for 1914–17 and 1920 Reichsbank deposits were split between cols. 8 and 9 in the ratio 1 : 3.5 – the rather constant average ratio for the preceding and following years.

** bank and non-bank.

Tables 10 and 11 demonstrate that for the period of the inflation (1914–1923) information on bank deposits is not available in the detail required for the construction of the M_1, M_2, or M_3 definitions of the money supply. One of the problems is the impossibility of distinguishing between cash held by the banks and public authorities on the one hand and cash held by the private non-bank sector on the other – only the latter counts as part of the money supply. A further problem lies in the impossibility of excluding inter-bank deposits and liabilities from published deposit totals. Deposits at the Reichsbank too require a finer classification than that undertaken in Table 10. Yet another problem, though not in practice a major one, arises out of the existence in Germany of four private note-issuing banks besides the Reichsbank – those of Bavaria, Saxony, Württemberg and Baden,[13] and it is no more

[13] A brief overview of the various types of bank in Germany will be found in P. Barrett Whale: *Joint Stock Banking in Germany. A Study of the German Credit Banks before and after the War*

Private Banks of Issue	*Total*	Monetary base (7 + 11 − 8)	Deposits at various credit institutions *Joint stock credit banks* Berlin great banks	Provincial banks	Total	*Mortgage banks* (incl. mixed)	*Savings banks*	*Co-op. credit societies*	*Postal giro accounts*
10	11	12	13	14	15	16	17	18	19
63	774	6628	4882	4241	9123	705	16781	3619	111
61	771	6839	4969	4444	9413	782	17882	3908	162
61	807	7266	4920	4441	9360	773	18680	4386	180
59	852	7223	5149	4493	9642	809	19689	4735	230
89	1846	10157	5321	4324	9645	888	20547	4656	278
35	2394	11918	6856	4913	11769	1041	20381	5301	315
51	4615	15912	9396	5982	15378	980	21433	6137	529
76	8126	24789	15210	7971	23182	1324	25403	7738	837
149	13429	43608	19696	10285	29981	2070	31834	10332	1202
181	17253	63632	39141	15460	54601	2274	36981	11832	3388
334	22661	99252	62566	21960	84526	3835	44563		7571
626	33532	148853	115569[1]				49932[2]		11000[3]
6695	537221	1678778	1618230				163020		173732
$18 \cdot 10^{12}$	$566 \cdot 10^{12}$		$1089 \cdot 10^{12}$				$189 \cdot 10^{12}$		

[1] from 1921: P. B. Whale: *Joint Stock Banking* ..., p. 216.
[2] from 1921: extrapolated from data on Prussian savings banks in *Zeitschrift d. Preuss. Stat. Landesamts*, current issues.
[3] from 1921: *Stat. Jahrbuch f. d. deutsche Reich*, 24 (1924/5), p. 314.

possible to estimate the proportion of their notes in private non-bank hands, or to analyze the deposits with them in the required manner, than it is for the Reichsbank. Since, however, the maximum note issue of these institutions was fixed in nominal terms, their proportionate influence on the money supply vanished into insignificance as inflation accelerated.

Let us now more specifically inquire into what can be said about the development of the money supply during the inflation period under one definition – M_2. Under the actual institutional arrangements current in Germany at the time, M_2 would consist of the following components.

(1) Cash in circulation: coin plus banknotes of the Reichsbank and the private note-issuing banks minus the cash balances of the commercial banks and public authorities, also minus notes of other banks of issue in the possession of note-issuing banks.

(London, 1930), pp. 1–6. An analysis of the structure of the credit banks' balance sheet will be found on pp. 143ff. of the same work.

Tabelle 11. Components of the money supply 1913–23: monthly data in mill. marks

	Cash			Deposits			
End of month	Notes	Coins	Total	Reichsbank	Joint stock credit banks	Savings banks	Postal giro accounts
	(1)	(2)	(3)	(4)	(5)	(6)	(7)
1913							
January	2198.4	3741.9	5940.3	533.2			
February	2109.0	3725.3	5834.3	564.5	7859		
March	2489.9	3759.4	6249.3	743.8			
April	2293.8	3715.4	6009.2	587.4	8181		
May	2147.0	3674.1	5821.1	608.8			
June	2577.6	3686.4	6264.0	696.4	7991		
July	2188.7	3643.2	5831.9	598.9			
August	2154.2	3675.8	5830.0	611.6	8134		
September	2738.8	3724.5	6463.3	703.5			
October	2385.3	3679.6	6064.9	775.2	8225		
November	2246.7	3653.4	5900.1	631.4			
December	2902.0	3729.9	6631.9	793.1	9642	19689	
1914							
January	2321.8	3601.6	5923.4	699.6			224
February	2226.0	3576.1	5842.1	905.8	8461		224
March	2732.6	3628.8	6361.4	890.5			244
April	2381.9	3568.5	5950.4	825.0	8623		234
May	2293.1	3600.4	5893.5	842.3			242
June	2709.5	3613.5	6323.0	858.3	8392	20302	258
July	3236.6	3732.3	6968.9	1258.5			232
August	4703.9	3624.3	8328.2	2441.3			240
September	5007.9	3428.4	8436.3	2350.7			307
October	4783.3	3188.9	7972.2	1305.5	7779		283
November	4900.3	2980.8	7881.1	1397.4		20424	279
December	5861.6	2841.4	8703.0	1756.9	9645	20547	295
1915							
January	5493.8	2700.7	8194.5	1452.6			306
February	5766.0	2537.9	8303.9	1581.5	9555	21389	302
March	6637.0	2409.5	9046.5	4037.0			335
April	6335.8	2303.6	8639.4	1463.9	9747		313
May	6383.5	2216.0	8599.5	1506.9		21176	293
June	6972.9	2142.4	9115.3	1799.3			299
July	6689.7	2065.7	8755.4	1651.6			303
August	6750.3	1987.0	8737.3	1736.3	10851	21006	289
September	7429.7	1915.2	9344.9	4416.3			311
October	7261.0	1836.0	9097.1	1622.7	9631		320
November	7347.6	1760.9	9108.5	1587.8		20597	321
December	8360.0	1690.1	10050.1	2359.0	11769	20381	351
1916							
January	7935.4	1605.5	9540.9	1785.9			345
February	8062.1	1530.3	9592.4	1986.8	11802	20967	357
March	8625.5	1461.6	10087.1	4357.8			396
April	8304.8	1393.2	9698.0	1736.9	12542		382
May	8350.6	1340.4	9691.0	1728.4		21149	355
June	9035.0	1268.6	10303.6	2370.7			369
July	8862.7	1204.0	10066.7	2395.6			388
August	9204.3	1144.0	10348.3	2835.5	13644	21141	398
September	9856.6	1084.9	10941.5	6266.5			422
October	9951.4	1014.7	10966.1	3458.4	13196		462
November	10311.5	946.1	11257.6	3661.9		21028	470
December	11437.9	877.4	12315.4	4564.2	15378	21433	502

Tabele 11. (continued).

	Cash			Deposits			
End of month	Notes	Coins	Total	Reichs-bank	Joint stock credit banks	Savings banks	Postal giro accounts
	(1)	(2)	(3)	(4)	(5)	(6)	(7)
1917							
January	11428.8	790.2	12219.0	3452.4			553
February	11982.1	738.3	12720.4	4076.6	15833	22992	536
March	12872.9	671.5	13544.4	8405.5			578
April	12709.1	604.9	13314.0	3981.0	17416		634
May	12889.6	520.0	13409.6	4538.2		23468	612
June	13719.0	487.8	14206.8	5692.7			649
July	14073.9	438.5	14512.4	5848.0			661
August	14921.2	384.0	15305.2	5890.6	19248	23934	663
September	16139.0	349.0	16488.0	9540.9			705
October	16512.4	330.4	16842.8	5686.1	19386		760
November	16989.8	201.6	17191.5	6045.3		24550	764
December	18245.2	212.3	18457.5	8050.4	23182	25403	797
1918							
January	17934.2	92.5	18026.7	6676.3			839
February	18351.6	84.1	18435.7	6490.1	23265	26886	775
March	19482.6	76.2	19558.8	9029.7			807
April	19263.5	68.8	19332.3	7055.1	23220		885
May	19678.7	69.5	19748.2	7634.8		27984	852
June	20597.2	71.1	20668.3	9181.3			888
July	20944.6	65.8	21010.4	8504.9			926
August	22402.1	70.9	22473.0	9432.1	25744	29082	903
September	24595.0	77.9	24672.9	14538.1			962
October	26561.5	142.0	26703.5	10733.8	27432		997
November	29103.5	179.3	29282.8	10683.0		29655	1023
December	32936.7	169.5	33106.2	13280.4	29981	31834	1121
1919							
January	34452.8	83.1	34535.9	12522.7			1310
February	35169.4	84.8	35254.2	11830.6	28527	32294	1313
March	37149.5	87.2	37236.7	14502.9			1424
April	38428.7	88.8	38517.5	14537.3	30663		1511
May	39825.3	91.5	39916.8	9987.9		33740	1622
June	42605.8	94.7	42700.5	13729.6			1723
July	41806.5	98.0	41904.5	10362.1			1964
August	40781.0	99.9	40880.9	10885.3	33779	35636	1900
September	42196.2	102.4	42298.6	13019.5			1948
October	43300.2	104.4	43404.6	12033.3			2166
November	45310.8	106.2	45417.0	11137.6		36032	2353
December	50064.7	108.2	50172.9	17071.9	54601	36981	2763
1920							
January	50959.7	119.5	51079.2	14121.5			3287
February	54329.9	126.5	54456.4	12142.3		35604	3304
March	59474.8	132.2	59607.0	18498.4			3894
April	62285.5	138.3	62423.8	16498.9			4459
May	64149.6	146.2	64295.8	17023.7		37354	4616
June	68154.3	155.6	68309.9	23414.0			4343
July	69655.0	168.9	69823.9	17281.8			4352
August	72223.0	181.4	72404.4	15771.8			4309
September	75635.1	196.1	75831.2	20053.6			4751
October	77167.9	211.4	77379.3	17945.4			5924
November	77202.2	226.5	77428.7	17339.9			6602
December	81387.3	241.1	81628.4	22327.1	84526	44563	7108

Table 11. (continued).

	Cash			Deposits			
End of month	Notes	Coins	Total	Reichs-bank	Joint stock credit banks	Savings banks	Postal giro accounts
	(1)	(2)	(3)	(4)	(5)	(6)	(7)
1921							
January	78506.3	257.6	78763.9	15834.0			7498
February	79720.3	274.2	79994.5	17357.1			6701
March	80118.0	294.2	80412.2	28042.7			6662
April	80911.6	308.0	81219.6	20855.9			6990
May	81409.7	325.4	81735.1	14093.7			6718
June	84556.3	345.6	84901.9	20392.7			6505
July	86.297.5	366.7	86664.2	15824.1			6756
August	88445.7	387.6	88833.3	13649.6			6864
September	94533.5	407.6	94941.1	19980.3			7519
October	99383.6	428.0	99811.6	18302.6			8690
November	108814.9	445.7	109260.6	25313.1			10085
December	122496.6	466.2	122962.8	32905.6		49932	11019
1922							
January	123938.4	487.5	124425.9	23413			11514
February	128507.0	509.5	129016.5	26526			12130
March	139958.9	535.2	140494.1	33359			15029
April	150197.8	554.4	150752.2	31616			18093
May	161.970.7	574.8	162545.5	33128			19213
June	180169.0	597.5	180766.5	37174			21476
July	202625.7	620.6	203246.3	39976			23146
August	252212.1	645.5	252857.6	56124			31350
September	331875.6	686.9	332562.5	110012			42949
October	484685.3	–	484685.3	140779			64407
November	769499.6	–	769499.6	240970			102666
December	1295228.1	–	1295228.1	530526		163020	173552
1923	in bn.		in bn.				
January	1999.6	–	1999.6	762			
February	3536.3	–	3536.3	1583			
March	5542.9	–	5542.9	2273			
April	6581.2	23.27	6604.5	3854			
May	8609.7	34.09	8643.8	5063			
June	17340.5	52.35	17392.8	9953			
July	43813.5	79.17	43892.7	27857			
August	668702.6	95.19	668797.8	591080			
September	28244405.8	–	28244405.8	16966617			
		in trillion		in trillion			
October	2504955.7	–	2504955.7	3868086			
November	400338326.4	–	400338326.4	373976741			
December	496585345.9		496585345.9	548024197			

Sources:

Cols. 1–4 Stat. Reichsamt: *Zahlen zur Geldentwertung in Deutschland 1914–1923* (Berlin, 1925) pp. 45–52. Col. 4, Sept. to Dec. 1923 J. P. Young: *European Currency* ..., vol. 1, pp. 528–529. From January 1921 on Young presents the data on public and private Reichsbank deposits separately.

Cols. 5–6 Politisches Archiv des Auswärtigen Amts Bonn, Abt. W. Rep., Akten betreffend Verhandlungen zur Ausführung des Friedensvertrages in Spa, 9125/242450-242595 (Kent Catalogue). On microfilm: National Archives, Washington D.C., T. 120 Reel no. 3462. Also Table 10. Monthly data for before June 1914: Stat. Reichsamt: *Die deutschen Banken 1924 bis 1926*, p. 107.

Col. 7 F. Hesse: *Deutsche Wirtschaftslage* ..., pp. 426ff.

(2) The amounts in circulation of various state liabilities which were accepted as money: the *Reichskassenscheine* and *Darlehnskassenscheine*, which bore no interest and were accepted as means of payment by all government agencies. Again, that part of the circulation of these notes which was held in the portfolios of the note-issuing and commercial banks must be subtracted. Since they were not interest-bearing we may perhaps assume that the proportion of their circulation held by commercial banks was the same as the corresponding proportion of banknotes. The Reichsbank and other note-issuing banks held them because – just like gold – they could count as part of the legally required reserves against the note issue.[14]

(3) Deposits with the Reichsbank and the four issuing banks, excluding those made by the banking system, other note-issuing banks, and the public authorities.

(4) Deposits with the banking system, excluding savings deposits and inter-bank deposits.

From each of these components of M_2 the amounts in foreign ownership are to be deducted since they do not count as part of the money supply. Table 62 supplies some particulars on this subject.

Some points of reference for analyzing the aggregates of Tables 10 and 11 into these components of M_2 may now be suggested. In 1913 the notes of other note-issuing banks in the Reichsbank's portfolio came to no more than 0.5 % of the Reichsbank's own note issue, in 1914 only 0.1 % and in subsequent years even less.[15] The impossibility of excluding these items from component (1) will therefore have little effect on our money supply calculations. The amounts of Reichsbank notes held by the other four banks of issue presumably constituted a much larger part of their portfolios. But since the notes of these banks accounted for only 4 % of the total circulation of paper money in 1914, 0.7 % in 1919 and less than 0.2 % in 1922,[16] errors in our estimate of Reichsbank notes in their possession will also make little difference to our calculations. The assumption may be made that the relationship between private note-issuing banks' cash balances and their chief liability – their own notes in circulation – was the same as that between the cash balances of

[14] On the reserve requirements governing the issue of notes by the Reichsbank, see S. Flink: *The Reichsbank and Economic Germany* (New York, 1929), pp. 1–15; or J. Riesser: *The German Great Banks and their Concentration in Connection with the Economic Development of Germany* (Washington, D.C., 1911), pp. 141 ff.

[15] Calculated from data in: *Die Reichsbank 1901–1925*, Pt. II, p. 12.

[16] Statistisches Reichsamt: *Zahlen zur Geldentwertung in Deutschland 1914 bis 1923* (Berlin, 1925), pp. 45–46.

commercial banks and *their* deposit liabilities. This relationship may be estimated from the following information.

For the eight Berlin great banks (seven after the amalgamation in 1921 of the Darmstädter with the Nationalbank) this ratio can be inferred from their annual balance sheets.[17] For all taken together it averaged as follows:

1912 7.6 %	1913 7.4 %	1914 10.8 %	1915 10.7 %
1916 9.2 %	1917 8.3 %	1918 7.2 %	1919 6.5 %
1920 6.9 %	1921 5.3 %	1922 6.3 %.	

These year-end cash ratios were of course affected by 'window dressing' and were consistently higher than the average ratios as calculated from the interim bimonthly balance sheets – for example 7.6 % as against 4.7 % in 1912, 7.4 % as against 4.7 % in 1913. Moreover the prewar cash ratios of the Berlin great banks were higher than the average ratio of all joint stock credit banks reporting to the Reichsbank: for the interim bimonthly balance data excluding December, 4.7 % (Berlin banks) as against 4.2 % (all reporting banks) in 1912 as well as in 1913.[18] This may be connected with the reserve function exercised by the Berlin banks on behalf of the provincial banks,[19] a function also betrayed by the fact that deposits by other banks were more prominent among the Berlin banks' liabilities than among other banks' liabilities.[20]

Having considered the extent to which the note-issuing banks held cash and each other's notes, I now turn to a deduction to be made under component (3): commercial banks' deposits at the Reichsbank. The sectoral origins of total deposits at the Reichsbank before the outbreak of war and after the end of the inflation may be studied in Table 12. Before the war commercial bank deposits accounted for between 25 % and about 40 % of the total but after the stabilization of the mark for only about 15 % – a reduction which perhaps reflects the weakened financial position of commercial banks following the inflation. The counterpart of commercial banks' reduced share in deposits at the Reichsbank is the increased share of public sector deposits.

Let us now investigate what can be known about savings and interbank deposits with the banking system – items to be deducted under component (4) of M_2. Savings deposits declined greatly as a proportion of total bank deposits during the inflation, and even as a proportion of all deposits with savings banks, which at one time had offered only this type of account. Following the

[17] P. B. Whale: *Joint Stock Banking*... pp. 340ff.

[18] Statistisches Reichsamt: *Die deutschen Banken 1924–1926* (Berlin, 1927), pp. 11–12.

[19] *Ibid.*, p. 15.

[20] *Ibid.*, p. 13

Table 12. Deposits at the Reichsbank by class of depositor 1900, 1910, 1914, 1925

Date	Total deposits	Banking sector: Total	Banking sector: Joint stock credit banks	Banking sector: Other banks	Non-bank businesses and individuals: Total	Trade, transport, insurance	Industry	Agri-cultural and related activities	Other (non-profit-making trusts, individuals)	Public sector
	Value of Giro deposits: mill. marks / reichsmarks									
May 7, 1900	388	142			98	37	52	1	8	148
June 15, 1910	563	143	90	53	117	36	72	2	7	303
July 23, 1914	834	321	246	75	139	36	97	2	4	374
July 31, 1925	582	90	42	48	114	16	49	2	47	378
	in %									
May 7, 1900	100	36,6			25.3	9.5	13.4	0.3	2.1	38.1
June 15, 1910	100	25.5	16.0	9.5	20.6	6.4	12.8	0.3	1.1	53.9
July 23, 1914	100	38.5	29.5	9.0	16.6	4.3	11.6	0.2	0.5	44.9
July 31, 1925	100	15.4	7.2	8.2	19.6	2.8	8.4	0.3	8.1	65.0

Source: Deutsche Bundesbank: *Deutsches Geld- und Bankwesen in Zahlen 1876–1975* (Frankfurt/M, 1976), p. 42.

recommendations of the Banking Inquiry of 1908 savings banks had been permitted to enter the field of short-term deposit banking, and the increase in current account deposits as a percentage of all deposits at Prussian savings banks may be observed in Table 13. Prussian savings banks held two-thirds of total German savings banks deposits.

Table 13. Current account (sight) deposits as a percentage of total deposits at Prussian savings banks 1909–25

End of year	%	End of year	%
1909	0.11	1918	4.74
1910	0.16	1919	5.75
1911	0.25	1920	10.08
1912	0.43	1921	14.94
1913	0.49	1922	82.95
1914	0.99	1923	83.69
1915	1.69	1924	51.0
1916	2.50	1925	25.9
1917	4.08		

Computed from the savings banks statistics in the *Zeitschrift des Preussischen Statistischen Landesamts*, current issues.

The tendency of deposit business during the course of the inflation to shift toward types requiring shorter notice of withdrawal is also evident in the changing structure of the Berlin great banks' deposit liabilities (cp. Table 14). This structure had been relatively stable up to 1918 but in 1919 a sudden shift

Table 14. Distribution of deposits at Berlin great banks by required notice of withdrawal, 1913–25

End of year	up to 7 days (current account) %	7 days–3 months %	above 3 months %
1913	56.8	29.8	13.3
1918	60.6	26.1	13.1
1919	78.1	14.0	7.8
1920	76.7	15.1	8.2
1921	77.1	15.0	7.9
1922	93.0	4.9	2.1
1923	92.6	3.3	4.0
1924	57.5	40.0	2.5
1925	51.5	44.5	3.9

Source: P. B. Whale; *Joint Stock Banking*..., p. 218; Stat. Reichsamt: *Die deutschen Banken 1924–26*, p. 25. Categorization is according to the scheme followed in the bimonthly bank balances.

can be observed. In 1922 a further dramatic increase occurred in the value of current account deposits as a percentage both of all deposits at Berlin great banks and of all deposits at savings banks. This can be explained by the onset of hyperinflation.

Interbank deposits are also to be subtracted from total bank deposits in calculating M_2, but the ratio between the one and the other cannot be accurately calculated for the inflation period. Table 15 contains data for the years 1913, 1924 and 1925. They suggest that the ratio of interbank to total deposit liabilities was significantly higher after the stabilization than in 1913.

Table 15. Deposits by other banks as a percentage of total non-bank deposit liabilities, 1913, 1924, 1925

End of year	1913	1924	1925
all credit institutions	3.7	22.4	27.1
joint stock credit banks	5.8	14.7	17.4
savings banks		2.1	5.9

Source: Stat. Reichsamt: *Die deutschen Banken 1924 bis 1926*, p. 179.

The rising importance of banks' deposits with other banks that can be inferred from the *assets'* side of bank balance sheets (see Table 16) may confirm that deposits by other German banks made up an increasing share of total deposit *liabilities* during the inflation as well as after it. If so, then in this case also 1922 was the year when the most dramatic shift was seen.

Table 16. Deposits at other banks as a percentage of the total assets of the Berlin great banks 1913–24

End of year	%	End of year	%
1913	4.1	1919	8.5
1914	4.3	1920	7.2
1915	4.5	1921	11.7
1916	5.6	1922	42.1
1917	7.7	1923	38.6
1918	4.8	1924	16.2

Source: to 1923: P.B. Whale; *Joint Stock Banking* ..., p. 200, 221. 1924: Stat. Reichsamt: *Die deutschen Banken 1924 bis 1926*, p. 139.

However the 'deposits with other banks' shown in Table 16 include the deposits which German banks made with foreign banks, and in Whale's view these deposits abroad accounted for most of the increase reported in 1922. They were "accumulated to finance imports, but to a much greater extent, in all probability, they served as investments which were both liquid and safe from depreciation."[21] Against this view it must be pointed out that an increase in the ratio which the sums deposited by banks with foreign banks bore to their own total assets must not be confused with an increase in the absolute gold value of such deposits with foreign banks. The gold value of the total deposit liabilities of the Berlin great banks at year's end fell from 2.6 bn. gold marks in 1921 to 0.9 bn. gold marks in 1922.[22] By definition their assets must have fallen accordingly. Thus even if the gold value of the sums deposited by the great banks with foreign banks remained constant, it would triple as a proportion of the total value of their assets. Supposing then that the gold value of these foreign deposits did not rise, the remainder of the increased share of deposits with other banks in total bank assets would be accounted for by increased deposits with *German* banks.

A further phenomenon affecting the calculation of the money supply remains to be mentioned, namely the growing importance of foreign currency deposits with the German banking system. This too is connected with the onset of hyperinflation in 1922 and forms a counterpart under bank liabilities to the deposits on the assets side with foreign banks which we have just discussed. The data is not available to determine whether the absolute value of these stable-currency deposits increased significantly during 1922,[23] but their relative importance certainly increased, owing to the rapid shrinkage of the gold value of the banks' paper-mark denominated liabilities and assets. Thus the rate of increase of the paper-mark denominated deposits with the banking system was less than the rate of increase of the (paper-mark value of) total deposits would suggest.

The foregoing discussion shows that a good deal of "guesstimating" would necessarily enter any attempt at a precise calculation of the money supply as a whole. However the data required for the calculation of the monetary base are preserved in adequate detail. The only exception is the lack of continuous information about the scale of public authority deposits with the Reichsbank – a quantity which should be excluded from the monetary base. The data presented in Table 10 show however that both during the inflation and before 1914 these formed between one fourth and one fifth of total deposits at the central bank.

---

21 P.B. Whale: *Joint Stock Banking*... p. 227.

22 *Ibid.*, p. 216.

23 *Ibid.*, p. 217.

I conclude my discussion of the money supply and the monetary base with some observations about the development of the structure of each during the inflation. The structure of the monetary base altered considerably during this period as Table 19 shows. Gold coins which represented about 40 % of the monetary base before 1914 were withdrawn from circulation by the Reichsbank after the outbreak of war and partially replaced by notes of smaller denomination than before. The circulation of small-change coins (which made up about 10 % of the base before the war) increased at the beginning of the war but subsequently declined in importance and during the last two war years played an insignificant role in the currency. The share of the notes of issuing banks other than the Reichsbank also declined into insignificance as did the share of deposits with them. The same is true of the *Reichskassenscheine*: the prewar limits on the issue of these were not adjusted during the inflation. However almost one quarter of the monetary base came during the war to consist of *Darlehnskassenscheine*, (Loan Bureau Certificates) which had not previously existed. The importance of *Darlehnskassenscheine* in the monetary base declined after the war was over however, and by 1922 was less than one per cent, most of it held by the Reichsbank which could employ it as part of the statutory reserve backing its own note issue. Reichsbank notes had represented rather more than one third of the monetary base in 1913; during the war years their share hovered around fifty per cent, climbing to more than 75 % in 1921 and 1922. Private sector deposits at the Reichsbank (i. e. those by banks, other businesses and private individuals) increased from about 8½ % of the monetary base in 1913 to approaching one quarter at the end of 1918. In the immediate postwar period this percentage fell somewhat, but returned to almost one quarter in 1922. The rising and sustained importance of private sector deposits at the Reichsbank reflects its efforts to promote the practice of giro in place of cash-payment methods.[24]

Broadening our attention to consider the structure of the money supply we must firstly note the substantial decline in the importance of "secondary" money (i. e. money created by the banking system) relative to central bank and state money (i. e. the monetary base). At the end of 1913 the aggregate value of deposits with the joint stock credit banks was about 133.5 % of the monetary base, and the total value of deposits with all types of credit institutions repre-

[24] The use of cash to effect payment was still more common in prewar Germany than in England, and following the German Banking Inquiry of 1908 the Reichsbank took steps to reduce Germany's backwardness in this respect by encouraging the use of non-cash payment methods. Cp. *Die Reichsbank 1901–1925*, pp. 27 ff. A summary survey of the various German giro systems is to be found in Whale, *op. cit.* appendix II.

sented in Table 10 about 500% of the same. But by the end of 1918 the corresponding ratios had declined to 68.8% and 173%, by the end of 1919 they stood at 85.8% and 171.4% (cp. Table 18). At the end of 1922 the sum of the deposits with Berlin great banks, the savings banks and accounts with the Postal giro system (*Postscheckämter*) was only 116.4% of the monetary base; at the end of 1921 the corresponding percentage had been 116.2%, 1920–115.5 %, 1919–124.9 % and 1918 – 121 %, as against 347.1 % at the end of 1913. The ratio between actual *mark* deposits and the monetary base (thus excluding foreign currency deposits) was probably even lower in 1922, for reasons already explained.[25]

The composition of "secondary money" also changed considerably during the period. The real value of deposits at institutions specializing in long term banking (mortgage banks, savings banks, co-operative credit societies) fell relatively much more sharply than the real value of deposits with the joint stock credit banks whose business was predominantly short term. Thus as Table 17 shows, aggregate savings bank deposit liabilities became a smaller proportion of the deposit liabilities of all banks over the inflation period and remained lower thereafter.

Table 17. Deposit liabilities of joint stock credit banks and savings banks as a percentage of the deposit liabilities of all credit institutions other than banks of issue 1913, 1924, 1925

End of year	*Joint stock credit banks*	*savings banks*
1913	27.7	56.3
1924	62.4	15.5
1925	53.9	19.0

Source: Stat. Reichsamt: *Die deutschen Banken 1924 bis 1926*, p. 179.

The changing structure of secondary money reflects the same tendencies as were at work to cause the deposit structure of the great credit banks to shift towards those types requiring shorter notice of withdrawal (Table 14). The effect of this latter shift was to disadvantage the provincial banks relative to the Berlin great banks. But the Post Office giro accounts benefited most of all because of their very short term nature, their undeveloped state at the start of the period, and the promotion of non-cash methods of payment by the Reichsbank.

[25] Cp. p. 60 *supra*.

Table 18. Deposits at various types of bank as a percentage of the monetary base 1913–22

	Joint stock credit banks			*Other banking institutions*			
End of of year	Berlin great banks	Provin-cial banks	Total	Mortgage banks	Savings banks	Co-op. credit societies	Postal giro accounts
1913	71.3	62.2	133.5	12.2	272.6	65.6	3.2
1914	52.4	42.6	95.0	8.7	202.3	45.8	2.7
1915	57.5	41.2	98.7	8.7	171.0	44.5	2.6
1916	59.0	37.6	96.6	6.2	134.7	38.6	3.3
1917	61.4	32.2	93.6	5.3	102.5	31.2	3.4
1918	45.2	23.6	68.8	4.7	73.0	23.7	2.8
1919	61.5	24.3	85.8	3.6	58.1	18.6	5.3
1920	63.0	22.1	85.1	3.9	44.9	–	7.6
1921	77.6	–	–	–	33.5	–	5.1
1922	96.4	–	–	–	9.7	–	10.3

Source: Table 10.

Table 19. The structure of the monetary base 1913–22 (%)

End of year	Gold coins	Other coins	Reichs-bank notes	Loan Bureau certificates*	Private sector deposits at the Reichsbank	Other items
1913	38.1	12.8	35.6	–	8.5	5.0
1914	–	28.0	49.7	4.4	13.4	4.5
1915	–	14.2	58.0	8.2	15.4	4.2
1916	–	5.5	50.6	18.0	22.3	3.6
1917	–	0.9	46.3	25.3	25.2	2.3
1918	–	0.4	50.9	23.2	23.7	1.8
1919	–	0.2	56.1	21.5	21.0	1.2
1920	–	0.2	69.3	12.1	17.5	0.9
1921	–	0.3	76.3	5.6	17.0	0.8
1922	–	–	76.3	0.8	22.5	0.4

* *Darlehnskassenscheine*
Source: Table 10.

Liquidity

The liquidity of the banking system, that is, the extent to which bank liabilities are covered by actual and potential central bank money, was generally high during the inflation, since money itself was generally so plentiful. The initial and final stages of the inflation were different however: crises of liquidity characterized both the first few weeks of war and the hyperinflationary phase that commenced in 1922.

The outbreak of war brought with it all the symptoms of panic and financial crisis.[26] Security prices fell heavily on the stock market[27] and there was a domestic run on the banks.[28] Prion estimates that the joint stock banks lost twenty percent of their deposits in the first few weeks of the war[29] and although the bimonthly balances now available (Table 11) register a reduction in joint stock credit bank deposit liabilities of no more than 7.3% (613 mill. M.) between the end of June and the end of October 1914, he may well be correct as regards the first few weeks of the war. The critical period "did not last beyond the middle of August and was followed by steady recovery during the autumn", says Whale.[30] But even the lesser decline as measured between the ends of June and October demonstrates the threat that the run posed to the banks' liquidity when one bears in mind that before the war banks' cash reserves were on average only about five percent of their liabilities.[31]

The Reichsbank, together with the government of the Reich, acted to overcome the liquidity crisis, the former by increasing its rediscounting of acceptances from bank portfolios,[32] the latter by establishing the Loan Bureaux (*Darlehnskassen*)[33] that were offering credit against the collateral of good stock or market securities. Reichsbank discount rate was raised from five to six percent at the beginning of August 1914 and, after the situation had calmed, reduced again to five percent on December 23rd: thus the Reichsbank, following Bagehot's celebrated maxim for coping with crises, had "lent freely,

---

26 Models and historical examples of this are to be found in C. P. Kindleberger: *Manias..., passim*.

27 Walter Klebba: *Börse und Effektenhandel im Kriege* (Berlin, 1920), p. 4. Cp. also *Die Bank*, 1914, p. 770.

28 P. B. Whale: *Joint Stock Banking...* pp. 185ff; Rudolf Stucken: *Liquidität der Banken* (Berlin, 1940), pp. 61–62. On the liquidity of banks before the war see also Ernst Loeb: *Wirtschaftliche Vorgänge, Erfahrungen und Lehren im Europäischen Krieg* (Jena, 1915), pp. 6–14. More generally on the role of the banks in the process of inflation Karl Erich Born: " Vom Beginn des Ersten Weltkrieges bis zum Ende der Weimarer Republik (1914–1933)", in Institut für bankhistorische Forschung (ed.): *Deutsche Bankengeschichte, Bd. 3: Vom Ersten Weltkrieg bis zur Gegenwart* (Frankfurt/M., 1983), pp. 29–32, 48–57.

29 Willi Prion: *Die deutschen Kreditbanken im Kriege und nachher* (Stuttgart, 1917), pp. 21–22, 32. Cp. also *Die Bank*, 1915, p. 301.

30 P. B. Whale: *Joint Stock Banking...* p. 189. Cp. also Ernst Hoppe: *Der Krieg und die deutsche Geldwirtschaft* (Essen, 1919), p. 17.

31 Cp. p. 56 *supra*; also Statistisches Reichsamt: *Die deutschen Banken 1924 bis 1926*, p. 12.

32 In *Die deutschen Kreditbanken...*, p. 24, W. Prion draws attention to the 2.2 bn. M. rise in the Reichsbank's holdings of commercial bills between 25th July and 25th August, 1914.

33 The functioning of the government Loan Bureaux is concisely described in P. B. Whale: *Joint Stock Banking...*, p. 187.

but at high interest rates."[34] The commercial banks for their part are said to have rationed withdrawals, that is, to have paid out only up to a certain percentage of sums deposited, to have refused to advance new credit, and to have demanded the repayment of some credit already granted.[35]

Thus the disruption of production and considerable unemployment that characterized the first few weeks of the war are to be attributed not just to the military requisitioning of men (i.e. the call-up) and of means of transport (especially railways): the credit difficulties just described also played a part.

During the years 1915 to 1921 business and the banks experienced general "abundance of funds."[36] Discount rate remained at five percent and money market rates were still lower[37] despite the pressure upon the market, especially during the second half of the war, of up to fifty billion marks' worth of Reich floating debt – the consequence of the increasing inability of the Reich to fund its fiscal deficits with War Loans (cp. Table 20). The non-bank private sector too could obtain credit from the banks at about five percent, using War Loans as collateral. The banks for their part reserved the right to use the War Loans thus deposited with them as collateral for their own borrowings from the government Loan Bureaux.[38] Insofar as the floating debt remained in the Reichsbank's portfolio, additional central bank money was made available, to the public sector in the first instance, but through its excess expenditures to the private sector. Business accumulated ever rising cash reserves in this manner, which for the most part they held as deposits with the banking system. As a result they required fewer loans from the banks. This also explains the decline of the commercial bill during the war as a form of trade credit.[39] Commercial banks were also extremely liquid and invested their funds mainly in Reich treasury bills.

The changing proportions in which these treasury bills were held by the Reichsbank on the one hand, and outside the Reichsbank – i.e. by the banking system – on the other, reflects therefore the degree of liquidity in the economy as a whole and particularly the liquidity of the commercial banks. The higher the proportion held outside the Reichsbank, the more liquid the money market must have been and the more willing the banks therefore to hold their

---

[34] Walter Bagehot: *Lombard Street. A Description of the Money Market* (London, 1873). Cp. R.S. Sayers: *Central Banking after Bagehot* (Oxford, 1957).

[35] P.B. Whale: *Joint Stock Banking*... p. 189.

[36] *Ibid.*, p. 190.

[37] *Ibid.*, p. 191.

[38] Willi Prion: *Die deutschen Kreditbanken*..., pp. 95, 100.

[39] Erich Renell: "Der Warenwechsel in Deutschland in der Geldentwertungszeit 1919–1923" (Dissertation, Berlin, 1926), p. 20.

liquid reserves in the form of potential rather than actual central bank money. According to Prion about 25% of treasury bills in circulation in 1920 for example were held by the Berlin great banks, representing about sixty percent of the value of their deposit liabilities.[40] A liquidity crisis, whether caused by withdrawal of deposits or by increased business demands upon the banking system for credit, will necessarily express itself in the conversion of potential into actual central bank money; in this case that would mean either the sale of Reich treasury bills from commercial bank portfolios to the Reichsbank or at least the refusal of banking institutions to increase their purchases of treasury bills in the money market despite growing deposits – a refusal which would also reduce the ratio of treasury bills held outside the Reichsbank to those held by it. Table 20 shows the month by month distribution of treasury bills between the Reichsbank and other holders from July 1914 to November 1923.

With these considerations in mind we can detect the symptoms of the onset of the credit crisis of 1922 in the fact that between the end of January and the end of May of that year the amounts of treasury bills held outside the Reichsbank declined not only proportionally but absolutely, even although the monetary base was continuing to expand and total deposits with the banking system were probably not declining.[41] The value of treasury bill holdings outside the Reichsbank fell from 129.7 bn. marks at the end of January 1922 to 121.7 bn. at the end of May, thereafter to 109.1, 100.1 and finally to 81.8 bn. marks at the end of August. The proportion held outside the Reichsbank fell still more steeply in the same period – from more than fifty percent to 24.7%, and although the absolute values (in current marks) held outside the Reichsbank began to climb in the later months of 1922 the proportion continued to fall. It rose again in December 1922 and in January 1923, jumped up from its lowest level (17.9%) in February to 31% in March, when the Reichsbank had succeeded in stabilizing the mark exchange rate by intervening on the foreign

---

[40] Willi Prion: "Deutsche Kreditpolitik 1919–1922", *Schmollers Jahrbuch*, 47 (1924), p. 177.

[41] During the summer of 1922 complaints about scarcity of credit were to be heard from credit institutions and business firms. Cp. the article "Kreditnot" in *Die Sparkasse*, No. 1067 of August 30th, 1922, p. 4: "A variety of forces has been denuding the savings banks of billions which under normal circumstances would have been deposited with them: hoarding of commodities to escape rapidly increasing prices, hoarding of banknotes in order to escape wealth tax and the compulsory [Reich] loan, as well as enormous speculation in foreign exchange and common stocks. The result has been that in July of this year savings deposits not only failed to increase but actually showed a slight decline. This obligates savings banks to pay all the greater attention to preserving their liquidity, primarily, that is, by advancing as little long-term credit as possible." On the credit crisis of 1922 see also Hans Wolf: "Inflationswirtschaft und Kreditmarkt. Dargestellt an der Entwicklung der deutschen Kreditkrise der Jahre 1922–1923" (Dissertation, Frankfurt, 1925).

Table 20. Development of the Reich's floating debt, and the proportion held outside the Reichsbank, 1914–23

End of month	Total value of treasury bills in circulation (bn. Mark)	Of which, percentage held outside Reichsbank	End of month	Total value of treasury bills in circulation (bn. Mark)	of which, percentage held outside Reichsbank
1914					
July	0.3	0			
Aug.	2.1	9.5			
Sept.	2.7	14.8			
Oct.	1.0	30.0			
Nov.	1.6	6.3			
Dec.	2.9	6.9			
1915			1918		
Jan.	4.3	34.9	Jan.	32.5	61.2
Feb.	5.9	42.4	Feb.	35.8	64.3
March	7.2	16.7	March	33.4	53.0
April	3.1	3.2	April	31.5	57.1
May	3.8	10.5	May	34.7	58.8
June	5.2	17.3	June	38.4	57.3
July	6.7	37.3	July	41.8	62.2
Aug.	8.2	46.3	Aug.	46.0	63.5
Sept.	8.6	20.9	Sept.	48.0	50.8
Oct.	3.6	2.8	Oct.	48.2	57.5
Nov.	4.1	0	Nov.	51.2	57.2
Dec.	5.7	8.8	Dec.	55.2	50.7
1916			1919		
Jan.	6.8	30.9	Jan.	58.6	54.3
Feb.	8.9	41.6	Feb.	61.6	56.0
March	8.6	14.0	March	63.8	53.1
April	4.8	10.4	April	67.2	53.4
May	5.9	20.3	May	70.4	59.5
June	7.2	18.1	June	73.4	54.9
July	8.8	34.1	July	76.1	60.1
Aug.	10.9	42.2	Aug.	78.2	60.4
Sept.	11.5	13.0	Sept.	80.6	58.3
Oct.	8.3	14.5	Oct.	83.3	59.5
Nov.	9.9	26.3	Nov.	85.2	60.3
Dec.	12.6	29.4	Dec.	86.4	52.2
1917			1920		
Jan.	15.0	49.3	Jan.	88.3	56.1
Feb.	17.7	52.0	Feb.	89.0	57.2
March	18.7	30.0	March	91.6	53.4
April	13.8	40.6	April	95.1	59.6
May	15.6	43.0	May	101.6	63.9
June	18.3	42.6	June	113.2	60.3
July	21.4	50.0	July	122.7	67.3
Aug.	24.7	55.6	Aug.	129.4	68.4
Sept.	26.0	41.5	Sept.	138.3	64.1
Oct.	22.9	50.7	Oct.	140.6	65.4
Nov.	24.8	52.4	Nov.	147.6	65.2
Dec.	28.6	50.4	Dec.	152.8	62.3

Table 20. (continued)

End of month	Total value of treasury bills in circulation (bn. Mark)	Of which, percentage held outside Reichsbank	End of month	Total value of treasury bills in circulation (bn. Mark)	of which, percentage held outside Reichsbank
1921			1923		
Jan.	155.5	67.5	Jan.	2 081,8	22.7
Feb.	161.8	66.8	Feb.	3 588.0	17.9
March	166.4	61.2	March	6 601.3	31.0
April	172.7	66.0	April	8 442.3	26.3
May	176.7	64.4	May	10 275.0	21.9
June	185.1	57.0	June	22 019.8	16.7
July	190.8	58.1	July	57 848.9	7.1
Aug.	202.9	58.6	Aug.	1 196 294.7	17.5
Sept.	210.5	53.3	Sept.	46 716 616.4	3.2
Oct.	218.0	54.7	Oct.	6 907 511 102.8	0.5
Nov.	226.7	49.7	15. Nov.	191 580 465 422.1	0.9
Dec.	247.1	46.5			
1922					
Jan.	255.9	50.7			
Feb.	263.0	48.9			
March	272.1	46.2			
April	281.1	44.7			
May	289.4	42.1			
June	295.3	37.0			
July	308.0	32.5			
Aug.	331.5	24.7			
Sept.	451.1	22.5			
Oct.	603.8	21.0			
Nov.	839.1	19.9			
Dec.	1 495.2	20.8			

Source: Deutschlands Wirtschaft, Währung und Finanzen (Berlin, 1924), p. 62.

exchange market. But from then on it declined rapidly (with the exception of August 1923), dwindling to insignificance in the final months of the inflation.

It seems paradoxical that bank liquidity as measured in this manner should improve in the middle of a period of credit restriction such as spring 1923, when the Reichsbank's "stabilization action" was under way. The explanation lies in the fact that throughout this period the Reichsbank continued to finance government deficits by accepting Reich treasury bills, whereas it required the credit banks to undertake a strict rationing of their advances to the private sector. Thus funds continued to flow into the banks but they were not permitted to invest them in advances to clients; so they placed them in treasury bills instead.

Table 21. The financing of Reich expenditure out of taxation and increase in the floating debt 1920–22. Expressed in mill. gold marks (converted at average dollar exchange rate for the month)

	Tax revenues	Increase in floating debt
April 1920 to March 1921	3178	6054
1921		
April	352.3	416.9
May	411.8	270.2
June	350.3	508.0
July	304.8	309.0
August	256.3	602.9
September	196.5	305.5
October	173.0	207.5
November	112.5	138.1
December	175.3	447.2
1922		
January	192.6	191.6
February	194.2	144.2
March	207.8	134.7
April	190.3	129.8
May	254.9	120.3
June	235.1	77.0
July	183.4	23.4
August	116.4	87.0

Source: Deutschlands Wirtschaft, Währung und Finanzen (Berlin 1924), p. 32.

This pinpoints the difference between the credit crisis of 1922 and the credit crisis of summer 1914. In July/August 1914 it was largely a case of a domestic run on the banks. Up till the actual outbreak of war there had been to some extent a foreign run, as foreigners rushed to withdraw deposits, but this was probably offset by an equivalent withdrawal of German deposits from foreign banks. Principally, the crisis of summer 1914 expressed a weakening of domestic confidence *in the banks*: a flight out of bank deposits into cash. The classic example of this type of run, occurring at a time when the purchasing power of money was actually rising, is the banking crisis in the U.S. during the 1929–33 depression. In 1914 the weakening confidence was occasioned by doubts about future bank liquidity, created by the political crisis. It was not occasioned by a weakening of confidence in the mark as such, i.e. not by a flight from the mark into foreign exchange or real commodities; there was no loss of confidence in the mark's future domestic and international purchasing power, whether on the part of foreigners or of German nationals.

The situation was reversed in 1922. During this latter year confidence in the currency was evaporating despite considerable success at the time in moving towards stabilization by bringing the fiscal deficit under control.[42] In consequence of this action the flow of funds to the banks was actually diminishing during the first half of 1922, as the proportion of Reich expenditures financed from taxation increased and the proportion financed by enlargement of the floating debt fell (see Table 21). This in turn retarded the growth of the monetary base (cp. Table 11) but was unable to arrest the upward drive of domestic prices or the downward plunge of the exchange rate, especially after June 1922. Temporarily, price and exchange rate movements had become detached from the development of the monetary base and the money supply. The explanation of the behavior of the currency at this time (and indeed of the transition from inflation to hyperinflation) lies, really, in the realm of the "psychology of money."[43] Expectations changed. It was an upsurge of pessimism about the mark's future domestic and international purchasing power that precipitated a "flight from the mark", not simply as a "store of value" but even as a "unit of account".

Businesses' accounting practices underwent a learning process through trying to cope with inflation. Prion describes the process roughly as follows: Because businesses, in preparing their balance sheets, were required to value their assets at cost of acquisition, they found themselves reporting high (paper) profits in times of rising prices. Nevertheless, when the time came to replenish stocks of materials or to replace plant and equipment, the funds available were not sufficient, because the real value of the money balances acquired in previous profit-taking had become eroded through the continuing currency depreciation. To remain in business, firms had to take up increased bank credits, and to insist on immediate payment from their customers. "The realization that in times of continuous currency depreciation firms suffer losses on outstanding claims but reap gains from the debts they owe led them to exploit the possibilities this opened up... As the inflation progressed the foremost business maxim became, to borrow as much credit as was obtainable but to offer no credit at all to others, or at least to keep outstanding claims on others in strict proportion to the credit one's own firm had received... Eventually, as everybody's prime objective became the exploiting of all available credit opportunities, commercial banks and the Reichsbank became 'lent up' and people began to talk about a 'credit crisis' and the problem of 'credit policy'."[44]

---

[42] Albert Hahn: "Die Frage des sog. Vertrauens in die Währung", *Archiv für Sozialwissenschaft und Sozialpolitik*, 52 (1924), Heft 2.

[43] Günter Schmölders: *Psychologie des Geldes* (Reinbek, 1966).

[44] W. Prion: "Deutsche Kreditpolitik...", p. 172.

Thus the liquidity crisis of spring and summer 1922 originated not so much in a loss of bank deposits in nominal terms as in an increase in the demands upon banks for advances – a quite different situation from that of summer 1914.

The liquidity required by firms rises, in nominal terms, during periods of inflation: they have to find the means to finance rising wage bills and increasingly expensive stocks of raw materials and capital goods. This had been true during the first phase of the postwar inflation – that is, up to spring 1920; nevertheless in that period business and the banks had remained very liquid. This was because the compensation paid by the Reich to business for properties confiscated in ceded territories, for the merchant marine and for other assets expropriated by the allies, had been financed by enlarging the floating debt. Thus liquid funds were flowing to firms either directly, or indirectly as increasing deposits enabled banks to relax their lending terms. Between February 1920 and May 1921 the currency entered a period of relative stability during which certain symptoms of a stabilization crisis were apparent. Business, but not bank, liquidity was impaired (cp. Table 20). This was followed by a second phase of currency depreciation, lasting until summer 1922 when the third phase, hyperinflation, began. During 1921 – even after the onset of the second period of postwar currency depreciation – banks were still able to satisfy the economy's demands for credit relatively easily as the Reich budget deficit continued to create generous supplies of liquidity.

In 1922 this changed as already indicated. Increasing illiquidity can be inferred from the behavior of a number of indicators.

(1) The proportion of the Reich treasury bill circulation held outside the Reichsbank (Table 20).

(2) The relationship between liquid assets and deposit liabilities in the banking system: the liquidity ratio. According to the schematic balance sheet below, liquid assets correspond to the difference between deposit liabilities and advances to customers. We can employ this difference, expressed as a percentage of deposit liabilities, as a measure of the liquidity ratio. This is done in Table 22.

Assets	Liabilities
Liquid assets	Deposits
Advances to customers	

Table 22. Deposit liabilities minus advances to clients expressed as a percentage of deposit liabilities: joint stock credit banks 1920–22 (January 1920 = 100)

	Joint stock credit banks
1920	
January	100
April	87.6
June	94.9
August	116.1
October	112.8
December	92.1
1921	
February	91.8
April	97.8
June	104.3
August	97.5
October	85.7
December	79
1922	
February	66.4
April	63.6
June	63
August	68.2
October	82.1

Source: Die Wirtschaftskurve, 1 (1922) and 2 (1923), *passim*.

(3) Interest rates. There were of course many different "interest rates", each relating to a different part of the market for credit, and they did not move uniformly.[45] Prion distinguished above all between the interbank rate for daily money and the interest rate upon current account advances. The market for daily money had collateral requirements identical to those of the Reichsbank and the Loan Bureaux (*Darlehnskassen*) set up by the government in 1914 – treasury bills or first class bonds – so that the interbank daily money rate would normally not rise above the Reichsbank discount rate. Insofar as business firms did not possess the required collateral, or commercial paper of equivalent quality, they were compelled to rely on other forms of credit,

[45] *Ibid.*, pp. 184–185. A description of the structure of the German money and credit markets at the time will be found in P. B. Whale: *Joint Stock Banking...*, chapters IV and V.

Table 23. A selection of short-term interest rates 1920–23. Percent p.a.

	Reichs-bank discount rate	Daily money rate	Forward margin against sterling*		Reichs-bank discount rate	Daily money rate	Forward margin against sterling*	Effective rate of interest on current account credit
	1.	2.	3.		1.	2.	3.	4.
1920				1922				
Jan.	5			Jan.	5	4.50	– 4.3	
Feb.	5			Feb.	5	4.28	– 3.0	10
March	5			March	5	4.54	– 0.8	
April	5			April	5	4.38	– 0.2	
May	5		– 5.5	May	5	4.34	– 0.6	
June	5		– 8.0	June	5	4.91	– 0.3	
July	5		– 4.0	July	5	5.40	+ 3.3	12
Aug.	5		– 7.5	Aug.	6	6.50	+ 12.5	
Sept.	5		– 3.4	Sept.	7	7.40	+ 43.3	
Oct.	5		– 5.6	Oct.	8	7.75	+ 92.3	
Nov.	5		– 2.3	Nov.	10	8.22	+163.6	50
Dec.	5		– 5.0	Dec.	10	9.21	+ 92.9	
1921				1923				
Jan.	5	3.70	–11.1	Jan.	12	11.05	+104.1	
Feb.	5	3.74	– 8.2	Feb.	12	25.67	+285.2	
March	5	3.85	– 9.9	March	12	11.00	+ 77.6	
April	5	4.25	– 7.6	April	18	12.70	+ 89.4	
May	5	4.07	– 7.1	May	18	20.15	+143.6	
June	5	4.13	– 6.0	June	18	19.35	+141.3	
July	5	4.09	– 4.1	July	18	92	+452.8	
Aug.	5	4.29	– 5.6	Aug.	30	283	+658.5	
Sept.	5	4.41	– 3.8	Sept.	90	1606		
Oct.	5	4.33	– 4.2	Oct.	90	1825		
Nov.	5	4.33	– 2.6					
Dec.	5	4.13	– 3.4					

* expressed as % p.a. of spot rate. Negative sign implies premium on the mark.

Sources:

Col. 1 *Die Reichsbank 1901–1925* (Berlin, n.d..); Tables, pp. 94–95.

Col. 2 *Die Wirtschaftskurve*, 1 (1922), 2 (1923), *passim*. Cp. also *Die Bank,* current vols.

Col. 3 For May–December 1920 calculated from data in: J. M. Keynes: "The Forward Market in Foreign Exchange", *Manchester Guardian Commercial Supplement: Reconstruction in Europe*, April 20th, 1922, pp. 11–14. From Jan. 1921 calculated from data in Paul Einzig: *The Theory of Forward Exchange* (London, 1937), pp. 450–455.

Col. 4 From data in: *Die Wirtschaftskurve*, 1 (1922), Heft 3, p. 5; also W. Prion: "Deutsche Kreditpolitik 1919–22", *Schmollers Jahrbuch*, 47 (1924), p. 185.

namely bank advances or the credit facilities which the banks offered to those who could furnish foreign currency balances as collateral – if they possessed such balances. Nominally, the interest charged by banks on current account advances was linked to the Reichsbank discount rate. However in practice the charges for handling the account (*Provisionen*) formed the major part of the true cost of the credit, so that in the last quarter of 1922, "the effective annual interest rate on a current account credit totaled fifty percent or more," at a time when the interbank daily money rate was still below ten percent.[46]

A third section of the credit market gained importance during the inflation, alongside the daily money market and market in current account credit. This was the market for credit against foreign currency collateral (*Devisenleihgeschäft*) alluded to in the last paragraph; it mushroomed as the flight from the currency gathered force and Germans converted their money balances into foreign currencies to protect their value. The loan was arranged as follows. The German holder of foreign balances required marks for the conduct of his business (to finance rising wage bills, etc.) but did not wish finally to relinquish these balances. So he sold to the bank foreign currency equivalent in value to the mark advance he required, simultaneously repurchasing the same sum of foreign currency from the bank in the forward market (for delivery, say, three months hence).[47] The repurchase price in marks which he would have to pay was of course different from the sum in marks which he had just received, and this difference between the spot and the forward exchange rate, expressed on an annual basis and as a percentage of the current spot rate, forms the so-called "swap rate". This was in effect the interest rate which the domestic borrower had to accept in order to obtain a loan on this market, and it is the third interest rate from whose behavior during 1922 increasing illiquidity may be deduced (Table 23).

The extent of credit scarcity was also reflected in the credit rationing practiced by the commercial banks in the spring and summer of 1922 and by both commercial banks and the Reichsbank in 1923.[48] The evidence for this is entirely qualitative however.[49]

For big firms, particularly, the liquidity crisis of the first half of 1922 was eased in the second half. After the Reichsbank signified in July 1922 its increased readiness to discount commercial bills, those sections of the non-bank private sector which were able to take advantage of this were placed on virtu-

---

[46] W. Prion: "Deutsche Kreditpolitik...", p. 185.

[47] Joachim Vogel: *Das Devisentermingeschäft* (Berlin, 1924).

[48] W. Prion: " Deutsche Kreditpolitik...", pp. 200–203.

[49] E.g. *Die Wirtschaftskurve*, 1 (1922), Heft 3, p. 5.

ally the same footing as the Reich itself in respect of the terms on which they could obtain credit. Such firms could dispense with the more expensive current account advances and the "foreign currency loan market" and refinance themselves at rates practically as low as those on the interbank daily money market. They even possessed direct access to the Reichsbank.

The extent of flight from the currency, to which the liquidity problems of this period may be traced, can be judged from the following assessment of the economic situation in October 1922, prepared by the *Frankfurter Zeitung.* "German economic life is now dominated by a struggle over the survival of the mark: is it to remain the German currency, or is it doomed to extinction?... During the past few months foreign currencies have replaced it as units of account in domestic transactions to a wholly unforeseen extent. The habit of reckoning in dollars, especially, has established itself, not only in firms' internal accounting practice, but above all as the method of price quotation in trade, industry and agriculture."[50] Foreign currency had, moreover, replaced the mark as the means of settlement of large transactions, though not of small ones or in retail trade. This discussion of the prospects for the mark concludes by emphasizing the degree to which foreign currencies also served as "stores of value", used to protect the real value of money balances.

The flight into foreign currencies was of course not merely a consequence of the collapse of the mark. It also played an important part in accelerating that collapse: to this aspect I now turn.

The key to the explanation of the various phases of the postwar inflation resides above all in the varying accessibility of foreign credit. Thus these phases were largely determined in the first instance by the behavior of the mark on the foreign exchanges; and the domestic price movements tracked exchange rate movements ever more closely as the inflation progressed. Now the mark's external exchange rate was determined by the supply of and demand for foreign currency, and the short run variations in supply and demand on the foreign currency market were primarily the result of changes in foreigners' willingness to invest short term balances in marks, and in German willingness to invest short balances abroad. The other determinants of excess supply or demand in this market were much less variable in the short run. Demand for foreign currency was a function of the demand for imports of goods and services, of the foreign currency required for the unilateral Reparations transfers to abroad, and of the foreign currency needed to effect German long and short term capital exports. The supply of foreign currency, insofar as not arising from foreign long and short lending to German firms, government

[50] *Die Wirtschaftskurve* 1 (1922), Heft 4, p. 3.

authorities or private individuals, was a function of foreign demand for German exports. The current account balance can, following Keynes,[51] be considered relatively "sticky" in the short run, except when major political changes disturb it – as for example when the allied blockade was lifted in 1919 and Germany re-entered international trade,[52] or when the Ruhr occupation in 1923 abruptly increased the German import demand for coal. The foreign currency requirements of Germany's Reparations commitments were politically predetermined to a large extent and – perhaps with the exception of the first heavy payment effected in the summer of 1921 – had no direct influence on the short term behavior of the foreign currency market. German capital exports were presumably small in this period, as the McKenna Committee believed, on the following *a priori* grounds: firstly, that Reparations obligations and a large import surplus during the early postwar years made heavy demands on Germany's capacity to earn foreign exchange and left little room in the balance of payments for capital exports, and secondly, that legal restrictions on the purchase of foreign currency impeded the possibility of investment abroad.

Thus in the short run only foreign lending to Germany – that is, willingness to sell goods or foreign currency in exchange for mark-denominated assets – possessed the flexibility to determine variations in the mark exchange rate.[53]

During 1919 and 1920 foreign suppliers displayed considerable readiness to accept German bank notes or mark deposits with German banks as payment for their exports to Germany. They then either retained these mark balances themselves in the expectation of a recovery of the mark in the foreign exchanges, or sold them to other foreign speculators who entertained such expectations. Part of these balances was invested in mark securities. By this means "liquidity" streamed into Germany from the outside world. Prion states that this was happening on a particularly large scale after August 1921.[54] Foreigners also used their mark balances to buy real assets in Germany, such as real estate or direct stakes in German companies. The effect was to create refinancing opportunities abroad for German firms and banks, for they could repair deficiencies in their liquidity at any time by selling securities or real assets to foreigners with mark balances. This in turn intensified inflationary

[51] J.M. Keynes: "The German Transfer Problem", *Economic Journal*, 39 (1929). Reprinted in *The Collected Writings of J. M. Keynes, edited by D. Moggridge et al.* (London, 1971 ff.), vol. XI, p. 457.

[52] This happened in November 1919, at which time German restrictions on exports were also relaxed: Cp. W. Prion: "Deutsche Kreditpolitik...", p. 175.

[53] This corresponds to the basic view of J.M. Keynes: "German Transfer Problem", p. 457.

[54] W. Prion: "Deutsche Kreditpolitik...", p. 177.

pressures within Germany, for the rising price of real estate and company stocks stimulated real investment, hence money incomes, aggregate monetary demand and the rate of increase of the price level.

As long as foreigners continued to have mark balances to dispose of, these foreign refinancing opportunities continued. Once foreigners were no longer prepared to buy German securities or real estate in return for their mark balances, or once the depreciation of the mark had so reduced the real value of these balances that they no longer mattered, this source of refinancing dried up. Germany became shut up to her own domestic sources of liquidity.

This point was reached in spring 1922. Proposals had been made at the Cannes conference of January 1922 for stabilizing the German public finances as the precondition for a Reparations moratorium; and accordingly, tax increases and a compulsory state loan were announced in Germany. Pessimism spread on the stock market[55] and security flotation could no longer count on rising prices. Foreigners held back from purchasing German securities as well, no doubt because the anticipation of stabilization measures and a consequent stock market recession made the holding of short term liquid assets more attractive. Between March and May 1922 there was also temporary respite in the external and internal depreciation of the mark (cp. Table 1) and this, coupled with the impossibility of selling securities, caused business to experience increasing illiquidity. The demand for bank credit increased, but since at the same time the flow of funds to the banks was diminishing, their only means of meeting their customers' credit demands was to reduce the level of their own liquidity. At the same time, however, as the banks were accepting reductions in their liquidity ratios, the structure of their deposit liabilities was shifting rapidly towards types requiring the least notice of withdrawal – a development that rather demanded the enhancement of their liquidity status. In June matters came to a head, in the sense that the bankers' committee, established under the chairmanship of J. P. Morgan by the Reparations Commission, postponed consideration of loans to Germany until after a revision of Reparations claims. This dashed hopes of an early stabilization of the mark and finally destroyed foreigners' willingness to accept payment in marks or to purchase mark securities. Foreigners now – a year after domestic citizens – embarked upon a flight from the mark into stable values – still German real estate to some extent, but mostly foreign exchange.

Thereafter the behavior of the mark exchange rate and of domestic prices entered the hyperinflationary phase. The economy's demand for credit intensified as price and cost increases accelerated; meanwhile in June and July 1922

[55] *Ibid.*, p. 180.

the supply of bank credit reached a standstill.[56] Savings banks actually experienced a relapse in the nominal value of their savings deposits during the latter month – the first for many years.[57] This may indicate at least that the level of deposits in all banking institutions was no longer increasing – hence point to a deterioration of their liquidity status. In this situation the Reichsbank saw itself compelled to try to encourage increased resort by business to commercial bills as a way of supplying business with the liquidity no longer flowing freely to the economy from the financing of the Reich's deficit or from foreigner's mark balances. It conveyed this encouragement both by signifying its own increased willingness to discount such bills and by a propaganda campaign in the press.[58]

Despite the prior success in reducing the Reich's deficit and the resultant illiquidity in the economy, the external depreciation of the mark started to accelerate in the second half of June 1922,[59] and the demands for credit to finance the purchase of higher-priced raw material imports increased yet further. In this situation the Reichsbank was faced with the alternatives either of permitting illiquidity to cause business collapse in the private sector whilst continuing to meet every demand of the public sector for liquid funds, or of allowing the non-bank private sector direct access to its own credit facilities, in order to prevent recession in the productive economy. The latter alternative was not necessarily more inflationary than the former. Insofar as evidence of illiquidity intensified the domestic and foreign flight from the currency it could accelerate the rate of mark depreciation and thus of wage and price increases. This led to higher public sector deficits whose financing by the central bank provided the monetary margin for inflation. An inflation proceeding ultimately from the fiscal balance could not be counteracted simply by creating liquidity shortages in the private sector. So simplistic a line of quantity-theoretic reasoning would overlook the repercussions of private sector illiquidity on real productive output, hence on the supply of goods, and also on the state of confidence in the currency, hence on the demand for money. As long as the rising domestic price level kept raising the paper mark value of government domestic expenditure and the falling exchange rate kept raising the paper mark value of Reparations obligations; as long as the Reichs-

[56] *Ibid.*, p. 181.

[57] Cp. note 41 on p. 66 *supra*.

[58] Especially on the part of the *Reichsbankdirektorium* member Karl Friedrich in "Kreditnot und ihre Bekämpfung", *Bank-Archiv*, 21 (1921/22), issue of July 15th, 1922, pp. 319–323.

[59] For the daily quotations of the dollar exchange rate see Statistisches Reichsamt: *Zahlen zur Geldentwertung*..., p. 9.

bank continued to finance the resultant Reich budget deficit without restraint thus holding the floodgates of inflation wide open – a liquidity crisis in the private sector could have practically no counterinflationary effect. Rather the converse: the liquidity crisis, by precipitating declines in production and flight from the currency, would have accentuated the decline in the demand for money and, given an undiminished pace of expansion of the money supply, would have accelerated the pace of price increase.

3.3. Measures of Monetary Overhang

For the war and early postwar years price statistics constitute an imperfect measure of the degree of inflation because the effect of legal maximum price regulations, as of other forms of state intervention on the market, was to hold actual prices below their market-clearing levels.[1] This was expecially true of the raw materials and foodstuffs markets and to this extent we are faced with a case of "suppressed inflation". This section of the chapter will confine itself to outlining the price and other administrative controls that developed in the foodstuffs sector, in view of the considerable and immediate effect of these on the cost of living and hence on the real income of the population. Controls in the raw materials sector will not be dealt with.[2]

The outbreak of war was followed by a spate of legislative measures designed to put the economy on a war footing, among other things empowering the Bundesrat to issue such decrees as were necessary to prevent economic dislocation and to safeguard the population's food supplies. One of the legislative measures was a "Law concerning Maximum Prices", passed by the Reichstag on August 4th.[3] This empowered the federal states, or authorities designated

---

[1] On wartime policy toward prices in general see Walter Le Coutre: *Die Grundgedanken der deutschen Preispolitik im Weltkriege 1914–1918* (Berlin, 1919).

[2] For detailed discussions of this see: Otto Goebel: *Deutsche Rohstoffwirtschaft im Weltkrieg* (Stuttgart, 1930); Kurt Wiedenfeld: *Die Organisation der Kriegsrohstoffbewirtschaftung im Weltkriege* (Hamburg, 1936); Alfred Müller: *Die Kriegsrohstoffbewirtschaftung 1914–1918 im Dienste des deutschen Monopolkapitals* (Berlin-East, 1955). Cp. also Dieter Baudis and Helga Nußbaum: *Wirtschaft und Staat in Deutschland vom Ende des 19. Jahrhunderts bis 1918/19* (Berlin-East, 1978), pp. 261–271. Hans Gotthard Ehlert: *Die wirtschaftliche Zentralbehörde des Deutschen Reiches 1914 bis 1919* (Wiesbaden, 1982), esp. pp. 34–52.

[3] *Reichsgesetzblatt* 1914, p. 339. Cp. also Gisela Gündell: *Die Organisation der deutschen Ernährungswirtschaft im Weltkriege* (Leipzig, 1939), p. 39.

by them, to establish legal maximum prices relating to necessities or other articles of mass consumption, and governing the activities of producers, wholesalers or retailers. Foodstuffs, animal feeds, industrial raw materials and fuel for heating and lighting were particularly in view, and offenders against the regulations were liable to fines or imprisonment. The authorities had the power to seize hoarded supplies of commodities and to sell them for the account of the hoarder.[4] This Law governed German official pricing policy for the early months of the war and its aim was made clear in the preamble. It was intended to prevent those price increases "which are not founded upon real changes in circumstances" and which occur "even when stocks adequate to supplying the population are available."[5] In other words the Law was designed to curb the attempts of traders to charge exploitative prices during periods of anxiety about general wartime scarcity or of temporary local shortages created by the military requisitioning of transport facilities. It was not designed to interfere with the fundamental market processes of price formation. Originally, then, the maximum price legislation aimed to enforce only upper limits on these processes and did not envisage that the maxima should become the prices at which transactions normally took place. The population was to receive its essential supplies at prices that were "reasonable" in the light of current availability and requirements; however in determining what was "reasonable" not only the interests of the consuming population, but also the interests of producers and traders were to be consulted. Otherwise trade would be crippled and possibly a worse evil brought about than that which the maximum prices were designed to prevent.[6]

Depending on local circumstances, some maximum prices were decreed by military or local civilian authorities in the same month as the Law was passed. Uncoordinated local determination of price maxima led to dislocating competition between authorities however; and where particularly severe shortages occurred as a result of war-related transport problems and the cessation of imports, the relevant local authorities were tempted to compensate by announcing "attractive" (i.e. relatively high) maximum prices. Price regulations in other localities were thus nullified: goods disappeared from these latter areas only to surface in the areas where more generous maxima ruled. The result was continuous week-by-week change in the relationship between max-

---

4 Karl Thiess: *Höchstpreispolitik. Beiträge zur Kriegswirtschaft,* Heft 1 (Berlin, 1916), pp. 3–6. Cp. also E. Stern: *Der Höchstpreis. Eine systematische Untersuchung auf Grund der Erfahrungen der deutschen Kriegswirtschaft* (Munich, 1923).

5 K. Thiess: *Höchstpreispolitik*... p. 6–7.

6 *Ibid.*, p. 7.

imum price levels in different areas. "The system of local determination of legal price maxima broke down, either because they were not imposed in all localities or because they were rescinded under the pressure of disappearing supplies.. But, at the same time, the very fact that prices were rising... was unleashing ever more insistent demands from the population that maximum prices be enforced."[7] Eventually on October 28th, 1914, the Bundesrat issued a decree giving itself the power to lay down uniform legal maximum prices for the entire Reich. Only in cases where it had not exercised its overriding right in this matter did the federal state governments retain the power to fix maximum prices. On the selfsame day the Bundesrat employed this power to issue decrees governing the supply of bread and bread grains.

The maximum prices which the Bundesrat fixed evidenced, for the first time, an intention to temper price increases on social grounds, even though general market conditions had caused them. Hence the price decrees had to be supplemented by flanking measures forbidding the use of bread grains and flour as animal feeds, controlling the wastage of grain in the milling process, and stipulating that a proportion of rye be added to wheat bread and of potato flour to rye bread. When these measures had failed to show the desired success, comprehensive state control of the distribution of bread and bread grains was instituted by a Bundesrat decree of January 25th, 1915. Production and distribution of bread, flour and bread grains was effectively transferred from private hands to the newly established Reich Grain Agency (*Reichsgetreidestelle*), which then re-employed the private producers and traders in a form of civilian war service.[8] The remuneration for this "service" consisted of the permitted profit margin or trade markup, now subject to the closest regulation. Thus organized, the grain sector became at this early stage "the corner stone of the system of civilian supply in wartime Germany."[9] Controls also survived longer into the postwar era in this than in any other sector – until the end of 1922,[10] and certainly worked better during that later period than the controls in other parts of the foodstuffs sector. Bread prices on the black market possessed "relatively little importance compared with official prices because the postwar official bread ration was usually adequate and as a result illegal deal-

---

7 *Ibid.*, p. 9.

8 Comprehensive accounts are to be found in: Otto Wiedfeldt: *Die Bewirtschaftung von Korn, Mehl und Brot im Deutschen Reiche, ihre Entstehung und ihre Grundzüge. Beiträge zur Kriegswirtschaft*, Heft 50/53 (Berlin, 1919); also Werner Pieper: "Die Versorgung Deutschlands mit Brotgetreide während des Weltkriegs 1914/18 und der Übergang zur freien Wirtschaft in den folgenden Jahren" (Dissertation, Berlin, 1927).

9 K. Thiess: *Höchstpreispolitik*..., p. 11.

10 Heinz Haushofer: *Die deutsche Landwirtschaft im technischen Zeitalter* (Stuttgart, 1963), p. 235.

ings in bread, when they occurred at all, usually took the form of the selling of bread ration cards."[11] Another source assesses the wartime situation thus: "Wherever it was possible for the authorities to organize the major portion of or the entire supply of a controlled commodity the maximum price system undoubtedly worked well. This is most clearly illustrated in the case of bread, which remained universally available at acceptable prices and in adequate quantities."[12]

A further extension of the August maximum price legislation occurred on December 17th, 1914, when articles "other than daily necessities" were brought within its purview.[13] By the end of 1914 maximum prices had been decreed for rye, wheat, barley, oats, potatoes and potato products, bran, animal feeds and sugar. This was in addition to the seizure and state administration of the supply of metals and industrial raw materials that had occurred after the outbreak of war.

As the war persisted into 1915, the tendency of prices to rise became increasingly apparent and it became more and more implausible to explain it in terms of speculative exploitation of temporary market disruption: clearly it reflected real underlying shortages. The enforcement of "socially just prices" began to replace the establishing of "reasonable prices, considering market conditions" as the overriding object of official price policy, and considerations such as the cost of production and the size of consumer disposable income began to supplant the relationship between available supplies and consumer requirements as the yardstick for determining maximum prices. The requisite administrative powers and machinery were created by two decrees: the Anti-profiteering Decree of July 25th, 1915[14] and the Decree of September 25th, 1915 concerning Price Investigation Offices and the Regulation of Supply.[15] The Anti-profiteering Decree (*Preiswucherverordnung*) represented a turning point in the conception governing official price policy inasmuch as penalties were now attached to price quotations which allowed an "excessive profit" to be made. The Supreme Court of the Reich defined this regulation in the sense that "nobody should gain more from the sale of his goods than he would receive under peacetime conditions."[16]

---

[11] Johannes Frenkel: "Zur Preisentwicklung der Nachkriegszeit", *Zeitschrift des Preussischen Statistischen Landesamts*, 61 (1921), p. 197.

[12] "Die amtliche Höchstpreispolitik", *Zeitschrift des Preussischen Statistischen Landesamts*, 61 (1921), p. 28^{+}.

[13] *Reichsgesetzblatt*, 1914, p. 516.

[14] *Reichsgesetzblatt*, 1915, p. 467.

[15] *Reichsgesetzblatt*, 1915, p. 607.

[16] K. Thiess: *Höchstpreispolitik...*, p. 13.

The implementation of this principle made it necessary to set up Price Investigation Offices staffed by experts who could subject business pricing policy to detailed scrutiny and, more generally, make recommendations regarding the ever-increasing mass of maximum price regulations governing the sale of "basic necessities". Such Offices were made obligatory in all local authority districts whose population exceeded ten thousand[17] and their field of activity was defined in the Decree as follows. They had the duty of

(1) employing their knowledge of local market conditions to determine reasonable prices on the basis of all relevant costs of production.

(2) assisting the appropriate authorities in the supervision of, and the prosecution of offenders against, the maximum price and other regulations governing trade in basic necessities.

(3) providing the courts and administrative authorities with reports regarding the justifiability of specific prices.

(4) assisting the appropriate authorities in their efforts to explain price movements and their causes to the population.

Higher level district, provincial and state Price Investigation Offices were also provided for in the Decree, as was a Reich Investigation Office for Foodstuffs Prices.

In the field of local supply local authorities were empowered, with the consent of the relevant administrative authorities at state level, to draw up regulations affecting producers and other manufacturers, dealers and other tradespeople in respect of their business operations and revenues, their purchases and marketing, even to the extent of transferring the organization of the supply of basic necessities into their own hands and excluding private businessmen. They had the power to conclude contracts for the delivery of articles of necessary consumption or to convey exclusive rights of supplying these either to municipal organizations or to individual producers and traders, under simultaneous stipulation of conditions of business operation, marketing and pricing. They were able to publish regulations affecting consumption and to require producers of basic consumer goods to unite in compulsory cartels.[18]

The creation of these powers and this administrative apparatus, coupled with the increasing supply scarcities and rising prices, had the result that

---

[17] Hans Stadthagen and Götz Briefs: *Die Preisprüfungsstellen. Beiträge zur Kriegswirtschaft*, Heft 22/23 (Berlin, 1917).

[18] *Ibid.*, p. 38. More generally on municipal food supply policies, see August Skalweit and Hans Krieger: *Die Nahrungsmittelwirtschaft großer Städte im Kriege. Beiträge zur Kriegswirtschaft,* Heft 7/8 (Berlin, 1917).

during the autumn of 1915 the range of goods for which legal maximum prices could be announced became substantially enlarged. In October for example petroleum, butter, fish and game were added to the list, in November milk, pigs (prices at slaughter) and pork, oils, fats, buckwheat and millet, vegetables and fruit, fruit purée, jams, natural and artificial honey, sugar beet syrup and emulsifying fats.[19]

In the winter of 1915/16 the food supply became more precarious and the incapacity of price controls on their own to cope with the problem became more obvious. The ancillary measures pioneered in the case of bread supplies were now applied to the supply of other common consumer goods, and the production and distribution of these became centrally organized. The first steps in this direction were the centralization of the supply of other basic foodstuffs: in spring 1916 the Reich Grain Agency was followed by a Reich Potato Agency, a Reich Meat Agency, a Reich Sugar Agency and a Reich Agency for Fruit and Vegetables – all equipped with comprehensive powers of intervention. As a result local authorities largely lost their power to regulate these commodities. The final step was the publication on May 22nd, 1916 of a "Declaration about Wartime Measures to Safeguard the National Food Supplies."[20] Among its provisions were the following.

> § 1. The chancellor of the Reich is empowered in the interests of the national food supply to acquire all stocks of foodstuffs as well as raw materials and other articles essential to the supply of food available in the German Reich. He has power to regulate import, export and transit traffic in such commodities.
>
> For the purpose of maintaining the livestock, he disposes of similar powers in respect of animal feedstuffs as well as raw materials and other commodities indispensable to livestock management.
>
> § 2. The chancellor of the Reich may issue such regulations as are necessary to the implementation of § 1; he has power to regulate traffic in such commodities, their consumption and also to regulate prices...
>
> § 4. The chancellor of the Reich may delegate the powers granted to him under this decree or other decrees concerning the safeguarding of food supplies, in whole or in part, to an agency subordinate to him. The detailed definition of the organization, field of activity and method of operation of such an agency is his responsibility.

---

[19] K. Thiess: *Höchstpreispolitik...*, p. 17–18. A survey of commodities subject to price control will be found in *Höchstpreise* (Berlin, 1917), issued by the *Volkswirtschaftliche Abteilung* of the *Kriegsernährungsamt* (i.e. the economic section of the War Nutrition Office).

[20] *Reichsgesetzblatt*, 1916, pp. 401–402.

The same day the War Nutrition Office was set up to take charge of these tasks. It was directly subordinate to the chancellor and in September 1916 it absorbed the Reich Investigation Office for Foodstuffs Prices. The supply of further goods was brought under central control in rapid order: pod vegetables, fresh water fish, eggs, edible fats, coffee, tea, cocoa, etc. On the price side central control was effected by maximum price stipulations; on the quantity side it was effected both by measures to stimulate supply – stretching of stocks, introduction of substitutes, powers to compel delivery and sale of commodities – and by measures to curb demand – consumer restrictions and prohibitions, and *per capita* rationing. From July/August 1916 ration cards were distributed for fats and meats; they had already been introduced for bread as far back as January 1915 in connection with the centralization of bread, grain and flour markets at that time.[21] The distribution of basic foodstuffs was thus largely withdrawn from market forces, and "the main rationale [of this transformation of the foodstuffs sector in 1916], given the situation of 'slender supplies which must suffice for all', necessarily was: systematic utilization of all stocks with a view to systematic administration and distribution according to definite and fixed principles."[22]

W. Wygodzinski[23] summed up the difference between the German and British systems of wartime agricultural control when he stressed that Germany's maximum price system "placed the interests of the urban consumer thoroughly in the foreground", whereas the minimum price guarantees provided for in the English Corn Production Act of 1917 "indicated a policy pursued undeniably in the interests of producers."[24]

The implications of the German system for the inflation are obvious: the maximum price regulations, especially in the second half of the war, prevented the full impact of the expansionist monetary policy from being registered in the movement of prices – or at least in the movement of official prices. Official prices were the only ones entering the calculation of wartime price indexes – for example Calwer's cost-of-living index[25] or the Reich Statistical Office's

[21] Wilhelm Weber: "Chronik der deutschen Agrarpolitik 1914–1932", in Fritz Beckman *et al.* (eds.): *Deutsche Agrarpolitik im Rahmen der inneren und äußeren Wirtschaftspolitik* (Berlin, 1932), Teil II, pp. 94–95. August Skalweit: *Die deutsche Kriegsernährungswirtschaft* (Stuttgart, 1927) provides a comprehensive survey: on the role of food ration cards see esp. pp. 196ff.

[22] H. Stadthagen and G. Briefs: *Preisprüfungsstellen…*, p. 81.

[23] W. Wygodzinski: "Agrarpolitik", in *Handwörterbuch der Staatswissenschaften*, (Jena, 8 vols. 1921–7), vol. 1, pp. 78–79.

[24] On the functioning of the foodstuffs sector in the economies of other belligerents see generally Ernst Wagemann: *Die Nahrungswirtschaft des Auslandes. Beiträge zur Kriegswirtschaft*, Heft 9 (Berlin, 1917).

[25] Cp. Table 9.

index of wholesale prices. To this extent the inflation was a suppressed one; but if the symptoms of inflation were partially suppressed in the price indexes they showed themselves in other ways characteristic of this type of inflation.

Firstly, they showed themselves in supply shortages and in the deteriorating quality of the goods supplied. Supply shortages arose not merely from the effect of the allied blockade on foodstuffs imports (before the war about one fifth of German food requirements had been met by imports)[26] but also from the decline of domestic production in the years 1915–24 by comparison with the years preceding and succeeding. Statistics of agricultural output show this clearly.[27] The reasons for this decline are to be found both in the maximum price policy itself and in the wartime shortages of labor and fertilizers[28] – the latter shortage persisting into the postwar years because of the lack of foreign exchange.[29]

Quality deterioration was to be observed for example in the coarser milling of flour as required by the regulations. It came out with particular crassness in the notorious "pig murder" of early 1915, when the state decreed a one-third reduction of the pig population on the grounds that the pig appears "to have become the human population's chief competitor in the consumption of grain and potatoes."[30] In other words the government of the Reich believed that the growing consumption of high protein foods that had developed during the last prewar decades must be rigorously cut back and the popular standard of consumption reduced to a bread-and-potatoes level. Lastly under this head, quality deterioration expressed itself in the displacement of fresh meat by canned meat and of fresh fruit by dried fruit.[31] "A Gresham's Law applied to the goods market: every gap in the graduation of quality promoted the inferior at the expense of the better – which disappeared from the shelves."[32]

---

26 Carl J. Fuchs: *Deutsche Agrarpolitik vor und nach dem Kriege* (Stuttgart, 1927), p.41.

27 Cp. Hans Wolfram Finck von Finckenstein: *Die Entwicklung der Landwirtschaft in Preussen und Deutschland 1800–1930* (Würzburg, 1960), pp. 313ff.; also Rudolf Berthold: "Zur Entwicklung der deutschen Agrarproduktion und Ernährungswirtschaft zwischen 1907 und 1925", *Jahrbuch für Wirtschaftsgeschichte*, 1974 II, pp. 83–111. Cp. also Table 33.

28 Heinz Haushofer: *Deutsche Landwirtschaft...*, p. 226. Friedrich Aereboe: *Der Einfluss des Krieges auf die landwirtschaftliche Produktion in Deutschland* (Stuttgart, 1927).

29 Gerhard Albrecht: *Zur Krisis der Landwirtschaft* (Jena, 1924), p. 13.

30 H. Haushofer: *Deutsche Landwirtschaft...*, p. 227.

31 Waldemar Zimmermann: "Die Veränderungen der Einkommens- und Lebensverhältnisse der deutschen Arbeiter durch den Krieg", in Rudolf Meerwarth *et al.*: *Die Einwirkung des Krieges auf Bevölkerungsbewegung, Einkommen und Lebenshaltung in Deutschland* (Stuttgart, 1932), pp. 447ff.

32 Götz Briefs: "Kriegswirtschaftslehre und Kriegswirtschaftspolitik", in *Handwörterbuch der Staatswissenschaften*, vol. 5 (1925), p. 1008.

The second symptom of suppressed inflation was the growing importance of the black market. In 1917/18, when the official per capita allocations of basic foodstuffs under rationing had fallen considerably below half the prewar consumption levels,[33] the black market became increasingly important as a source of supply even for these. Günther[34] states that, according to expert estimates relating to 1918, black market dealings disposed of between one seventh and one eighth of aggregate grain, flour and potato production, between one third and one fourth of total milk, butter and cheese output and between one half and one third of total egg, meat and fruit production. The same source estimated that black market prices stood at up to ten times prewar prices, in a period when official prices were two to three times the prewar levels. No detailed information on wartime black market prices has survived, to my knowledge, but the implication of this source is that they could have been as much as four times the official prices. On average however they were probably no more than twice as high.

After the war the Reich Statistical Office began to collect information on black market prices to incorporate in its cost-of-living statistics, given the importance of this market once the quantities of foodstuffs available as rations no longer met even subsistence requirements. Thus a partial comparison of black market and official prices becomes possible for the postwar period. Table 24 shows this comparison for the city of Berlin.

A third symptom of suppressed inflation was the adjustment of product mix in order to escape the effects of price regulations and other controls on profitability. "Commodities were transformed by one means or another into products not subject to maximum prices; this meant that they reached the market in a more expensive guise. In many cases they were offered as foreign goods and sold at the higher prices for these."[35] The maximum price regulations also distorted the relationship of prices and rates of return among controlled commodities, and this also caused adjustments in the product mix. One reason for

---

[33] Cp. the detailed comparative statistics in W. Bach: *Untersuchungen über die Lebensmittelrationierung im Kriege und ihre physiologisch-hygienische Bedeutung auf Grund der Lebensmittelversorgung in Bonn während der Zeit vom 1. Juli 1916 bis 28. Dez. 1918* (Munich, n. d.), cited in W. Zimmermann: "Die Veränderungen der Einkommens- und Lebensverhältnisse...", pp. 456–457.

[34] Adolf Günther: *Die gesunkene Kaufkraft des Lohnes und ihre Wiederherstellung* (Jena, 1919), p. 5, cited in W. Zimmermann: "Die Veränderungen...", p. 441. On problems connected with the black market see also Günther Plachetka, "Die Getreide-Autarkiepolitik Bismarcks und seiner Nachfolger im Reichskanzleramt. Darstellung und Auswirkungen insbesondere während des ersten Weltkrieges" (Dissertation, Bonn, 1969); also Robert Kalt: "Rationierung der Nahrungsmittel und schwarzer Markt in der Kriegswirtschaft" (Dissertation, Freiburg, 1949).

[35] G. Briefs: "Kriegswirtschaftslehre...", p. 1007.

Table 24. Retail and black market prices in Berlin (most common prices in pfg.), 1914, 1919–22. Col. 1: prices of (in bold type) and, after decontrol, free market prices

	Rolled oats 1 kg		Potatoes (retail price) 1 kg		Boiling beef with bone 1 kg		Belly pork (fresh) 1 kg		German butter (medium quality) 1 kg		Margarine (medium quality) 1 kg	
	1	2	1	2	1	2	1	2	1	2	1	2
July 1914				15		180		140		260		180
1919												
J				**21**		**440**		**380**		**1200**		
F				**24**		**440**				**1300**		
M				**24**		**480**				**1400**		
A				**24**		**480**		**380**		**1400**		
M				**29**		**480**	1320			**1400**		
J			30/50	**45**	1920	**480**	1480			**1400**		
J				**40**	950	**480**	950	**680**		**1400**		
A				**40**	910	**720**			2440	**1400**		
S				**30**	950	**720**	950			**1400**		
O				**30**	950	**720**	950	**680**		**1400**		
N				**38**	950	**720**				**1400**		
D			80	**40**	1600	**910**	3000		5800	**1400**	3200	
1920												
J		**184**		**50**		**760**		**680**		**2800**		
F	500		100		1900	**760**	3100		5800		4200	
M	800		200		2400	**760**	4400		6400		4800	
A	780	**184**	200	**70**	2200	**760**	3800	**2240**	6800	**3400**	5600	
M	740		170		2300	**760**	4200		7200		5200	
J	650		240		3000	**760**	4400		7200		3400	
J	520	**280**	250	**100**	3200	**2000**	3800	**2320**	6400	**3750**	2400	
A	490		120		2500	**2000**	3850		6400			2200
S	480			70	4000	**1680**	4200		6600			2290
O	600			80		3000		4100	6800	**3760**		2730
N		650		90		3085		4155	6970			2900
D		750		100		3200		4200	7000			2900
1921												
J		750		110		3200		4200	6700	**4000**		2770
F		700		110		3000		3600	6400	**4000**		2400
M		640		110		2800		3400	6400	**5000**		2280
A		580		110		2800		3300	6200	**5120**		2180
M		550		110		2800		3400	5800			2100
J		540		130		2800		3500		4800		2050
J		580		210		2800		3600		5000		2100
A		650		190		2800		3600		5800		2400
S		760		130		2800		3800		6000		2900
O		860		160		2800		3800		6400		3200
N		950		220		3000		4400		8200		5600
D		1000		250		3200		4600		8800		5700
1922												
J		1100		260		3600		4800		8800		4800
F		1200		560		4400		5400		10400		5200
M		1500		460		6000		7000		12400		6400
A		1800		660		7600		8800		12800		7200
M		2200		480		8800		9600		15200		7200
J		2400		400		11600		13600		14400		7600

municipally distributed imported foodstuffs (underlined), and black market prices. Col. 2: official maximum prices

Sugar (fine domestic) 1 kg		Eggs each		Unskimmed Milk (retail price) 1 Litre		Wheat flour 1 kg		Pork lard (foreign) 1 kg		Fat bacon 1 kg		Rye bread (war-time quality) 1 kg	
1	2	1	2	1	2	1	2	1	2	1	2	1	2
	45		8		24				130				28
	108		**38**		**48**		**64**				**580**		**54**
	108		**38**				**64**						**54**
	108		70				**64**						**54**
	108		136		**56**		**64**				**580**		**58**
	108		131			436	**64**			1320			**58**
	108		136			440	**64**						**58**
	108		140		**80**	168	**64**	1000			**580**		**58**
	116		138			168	**64**	1560		830			**58**
	116		139			168	**64**	1200		830			**58**
	116		151		**80**	168	**64**	1760	**1760**	830	**580**		**58**
			188			168	**92**	1760		1020			**80**
2000			213	300		1200	**92**	4200		4000			**80**
	208				**84**		**146**		**3360**		**580**		**118**
2400			185	400		900		5000		4900			**135**
3200			180	400		1100		6400		5600			**140**
3200	**288**		165	400	**200**	1200	**152**	6400	**4000**	5600	**580**		**140**
3200			170	400		1300		5400		5200			**237**
3400			180	400		1200		5600		5600			**237**
3200	**400**		180	450	**200**	1100	**280**	5400	**4000**	5400	**580**		**237**
3000			185	500									**237**
3000			210	400									**237**
3115	**400**		245	270	**200**		**280**		**4400**				**237**
3150			265	470									**237**
3100			320	400									**237**
3200	**760**		285	430	**220**				3060				**237**
3200	**760**		200	400	**220**				2475				**237**
2800	**760**		170	450	**300**				2300				**237**
2700	**760**		135	450	**300**				2180				**237**
2700	**800**		135	440	**300**				2140				**264**
2400	**800**		155		400				2100				**264**
2200	**800**		155		350				2400				**264**
2400	**800**		180		380				2800				**366**
2000	**800**		210						3100				**366**
	1600		260		440				4125				**374**
	1100		350		500				6900				**374**
	1200		400		620				5900				**391**
	1350		450		620				5200				**391**
	1500		540		620				6300				**674**
	1900		360		660				7700				**674**
	2200		400		960				9200				**760**
	3400		480		900				8900				**770**
	3600		600		1000				9500				**815**

Sources: Black market prices: "Schleichhandelspreise wichtiger Lebensmittel nach Angaben Grossberliner Gemeinden", in *Zeitschrift des Preussischen Statistischen Landesamts*, vol. 60 (1920), pp. 37*–42*. Johannes Frenkel: "Zur Preisentwicklung der Nachkriegszeit", in *Zeitschrift des Preussischen Statistischen Landesamts*, vol. 61 (1921), pp. 196–310. The latter source reports the freemarket prices that followed decontrol, up to June 1922, and, besides Berlin, contains particulars for all *Regierungsbezirke* in Prussia. Official maximum prices within Prussia were published in the *Amtliche Preisberichte zur Statistischen Korrespondenz* (Berlin, 1916ff.) They were also published in part in the *Statistische Jahrbücher für den Preussischen Staat*, in the *Vierteljahrshefte zur Statistik des Deutschen Reichs*, current volumes, and in the *Statistische Jahrbücher für das Deutsche Reich*, current volumes. Maximum prices for rye bread and beef will also be found in *Zahlen zur Geldentwertung in Deutschland 1914–1923*, p. 34.

---

this was "that generally speaking the later a maximum price had been fixed, the more generous it tended to be."[36] The earliest maximum prices had been decreed for commodities constituting the mass consumption of the lower income groups however (bread, potatoes). "The result of this was that despite numerous consultations, regulations, eventual increases in price maxima and forceful interventions by the state the quantities needed to meet the requirements of the population entitled to expect it could not be procured. This was especially true of the potato market during the autumns of 1914 and 1915. In both years maximum prices were so fixed that the return on selling potatoes for human consumption was far below that on selling them as animal feed. As a result it proved impossible even in spite of the excellent potato harvest of 1915 to secure sufficient potatoes for table consumption... The faulty gradation of maximum prices drove farmers to realize the higher returns on potatoes as feedstuffs."[37] Maximum prices for fresh milk were also particularly low in relation to the maxima for other foods. "The milk supply in many towns became increasingly endangered through this."[38]

Suppressed inflation also expressed itself as monetary overhang – as the accumulation of monetary assets by private households. Incomes which could not be spent legally because goods were rationed were either spent on the black market or saved. In the second half of the war especially this increased saving is reflected in the growth of savings deposits at savings banks. War Loans apart, these were the monetary assets in which households placed the bulk of their savings. Thus total deposits at all German savings banks rose

---

[36] Friedrich Aeroboe, H. Warmbold and A. Hesse: *Preisverhältnisse landwirtschaftlicher Erzeugnisse im Kriege. Beiträge zur Kriegswirtschaft,* Heft 6 (Berlin, 1917), p. 26.

[37] *Ibid.*, p. 27.

[38] *Ibid.*

from 21.4 to 31.8 bn. M. between the end of 1916 and the end of 1918[39] – an increase of about fifty percent, whereas during the earlier years of the war the level had scarcely changed. In part, of course, this simply reflects the steeper rise of money wages and salaries in the second half of the war: deflated by Calwer's cost-of-living index – which showed a 130% increase over the war period despite reflecting official prices only – the real value of aggregate savings deposits declined. But if we bear in mind that a large part of private savings was invested in government War Loans whose aggregate value was about 100 bn. M.[40] – then we can conclude that the rate of increase of household monetary savings far exceeded that of money incomes and rose considerably even in real terms.

State control of production and consumption was gradually dismantled during the postwar era. The obligation on producers to supply their produce was relaxed or in some cases supplemented by market incentives such as the payment of bonuses for grain deliveries.[41] After the 1921 harvest the comprehensive administration of grain production was abandoned in favor of an assessment procedure that obligated only the larger enterprises to supply stipulated quantities at official prices, subsidized to some extent out of the revenues other farmers received by selling grain on the free market.[42] A Decree of March 13th, 1920 secured the introduction of minimum prices for grain and potatoes, based on cost of production up to time of harvest:[43] an "index commission" continued to determine these up to the harvest of 1922.[44] Legal maximum prices reinforced by an obligation to sell were thus transformed into legal minimum prices with a guaranteed market; in this we may see an adumbration of the agricultural price support system of the Federal Republic and the Common Market.

---

[39] Cp. Table 10.

[40] Cp. Table 27.

[41] December 18th, 1919: "Verordnung über die Zahlung von Ablieferungsprämien für Brotgetreide, Gerste und Kartoffeln", *Reichsgesetzblatt*, 1919, p. 1990. On farmers' opposition to agricultural controls [*Zwangswirtschaft*], cp. Jens Fleming: *Landwirtschaftliche Interessen und Demokratie* (Bonn, 1978), esp. pp. 116ff. Robert G. Moeller: "Peasants, Politics and Pressure Groups in War and Inflation: A Study of the Rhineland and Westphalia, 1914–1924" (Dissertation, Univ. of California, Berkeley, 1980). Idem: "Winners as Losers in the German Inflation: Peasant Protest over the Controlled Economy, 1920–1923", in Gerald D. Feldman *et al.*(eds.): *The German Inflation Reconsidered. A Preliminary Balance* (Berlin, 1982), pp. 256–288.

[42] Lothar Meyer: *Die deutsche Landwirtschaft während der Inflation und zu Beginn der Deflation 1919–1923* (Tübingen, 1924), pp. 12ff. On the motivation underlying this policy, see *Akten der Reichskanzlei. Weimarer Republik. Das Kabinett Fehrenbach*, pp. LIIff.

[43] *Reichsgesetzblatt*, 1920, p. 325.

[44] W. Weber: "Chronik...", p. 99.

The transition from a food policy pure and simple to an active agricultural policy designed to promote agriculture was also signalized by the establishing of the Reich Ministry for Food and Agriculture. Founded by a Law of March 30th, 1920,[45] this ministry pressed on with the abolition of agricultural controls and hence of the maximum price system in retail markets. The dates at which specific foodstuffs were released from control can be found in Table 24 by looking for the months at which legal maximum prices and / or black market prices cease to be recorded. Thus margarine was decontrolled in July 1920, potatoes in September 1920, beef and pork in October 1920, rolled oats in November 1920, butter and milk not until May/June 1921 and sugar in October 1921. Eggs, vegetables, fruit and rice had already been freely saleable in 1919.

Bread and bread grains were not decontrolled until the end of 1922. Otherwise the *Zwangswirtschaft* – the pejorative name given to wartime controls – in the foodstuffs sector had been largely dismantled in 1920–21. Thereafter agriculture experienced a boom whose principal causes may be discerned in the shrinking real value of the burden of interest payments resting on the sector and in the ability to repay mortgages in devalued currency – windfall gains which accrued particularly rapidly once the London Ultimatum of May 1921 had added its fillip to currency depreciation. This upswing has rightly been described as "a prosperity as illusory as that in industry, a bubble which burst suddenly when the mark was stabilized."[46] Even so, while it lasted this short period was "among the best that modern German agriculture has experienced;"[47] and this apposite judgment sums up the short run significance of the termination of state controls for the sector. Currency depreciation was acting like a tariff barrier round agriculture, taking the place of the grain duties that had been suspended at the outbreak of war. This protection weakened and then disappeared during 1923, initially owing to the spread of various types of gold mark accounting and ultimately with the introduction of the *rentenmark*; with the result that in the absence of grain tariffs German agriculture experienced intensified import competition.[48] Industrial tariffs had been maintained and indeed in some cases intensified during the postwar inflation; and so once the mark was stabilized the terms of trade deteriorated between agricultural produce and the industrial inputs necessary to its cultivation. This

---

[45] *Reichsgesetzblatt*, 1920, p. 379. Cp. also W. Weber: "Chronik...", p. 93.

[46] Carl J. Fuchs: *Deutsche Agrarpolitik*..., p. 48.

[47] L. Meyer: *Deutsche Landwirtschaft*..., p. 17.

[48] Fritz Beckmann: *Die weltwirtschaftlichen Beziehungen der deutschen Landwirtschaft und ihre wirtschaftliche Lage 1919–1924* (Bonn, 1924).

deterioration was a material factor in agriculture's 'stabilization crisis' during 1923-4.[49] 1923 was moreover the year of the occupation of the Ruhr and of government-supported passive resistance; at that time the idea of reimposing the controls of the war years upon agriculture came under active discussion in government circles.[50] The refusal of agricultural producers in the summer of 1923 to market the harvest against payment in rapidly depreciating paper marks was to no small degree responsible for the spread of stable value substitute moneys, for the 'rye mark' currency reform proposals, and ultimately for the November currency stabilization.

If in conclusion we consider the extent to which price controls and other administrative measures kept food prices below their free market levels during and after the war, then the chronological limits of suppressed inflation should firstly be borne in mind: signs of it are evident in the economy only between 1916 and 1920. Next, its intensity within those years: the data in Table 24 suggest that in fact the degree of 'suppression' was fairly mild. Black market prices in 1920–21 were as a rule between one and one-half and three times the official maximum prices.[51] However the market prices that emerged once commodities had been decontrolled usually lay somewhere between these two price levels: and it is against these market prices that the degree of prior suppressed inflation should be measured, for the black market prices would also incorporate a risk premium. Official prices certainly do not reflect the full impact of inflation on the population, given the proportion of its food supplies it had to acquire on the black market; and no doubt black market price movements exaggerate the rate of price increase overall. The cost-of-living index of the Reich Statistical Office took account of both types of prices

---

[49] Carl J. Fuchs: *Deutsche Agrarpolitik...*, p. 49. Max Sering: *Agrarkrisen und Agrarzölle* (Berlin, 1925).

[50] *Akten der Reichskanzlei. Weimarer Republik. Das Kabinett Cuno,* p. 263. Cp. also W. Weber: "Chronik...", p. 102.

[51] By way of comparison: In the period between the end of the Second World War and the currency reform of 1948 the black market – in contrast to the "grey" market where goods are exchanged against other goods rather than against money – achieved no very great importance; "only about 10 % of the real volume of all transactions were completed on it. But because about 80 % of all money in circulation flowed through this market the prices on it became fantastic. For some goods in particular demand (e. g. edible fats) black market prices in Germany were up to one hundred times the official 'Stop-price'." Cp. Karl-Heinrich Hansmeyer and Rolf Caesar: "Kriegswirtschaft und Inflation (1936–1948)", in Deutsche Bundesbank (ed.): *Währung und Wirtschaft in Deutschland 1876–1975* (Frankfurt/M., 1976), p. 423. Cp. also Rudolf Stucken: *Deutsche Geld- und Kreditpolitik 1914–1963* (Tübingen, 3rd edn. 1964), p. 192; and Nicholas Balabkins: *Germany under Direct Controls. Economic Aspects of Industrial Disarmament* (New Brunswik, N. J., 1964), p. 108.

however – as explained above[52] – and may therefore be considered an accurate reflection of the true extent of postwar inflation.

But no price indexes taking account of black market prices exist for the actual war years. Since the population's dependence on black market sources of food supplies was increasing during the second half of the war, it follows that the available cost-of-living indexes understate the rate of inflation during that period. If however black market prices during 1917–18 were on average no more than twice as high as official prices – as suggested on p. 87 – and the population derived on average no more than one quarter of its food supplies from this source, then the available indexes will understate the true cost of living in 1917–18, relative to 1913, by no more than twenty-five percent.

In discussing suppressed inflation we should, finally, take note of the fact that during the postwar years official prices showed downward as well as upward flexibility (cp. in Table 24 potato prices in 1919, and the reduction of official beef prices between December 1919 and January 1920). From this, as well as from the general tendency of official prices to follow black market prices after a delay, we may deduce that at least in those years official price policy was sensitive to market trends, not least perhaps in view of the intention to proceed with decontrol.

[52] Cp. pp. 30–31 *supra*.

Part Two
Explaining the Inflation

Chapter 4
Theoretical Preliminaries

Economic science has traditionally regarded its task as one of providing economic explanations of economic phenomena – of explaining, for example, movements of the trade cycle or changes in the value of money by reference to changes in other economic variables such as the money supply, public expenditure, the balance of payments, the level of costs, the rate of investment, or consumer demand. A division of labor imposed by the rules of the discipline ensures that the infinite regression of causal analysis is interrupted at that point where political, psychological, sociological, legal, cultural and other phenomena have to be brought into consideration. Gottfried Haberler, for example, devotes only eight of the four hundred and eighty-two pages of his standard work *Prosperity and Depression* to non-economic explanations of the business cycle;[1] these eight deal solely with "psychological" theories, and quotation marks round "psychological" clearly differentiate between this type of explanation and all the rest.

Only in quite recent times have economists begun to incorporate political factors explicitly into their explanatory models. The idea of the "political business cycle" has entered the economist's vocabulary[2] – the idea that in parliamentary democracies the timing of macroeconomic policy changes is governed by electoral considerations, so that the periodicity of the business cycle becomes synchronous with the period between elections. Historical studies of economic crises, too, have recently begun to pay greater attention to the explanatory power of political considerations. Kindleberger ascribes the severity of the world depression of 1929–1939 to a failure of political leadership in the international economy: in Great Britain's case to loss of power to lead as a consequence of the First World War, and to lack of will to lead as far as the U.S.A. was concerned.[3] Borchardt recently analyzed the political "room for maneuver" of the Brüning government of 1930–32 and concluded that the unstable political equilibrium of the day left no feasible policy alternative to

[1] Gottfried Haberler: *Prosperity and Depression. A Theoretical Analysis of Cyclical Movements* (London, 5th edn. 1964), pp. 142–50.

[2] E.g. William D. Nordhaus: "The Political Business Cycle", *Review of Economic Studies*, 42 (1975), pp. 169–190. Bruno S. Frey: "Theorie und Empirie 'Politischer Konjunkturzyklen'", *Zeitschrift für Nationalökonomie*, 36 (1976), pp. 95–120.

[3] Charles P. Kindleberger: *The World in Depression* (London, 1973), esp. pp. 296ff.

the deflationary measures it actually pursued.[4] It was Borchardt, too, who stressed that the 1914–23 inflation "was no mere mechanical breakdown of the capitalist economy. On the contrary, it was primarily a political phenomenon...Consequently the abstract models suggested by monetary theory can contribute little toward explaining it."[5]

In this part of the book, I will endeavor to get behind the economic categories, to identify the remote political determinants influencing the proximate economic determinants of Germany's great inflation. The term "political determinants" embraces both political choices, whose outcome can be analyzed in terms of domestic and foreign power constellations together with the interests these reflect, and also institutional structures whose forms and "biases" can be reduced to the same elements. The unrealistic determination of the total Reparations liability is an example of the former; the structure of the Reich's wartime budgets is an example of the latter.

My analysis of these economic and political variables can be made more specific if I adopt, as its basis, the modern version of Irving Fisher's "equation of exchange":

$$M \cdot V = P \cdot Y_r$$

$$\text{or } P = \frac{M \cdot V}{Y_r}$$

P = the price level
M = the stock of money
V = the (income) velocity of circulation of money
Y_r = the real national income – a function of the level of domestic productive activity and of the current account balance with abroad.

[4] Knut Borchardt: "Zwangslagen und Handlungsspielräume in der grossen Wirtschaftskrise der frühen dreissiger Jahre: Zur Revision des überlieferten Geschichtsbildes", *Jahrbuch der Bayerischen Akademie der Wissenschaften*, 1979, pp. 1–47, reprinted in Knut Borchardt: *Wachstum, Krisen, Handlungsspielräume der Wirtschaftspolitik. Studien zur Wirtschaftsgeschichte des 19. und 20. Jahrhunderts* (Göttingen, 1982), pp. 165–182. For a critical assessment of Borchardt's results cp. C.-L. Holtfrerich: "Alternativen zu Brünings Wirtschaftspolitik in der Weltwirtschaftskrise?" *Historische Zeitschrift*, 235 (1982), pp. 605–631. Idem: "Zu hohe Löhne in der Weimarer Republik? Bemerkungen zur Borchardt-These", *Geschichte und Gesellschaft*, 10 (1984), pp. 122–141.

[5] Knut Borchardt: "Die Erfahrung mit Inflationen in Deutschland", in J. Schlemmer (ed.), *Enteignung durch Inflation? Fragen der Geldwertstabilität* (Munich, 1972), pp. 17, 22.

This "equation" is a tautology: in itself it has no explanatory power. Its advantage is that it "factorizes" price change – i.e. the concrete reality of inflation – into definitionally exhaustive categories which constitute in effect its coordinates in the spheres of production and monetary relationships. The search for the political origins of the inflation then resolves itself into an investigation of the political determinants of these components of price change – changes in the money supply, in the velocity of circulation of money, or in the real national income. Chapter 5 will investigate the determinants of change in the money supply and chapter 6 the variables affecting velocity and real national income (domestic production plus current account balance). A short, general conclusion to chapter 6 brings the analysis together.

Diagram 3 shows that a close relationship existed over the long run between wholesale prices and the money supply during the German inflation. Over the short run this was not necessarily so however: divergent movements can be observed. This is the background against which the various theoretical accounts of the effect of the money supply upon price change must be evaluated. These explanations operate by imposing exogenous restrictions upon one or more of the elements of Fisher's identity, thus turning it into a causal hypothesis. Older versions of the quantity theory of money started from the assumption that both the velocity of circulation and the real national income were relatively invariant, in the short run at least: thus the chief determinant of price-level change was change in the stock of money.[6] The "neo-quantity" theory of the 1950s, championed above all by Milton Friedman[7] recognizes that the velocity of circulation, which – assuming a constant real national income – changes inversely proportional to the demand for real cash or money balances, may be subject to considerable variation, but it maintains that during rapid inflations this velocity and the demand for money exhibit a stable functional dependence particularly upon past price developments. Thus this theory continues to accord the money supply a decisive role in the explanation of price movements. Other theories, standing in the Keynesian tradition, ascribe an independent influence upon price movements to changes in the demand for cash balances, or velocity, relating these changes in turn to instability of expectations, especially of expectations about future price move-

[6] Otmar Issing: *Einführung in die Geldtheorie* (Munich, 3rd edn. 1977), p. 122. Cp. Joseph A. Schumpeter: *History of Economic Analysis. Edited from Manuscript by E. B. Schumpeter* (New York, 1954), pp. 1100ff. H.G. Johnson: *Macroeconomics and Monetary Theory* (London, 1971), pp. 59–62.

[7] Milton Friedman: "The Quantity Theory of Money – A Restatement", in M. Friedman (ed.): *Studies in the Quantity Theory of Money* (Chicago, 1956). Petros A. Gemtos: *Die Neubegründung der Quantitätstheorie durch Milton Friedman* (Tübingen, 1975).

Diagram 3. Growth of the money supply and movements of wholesale prices in Germany 1914–23. 1913 = 1 (semi-logarithmic scale)

Sources: Central bank money (cash in circulation + deposits at the Reichsbank): Table 11, columns 3 + 4. Wholesale prices: Table 1.

ments.[8] These price expectations are not solely a function of past price changes or of current changes in the stock of money; this is why they can exert an influence upon actual price movements that acts independently of other elements of the Fisherian identity.

Finally, the fact requires no lengthy elaboration that changes in real income can exert an influence on price change, which, though not cumulative, may nevertheless be sizeable in the short run. Particularly in periods marked by exceptional disturbance of economic life – war, revolution, above average strike activity, or disruption of international trade, occurrences in the sphere of production and exchange can gain a momentum of their own as explanations of the movement of prices. 1914, 1919 and 1923 were years when this was the case.

[8] See O. Issing: *Einführung in die Geldtheorie*, pp. 21 ff. H. G. Johnson: *Macroeconomics and Monetary Theory*, pp. 63–74.

Chapter 5
The Determinants of Monetary Expansion

5.1. The Fiscal Policy of the Reich

War financing: some theoretical considerations

Haller estimates that the requirements of the First World War claimed half or more of the productive potential of the principal belligerents; such demands had no precedent in the history of industrial economies.[1] This degree of economic mobilization lasted for four years, and economic science and governments alike had been inadequately prepared for it – both in terms of the theoretical apparatus for formulating the problems it posed and of the contingency planning for coping with its practical aspects. No existing theoretical or applied studies examined the mobilization of production for total war from the real side. "The outbreak of the First World War, as fateful as it was to prove for the course of subsequent history, found the belligerent nations virtually clueless about its economic implications."[2]

The aim of war financial policy is to mobilize or redirect an economy's productive potential towards those activities essential to the conduct of the war. Economic priorities become rearranged: the importance of the present rises relative to the importance of the future, so that production for "consumption" takes precedence over the production of investment goods while within "consumption" the consumption requirements of the state take precedence over those of the general population. Although aggregate demand for what the economy can produce rises abruptly during wars, the conditions for maintaining, let alone improving, productive potential often deteriorate appreciably, as a result of the loss of manpower in precisely its most productive age groups to the armed forces, of the interruption of the raw material supply through domestic and international transport difficulties, and of the loss of output of areas occupied or in the war zone. As demand mounts on the goods market and the damage or threat to productive potential constrains supply, a

[1] Heinz Haller: "Die Rolle der Staatsfinanzen für den Inflationsprozess", in Deutsche Bundesbank (ed.): *Währung und Wirtschaft in Deutschland 1876–1975* (Frankfurt/M. 1976), p. 136.
[2] *Ibid.*, p. 115.

"goods gap" opens up. The task of economic planning for war is to find the most efficient methods of closing this gap, whilst ensuring that at the same time the priorities dictated by the requirements of war are satisfied.

Macroeconomics indicates that the "goods gap" may be closed if a variety of adjustments can be brought about:[3]

(i) If productivity can be raised by the more intense utilization of labor and capital.

(ii) If the share of aggregate output devoted to current consumption can be increased by the neglect of such net or replacement investment as is not essential to the war effort: thus the cost is registered in the deteriorating national capital stock.

(iii) If the consumer demand of the general population can be limited.

(iv) If imports can be increased.

In modern wars, requiring a virtually "total" mobilization of economic resources, direct intervention to regulate production and consumption forms an indispensable aspect of the state's efforts to bring about the required economic adjustments. Rationing of consumption, foreign exchange and foreign trade controls, investment permits, controls on the use of raw materials and of the labor force, civilian conscription: these measures become the sinews of the "war economy" (although some of them were not thought necessary in Germany before the second half of the war and the introduction of the so-called "Hindenburg program"[4]). War financial policy is the counterpart in the monetary sphere of this direct state intervention in the "real" economy. Its aim is to transfer the purchasing power which the state requires for the conduct of the war from the private sector or from abroad. At the same time it has the task of distributing the fiscal burden of the war both over time and between individuals in a manner which most people will think just. Finally, it should aim to stimulate productive activity, or at least not diminish it, to stimulate war production at the expense of civilian production, and to suppress private and inessential consumption and investment.

Four types of war financial policy may in principle be distinguished:[5]

---

[3] Cp. Horst Jecht: *Kriegsfinanzen* (Jena, 1938), p. 38. Max Lanter: "Kriegsfinanzen", article in the *Handwörterbuch der Sozialwissenschaften* (Stuttgart, 13 vols. 1956–68), vol. 6 (1959), p. 357. Cp. Arthur C. Pigou: *The Political Economy of War* (London, 1921), pp. 30ff.

[4] Gerald D. Feldman: *Army, Industry and Labor in Germany 1914–1918* (Princeton, 1966), pp. 149ff. Gerd Hardach: *The First World War* (London, 1977), pp. 63ff. (German original, 1973). Alfred Schröter: *Krieg – Staat – Monopol 1914–1918* (Berlin-East, 1965), pp. 94ff.

[5] H. Jecht: *Kriegsfinanzen*, pp. 43ff. Max Lanter: *Die Finanzierung des Krieges, Quellen, Methoden und Lösungen seit dem Mittelalter bis Ende des Zweiten Weltkrieges 1939 bis 1945* (Lucerne, 1950), pp. 68ff. M. Lanter: "Kriegsfinanzen", p. 357.

(i) The prior accumulation of bullion (a "war chest").
(ii) Increased taxation.
(iii) Flotation of war loans.
(iv) Short-term borrowing at the central bank or from the private banking system – processes which normally bring additional money creation and inflation in their train.

Let us now consider each of these in turn.

(i) In a pre-industrial world where princes had to pay mercenary armies in coins which they could not themselves create at will, and where the costs of war were still small in relation to aggregate social income, the prior accumulation of bullion played an important part in the financing of wars. Wherever functioning credit markets had developed however, borrowing took its place. This explains why borrowing replaced bullion accumulation as the method of war finance in England and France earlier than in Prussia with its relatively backward agrarian and semi-subsistence economy and its undeveloped money markets. Here, even in the eighteenth century, wars were still entirely or largely financed out of previously accumulated "war chests". According to Schmoller this tradition is "the grounds of that parsimony and exactness which has been the staple feature of Prussian state finance ever since."[6] It also explains why the government of the Reich employed part of the French reparation for the war of 1870/71 to establish a "war chest", despite the fact that developments in the credit markets had long since opened up other methods of war finance more appropriate to the degree of economic mobilization for war between industrial states. The advent of "total war"[7] made this primitive method of war finance wholly irrelevant; by 1914 the bullion locked in the "Juliusturm" at Spandau had grown from its 1870/71 origins to a total slightly more than two hundred million marks in value, yet it would have defrayed the expenses incurred in only a few days of the coming war, whose costs, averaged over its four year duration, came to 98 million marks per day.[8] "If the war treasure had any significance, it was the disadvantage that it en-

[6] J. Jecht: *Kriegsfinanzen*, p. 25. Cp. Gustav Schmoller: *Umrisse und Untersuchungen der Verfassungs-, Verwaltungs- und Wirtschaftsgeschichte bes. des Preussischen Staates im 17. und 18. Jahrhundert* (Hildesheim, 1974), pp. 175ff. (original edition, 1898).

[7] The First World War opened this era not merely because of the "totality" of the claims it imposed upon economic resources, but also because the resort to elements of global economic planning finally marked the end of the era of "laissez-faire" which had anyway been in perceptible decay in the preceding decades. Cp. Friedrich Zunkel: *Industrie und Staatssozialismus* (Düsseldorf, 1974).

[8] M. Lanter: *Die Finanzierung des Krieges*, p. 98.

couraged bellicosity and poisoned international relations."[9] Apart from its political significance for the unity of the Reich and as a weapon of diplomatic intimidation, the bullion could have been employed as collateral for a foreign loan or as payment for purchases abroad. For the state's domestic purchases it had (assuming a closed economy) effects on production and prices no different from those of money creation – i.e. from the method to be discussed under (iv).

This being the case, the belligerent nations relied effectively on combinations of the second, third and fourth of the methods of war finance listed above. The precise specification in practice of each method, and the actual combination in which they were employed, helped to determine the degree of wartime economic mobilization reached, and the interpersonal and intergenerational distribution of its costs. More germane to our study: they had a determinative influence on changes in the value of the currency, not only during but also after the war. The fact that in Great Britain for example taxation supplied between twenty and thirty percent of the costs of the war (estimates vary) is to no small extent responsible for her successful postwar financial stabilization and ability to restore convertibility at prewar parity. In Germany, taxation supplied between zero and six percent of the costs of the war,[10] and after the war a currency depreciation sliding into hyperinflation could not be halted.

(ii) The question whether wars should be financed out of taxation or by borrowing had been a subject of theoretical debate before the war. What arguments were advanced on each side?

The belief that wars should be tax-financed had a respectable intellectual pedigree in England, going back to Adam Smith and Ricardo.[11] Classical economists regarded all borrowing by the state as the harbinger of unwelcome increments of state activity. They also believed that taxation was exacted more particularly at the expense of consumption whereas borrowing had the effect of crowding out private investment activity, and was thus the more injurious

[9] A. Schär: "Aufwand- und Deckungsgrundsätze im schweizerischen Bundeshaushalt, insbesondere in der Kriegs- und Nachkriegszeit" (Dissertation, Zürich, 1930), p. 53, cited according to M. Lanter: *Die Finanzierung des Krieges*, p. 69.

[10] Robert Knauss: *Die deutsche, englische und französische Kriegsfinanzierung* (Berlin, 1923), p. 175. Knauss estimated the proportion of war expenditure financed out of taxation at 6% for Germany and at about 20% for the U.K. But Rudolf Will: *Die schwebenden Schulden der europäischen Großstaaten* (Tübingen, 1921), pp. 28 and 109, estimated the proportions at 0% and 28% respectively.

[11] Cp. H. Jecht: *Kriegsfinanzen*, pp. 26ff.

to the development of productive potential. Further advantages of taxation have been added to the list:

- that postwar taxpayers were thereby relieved of the burden of servicing a war debt.
- that careful adaption of types and rates of taxation according to individuals' capacities to pay facilitated a fairer distribution of the costs of the war.

However the following disadvantages to the tax-financing of wars also figured in the debate:

- that the ultimate material burden of the war rests on those whose purchasing power the state expropriates by this means.
- taxation expropriates the purchasing power of the liquid and the illiquid alike. This may disrupt productive activity.
- that by the same token the criteria by which tax liability is assessed may leave reserves of liquidity untapped which would be useful to the state.
- that the introduction and assessment of new taxes takes time. Borrowing is a speedier method of effecting the required transfer of purchasing power.

(iii) Whereas in England not only theory but also policy favored taxation as the method of war finance,[12] the German tradition of public finance ran along different lines. There borrowing was believed to be the better method according to arguments first comprehensively worked out by Carl Dietzel.[13] Unlike the liberal economists in England, Dietzel regarded the extension of state activity which borrowing portended not as an evil but as a good. He conceived of it as the accumulation of "non-material national capital". Among the other advantages of debt financing he emphasized:

- the opportunity it afforded for distributing the cost of the war over a period longer than the war itself.
- its power to mobilize exclusively the liquid capital available.
- the rapidity with which it can satisfy very large fiscal requirements.

With these arguments Dietzel advocated exclusive reliance on borrowing during wars. More cautiously Adolf Wagner viewed it as the most important source of war finance, on the first of the grounds mentioned above – intertemporal distribution of the burden which he expected to be very heavy. He also advocated the building up of state bullion reserves and the levying of special

[12] Taxation met 53% of the cost to the U.K. of the Crimean War, and 32.5% of the cost of the Boer War. Cp. Willi Prion: *Steuer- und Anleihepolitik in England während des Krieges* (Berlin, 1918), p. 25. M. Lanter: "Kriegsfinanzen", p. 360. Olive Anderson: *A Liberal State at War. English Politics and Economics during the Crimean War* (London, 1967), p. 201.

[13] Carl Dietzel: *Das System der Staatsanleihen im Zusammenhang der Volkswirtschaft betrachtet* (Heidelberg, 1855).

taxes. Resort to money creation was, in his eyes, the least desirable method of war financing; nevertheless in some circumstances he believed it would prove unavoidable.[14]

A further advantage of loan flotation over taxation as a method of war financing may reside in the fact that it diverts the flow of savings from meeting private investment demands to meeting the state's military requirements, thus reinforcing the desired reorientation of productive activity toward war production. Loan financing also opens up the possibility of foreign borrowing, whether by flotation on foreign capital markets or by sale of debt denominated in domestic currency to foreigners. Both types of foreign borrowing provide supplies of foreign exchange and permit an increase in net imports without directly endangering the currency. An increase in net imports enlarges the real supply of goods – military and civilian – to the economy.

The chief practical drawback to loan flotation as a method of war financing is however the obverse of what Wagner regarded as its primary advantage: it burdens postwar budgets and necessitates the tightening of the tax screw at a time when this is psychologically and politically harder to achieve than during the war itself. Thus it is not often that the debt is satisfactorily amortized, and in any case the deflationary implications of doing so may not be desirable. Loan financing, moreover, imports a socially undesirable redistributive bias into postwar public finance – from the broad mass of tax payers to the smaller and wealthier class of war loan subscribers. Loan financing cannot easily be tailored to the principles of social justice.[15]

Finally, the existence of a large governmental debt can pose a considerable threat to monetary stability, even where it is predominantly long term. If for example debt holders sell government securities for money in order to be able to make good consumption and investment opportunities foregone during the war, the central bank may have to take steps to prevent their price from falling, since this would injure the credit worthiness of the state. It may engage in open market purchases of state paper, or extend the opportunities for borrowing on its collateral, and since they tend to enlarge the monetary base, both courses of action could create a more permissive climate for inflation.[16]

(iv) The printing of money is the final – and most inflationary – method of war finance. In Germany during the First World War it was pursued under the

---

[14] Adolph Wagner: *Die Ordnung des österreichischen Staatshaushalts* (Vienna, 1863). Cp. H. Jecht: *Kriegsfinanzen*, p. 28.

[15] Cp. Heinz Haller: *Finanzpolitik. Grundlagen und Hauptprobleme* (Tübingen, 5th edn. 1972), p. 202.

[16] *Ibid.*, pp. 203–205.

guise of borrowing from the Reichsbank. In Britain in the same period it was achieved by the more direct expedient of issuing government money – "currency notes" – and declaring them legal tender; the same had been done during the American Civil War ("greenbacks"). The following advantages were claimed for this method.[17]

- rapidity: there is no speedier method of meeting the state's financial requirements. Hence it is particularly advantageous during the early stages of adjustment to war.
- its anti-deflationary tendency. Hoarding increases during the early stages of wars and this, as well as the military mobilization, tends to disrupt production. Money creation can counteract this.
- its stimulative properties. Money creation "lubricates" the economic system and may even encourage private productive activity during the course of the war.
- political advantages. The price increases induced by monetary expansion act to restrain real consumption as required, but in a manner bringing less odium on the government than increases in taxation; rising prices are accepted with greater resignation as the inevitable concomitant of war.

The main disadvantage of this method of war finance lies in its redistributive implications, when pursued relentlessly under conditions of full employment of resources. Formal taxation can be graduated according to individual capacity to pay; inflation acts as a tax bearing most heavily on those whose money incomes are rising most slowly, and on those who hold their wealth mainly in monetary assets, having neglected to exchange them for real assets quickly enough.

War financing: practical proposals, measures and results

In 1914 the authorities in Germany were poorly prepared both for the fiscal problems of a modern war and for its effects on the real economy. More thought had nevertheless been given to the technical aspects of war financing than to any of the other problems. The possibilities of "financial mobilization" for war had been discussed in detail during the closing prewar years by military strategists, academics and bankers. Among early contributions to the debate were those of Moritz Ströll[18] and Josef von Renauld.[19] The latter was

---

[17] H. Jecht: *Kriegsfinanzen*, pp. 52ff.

[18] Moritz Ströll: "Über das deutsche Geldwesen im Kriegsfall", *Schmollers Jahrbuch*, 23 (1899).

[19] Josef von Renauld: *Die finanzielle Mobilmachung der deutschen Wehrkraft* (Leipzig, 1901).

the only prewar writer to suggest even an approximately accurate forecast of annual war expenditure: assuming an army establishment of ten million men, he suggested twenty two billion marks. Subsequently however he retracted this forecast on the grounds of its financial impossibility.[20] Heinrich Dietzel,[21] Magnus Biermer,[22] Fritz Neubürger[23] and C. Henke[24] tended to advocate long or short-term debt financing. Jakob Riesser,[25] Johann Plenge,[26] Julius Wolf[27] and Wilhelm Gerloff[28] argued on the other side for greater reliance on taxation. In the event, of course, Germany relied less on taxation than England did. Why was this?[29]

Adolph Wagner had recommended a reform of the peacetime tax system which would facilitate the rapid imposition of surcharges on existing taxes if war broke out, thus assuring the state of a rapid increase of revenue.[30] Such a reform was particularly necessary in prewar Germany. According to the 1871 constitution of the Reich, central government had very limited powers to tax. Initially it could levy only certain indirect taxes – customs duties and a number of excises (especially those on tobacco, beer, spirits and salt): beyond this it enjoyed the operating surpluses of the enterprises it owned.[31] Reich expenditure in excess of these revenues was to be covered by so-called "matricular contributions" from the federal states and this effectively turned the Reich into their fiscal dependant. In this arrangement the government of the Reich

---

20 Josef von Renauld: "Finanzielle Mobilmachung", *Bank-Archiv*, 4 (1904/05). Cp. H. Haller: "Rolle der Staatsfinanzen", p. 116.

21 Heinrich Dietzel: *Kriegssteuer oder Kriegsanleihe?* (Tübingen, 1912).

22 Magnus Biermer: *Die finanzielle Mobilmachung* (Giessen, 1913), p. 51: "The treasury certificate is the most appropriate credit instrument while the war lasts."

23 Fritz Neubürger: *Die Kriegsbereitschaft des deutschen Geld- und Kapitalmarktes* (Berlin, 1913).

24 C. Henke: "Das deutsche Geldwesen im Kriege", *Vierteljahreshefte für Truppenführung und Heereskunde*, 10 (1913), pp. 260–279.

25 Jakob Riesser: *Finanzielle Kriegsbereitschaft und Kriegsführung* (Jena, 1909, 2nd edn. 1913).

26 Johann Plenge: "Zur Diagnose der Reichsfinanzreform", *Zeitschrift für die Gesamte Staatswissenschaft*, 65 (1909), esp. pp. 322–323.

27 Julius Wolf: *Die Steuerreserven in England und Deutschland* (Stuttgart, 1914).

28 Wilhelm Gerloff: *Matrikularbeiträge und direkte Reichssteuern* (Berlin, 1908).

29 Cp. p. 105, note 10 *supra*. For international comparison see the Table in Jens Jessen: "Kriegsfinanzen", article in Ludwig Elster (ed.): *Wörterbuch der Volkswirtschaft* (Jena, 3 vols. 4th edn. 1932–3) vol. 2 (1932), pp. 674–682. See too Karl Theodor Eheberg: "Finanzen im Weltkrieg", article in the *Handwörterbuch der Staatswissenschaften* (Jena, 4th edn. 8 vols. 1921–7), vol. 4 (1927), pp. 75–86. Gerhard Colm: "War Finance", article in the *Encyclopedia of the Social Sciences* (New York, 15 vols. 1930–35), vol. 15 (1935), pp. 347–52.

30 Cp. H. Haller: "Rolle der Staatsfinanzen", p. 115.

31 Peter-Christian Witt: *Die Finanzpolitik des Deutschen Reiches von 1903 bis 1913* (Lübeck, 1970), pp. 18–19.

found itself beholden to the Reichstag as well, for the Reichstag had the duty, as part of its general responsibility to approve the budget, of determining aggregate matricular contributions each year, which were then distributed among the states according to a key based on their relative populations. Under the second empire, taxing powers had been allocated according to the principle, "indirect taxes to the Reich, direct to the states."[32] By securing acceptance of this rule in the state whose constitutional relations he influenced so decisively, Bismarck's aim had not been to perpetuate a fiscally weak Reich. On the contrary: in 1875 he had stated, "I declare myself innately in favor of raising revenue entirely out of indirect taxation wherever possible."[33] His intention was not that the Reich should ultimately exploit the sources of direct taxation currently worked by the states, but rather that direct taxation should be pushed back, and indirect taxation extended – thus advantaging the Reich.[34]

From the 1890s the yield of a growing number of stamp duties became increasingly important to the Reich. Eventually, in the years just before the war, it entered the field of wealth taxation.[35] In 1906 a Reich inheritance tax was introduced, but its yield was low. In 1913 a non-recurrent capital levy, the so-called "Defense Contribution", was imposed. Those liable could pay in three annual installments between 1913–15; its eventual yield was pretty near the one billion marks it had been designed to raise. Lastly, a capital gains tax was introduced in the same year, with an intended annual yield of 185 million marks.

The two 1913 taxes were introduced solely in connection with the armament policies of the Reich and must be attributed rather to international tensions and the threat of war than to any reform of fiscal principles designed to improve the Reich's powers of direct taxation.[36] The fact, however, that the demands of the military build-up were met by enlarging the direct tax base and not the indirect, "signifies the victory of a social-democratic/liberal coalition

32 Fritz Terhalle: "Geschichte der deutschen öffentlichen Finanzwirtschaft vom Beginn des 19. Jahrhunderts bis zum Schlusse des Zweiten Weltkrieges", article in the *Handbuch der Finanzwissenschaft* (Tübingen, 2nd edn. 4 vols., 1952–65), vol. 1 (1952), p. 280.

33 Cited according to Wilhelm Gerloff: "Der Staatshaushalt und das Finanzsystem Deutschlands", article in the *Handbuch der Finanzwissenschaft* (Tübingen, lst edn. 3 vols. 1925–9), vol. 3 (1929), p. 25.

34 *Ibid.*

35 F. Terhalle: "Geschichte", p. 286.

36 *Ibid.* Also Konrad Roesler: *Die Finanzpolitik des Deutschen Reiches im Ersten Weltkrieg* (Berlin, 1967), p. 17.

over the conservatives."[37] Rates of direct taxation can be graduated according to capacity to pay – they can be made progressive; whereas indirect taxation tends to act regressively, bearing more heavily on the lower income groups who consume more and save less. This is an important observation; it means that had taxation played a larger part in financing the war, the additional burden would have been distributed regressively across the population, unless the Reich's fiscal foundations had shifted drastically.

Inelasticity is a further property of a system based on indirect taxation. The yield of the Reich's tax base at the outbreak of war could not be rapidly expanded by the imposition of surcharges. Customs revenue was likely to fall in the event of war, as cross-border trade fell, and in any case certain import duties were suspended – especially on foodstuffs and raw materials – soon after war began, in order to attract urgently required commodities into the country. Excises on non-necessities (especially tobacco, beer, spirits) are also likely to yield falling revenues as the consumption of such goods declines. These things happened in the event: the ordinary revenues of the Reich fell about 25 % between 1914 and 1915 – from 2.47 to 1.83 billion marks (cp. Table 25). The ordinary budget could be balanced only because military expenditure – traditionally by far the largest item on the expenditure side of the Reich budget even in peacetime[38] – was mainly transferred to the extraordinary budget for the duration of the war. Interest payments on the swelling debt by which the "extraordinary war expenditures" were financed were however charged to the ordinary budget, and came to dominate it; debt servicing rose from 26.5 % of ordinary expenditure in 1914 to about 90 % in 1918 (cp. Table 26).

In Great Britain it proved possible to meet a considerable part of war expenditure out of current taxation. The "centrally and efficiently organized English tax system"[39] already possessed powers of direct taxation – income tax in particular.[40]

---

[37] Fritz Neumark: "Die Finanzpolitik in der Zeit vor dem Ersten Weltkrieg", in Deutsche Bundesbank (ed.): *Währung und Wirtschaft in Deutschland 1876–1975*, p. 91.

[38] In 1886/90 military outlays amounted to over 95% of total Reich expenditures, and in 1911/13 still to about 90%. P.-C. Witt, *Finanzpolitik*, p. 380. Cp. also F. Terhalle: "Geschichte", p. 279. A concise survey of the structure of the finances in the last prewar year (1913/14) can also be found in Statistisches Reichsamt: *Die deutsche Finanzwirtschaft vor und nach dem Kriege. Einzelschriften zur Statistik des Deutschen Reichs,* Nr. 14 (Berlin, 1930), pp. 56–57.

[39] H. Jecht: *Kriegsfinanzen*, p. 59.

[40] On U.K. public finances before and during the First World War see, among many works, Paul Haensel: "Der Staatshaushalt und das Finanzsystem Grossbritanniens", article in *Handbuch der Finanzwissenschaft*, 1st edn. vol. 3 (1929), esp. pp. 79–87. Ursula K. Hicks: "Die öffentliche Finanzwirtschaft Grossbritanniens 1799–1949", article in *Handbuch der Finanzwissenschaft*, 2nd

Table 25. Ordinary revenues of the Reich 1914–19. Million marks

	1914	1915	1916	1917	1918	1919
Customs	560.8	359.9	348.3	234.4	133.0	1088.8
Excises	775.8	516.2	668.8	1200.2	2032.8	3334.5
of which: Tobacco, cigarettes	68.3	79.7	202.9	419.5	699.4	716.4
Sugar	214.6	168.4	194.7	163.2	184.1	158.7
Brandy	228.0	95.6	73.1	19.6	29.2	120.4
Beer	130.7	78.5	55.2	20.2	33.9	136.8
Wine	–	–	–	–	159.6	414.9
Mineral waters	–	–	–	–	18.1	51.9
Coal	–	–	–	412.9	751.3	1552.2
Stamp duties	183.1	167.1	252.8	468.7	510.8	797.2
of which: on commodity transactions	–	–	24.3	111.7	84.5	–
Turnover tax	–	–	–	–	150.5	823.4
Duty on passenger and freight transport	–	–	–	64.5	291.6	468.3
Duty on postal charges	–	–	89.6	146.8	235.7	173.9
Capital gains tax	2.8	0.7	0.5	1.2	0.7	0.5
Wealth tax	–	–	–	101.5	89.1	76.8
Inheritance tax	43.6	48.8	65.0	69.8	77.8	87.0
Defense contribution	637.4	307.8	19.5	10.4	1.3	–
Extraordinary War levy of 1916	–	–	45.6	4842.7	791.8	93.2
Extraordinary War levy of 1918	–	–	–	–	1617.2	1072.9
Matricular contributions from the states (net)	51.9	51.9	51.9	51.9	51.9	–
Other	215.7	372.8	580.2	818.0	1411.0	2946.7
of which: from the profits of the Reichsbank	43.6	199.7	190.3	206.9	390.5	1550.0 (both items)
from the profits of the Loan Bureaux	–	60.0	60.0	275.0	495.0	
Export duties	–	–	25.2	281.4	516.9	849.5
Surpluses from previous years	53.8	71.0	219.7	–	–	–
Total Ordinary Revenues (Excl. Gross revenues of Railways and Post Office)	2471.1	1825.2	2122.2	8010.1	7395.2	10963.2

Source: K. Roesler: *Die Finanzpolitik des Deutschen Reiches im Ersten Weltkrieg* (Berlin, 1967), p. 196.

edn. vol. 1 (1952), esp. pp. 331–334. Ursula K. Hicks: *British Public Finances. Their Structure and Development 1880–1952* (Oxford, 1954). A. W. Kirkaldy: *British Finance during and after the War* (London, 1921). E. V. Morgan: *Studies in British Financial Policy 1914–1925* (London, 1952). Gaston Jèze: *Les finances de guerre de l'Angleterre 1915–1918* (Paris, 1919). Willi Prion: *Steuer- und Anleihepolitik in England während des Krieges* (Berlin, 1918)

Germany's financial preparations for war had been chiefly governed by her experiences during the war with France in 1870/71.[41] The difficulty proved to be that whereas that had been a short war ending in German victory, the war Germany was now entering would be protracted and end in her defeat. The Franco-Prussian war lasted only half a year and cost no more than about one sixth of German national income at the time.[42] These costs were financed initially through loans of the North German Confederation, and of the belligerent German states,[43] and were ultimately more than offset by the French reparations of five billion francs. Over the four years of the First World War however German war expenditure amounted to about one hundred and fifty billion marks[44] – in nominal terms about four times Germany's 1913 national

Table 26. Ordinary expenditures of the Reich 1914–19. Million marks

	1914		1915		1916		1917		1918		1919	
	Marks	%	Marks	%	Marks	%	Marks	%	Marks	%	Marks	%
Deficits of Post Office, Railways, etc.	46.3	2.6	33.0	1.8	40.4	1.3	132.4	1.9	351.5	4.7	–	–
Military Expenditures (Army, Navy)	790.4	44.6	147.0	7.8	73.0	2.4	45.1	0.6	25.4	0.3	469.1	3.5
Costs of servicing the Reich debt	470.4	26.5	1346.0	71.7	2616.8	85.3	6518.8	92.2	6770.5	89.7	8397.1	62.9
Other ordinary expenditures	466.4	26.3	349.9	18.7	336.6	11.0	377.0	5.3	398.2	5.3	4512.8	33.6
Total ordinary expenditures	1773.5	100.0	1875.9	100.0	3066.8	100.0	7073.3	100.0	7545.6	100.0	13379.0	100.0
Surplus (+) or deficit (−) of ordinary revenues over ordinary expenditures	+697.6		−50.7		−944.6		+936.8		−150.4		−2415.8	

Source: K. Roesler: *Finanzpolitik, p. 197.*

[41] Reichsarchiv: *Der Weltkrieg 1914–1918. Kriegsrüstung und Kriegswirtschaft, Bd. 1: Die militärische, wirtschaftliche und finanzielle Rüstung Deutschlands von der Reichsgründung bis zum Ausbruch des Weltkrieges* (Berlin, 1930), p. 417. Cp. also Karl Helfferich; *Der Weltkrieg* (Berlin, 3 Bde. 1919), Bd. 2 pp. 34 ff. On the war of 1870/71, see Rudolf Lenz: *Kosten und Finanzierung des deutsch-französischen Krieges 1870/71* (Boppard am Rhein, 1971).

[42] M. Lanter: *Die Finanzierung des Krieges,* p. 46.

[43] H. Jecht: *Kriegsfinanzen,* pp. 29, 74.

[44] R. Knauss: *Die deutsche, englische und französische Kriegsfinanzierung,* p. 175.

income.[45] Over and above this came Reparations: rather than Germany's enemies defraying her war costs, she was required to help to defray theirs.

It was clear, both from the experience of 1870 and from the tenor of theoretical discussion that the declaration of war would probably be accompanied by a shortage of cash, partly because of hoarding, at the same time as the cash requirements of the Reich would be increasing enormously. Steps had been taken to cope with this eventuality. Certain of the measures for strengthening the credit system recommended by the Bank Inquiry of 1908,[46] and subsequently acted upon, owe their impetus to this consideration – for example the declaration in the Bank Act of 1909 that bank notes were legal tender, the steps taken to centralize gold reserves at the Reichsbank through the issue of smaller denomination notes as substitutes for coin (this began in 1906), and the encouragement of non-cash payment methods. Other measures of this type included the decision, announced in the "Law amending the Fiscal System" of July 3rd, 1913, to add 120 million marks worth of silver to the war bullion reserves, and to increase the circulation of state paper money (*Reichskassenscheine*) by the same amount.[47]

Further steps were taken at the outbreak of war to prevent a domestic run on the gold stock and on the banks, to reinforce the position of the Reichsbank, and to secure direct access for the Reich to the credit and money-creating facilities of the bank of issue. The first step was to suspend the gold convertibility of bank notes; this was done at the end of July 1914. On August 2nd the government turned its war bullion reserves over to the Reichsbank to serve as additional backing for the currency.[48] On August 4th the Reichstag

[45] W. G. Hoffmann *et al.*: *Das Wachstum der deutschen Wirtschaft seit der Mitte des 19. Jahrhunderts* (Berlin, 1965), p. 455.

[46] *Bankenquete 1908–1909, Stenographische Berichte nebst Materialien*, H. 1–3 (Berlin, 1909–1910). Summary of findings in L. Cohnstaedt: *Ergebnisse der Bankenquete* (Frankfurt/M., 1908). *Die Reichsbank 1901–1925* (Berlin, n.d.), pp. 26–38. Cp. Alfred Lansburgh: *Die Massnahmen der Reichsbank zur Erhöhung der Liquidität der deutschen Kreditwirtschaft* (Stuttgart, 1914) and the criticisms of the measures by Johann Plenge: *Von der Diskontpolitik zur Herrschaft über den Geldmarkt* (Berlin, 1913).

[47] Goetz Briefs: "Kriegswirtschaftslehre und Kriegswirtschaftspolitik", article in *Handwörterbuch der Staatswissenschaften*, vol. 5 (Jena, 1923), pp. 995–996. All preparatory measures were based on the presumption that the war would be short. "The fact that [the war] became more than we could manage both in its material demands and in its duration showed that we were not adequately prepared for it". Reich Finance Minister E. Schiffer: *Deutschlands Finanzlage nach dem Kriege. Rede gehalten in der Deutschen Nationalversammlung am 15. Februar 1919* (Berlin, 1919), p. 9. On the prevalent prewar expectations about the war's duration, see too Lothar Burchardt: *Friedenswirtschaft und Kriegsvorsorge* (Boppard am Rhein, 1968), pp. 14ff.

[48] G. Briefs: "Kriegswirtschaftslehre", p. 997.

dispatched a number of laws placing the relationship between Reichsbank and credit system, and Reichsbank and central government, on a new basis. The salient provisions were as follows.[49]

(i) The Reichsbank was released from its duty to redeem its own notes and the *Reichskassenscheine* in gold on demand.

(ii) The tax levied on the Reichsbank when the circulation of its notes exceeded the legal maximum was abolished.[50]

(iii) Treasury bills (*Reichsschatzwechsel*) and interest-bearing treasury certificates (*Reichsschatzanweisungen*) were declared eligible secondary reserves against the note issue, on the same basis as good commercial bills.

(iv) Loan Bureaux were established, and subordinated to the Reichsbank. Their task would be to extend credit to the private sector as well as to public authorities, against the collateral of commodities or stock market securities. Against such collateral they issued non interest-bearing claims upon themselves – *Darlehnskassenscheine* (Loan Bureau Certificates) – which all public offices were obligated to accept at full face-value in discharge of debts. Thus these claims functioned effectively as money. Furthermore, the Reichsbank was empowered to substitute them, along with *Reichskassenscheine*, for bullion in the primary one-third reserve against its note issue. This power gave the Reichsbank autonomy in determining the size of the monetary base, for by varying the credit policy of the Loan Bureaux, it could control the legal limits to its own note issue.[51]

Table 20 reveals the extent to which the government of the Reich took advantage of the opportunities for recourse to the printing presses created by this legislation. During the first half of the war the Reich had considerable success in funding the floating debt that had initially been taken up by the Reichsbank. Successful War Loan flotations (cp. Table 27) were intended by the government to awaken the impression that the economy's excess and inflationary purchasing power was being absorbed, and hence to strengthen

[49] Rudolf Stucken: *Deutsche Geld- und Kreditpolitik 1914–1963* (Tübingen, 3rd edn. 1964), pp. 17ff. Hermann Bente: "Die deutsche Währungspolitik von 1914–1924", *Weltwirtschaftliches Archiv*, 23 (1926), I. pp. 117+ff.

[50] On prewar statutory requirements regarding the note issue, see Jakob Riesser: *The Great German Banks and Their Concentration in Connection with the Economic Development of Germany* (Washington, D.C., 1911), pp. 143ff.

[51] As early as 1915 Friedrich Bendixen made critical notice of this implication, in his *Währungspolitik und Geldtheorie im Lichte des Weltkrieges* (Munich, 1915, 2nd edn. 1919), p. 28. On previous German experience with Loan Bureaux during political crises (1848, 1866, 1870), see Walter Lotz: "Darlehnskassen", article in *Handwörterbuch der Staatswissenschaften*, vol. 3 (Jena, 1926), pp. 209ff.

confidence in the currency. The reality was however that purchasing power placed in War Loans was no less liquid than that placed in treasury bills; the obligation upon the Loan Bureaux to accept them as collateral meant that up to the prescribed limit of 75 percent their cash value could at any time be realized without risk of capital loss. Thus, during the first half of the war more than fifty percent of the Loan Bureau Certificates entering circulation did so against the collateral of War Loan stock.[52] While it is true that only three billion marks worth of such Certificates had been issued by the end of 1916, implying that only a small fraction of aggregate War Loan stock had been employed in this fashion, the important point is the possibility this represented. By it War Loan was constituted as efficient a "potential money" as Reich treasury bills. Indeed the potential of War Loan stock as a source of monetary expansion was theoretically even greater than that of the floating treasury bill stock. The Loan Bureau Certificates which War Loan stock could command were eligible components of the primary reserve cover of the note issue; treasury bills were eligible only as secondary reserves and hence (until 1921) rediscountable only up to the limits dictated by the size of the primary reserves. There was a legal limit on the issue of Loan Bureau Certificates which stood initially at 1.5 billion marks. But a Bundesrat decree was sufficient to raise this limit,[53] and this is what happened whenever the liquidity requirements of the state or the private sector demanded it.

In the spring of 1916 the projections even for the ordinary budget slipped into deficit, despite the fact that military expenditures in their entirety were now debited to the extraordinary budget. The reason was that the cost of servicing the debt now exceeded what the existing sources of taxation could be expected to yield. With the intensified armaments drive called for by the new High Command in the so-called "Hindenburg program" of autumn 1916, this problem could only get worse. Beginning in the spring of 1916, then, the Reichstag agreed to a variety of tax rate increases and new taxes. These new taxes lay within the limits of the Reich's prewar fiscal base however: indirect

---

[52] Monthly data are to be found in a Table on p. 212 of K. Roesler: *Finanzpolitik*. For the 75 percent limit on Loans against the collateral of stock market securities cp. E. Hoppe: *Der Krieg und die deutsche Geldwirtschaft* (Essen, 1919), p. 22. General information on the role of the Loan Bureaux and their relationship with the Reichsbank is to be found in Robert A. v. Ruedorffer: "Reichsbank und Darlehnskassen in der Kriegsfinanzierung 1914–1918" (Dissertation, Cologne, 1968). Cp. also Reinhold Zilch: "Reichsbank und finanzielle Kriegsvorbereitung des deutschen Imperialismus 1907–1914" (Dissertation, Berlin-East, 1976). Rudolf Will: *Die schwebenden Schulden*, pp. 101 ff.

[53] K. Roesler: *Finanzpolitik*, p. 41. Leo Feuchtwanger: *Die Darlehnskassen des deutschen Reiches* (Stuttgart, 1918).

Table 27. Over- or undersubscription of War Loans 1914–18. Million marks

At the flotation of the ... War Loan (W. L.)		Short term treasury paper in current circulation	Amount of War Loan subscriptions	(+) Over- or (−) under- subscription
First	W. L. 1914	2.6 M	4.5	+ 1.9
Second	W. L. 1915	7.2 M	9.1	+ 1.9
Third	W. L. 1915	9.7 M	12.1	+ 2.4
Fourth	W. L. 1916	10.4 M	10.7	+ 0.3
Fifth	W. L. 1916	12.8 M	10.7	− 2.1
Sixth	W. L. 1917	19.9 M	13.1	− 6.8
Seventh	W. L. 1917	27.2 M	12.6	−14.6
Eighth	W. L. 1918	38.9 M	15.0	−23.9
Ninth	W. L. 1918	49.4 M	10.4	−39.0

Source: "Die Finanzen des Deutschen Reiches in den Rechnungsjahren 1914–1918. Denkschrift der Reichsregierung vom 12. März 1919 (Drucksache der Nationalversammlung Nr. 158)", in *Finanzarchiv*, 36 (1919), pp. 797–798.

taxes and stamp duties and, of direct taxes, only an elaboration of the capital gains tax of 1913.[54] No further direct taxes were introduced by the Reich. The highly productive income and wealth taxes remained the preserve of the states and local governments: this did not change till after the war.[55]

The elaboration of the 1913 capital gains tax was the war profits tax of 1916. Under it, private individuals suffered a fifty percent tax rate on the nominal increase in the value of their assets between 31.12.1913 and 31.12.1916. For business companies the tax was assessed on the amount by which their war-time profits exceeded their average profits during the last prewar quinquennium. In 1916 the Reichstag also agreed to a turnover tax, at first confined to the sale of goods but extended in 1918 to the sale of services; the initial rate was one per mille. Consumer excises were increased on tobacco, cigarettes and beer, as were the customs duties on tea and coffee; eventually in 1918 new excises were even imposed on lemonade and mineral waters. A coal tax was

[54] Walther Lotz: *Die deutsche Staatsfinanzwirtschaft im Kriege* (Stuttgart, 1927), pp. 59 ff. K. Roesler: *Finanzpolitik*, pp. 105–106 and a summary of tax legislation on pp. 189–194.

[55] Erwin Respondek: *Die Reichsfinanzen auf Grund der Reform von 1919/20* (Berlin, 1921). Klaus Epstein: *Matthias Erzberger and the Dilemma of German Democracy* (Princeton, 1959), pp. 334–348. Johannes Popitz: "Die deutschen Finanzen 1918–1928", in *Zehn Jahre deutsche Geschichte 1918–1928* (Berlin, 1928), pp. 187 ff. Franz Menges: *Reichsreform und Finanzpolitik. Die Aushöhlung der Eigenstaatlichkeit Bayerns auf finanzpolitischem Wege in der Zeit der Weimarer Republik* (Berlin, 1971), pp. 184–228.

introduced in 1917 and proved to be the most productive of the new excises. Various stamp duties were also increased or first imposed after 1916.

These fiscal measures did raise the ordinary revenues of the Reich from 2.1 billion marks in 1916 to 8 billion in 1917 and 7.4 billion in 1918 (see Table 25). This was no more than was required to keep pace with the mounting burden of interest payments on Reich debt. In other words the one hundred and fifty billion marks of German war expenditure over four years were met almost entirely out of War Loan subscriptions (about one hundred billion marks) and, especially during the second half of the war, by increases in the floating debt (fifty billion). The Reich's rising ordinary revenues in the second half of the war did no more than pay the interest on this debt.

The contrast with Great Britain is striking. There tax increases were announced shortly after the commencement of hostilities. In 1914 the rate of income tax was doubled, the excise on beer tripled and that on tea raised by sixty percent.[56] In the following years too the tax screw was turned more tightly than in Germany. The earlier resort to, and the greater success of, taxation policy in Britain than in Germany are alike explained by the differential importance of direct taxes as sources of central government revenues in the two countries; their much greater role in Britain not only before but also during the war can be seen in Table 28. England however also enjoyed the additional advantage that part of her borrowing could be undertaken abroad, particularly in the empire and in the U.S.A., especially after that country had entered the war.

French wartime taxation resembled German: the central government was mainly dependent on indirect taxation for its ordinary revenues, and the taxable base shrank owing to the hostilities on her own territory. As a result tax revenue scarcely increased: it stood at 4.1 billion francs in 1913 and at 4.2

Table 28. Composition of central government ordinary tax revenues in Germany and Great Britain in 1913 and 1918 (%)

	Great Britain		Germany	
	1913	1918	1913	1918
Direct taxes	47.5	77.2	3.5	43.4
Indirect taxes	46.0	21.2	81.3	47.9
Stamp duties	6.5	1.6	15.2	8.7

Source: Robert Knauss: *Die deutsche, englische und französische Kriegsfinanzierung* (Berlin, 1923), p. 148.

[56] Karl T. Eheberg: "Finanzen im Weltkrieg", p. 80.

billion francs in 1918,[57] and in fact war costs were met entirely by borrowing. However in her ability to borrow abroad France resembled England and met 21 % of the war-related expenditures in her extraordinary budget from this source.[58] Germany, by contrast, could not borrow abroad at any time during the war; rather, she herself had to make loans to her south-east European allies, and under the terms of the Treaty of Versailles these loans were entirely written off in the end.

Fiscal and monetary policy options in 1919

The German government had financed the war by readier resort to the printing presses than Great Britain, the United States or France. It had turned the tax screw more gently than the British or American governments, and been less able to rely on foreign loans than the British or French. Funding of the floating debt had been less successful in Germany than in any of the three Allied countries, particularly in the second half of the war. Inevitably, then, there *was* a "tax" which had played a larger role in German war finance than in that of her three principal opponents. Price inflation, which suppresses private claims on the domestic product thus releasing productive capacity for war purposes, can itself be viewed as a "tax".[1]

"Inflation tax" falls indiscriminately on everyone with a net creditor position in domestic currency assets. Those whose access to credit enables them to contract domestic currency debts in excess of their domestic currency assets can easily evade it or indeed convert it into a subsidy, at the cost of very low,

---

[57] R. Knauss: *Die deutsche, englische und französische Kriegsfinanzierung*, p. 148.

[58] Cp. R. Will: *Die schwebenden Schulden*, p. 107.

[1] The conception of inflation as a species of taxation can be traced back to the classical economists. Cp. John Stuart Mill: *Principles of Political Economy. The Collected Works of J. S. Mill, vols. III–IV* (Toronto, 1965), vol. IV, p. 565 (original edition, 1848). Keynes in particular was responsible for reviving the conception during the 1920s in *A Tract on Monetary Reform. The Collected Writings of J. M. Keynes, ed. E. Johnson and D. E. Moggridge, vol. IV* (London, 1971), p. 37: Inflation "is the form of taxation which the public find hardest to evade and even the weakest government can enforce when it can enforce nothing else". The *Tract* was first published in 1923. Philip Cagan also emphasizes the same idea. "In the unsettled conditions following the two world wars governments were too weak to enact adequate tax programs and to administer them effectively. Issuing money was a method of raising revenue by a special kind of tax – a tax on cash balances. This tax is often appealing because it does not require detailed legislation and can be administered very simply." See his "Monetary Dynamics of Hyperinflation", in Milton Friedman (ed.): *Studies*, p. 78. With particular reference to the German inflation, see Friedrich Sommer: "Die Inflationssteuer" (Dissertation, Frankfurt/M., 1924).

even negative, real interest rates. Primarily, then, those whom "inflation tax" affects are those who hold the greatest share of their wealth in assets with fixed domestic-currency value. Real assets, foreign currency assets and "human capital" are not directly "taxed" by inflation, although the income which these yield may be affected as for example when wage, salary or permissible rent increases fail to keep up with the general rise of the price level. Secondly, the incidence of "inflation tax" varies inversely with ease of access to cheap domestic-currency credit. As a result, those who are versed in financial matters are generally speaking in a better position to evade the exactions of "inflation tax" than those who are not. Those who are wealthy to begin with are in a better position than those who are poor, because their wealth improves their ability to borrow. For those whose wealth is in real assets, hard foreign currency assets, or "human capital" and who can use this wealth to command credit in domestic currency, the "inflation tax" shifts into reverse, and becomes a subsidy. Obviously wealth is not *in itself* the passport to evasion of the tax however; many wealthy charities, universities, trade unions and associations, holding their wealth in the form of fixed value domestic-currency assets and not using it to obtain credits, had it wiped out by the inflation, as did wealthy individual rentiers, including many academics.[2]

Thus the incidence of this "tax" is not under the control of the taxing authorities. They can neither determine the class of people to be taxed nor do they determine the distribution of burden between them on the normal equita-

---

[2] Georg Schreiber: *Die Not der deutschen Wissenschaft und der geistigen Arbeiter* (Leipzig, 1923). Alfred Weber: "Die Not der geistigen Arbeiter", in *Schriften des Vereins für Socialpolitik*, Bd. 163 (Munich, 1923), p. 173: "The modern intelligentsia are a rentier-intelligentsia. They depend for their subsistence on their possession of small or moderate independent means – not in the sense (as far as most of them are concerned) that thereby they maintain themselves in professional idleness, but on the contrary that these means enable them to survive the early periods of training in the professions of which I have spoken, until the stage in their careers where they reach their full earning potential. For some, the possession of independent means serves as a permanent supplement to their professional earnings and as such formed the foundation of the intellectual liberty of the prewar intelligentsia...", [p. 174] "... [G]ermany's financial capital has as good as disappeared, and with it, as I have already drawn attention to, the foundation of the intellectual liberty of the intellegentsia". The same matter is dealt with in a larger chronological context by Fritz Ringer: *The Decline of the German Mandarins. The German Academic Community 1890–1933* (Cambridge, Mass., 1969), esp. pp. 62–66, and in a larger social context by Franz Eulenburg:" Die sozialen Wirkungen der Währungsverhältnisse", *Jahrbücher für Nationalökonomie und Statistik*, 122 (1924), pp. 748–794. The importance of the problem in contemporary eyes is shown by the fact that the Provisional Reich Economic Council set up a "Subcommittee for the Economic Advancement of Intellectual Labor" (Unterausschuß zur wirtschaftlichen Förderung der geistigen Arbeit) on October 9, 1920. Cp. Harry Hauschild: *Der vorläufige Reichswirtschaftsrat 1920–1926* (Berlin, 1926), p. 241.

ble principles of equality of sacrifice or ability to pay. The incidence in fact bore no calculable relation to any measurable criterion such as wealth. Rather it depended on the financial adroitness of the individual or of the institutions which he had made responsible for securing his investments and income – banks, business companies or (for the wage earner) trade unions. Under inflation, financial proficiency matters more than status or long established fortune, and the state's power to exact taxation is partially abdicated to its citizens, the most expert of whom turn to profit and subsidy what others experience as severe expropriation.

Periods of high inflation, therefore, resemble those of the classical "laissez-faire" relationship of power between the individual and the state. Such social conditions have been applauded as well as condemned, depending on the individual's political preferences.

In purely economic terms inflation has the following advantage over conventional taxation as a method of converting an economy from a peace to a war footing and back again, that it does not precipitate private sector illiquidity, bankruptcy and unemployment. The adjustments inherent in such large scale changes in the composition of output involve big enough costs without being intensified through illiquidity; resort to the "inflation tax" ensures that the adjustments are undertaken at maximum levels of aggregate output and employment. The economic costs of this method of "taxation" are of course registered in the weakening power of the currency to fulfil its traditional functions, particularly of serving as a store of value. While the war lasts however the time horizon relevant to economic policy-making becomes foreshchtened; "the great importance that in normal times is correctly attached to currency stability has to give way to the more urgent objectives dictated by the war."[3] "With the return of peace, however, currency policy objectives which have often been forced into second place by wartime military and political objectives, will regain their former importance. The question then arises, whether official policy should regard as its goal the maintenance of the value which money has acquired during the course of the war, or whether it should seek to bring its value back to what it was before the war."[4] This sums up the currency problem created by the war, already discussed in all the belligerent countries during it, and ultimately requiring to be faced when the war ended and the ground rules for postwar currency policy needed to be fixed.

In the United States the decision to prevent internal currency collapse was taken in December 1919. In that month the Federal Reserve Board, supported

[3] Richard Hauser: "Unsere Währung nach dem Kriege", *Bank-Archiv*, 17 (1917/18), p. 3.
[4] *Ibid.*

by the Treasury, acted to break the inflationary pressures set up by the wartime and postwar boom. A high interest rate policy precipitated a fall in economic activity, culminating in the world slump of 1920–21.[5] The recession was sharper than that of 1929–32,[6] as also, however, was the subsequent recovery.

The *external* stability of the dollar and its convertibility into gold was never in question. The war had strengthened the financial solidity of the U.S.A. and substantially enlarged its gold reserves, and postwar developments only reinforced this tendency. The war had the opposite effect on the British financial position and bullion reserves. In Britain the currency debate revolved round the question of whether or not to restore sterling's prewar international parity; a decision on this question also necessarily determining the extent to which the pound's domestic purchasing power could be allowed to depreciate. In 1918 the British government established the so-called Cunliffe Committee to examine the question and make recommendations. It decided that policy should aim to restore the prewar parity under conditions of convertibility (during the war exchange controls and practically unlimited U.S. credits had enabled the near-maintenance of parity), and that exchange controls should be abolished forthwith.[7] Since the floating pound was well below parity after the war, these recommendations dictated a deflationary course for domestic prices and economic activity. The inadequacy of Britain's own bullion reserves compelled her to subordinate her currency policy strictly to that of other major gold standard countries, chief among which was the U.S.A. It forced the United Kingdom to accommodate her own policy fully to the contractionary policy introduced by the U.S.A. at the end of 1919; no other course of action

---

[5] Elmus R. Wicker: *Federal Reserve Monetary Policy 1917–1933* (New York, 1966), pp. 42–43. Milton Friedman and Anna J. Schwartz: *A Monetary History of the United States 1867–1960* (Princeton, 1963), p. 227.

[6] Derek H. Aldcroft: *From Versailles to Wall Street 1919–1929* (London, 1977), pp. 68–9. Cp. also p. 209 *infra*. On the development of economic conditions outside Germany after the war see also Statistisches Reichsamt: *Die Wirtschaft des Auslandes 1900–1927. Einzelschriften zur Statistik des Deutschen Reichs*, Nr. 5 (Berlin, 1928). More particularly on fiscal developments see Statistisches Reichsamt: *Die Staatsausgaben von Grossbritannien, Frankreich, Belgien und Italien in der Vor- und Nachkriegszeit. Einzelschriften zur Statistik des Deutschen Reichs*, Nr. 2 (Berlin, 1927).

[7] Committee on Currency and Foreign Exchanges after the War: *First Interim Report* (London. 1919). This "interim report" contains the essential recommendations. The documents collected by the Committee – submissions from experts, discussions within the Committee, statements by interest groups – are to be found in the Public Record Office, London, T185/1–3. A recent discussion and assessment of the Committee's deliberations and recommendations is offered by Donald E. Moggridge: *British Monetary Policy 1924–31. The Norman Conquest of $ 4.86* (Cambridge, England, 1972), pp. 17–21. Cp. also Albert Feavearyear: *The Pound Sterling. A History of English Money* (Oxford, 2nd edn. 1963), pp. 348–50.

was possible if the depreciation of sterling against the dollar that had followed the lifting of currency controls in 1919 was to be halted (cp. Diagram 2).

The basis of the British decision was the calculation that the fiscal economies necessary for the domestic stabilization of the pound were both achievable and politically desirable and that the deflationary costs of the action would be compensated both by the restoration of London's role as an international financial center and by the improvement this in turn would cause in Britain's capacity to trade on world markets. But reality proved different from the calculation. Britain's international position continued to weaken, partly because America's policy ran counter to the "rules" of the gold standard. Gold flows into the U.S.A. were "sterilized" to prevent their causing domestic price rises, and tariff barriers were increased, thus limiting other countries' capacities to earn the gold and dollars they needed to buy imports and repay debts. These measures to insulate the American money and goods markets from outside influences stood in the way of any permanent improvement of the British external trading position and hence of the position of sterling. At the same time U.S. policy set its face steadily against European, especially French, demands for the cancellation of inter-allied debts.[8] In Gottfried Haberler's view, the increasing protectionism of the U.S.A., the world's greatest creditor nation, during this period could only be described as "sadistic."[9] The American economist B.M. Anderson described the U.S. government's schizoid economic policy – demanding repayment of debts but preventing the corresponding real transfers – with the following metaphor: "The debts of the outside world to us are ropes about the necks of our debtors, by means of which we pull them toward us. Our trade restrictions are pitchforks pressed against their bodies, by means of which we hold them off. This situation can obviously involve a very painful strain for the foreign debtor."[10] These were the external strains to which the British economy was exposed in the twenties and which constrained her economic development.

The decision to "return to gold" not only exposed the British economy to these deflationary impulses from abroad; it also created a domestic environment inimical to enterprise. The falling price level conferred a bonus on net holders of fixed value domestic-currency assets – the rentiers who held conser-

---

[8] Statistisches Reichsamt: *Die interalliierten Schulden. Ihre Entstehung und ihre Bedeutung im Youngplan* (Berlin, 1930), esp. the documents on pp. 115ff. Cp. H.G. Moulton and L. Pasvolsky: *War Debts and World Prosperity* (Washington, D.C., 1932), chapters III.–V.

[9] Gottfried Haberler: *The Theory of International Trade with its Applications to Commercial Policy* (London, 1936), p. 80 (German original, 1933).

[10] In Chase National Bank (ed.): *The Chase Economic Bulletin* (New York), March 14, 1930. Cited from G. Haberler: *International Trade,* p. 80.

vatively selected asset portfolios including a high proportion of War Loans and other government stocks and who had not used their wealth to contract large debts. Such people, earning nominally fixed-interest incomes, were the beneficiaries of falling prices, whereas the same price falls discouraged the enterprising elements in society from extending their business activities by borrowing to invest in real or "human" capital. Since the state was the largest debtor of all, the chosen deflationary policy entailed an "austerity" policy; debt service charges increased with higher interest rates while tax revenues tended to fall; this compelled so much the greater savings on other classes of expenditure. The "Geddes" axe fell on personnel and infrastructural investment projects. Employment of labor and utilization of capital suffered as a result; business willingness to invest was weakened and the rate of economic growth diminished. An environment was created in which the required adjustments of economic structure necessarily brought heavy structural unemployment in their train.

These comparisons furnish a background against which to consider the corresponding discussion in Germany. The alternatives, "return to the prewar parity" or "stabilization at a depreciated exchange rate", were already being debated during the war itself.[11] Initially, the fiscal implications of the choice played a subordinate part in the discussion; however as early as 1916 the Swedish economist Gustav Cassel[12] had made them the basis of his argument that after the war the mark ought to be stabilized at a lower parity. Drawing attention to the great rise in the national debt during the war he pointed out, "The real burden of an annual interest charge of one billion marks must obviously double, if the purchasing power of the currency unit doubles in which the debt is denominated."[13] German discussion recognized that restoration of the prewar parity would penalize the public household with reduced tax revenues out of which unaltered debt servicing obligations would have to be met.[14] Nevertheless it was steadfastly maintained that domestic prices must be reduced to their prewar level in order to protect the real wealth of prewar creditors. The "goal of speedy restoration of the external parity"[15] of the mark was equally undisputed: restoration of convertibility at a lower parity or, worse still, the retention of an inconvertible paper currency would

[11] R. Hauser: "Unsere Währung nach dem Kriege", pp. 2–6.

[12] Gustav Cassel: *Deutschlands wirtschaftliche Widerstandskraft* (Berlin, 1916), pp. 155–156. Subsequently, Gustav Cassel, *Money and Foreign Exchange after 1914* (London, 1922), pp. 254ff.

[13] G. Cassel: *Deutschlands wirtschaftliche Widerstandskraft*, p. 151.

[14] R. Hauser: "Unsere Währung nach dem Kriege", p. 4.

[15] *Ibid.*

"seriously jeopardize the reputation of our currency as an international means of settlement, as well as the international position of our banking system... For more than a generation our banks and great merchant houses have been endeavoring to secure recognition for the mark as an international currency alongside the pound and the franc. Success crowned their efforts, so that not only the greater part of German foreign trade but even a portion of the foreign trade of neighboring countries to the south and east was settled in mark currency – a situation bringing German banks pecuniary and other advantages that had previously been enjoyed by London."[16] These sentiments are reminiscent of those which in Great Britain led the Cunliffe Committee to make its – eventually realized – currency recommendations.

However during the war currency theorists in Germany – as in England – did debate whether the return should take the form of a full "gold currency" system or merely a "gold reserve" system in which the nation's gold stocks would be centralized at the Reichsbank and the currency would be convertible only for the purposes of foreign transactions.[17] On the question of the parity itself and of the domestic price level to be aimed at, virtual unanimity reigned – as in the Cunliffe Committee: return to prewar conditions. "Our postwar currency policy must aim at as rapid as possible a restoration of the parity – this is the overwhelming consensus among those practically and theoretically concerned with the question." So wrote Friedrich Bendixen as late as October 18th, 1918.[18]

But in 1919 a fundamental change of opinion came across the discussion. From now on the debate about how to restore currency stability revolved, in principle, round three distinct possibilities. Common to all of them was the long-term goal of pegging the mark to some gold or foreign exchange parity, thereby also securing domestic price stability. They differed however as to the external parity and domestic price level to be aimed at. Disregarding minor differences of detail, the proposals discussed can be reduced to one or other of the following three schools of thought.

(i) Return to the prewar parity, i.e. (relative to the actual situation at the war's end) reduction of the price level and appreciation of the exchange rate. This type of proposal entailed a rigorous fiscal deflation yielding the budget surpluses out of which the state could retire both the floating debt and the long-term debt as it matured.

---

[16] *Ibid.*, pp. 5–6.

[17] The gold reserve currency was explicitly recommended by e.g. Robert Liefmann, Johann Plenge, Otto Heyn and Friedrich Bendixen.

[18] Friedrich Bendixen: "Die Parität und ihre Wiederherstellung", *Bank-Archiv*, 18 (1918/19), p. 9.

(ii) Stabilization at the existing price level, thus avoiding the need for domestic price deflation and external exchange rate appreciation. Contemporaries applied the word, "devaluation" (*Devalvation*) to this course of action; in currency history it was sometimes associated with proposals designed to reconstitute original currency relationships in nominal terms: by overprinting banknotes or exchanging existing notes for new in a fixed ratio, and by converting nominal debt values.[19] This type of proposal merely involved the government's renouncing the right to pursue further inflationary financial policies.

(iii) Continued price inflation and exchange rate depreciation. This policy entailed yet further increases in governmental indebtedness at the Reichsbank, hence in the monetary base, using either premature retirement of War Loan stock or continued budget deficits to bring the cash thus created into general circulation. Its advocates recommended this strategy as an alternative to a regular "state bankruptcy,"[20] under which the state suspends retirements of, and interest payments upon, its debt, thus permitting nominal public debt values to collapse. Inflation by contrast reduces the real value not only of public but also of private debts.

This last argument is sufficient to show that the fiscal dilemma of the Reich was becoming an increasingly central element in the currency debate as the war ended. At the heart of the discussion was the question whether and how the Reich was to service and redeem the long term debt of around one hundred billion marks which it had contracted during the war. Including the floating debt, the aggregate had increased to 175 billion marks by the middle of 1919, representing annual interest charges of about 9 billion marks. Helfferich estimated national wealth on the eve of the war at about three hundred billion marks.[21] This gives a perspective on the size of the problem: were prices reduced to the prewar *status quo ante*, the state would have to appropriate more than half the nation's assets to redeem its debts. The nine billion marks interest charges (175 bn. marks at five percent) were four times the Reich's

[19] Friedrich Bendixen: "Devalvation, Eine Richtigstellung", *Bank-Archiv*, 19 (1919/20), pp. 163–169. Carl Weill: "Betrachtungen zum Devalvationsproblem", *Bank-Archiv*, 19 (1919/20), p. 183. Cp. too Karl Diehl: "David Ricardo und der finanzielle Wiederaufbau Englands nach den napoleonischen Kriegen", *Bank-Archiv*, 19 (1919/20), p. 122.

[20] Alfred Manes: *Staatsbankrotte. Wirtschaftliche und rechtliche Betrachtungen* (Berlin, 1918). Waldemar Haefner-Hainen: *Der Staatsbankrott in Deutschland unvermeidlich. Ein ernster Mahnruf an die Nationalversammlung in Weimar* (Leipzig, 1919). Paul Bang: *Staatsbankrott oder -erneuerung?* (Munich, 1920).

[21] Karl Helfferich: *Deutschlands Volkswohlstand 1888–1913* (Berlin, 6th edn. 1915), p. 122.

total 1913 revenues of 2.2 billion marks.[22] This was the essence of the fiscal dilemma that had built up by the end of the war. The strategy selected to resolve it simultaneously determined postwar currency policy, as we shall see by further examination of each of the three schools of thought on the subject.

(i) Those who proposed the first type of policy – restoration of prewar parity plus domestic price deflation – generally supported it with a two-stage policy for dealing with the debt problem. They proposed that the floating debt be dealt with as soon as possible, by funding loans. Steps should then be taken to reduce the principal of the funded debt, preferably by means of a non-recurrent capital levy.[23]

The only attempt at a funding loan by the Reich after the war ended however in failure. This was the so-called *Sparprämienanleihe* of 1919[24] and its undersubscription registered the decline of the state's credit worthiness in the eyes of the public. War Loan stock traded at very depressed prices on the stock market;[25] this was a symptom of the same ailment, as Karl Elster confirmed in an article published on July 15th, 1919: "A single observation tells all. On the stock market the price of five percent War Loan stands almost twenty five percent below that of the four percent mortgage bonds of commercial mortgage banks (*Hypothekenpfandbriefe*). There exists only one explanation for this unhappy, indeed shameful state of affairs: War Loan is no longer regarded as a secure investment."[26] The "observation" Elster refers to reflects public anxiety about possible state bankruptcy of the classic type, affecting governmental debts only or at least not affecting private debts in the same measure.

But even had it proved possible to place long-term Reich debt, it must be questioned whether such a "funding" operation would have had a significant counterinflationary impact. This is because of the high liquidity of Reich Loan stock as already described, in virtue of its eligibility as collateral at the Loan Bureaux and of the admissibility of the Loan Bureau Certificates it could thus command as components of the primary currency reserve.[27] The expansionary implications of funded debt for the monetary base were not much less than

---

22 Peter-Christian Witt: *Die Finanzpolitik des Deutschen Reiches von 1903 bis 1913* (Lübeck, 1970), p. 379.

23 Fritz Terhalle: "Zum Inflationsproblem der Übergangswirtschaft", *Bank-Archiv*, 18 (1918/19), p. 93 (February 15, 1919).

24 F. Hesse: *Die deutsche Wirtschaftslage von 1914 bis 1923. Krieg, Geldblähe und Wechsellagen* (Jena, 1938), p. 137.

25 The stock market prices of War Loans are reproduced in the *Statistische Jahrbücher für das Deutsche Reich*, 1920–1923.

26 Karl Elster: "Kriegsanleihen und Finanznot", *Bank-Archiv*, 18 (1918/19), p. 212.

27 See p. 115 *supra*.

those of the floating debt; subscription to the former reduced lenders' liquidity only somewhat more than purchase of the latter. It seems astonishing, then, that to my knowledge not one of the postwar anti-inflationary proposals for consolidating the floating debt even discussed its necessary corollary: the closing of the Loan Bureaux.

Against this it must be conceded that wartime funding issues may have achieved a counterinflationary result by a different route: by building confidence in the solidity of the Reich's financial policy and hence, more generally, in the currency. As long as the Loan Bureaux existed, Reich funding policy could hardly damp inflationary pressures from the supply side (by reducing lender liquidity and the potential growth of the monetary base); it could however act to support the demand for money, by its psychological effect on confidence, and this would help to contain inflation. After the war however general confidence in the Reich's credit worthiness had so much deteriorated that even this effect could not operate.

The second part of this proposal for creating the fiscal prerequisites of a return to prewar currency relationships involved a tax measure: the non-recurrent capital levy.[28] Even before the war ended this possibility had been faced and thoroughly ventilated.[29] Its aim would be to "lighten the burden" of the war debt and it was to be undertaken in the context of wider fiscal reform designed to mobilize new sources of taxation. By making it *non-recurrent*, the *continuing* burden of postwar taxation required to service the remaining part of the debt could be rendered bearable. "Had we the choice between gradual amortization on the basis of a moderate burden of annual taxation, and a non-recurrent capital levy, the gradual amortization would unquestionably be preferable. But in fact we face a different choice: between gradual amortization coupled with an intolerable tax burden, and the non-recurrent levy. The levy is a severe measure indeed, but justifiable as it reduces the permanent burden of taxation considerably."[30]

The proposed levy was partially realized in the "Reich Emergency Contribution" (*Reichsnotopfer*) exacted from the wealthier classes as part of the great Erzberger tax reforms. It was, however, payable in installments, contrary to the original conception, and became a recurrent charge on wealth additional

---

[28] Otto Heyn: "Die Geldentwertung; ihre Ursache und die Mittel zu ihrer Beseitigung", *Bank-Archiv*, 18 (1918/19), p. 72 (January 15, 1919).

[29] Cp. the various contributions on the question of the "non-recurrent capital levy" from Karl Diehl und Felix Somary (both in favor) and from Heinrich Dietzel and Paul Homburger (both against), plus the annexed discussions, in Heinrich Herkner (ed.): *Die Neuordung der deutschen Finanzwirtschaft. Schriften des Vereins für Socialpolitik Bd. 156 I–III* (Munich, 1918).

[30] Karl Diehl in *ibid.*, Bd. 156 I, p. 11.

to wealth holders' existing liabilities under the "Defense Contribution" of 1919[31] and the extraordinary 'War levy' of 1917. The assessments under the Emergency Contribution were made in nominal terms and the first installment was not due until 1920 by which time the swelling of the floating debt and consequent diminution in the value of the currency had assumed considerably larger proportions than in November 1918 (cp. Tables 1 and 20).

This is the astounding thing. All the time that people were discussing the *reduction* of the floating and funded debt resulting from the war, the Reich in 1919 was finding it impossible to operate without continuing to contract new floating debt at a rapid rate. Reich expenditures in 1919 did show a decline against the last year of the war: 55 as against 76 billion marks.[32] Expenditures by state and communes on the other hand were considerably higher: in Prussia they were 17.3 billion marks in 1919 as against 9.7 billion marks in 1918.[33] Meanwhile the ordinary revenues of the Reich showed only a modest increase: from 7.4 billion marks in 1918 to 11.0 in 1919 (cp. Table 25) and did little to reduce the overwhelming reliance on deficit financing, now almost exclusively through short-term borrowing. The fighting and maintenance costs of a military establishment formed a much smaller proportion of Reich expenditures in 1919 than in the previous year; in their place however came the costs of demobilizing the armed forces and reintegrating them into employment, also the costs imposed by the Armistice terms and the Peace Treaty.

It may be concluded then that the strategy of "lightening the burden" of Reich debt and restoring prewar currency conditions was no longer a realistic alternative even as early as 1918/19, once Germany had lost the war and the burden of Reparations had been superimposed on the crushing load of the Reich's internal debt. Any attempt not only to service but also to redeem this debt out of taxation – recurrent or non-recurrent – would have involved a deflation and depression of unimaginable severity – if it had not first burst the bounds of all tax morality and administrative capacity. No government could have survived such a policy; the newly constituted republic would have been no exception to this judgment. Richard Hauser, who in October 1917 had still been advocating resumption of the prewar parity, came to recognize that circumstances alter cases. In July 1919 he wrote that, "the preconditions on which the judgment [i.e. restoration of the parity] rested have now altered fundamentally."[34] Restoration was now no longer desirable since the greater

[31] Boleslav Fux: "Die Vermögenssteuer", article in *Handbuch der Finanzwissenschaft* (Tübingen, 1st edn. 3 Bde. 1925–9), Bd. 2 (1927), p. 153.

[32] F. Hesse: *Deutsche Wirtschaftslage*, p. 422.

[33] A. Jessen: *Finanzen, Defizit und Notenpresse 1914–1922* (Berlin, 1923), Tafel (i.e. Table) 1.

[34] Richard Hauser: "Zur Währungsfrage", *Bank-Archiv*, 18 (1918/19), p. 197 (July 1, 1919).

part of the state's wartime debt had been contracted after the currency had already begun to depreciate; return to 1914 prices would bring the creditors unjustifiable windfall gains. But in any case, Hauser argued, the restoration of the original parity was "simply not possible", in view of the condition of the Reich's finances. Using the argument already expounded that at 1913 prices the Reich's current internal debt would amount to half the aggregate prewar German national wealth, and adding that interest charges on the same debt at a rate of five percent would represent one quarter of the prewar national income at the prewar price level,[35] he concluded, "Annual interest charges to the tune of ten billion gold marks would, in view of the additional obligations toward the Entente, prove a greater burden than the German national income could bear and would inevitably lead to collapse. Consideration of the internal debt problem rules out categorically the restoration of the former parity of our currency."

Richard Hauser emphasized other problems of returning to the prewar parity, notably the implied pressure on wages and prices. "The attempt to reduce workers' wages would create insuperable difficulties... Conflict between wage earners and employers would be interminable... Under present political circumstances such a measure could not be achieved without great damage being done."[36] In October 1918, just before the war ended, Friedrich Bendixen had already warned against restoring the gold parity of the mark, and his reservations had less to do with the associated fiscal problems than with its probable effects on production, social relations and politics. Bendixen's arguments sound in places like a criticism of the English Cunliffe Committee proposals: it would be perverse, he wrote, "to regard the gold value of the currency in itself as a good, directly enhancing the welfare and honor of the people, and worth paying any economic price to achieve."[37] As if passing premonitory judgment on Brüning's policy of deflation, he opined, "No statesman would want to incur responsibility for the odious policy of depressing wages. To drive prices down is, however, likewise the reverse of good policy."[38] Bendixen recommended that those who formulated postwar financial and currency measures pay attention to the consequences of alternative policies for national production. He warned of the effects of traumatic tax increases designed to reduce the quantity of money and the price level. "Un-

[35] Cp. Karl Helfferich: *Deutschlands Volkswohlstand*, p. 122, who estimated German prewar national income at forty billion marks.

[36] R. Hauser: "Zur Währungsfrage", p. 198.

[37] F. Bendixen: "Die Parität und ihre Wiederherstellung", p. 13 (October 15, 1918).

[38] *Ibid.*

employment, devaluation of real production and credit crisis would be the hallmarks of this fateful policy. On the contrary, nothing will in fact be so bitterly necessary in Germany after the war as the harnessing of our entire economic capabilities to the task of production."[39]

Thus the first school of thought about postwar currency policy no longer enjoyed serious support after the end of the war, mainly on account of its fiscal implications. Advocates of the second and third types of proposal – stabilization at present price levels or continued inflation – were not lacking: what distinguished them was the importance they attached to production policy.

(ii) Willi Prion may be regarded as the most prominent representative of the second school of thought. In 1918 he had, it is true, prepared a memorandum for the Reich Finance Ministry that bore the title, "Financial Measures for Reducing Prices", but in it he had reached the conclusion that, "price stability would be more advantageous than the objective of achieving a lower price level at some future date, both for the economic life of the country and for the public finances. The same conclusion applies to exchange rate policy."[40] Like Hauser and Bendixen he justified his recommendation with economic, social and political arguments on the one hand, and with reference to fiscal considerations on the other. "The process of reconstituting the former (prewar) price level would set in motion a whole train of new economic disturbances. In particular, owners of real goods... would suffer losses, the production of new goods would come to a standstill, commodity markets would be dislocated, and wage disputes would threaten economic and social life with incalculable damage. It would have the most far-reaching consequences for public finance. The enormous debts contracted by public authorities in depreciated currency would have to be paid back with good money. Creditors would do good business, for they would get back their principal at the same face value, but with greater purchasing power. Quite apart from the harshness and injustice of such a distribution of burdens and benefits, the raising of the required taxation would weigh intolerably on those who shared only the burden."[41] Price reductions should therefore occur only when they could be generated from the side of real supply – that is, from increasing production.[42]

Prion recommended forced loans, income taxes and excises on consumer

---

[39] *Ibid.*

[40] Willi Prion: *Inflation und Geldentwertung. Finanzielle Massnahmen zum Abbau der Preise. Gutachten erstattet dem Reichsfinanzministerium* (Berlin, 1919), p. 108.

[41] *Ibid.*, p. 113.

[42] *Ibid.*, p. 108.

goods as the method of meeting the state's fiscal requirements and hence of attacking the root cause of inflation; the tax increases were to be introduced once increases in production were depressing prices and thus creating an environment where they could be passed on in a non-inflationary manner. Finally he recommended a non-recurrent capital levy, to be paid in a lump sum and not by installments, thus preventing its being passed on in higher prices. He believed that the upward pressure on prices of a capital levy payable in installments would be greater than the corresponding upward pressure exerted by income and consumption taxes. The latter taxes bore on the mass of the population, reducing its purchasing power and this effect would counteract attempts to pass them on in higher prices. A capital levy affects the rich only who would react by cutting back on saving and hence investment, thus protecting their level of consumption; lump-sum payment would prevent its being passed on. Nonetheless the Reich Emergency Contribution was in the event levied in installment form; it was payable over a maximum of fortyseven years.

(iii) The third school of thought regarding currency policy – that advocating further inflation – remains to be discussed. Prion, Hauser and Bendixen had all at first argued that the price level should be stabilized at its current, depreciated level, but towards the middle of 1919[43] Bendixen[44] made public a proposal which had been the subject of private discussion since March.[45] His immediate concern was simply to propose a method of eliminating the enlarged discount at which the Reich's long-dated issues were standing in the aftermath of the announcement of the Allied peace treaty conditions; in doing so however he explicitly advocated accelerated inflation as a mode of taxation: the Reich should redeem its long-term debt prematurely and at par value, obtaining the requisite cash by recourse to the central bank; alternatively it should convert its long-dated stocks into treasury bills, thus giving the holders immediate access to central bank credit and to additional newly created money. This course of action would remove the threat of state bankruptcy; at the same time the productive economy could enjoy the benefits of plentiful and depreciating currency. For it was preferable, "to exploit to the full the opportunities afforded by money creation, than to cripple the forces of production and the spirit of enterprise by a confiscatory tax policy."[46]

[43] This is clear from an article discussing the proposal: Karl Elster: "Kriegsanleihen und Finanznot" (July 15, 1919). Elster is ultimately unsympathetic to the proposal.

[44] Friedrich Bendixen: *Kriegsanleihen und Finanznot. Zwei finanzpolitische Vorschläge* (Jena, 1919).

[45] *Ibid.*, p. 18.

[46] *Ibid.*, p. 9.

Keynes drew a similar contrast between the two alternatives a few years later: "Thus inflation is unjust and deflation is inexpedient. Of the two perhaps deflation is...the worse, because it is worse in an impoverished world to provoke unemployment than to disappoint the rentier."[47] Whereas Keynes however saw evils in both alternatives, and believed they could be avoided by a policy of price stabilization,[48] Bendixen regarded stabilization in the existing circumstances as a good deal worse than inflation. "I have never denied that what I propose is an evil, but it is the only means of preventing a still worse evil... We may deprecate the fraudulent excesses of speculation and of entrepreneurial activity that inflation would bring – and not without reason: but are we on this account to prefer the corpse-strewn battlefield into which the repudiation of the War Loans would turn our economy?"[49] Bendixen believed it would be impossible, or at least extremely injurious to the economy, to repay the War Loans out of taxation. He also regarded inflation as preferable to the type of tax system that – under existing political conditions – was threatening wealth holders and high income groups in the manner proposed and partly effectuated under the Erzberger tax reforms. Bendixen's prejudice against the *soziale Republik* and its tax schemes is unmistakable:[50] whether his inflationary proposals flow more from his anxieties regarding government tax proposals, or from his concern about growth and employment, is difficult to decide. It is significant however that even the government itself and the higher levels of the bureaucracy undoubtedly formulated and discussed currency proposals on the lines of Bendixen's, as Prion remarks in his memorandum of 1919.[51]

Bendixen's proposals to convert War Loan stock into cash were never put designedly into effect. The Reich did occasionally make open market purchases of its bonds and sometimes accepted them in discharge of tax liabilities – practices which reduced the one hundred billion marks' worth outstanding at the end of the war to around seventy billion in early 1924[52] – but these were not the principal inflation-accelerating and production-stimulating forces in the early postwar economy. Rather Bendixen's results were achieved by a

---

[47] J. M. Keynes: *A Tract on Monetary Reform. The Collected Writings of J. M. Keynes, ed. E. Johnson and D. E. Moggridge, vol. IV* (London, 1971), p. 36 (original edition, 1923).

[48] Thus too Willi Prion: *Inflation und Geldentwertung*, p. 114.

[49] Friedrich Bendixen: " Die Inflation als Rettungsmittel", *Bank-Archiv*, 19 (1919/20), p. 54 (December 1, 1919).

[50] *Ibid.* where the polemical tone is manifest.

[51] W. Prion: *Inflation und Geldentwertung*, p. 113.

[52] Cp. p. 327 *infra*.

different route – as continuing budget deficits necessitated a continuous expansion of the floating debt. Constantly increasing prices eroded the real receipts from taxes assessed on a nominal basis and payable, as is customary in the case of wealth taxes and taxes on higher incomes, only after a certain lapse of time from the assessment. Even the servicing of War Loans, regarded by Bendixen as a primary cause of the Reich's fiscal difficulties, became an ever more minor element of Reich expenditure as the inflation progressed. Indeed the goal he pursued was far more effectively achieved by the route actually followed than by the means he proposed. Repayment of War Loan would not have greatly increased liquidity in the economy. As long as it could be lodged as collateral at any time at the Loan Bureaux, official repurchase was not necessary to create this effect – War Loan was almost "as good as money" anyway. It was the pressures exerted by a deficitary public household that had the greatest impact on inflation and production, and this mechanism played no part in Bendixen's scheme; he may have envisaged a balanced budget.

Whatever the positive advantages claimed for the postwar inflation as a means of easing the transition to peacetime production, of promoting full employment and of stimulating private investment, its power to rescue the private economy from the clutches of an unacceptable tax system, based on socially equitable criteria and aiming at income and wealth redistribution, is vividly illustrated by the history of the Reich Emergency Contribution. Announced in December 1919 as the successor to two provisional measures of that year – the 'War Levy on Capital Gains' and the 'Extraordinary War Levy for Fiscal Year 1919' – its tax rates were strongly progressive: rising from 10% of the value of assets at five thousand marks to 65% at above seven million marks.[53] According to original estimates the tax would cream off up to one

[53] Fritz Terhalle: "Geschichte der deutschen öffentlichen Finanzwirtschaft vom Beginn des 19. Jahrhunderts bis zum Schlusse des Zweiten Weltkrieges", article in *Handbuch der Finanzwissenschaft* (Tübingen, 2nd edn. 4 Bde. 1952–65), Bd. 1 (1952), p. 298. Cp. also Johannes Popitz: "Die deutschen Finanzen 1918–1928", *Zehn Jahre Deutsche Geschichte 1918–1928* (Berlin, 1928), pp. 189–190. More detailed: Robert Eichhorn: *Die einmaligen Vermögensabgaben im Deutschen Reiche* (Jena, 1925), esp. pp. 16 ff. Cp. also *Akten der Reichskanzlei. Weimarer Republik. Das Kabinett Fehrenbach*, pp. 265–266, note 1. Detailed statistical material on the effects of the Reich's financial policies during the war is to be found in the state memoranda: "Die Finanzen des Deutschen Reiches in den Rechnungsjahren 1914 bis 1918", in *Verhandlungen der Verfassungsgebenden Deutschen Nationalversammlung, Bd. 335* (Berlin, 1920), Drucksache Nr. 158. "Der künftige finanzielle Bedarf des Reichs und seine Deckung", in *Verhandlungen der Verfassungsgebenden Deutschen Nationalversammlung, Bd. 338* (Berlin, 1920), Drucksache Nr. 760. "Die finanzielle Lage des Reichs", in *Verhandlungen des Reichstages, Bd. 363* (Berlin, 1924), Drucksache Nr. 254.

third of German national wealth,[54] which could then be applied to redeeming the state's war debts; it would have been a fiscal exaction without parallel in the history of German public finance. Since the Levy was for the most part payable in cash,[55] the Reich had no choice but to permit payment by installment, and in fact according to its provisions payment could normally be spread over up to twenty-eight and a half years, or in the case of landed property up to forty-seven years. Since aggregate liability was determined according to assessed nominal value of assets on a date fixed at the direction of the tax authorities, the real value of the installments which the exchequer was receiving dwindled rapidly into insignificance. The gold value of what had been paid up to 1922 was only a little more than one billion marks. In this way the currency depreciation made the capital levy into "a sham...indeed a comedy."[56] In 1922 the collection of the now pointless tax ceased; it was replaced by surcharges on the recurrent wealth tax.

A further, more modest, attempt at conscripting the resources of the rich for the financing of the Reich on a non-recurrent basis was the "compulsory loan," announced in the Reichstag in April and agreed to in July 1922. The one billion gold marks it was supposed to raise were earmarked to meet certain Reparations commitments accepted at the Cannes Conference of January 1922. The Loan was actually subscribed in paper marks however at the fixed ratio of seventy paper marks to one gold mark (this corresponded to the dollar rate in April); subscriptions were paid between July 1922 and March 1923, and because of the simultaneous slide into hyperinflation after June 1922 the real value of the sums raised was pitiful. Only fifty million gold marks were ultimately received by the exchequer – a fiasco hardly less total than that of the Reich Emergency Contribution.

This discussion of the options facing fiscal policy in 1919 cannot be concluded without discussion of the question whether those who found the inflation a welcome alternative to confiscatory taxation can be considered responsible for the fiscal policy that stimulated it. This question was heard only indirectly in the contemporary debate itself – namely in discussion of the limits of taxable capacity.

Before answering the question it needs to be spelt out more clearly. Debt servicing out of tax revenue does not enlarge public sector demand at the

[54] Heinrich Dietzel: "Abbürdung der Kriegsschuld", in H. Herkner (ed.): *Die Neuordnung der deutschen Finanzwirtschaft*, p. 107.

[55] Criticism of this stipulation can be found in Robert Nöll von der Nahmer: *Lehrbuch der Finanzwissenschaft* (Cologne, 2 Bde. 1964), Bd. 2: *Spezielle Steuerlehre*, p. 38.

[56] Gaston Jèze, cited in F. Terhalle: "Geschichte", p. 298.

expense of private sector demand in the way that the expenditures do which give rise to the debts in the first place. Rather it represents a transfer of purchasing power from the tax payer to the debt holder.[57] As the sums transferred grow larger so does the share of national income subject to state discretion (assuming constant real value of other public expenditures); specifically, the scope widens for employing taxation policy as an instrument of social goals.

Evidence that taxation was beginning to be governed by such considerations, already apparent during the war, became unmistakable after the November 1918 revolution, and many, particularly in business circles, perceived it as a threat. The foregoing discussion of the tax implications of a deflationary policy shows how immeasurably more threatened they would have felt, had a tax-financed policy of funding and redeeming the debt and of restoring the prewar parity been carried through by a state they perceived as hostile to their interests. Inflation however was a form of taxation[58] against which the individual could more or less shield himself, and in any case its incidence could not be controlled according to social criteria. Over the long run inflation could only tend to weaken the state, initially in the measure that rising prices eroded the real value of its conventional tax revenues, and ultimately as the accelerating pace of price increase reduced the resources which the "inflation tax" itself could command.

For those who feared the expansion of state activity – especially of the kind involving fiscal expropriation of private property – inflation acted as a loophole through which they could defend their assets and ward off state interference. Can they on this account be held responsible for it? Were they the authors of the fiscal policy that engendered it? Clearly the propertied classes were not *en masse* its beneficiaries. Those whose wealth was sunk in fixed value monetary assets and who did not learn to protect it by shifting into real assets or by contracting equivalent debts, suffered capital losses through the inflation far greater than the most rigorous tax policy would have caused them. Obviously this group cannot be accused of having fostered inflation to protect their wealth. Nor on the other hand can owners of real assets or paper-mark debtors, however much they gained by inflation, be held responsible that a government, conducted largely by the Social Democrats who at one time had strongly advocated a capital levy,[59] added large demobilization and social expendi-

[57] Heinz Haller: *Finanzpolitik. Grundlagen und Hauptprobleme* (Tübingen, 5th edn. 1972), p. 198–199.

[58] Cp. p. 119 note 1 *supra.*

[59] Heinrich Dietzel in H. Herkner (ed.): *Die Neuordnung*, p. 107.

tures to the Reparations outlays it could not escape. These expenditures bore much of the responsibility for the failure to gain control of the budget deficit after the war, and by fuelling inflation reduced the chances of effective progressive taxation of income and wealth. Whether the new republican government had any real alternative, in view of the economic and political exigencies under which it took office and the small confidence placed in it by precisely those wealthier classes from whom the bulk of tax revenues would have to flow, must be doubted. Haller recently calculated that a level of taxation equal to thirty-five percent of national income would have been required to defray postwar expenditures on Reparations, social welfare and the general running costs of government in a noninflationary manner, as against 11–12% before the war. The decisive precondition for such taxation "would have been a strong government that had the entire population behind it and was thus in a position to demand great sacrifices.... The legislative apparatus and machinery of government would have to have been intact and in possession of the sheerly technical competence to devise and organize the collection of new high-yielding taxes in a short space of time. Scarcely any country that had just lost a war would have been in a position to satisfy this precondition... And so, in the circumstances, the Reich had no other means of defraying the flood of expenditure than by further short-term borrowing."[60] "The inflation", according to Haller, had "the great positive effect" that it secured the parliamentary form of government for the duration of the Weimar republic.[61] While Terhalle[62] merely opined that the national exchequer was both author and chief beneficiary of the inflation, Haller stressed the political dilemma which narrowly constrained the spectrum of feasible options for financial policy. "If the state did cause the inflation, it did so in self-defense."[63]

The influence of Reparations

Defeat was one of the primary constituents of this "situation of self-defense", most materially because it transformed Germany from a nation expecting to receive reparations into a nation required to pay them. In place of the expected

---

60 Heinz Haller: "Die Rolle der Staatsfinanzen für den Inflationsprozess", in Deutsche Bundesbank (ed.), *Währung und Wirtschaft in Deutschland 1876–1975* (Frankfurt/M., 1976), pp. 140–141.

61 *Ibid.*, pp. 151–152.

62 F. Terhalle: "*Geschichte*", p. 304.

63 H. Haller: "*Rolle*", p. 152.

relief of the Reich's fiscal difficulties, the Armistice and Peace Treaty brought added burdens.[1]

Germans always represented the terms of the Peace Treaty as the reason for the inflation. This charge was not confined to the public utterances of politicians;[2] it also governed the contemporary academic debate about the inflation's causes. Both balance of payments and quantity theorists saw in Reparations the disequilibrating factor, acting either on the external balance

---

1 On the tug of war over the Versailles peace terms, not only between Germany and the Allies, but also amongst the Allies themselves, see above all the accounts of the conference participants: Bernard M. Baruch: *The Making of the Reparation and Economic Sections of the Treaty* (New York, 1920), esp. pp. 45–55. Edward M. House and Charles Seymour (eds.): *What Really Happened at Paris: The Story of the Peace Conference by the American Delegates, 1918–1919* (New York, 1921). Andrew MacFadyean: *Reparation Reviewed* (London, 1930). André Tardieu: *La Paix* (Paris, 1921). David Lloyd George: *The Truth about the Peace Treaties* (London, 1932).
For comprehensive accounts of the Peace Settlement and Reparations, see H. W. V. Temperley (ed.): *A History of the Peace Conference of Paris* (London, 6 vols. 1920–1924). John W. Wheeler-Bennett and Hugh Latimer: *Information on the Reparation Settlement. Being the Background and History of the Young Plan and the Hague Agreements 1929–30* (London, 1930). Philip M. Burnett, *Reparation at the Peace Conference. From the Standpoint of the American Delegation* (New York, 2 vols. 1940). William M. Jordan: *Great Britain, France and the German Problem 1918–1939* (London, 1943). Etienne Weill-Raynal: *Les Réparations Allemandes et la France* (Paris, 3 vols. 1947). A short, suggestive account of the first five years is: "History of the Reparations Question", in *The Economist Reparations Supplement*, 1924 – copy in Thomas W. Lamont Papers 176–5 (Reparations and the Dawes Plan May-July 1924), Harvard University, Cambridge, Mass. Among more recent studies on Versailles are: Arno J. Mayer: *Politics and Diplomacy of Peacemaking. Containment and Counterrevolution at Versailles 1918–1919* (New York, 1967). Peter Krüger: *Deutschland und die Reparationen 1918/19. Die Genesis des Reparationsproblems in Deutschland zwischen Waffenstillstand und Versailler Friedensschluß* (Stuttgart, 1973). Leo Haupts: *Deutsche Friedenspolitik 1918–1919. Eine Alternative zur Machtpolitik des Ersten Weltkrieges?* (Düsseldorf, 1977). Marc Trachtenberg: "Reparations at the Paris Peace Conference", *Journal of Modern History*, 51 (1979), pp. 24–55. Idem, *Reparation in World Politics. France and European Economic Diplomacy, 1916–1923* (New York, 1980).
More particularly on the economic consequences: Erich Wuest: *Der Vertrag von Versailles im Licht und Schatten der Kritik. Die Kontroverse um seine wirtschaftlichen Auswirkungen* (Zürich, 1962). On the Franco-German relationship in particular, Ludwig Zimmermann: *Frankreichs Ruhrpolitik von Versailles bis zum Dawes Plan* (Göttingen, 1971). Jacques Bariety: *Les Relations Franco-Allemandes après la Première Guerre Mondiale, 10 Nov. 1918–10 Janv. 1925: De l'Exécution à la Négociation* (Paris, 1977).

2 Thus the Hamburg banker and government advisor Max Warburg remarked at the Fifth General German Bankers' Congress in October 1920 that as long as German obligations under the Peace Treaty remained uncertain, it would be impossible "to put the budget on a proper footing, to construct a proper tax system, to consolidate the floating debt and to take up the credits we require". *Verhandlungen des 5. Allgemeinen Deutschen Bankiertages* (Berlin, 1920), p. 158.

or on the fiscal balance, and thereby precipitating currency depreciation.[3] Voices echoing this opinion were not lacking in the lands of the victors either. Even in connection with the Peace Conference Allied experts were warning against the idea of exacting immediate compensation in excess of German capacity to pay while still leaving German aggregate liability undetermined. The American Norman Davis composed a memorandum along these lines to President Wilson on June 1st, 1919.[4] More famous are the polemics of Keynes:[5] Such a policy would remove all incentive to make efforts even to create the fiscal basis for payment and inhibit foreigners from subscribing to German loans and thus raising her capacity to pay. "Those responsible for the financial policy of Germany have a problem of incomparable difficulty in front of them. Until the reparation liability has been settled reasonably it is scarcely worth the while of anyone to trouble his head about a problem which is insoluble."[6] W.M. Jordan later described the problem as follows: "The true situation appears to have been that, while the governments of the newly born Republic possessed all too little authority to impose the measures of financial reorganization which would in any event have been indispensable, their task was rendered quite hopeless by the remorseless pressure of Allied demands."[7]

The contrary position was espoused in France, particularly by Poincaré who became Prime Minister in January 1922. He never tired of asserting that the German government was under pressure from industrialists to keep its finances in disorder with the aim of promoting inflation and demonstrating an apparent inability of Germany to pay.[8] To the extent that the fall in the mark

---

[3] Cp. Walter Eucken: *Kritische Betrachtungen zum deutschen Geldproblem* (Jena, 1923). Cp. also pp. 155 ff. *infra.*

[4] P.M. Burnett: *Reparation*, vol. 1, p. 101. The part played by Reparations in German-American relations is examined by Klaus Schwabe: *Deutsche Revolution und Wilson-Frieden* (Düsseldorf, 1971), and by Werner Link: *Die amerikanische Stabilisierungspolitik in Deutschland 1921–1932* (Düsseldorf, 1970).

[5] J.M. Keynes: *The Economic Consequences of the Peace. The Collected Writings of J. M. Keynes, ed. E. Johnson and D. E. Moggridge, vol. II* (London, 1971), pp. 106–31, esp. pp. 126 ff. The first English edition was 1919, the first German edition 1920. Germans regarded Keynes as a key witness to the unfulfillability of the Peace Treaty, as is strikingly exemplified in the speech of the banker Georg A. Solmssen on October 26, 1920 at the Fifth Bankers' Congress: *Verhandlungen des 5. Allgemeinen Deutschen Bankiertages*, (Berlin, 1920), pp. 36 ff. The offense caused to the French by Keynes' impact in Germany is shown by Etienne Mantoux: *The Carthaginian Peace or the Economic Consequences of Mr. Keynes* (London, 1946).

[6] J.M. Keynes: *The Revision of the Treaty. The Collected Writings of J. M. Keynes, ed. E. Johnson and D. E. Moggridge, vol. III* (London, 1971), pp. 67–68. (First English edn. 1922, first German edn. 1922).

[7] W.M. Jordan: *Great Britain*, p. 122.

[8] Carl Bergmann: *A History of Reparations* (London, 1927), pp. 148, 203 (German original 1926).

promoted Geman exports, the Allied governments were indeed experiencing pressure through their trading relations which might force them to moderate their demands. Primarily this pressure was affecting the depressed British economy during and after the world slump of 1920–22. As a result "the revival of trade became the *summum bonum* of British policy towards Europe... Great Britain's first need was the stabilization of currencies, and of the mark above all. To this end a moratorium on reparation payments and – so it was widely believed – an amputation of the total liability were essential."[9]

These interrelations were understood in Germany and it was recognized that the "burden of reparations" was not without its advantages. At the start of 1922 the *Frankfurter Zeitung* analyzed the position as follows. The inflation conferred a foreign currency advantage that stimulated German exports and reduced German unemployment. It was impossible to deny that "we face more difficult conditions in the labor market, once an easing of the Reparations burden has opened the way to some improvement of the exchange rate. The wish to offload some English and American unemployment on to Germany is one of the motives behind the current calls for revision of Reparations."[10]

So much for contemporary perceptions of the matter. How much did Reparations do to disequilibrate the Reich's finances in reality? The following remarks and figures may serve to illuminate the dimensions of the problem.

Reparations originated in the acceptance by Germany, as a condition of armistice and on the basis of the Wilson Program and U.S. Secretary of State Lansing's interpretative Note of November 5, 1918, that "compensation will be made by Germany for all damage done to the civilian population of the Allies and their property by the aggression of Germany by land, by sea and from the air."[11] Postwar Germanophobia[12] in their own countries caused Allied politicians to widen the extent of German liability by demanding reparation for all costs of the war and not merely direct damage. The pressure came particularly from England where, in contrast to France, civilian injury and

Cp. also *Akten der Reichskanzlei. Weimarer Republik. Die Kabinette Wirth I und II. Dokument Nr. 329.* Stephen A. Schuker: *The End of French Predominance in Europe. The Financial Crisis of 1924 and the Adoption of the Dawes Plan* (Chapel Hill, 1976), p. 178. Schuker demonstrates that this opinion was also prevalent among experts in the French Ministry of Finance. W. M. Jordan: *Great Britain*, p. 122 assesses the role of the German industrialists. Cp. also Gert von Eynern: *Die Reichsbank* (Jena, 1928), p. 79.

[9] W. M. Jordan: *Great Britain*, p. 112.

[10] *Die Wirtschaftskurve* 1 (1922), Heft 1, pp. 29–30.

[11] Cited from J. M. Keynes: *Economic Consequences*, p. 71. Cp. Carl Bergmann: *History*, pp. 3–4.

[12] Roy F. Harrod: *The Life of John Maynard Keynes* (London, 1951), p. 266.

damage to civilian property had been slight. With the slogans, "L'Allemagne / Le boche payera tout,"[13] and "Squeeze the orange till the pips squeak,"[14] French and English politicians bowed to increasingly hysterical public opinion, thereby circumscribing their own freedom of maneuver in the actual Reparations negotiations. Thus the mood in the Allied countries dictated a level of Reparations demands far in excess of that anticipated by the German government at the time when it accepted liability on the basis of Wilson's Fourteen Points. The Office of the Reich Treasury (shortly to be renamed the Reich Finance Ministry) was working at the end of December 1918 on the basis of an aggregate liability of thirty billion gold marks.[15] However even the terms of the Armistice had already imposed heavy burdens, including agreement to meet the costs of the Allied occupation of Germany, surrender of five thousand locomotives, one hundred and fifty thousand railroad freight cars, and five thousand road freight vehicles as well. The cession of the Alsace-Lorraine railroads involved the further loss of 3036 locomotives, 4613 passenger coaches, and 77,087 freight cars.[16] German estimates put the value of transport equipment surrendered at 1.1 billion gold marks.[17] Farm tools and machinery worth 31 million gold marks plus the high seas fleet and other war matériel (German valuation: 6.38 billion gold marks) were also to be surrendered. The signs were, even at the Armistice, that the final Reparations claim would reach forbidding proportions.

At the end of the war Lloyd George had appointed a committee in England to determine the compensation to be demanded of Germany and her allies, taking into consideration Germany's capacity to pay. Among its members were, "Sir G.E. Foster the Canadian Finance Minister a statesman of recognized sanity and moderation and with great experience in public finance, Mr. W.A.S. Hewins the economist, Lord Cunliffe the Governor of the Bank of England, and the Hon. Herbert Gibbs of the firm of Antony Gibbs and Sons. These last two were specially nominated to serve in the Committee as busi-

---

[13] Jens Jessen: "Reparationen", article in Ludwig Elster (ed.): *Wörterbuch der Volkswirtschaft* (Jena, 4th edn. 3 Bde. 1932–3), Bd. 3 (1933), p. 37.

[14] Roy F. Harrod: *Life*, p. 266.

[15] Ernst Meier: *Handbuch der deutschen Reparationen* (Leipzig, 1927), p. 22. Carl Bergmann: *History*, p. 6.

[16] Statistisches Reichsamt: *Deutschlands Wirtschaftslage unter den Nachwirkungen des Weltkrieges* (Berlin, 1923), p. 10. The initially debilitating effects of the terms of the Armistice and Peace Treaty on German economic power are detailed in the memoranda commissioned or prepared by the German government: *Deutschlands wirtschaftliche Leistungsfähigkeit* and *Denkschrift über die Zahlungsfähigkeit Deutschlands für die Wiedergutmachung* (both Berlin, 1920).

[17] Ernst Meier: *Handbuch*, p. 18

nessmen of high repute."[18] The recommendation of this committee was that the compensation claim be based on the total costs of the war – and considering only direct costs they estimated these at twenty-four billion pounds sterling (i.e. 480 bn. gold marks). Interest at five percent on this sum was to be charged to the former central powers; the committee considered £ 1.2 billion per annum a manageable sum "when normal conditions are restored."[19] The significant point is that this committee was not composed of financially naive politicians, anxious to please the public mood; even so its financially competent and supposedly dispassionate members were prepared to recommend sums of this order. "No protest was raised here from the City as to the fantastic amount of Reparations suggested by their foremost authority."[20]

Others of course did raise cautionary voices. "To the credit of the British Treasury I must state that in their view, expressed at that moment of triumphant exultation, £ 2,000,000,000 was the full amount of repayment we could possibly expect Germany to make."[21] Small heed was paid to such opinions at the Peace Conference however;[22] the British delegation demanded compensation for all costs of the war.[23] The U.S. delegation opposed this because of the terms of the Armistice; eventually agreement was reached by making compensation for war *damage* the basis of the claim, but interpreting 'damage' in an extremely broad manner.

In particular the British government had insisted, and succeeded in securing agreement, that pensions to military personnel and their surviving dependants should be treated as compensation for injury to the civilian population and debited to Germany – a principle that increased the British share of Reparations. This accepted, French claims on Germany had to be increased by the amount of the same item. At the meeting of the Supreme Council of the Allied Powers on April 12th, 1919 Klotz, the French Minister of Finance, demanded the sum of twenty four billion gold marks as a first installment on Reparation account, of which sixteen billion was to be paid within three months and the remainder in the first year following the conclusion of the Peace Treaty. A further eight billion should fall due during the second year after the signing of the Treaty and in subsequent years this sum should rise by

---

[18] David Lloyd George: *The Truth about Reparations and War Debts* (London, 1932), p. 12.

[19] *Ibid.*, p. 13.

[20] *Ibid.*, p. 11.

[21] *Ibid.*, p. 13.

[22] Among such was Keynes, who was provoked into writing his *Economic Consequences* by this experience. Cp. R.F. Harrod: *Life*, pp. 254ff.

[23] C. Bergmann: *History*, p. 5.

two percent per annum.[24] The provisional determination of Reparations in the Versailles Treaty did not quite reach these extravagant heights; nevertheless the stipulation that Germany had to pay the equivalent of twenty billion gold marks by May 1st, 1921 – the date by which her aggregate liabilities were to be finally determined – was not much more moderate than Klotz's proposal. Eventually the London Ultimatum of May 1921 fixed Germany's aggregate liability at 132 billion gold marks plus the Belgian war debts, estimated by the Allies at five to six billion gold marks. The Reparations Commission believed this sum within Germany's capacity to pay. However for the time being only a first tranche of twelve billion gold marks, together with a second of thirty-eight billion were to be serviced, at a rate of five percent interest plus one percent amortization. This annuity was to be raised by an annual charge on the budget of the Reich of two billion gold marks plus a sum equal to twenty-six percent of the value of German exports. In existing conditions this would yield a total of about three billion gold marks, payable to the Allies in cash (bullion or foreign exchange) or kind.

This annuity was not very different from an offer made, surprisingly, by Germany herself under Allied pressure in the spring of 1921. By it Germany had offered to acknowledge liability for Reparations to a present value of fifty billion gold marks to be paid off with interest in annuities totaling two hundred billion gold marks, if desired. This German proposal also provided for a so-called "recovery index" (*Besserungsschein*) by which the Allies would participate in future improvements in the performance of the German economy and public finances.[25] The Allies rejected this proposal; they had already worked out their own plan whose most oppressive aspect in German eyes was not its immediate schedule of annual payments but its "third tranche", amounting to eighty-two billion gold marks – the so-called "C bonds". The Reparations Commission was empowered to demand interest on this tranche when it considered Germany capable of paying it. Thus a financial "sword of Damocles" was suspended over the German economy, despite the warnings about the implications of such an arrangement already delivered in June 1919 by the Financial Commission of the German delegation at Versailles. In their Observations on the peace terms proposed by the Allies they had written, "If they [the victorious powers] impose such a burden on Germany as blights all her future prospects; if consequently every improvement achieved by the strenuous endeavor and most spartan economy on the part of

[24] *Ibid.*, p. 6.

[25] *Ibid.*, pp. 71, 77. Cp. also: *Die den Alliierten seit Waffenstillstand übermittelten deutschen Angebote und Vorschläge zur Lösung der Reparations- und Wiederaufbaufrage* (Berlin, 1923), pp. 17–18.

her people leads merely to the exacting of yet greater payments in liquidation of this debt – then all will to work, all pride of craft, all boldness of enterprise must for ever be extinguished in Germany. The German people would feel itself condemned to slavery, for the beneficiaries of their labors would be neither themselves nor their children, but strangers."[26]

The "C bonds" served a variety of objectives. They served to assuage inflamed public opinion in Allied countries by the appearance of enormous German Reparations liabilities. They also served as a "financial pledge"[27] at the disposal of the Reparations Commission, which could be employed to exert pressure on Germany to extract not merely economic, but also political advantages. Anxieties about security and apprehensions about a revival of German power made France anxious for this latter class of advantages, after the promised Anglo-American military guarantees of her eastern frontier had foundered on the opposition of the U.S. Congress.[28] Lastly the "C bonds" also served as a French bargaining counter in their attempts to persuade their creditors – the U.S. directly or indirectly, and the U.K. – to cancel debts. Plans existed for applying the yield on "C bonds" toward the redemption of inter-allied debt.[29] Had Great Britain and the U.S.A. wished to reduce the German Reparations obligation they would thus have had the opportunity of canceling "C bonds". With the celebrated Balfour Note of August 1st, 1922, in which the British government declared that it would insist on Reparations only in the measure that the American government laid claim to the debts owed to the U.S. by Britain, the "buck" was passed to the U.S.A. However Congress had required the U.S. government to insist that war debts be paid. When the French demanded debt cancellation in return for agreement to a reduction of Reparations C. E. Hughes, the U.S. Secretary of State, replied, "Germany cannot pay one mark more or less because of what France may owe, and France cannot collect what Germany is unable to pay."[30]

France, left in the lurch by her allies on the question of her security and

---

[26] "Das Gutachten der deutschen Finanzkomission zu den gegnerischen Friedensbedingungen", *Bank-Archiv*, 18 (1918/19), p. 187 (June 15, 1919).

[27] I.e. in contrast to the "productive pledges" demanded by the French government in 1922 under Poincaré, once it could be seen that the inflation had indeed impoverished Germany financially but stimulated her productive activity. This French search for "productive pledges" culminated in the occupation of the Ruhr in 1923.

[28] W. M. Jordan: *Great Britain*, p. 38.

[29] As for example under the Poincaré government in July 1922. Cp. W. M. Jordan: *Great Britain*, pp. 117–118.

[30] Communication of Hughes to Herrick of October 17, 1922, in: *Papers Relating to the Foreign Relations of the United States 1922* (Washington, 1938), p. 169.

disappointed in her hopes of a remission of war debts, steadily maintained her claims against Germany. Once Anglo-French relations had deteriorated in the summer of 1922 she was prepared to pursue them even in the face of British opposition. This attitude culminated in the occupation of the Ruhr in January 1923. "The secret of the Ruhr must be sought in the Mississippi plain," was the trenchant observation of a British journalist:[31] mid-West congressmen above all had both objected to U.S. involvement in European security arrangements and insisted on the payment of inter-allied debts.[32]

In the German financial situation between 1918 and 1923 uncertainty about the *future* level of reparations requirements was probably the principal destabilizing agent. However this uncertainty cannot be quantified. Instead, what follows will attempt to estimate the importance of Reparations actually paid in the inflationary process, by quantifying their contribution to the scale of the Reich's budget deficits.

In explaining the behavior of the mark exchange rate, the distribution of Reparations payments between cash and kind is a relevant variable; not so in explaining the behavior of the budget. Cash payments require the application of government revenues for the purchase of foreign exchange while payments in kind require it for the purchase of the commodities for delivery (e.g. coal, livestock, machinery, wood products, chemical products, etc.) or for the reimbursement of the former owners of sequestrated property (e.g. owners of the expropriated merchant vessels, or of mines and factories in ceded territories). The German government had already drawn attention to the inflationary implications both of payments in kind and of compensation to Germans in its observations on the Allied peace terms: "Since the floating of domestic and foreign loans will not be a feasible method of raising the required sums in the immediate future, it will be possible to pay compensation only through enlargement of the note issue. Inflation is already much too rapid in Germany: if the proposed Peace Treaty conditions are carried through, its further increase will know no bounds. Large commodity deliveries to abroad, too, can only take place if the Reich reimburses their producers and this means yet further enlargement of the note issue. Stabilization of the German currency, even at the present level, would be unthinkable as long as these deliveries continue."[33]

---

[31] William Martin, in the *Revue de Genève*, Mai 1923; cited in W. M. Jordan: *Great Britain*, p. 119.

[32] Thus earning the U.S. the nickname of "Uncle Shylock" rather than "Uncle Sam".

[33] C. Bergmann: *History*, p. 19. Stephen A. Schuker examines and documents the relationship between Reparations demands and inflation as it was perceived by German industrialists and politicians in his "Finance and Foreign Policy in the Era of the German Inflation", in O. Büsch and G. D. Feldman (eds.): *Historische Prozesse der deutschen Inflation 1914 bis 1924. Ein Tagungs-*

Calculations of the Reparations actually paid by Germany before the end of the inflation diverge sharply. Payment proceeded effectively until the middle of 1922 – the period of transition to hyperinflation. Moratoria and Germany's unilateral suspension of payments in response to the occupation of the Ruhr meant that thereafter only insignificant sums were transferred. The Reparations Commission credited Germany with the payment of about 8 billion gold marks up to August 1924, 1.7 billions of it in cash (cp. Table 29). Of actual payments under the schedule imposed by the Versailles Treaty, the Commission acknowledged only transfers made between May 1st, 1921 and December 31st, 1922, which it put at 2.75 billion gold marks[34] – much less, that is, than the anticipated three billions per annum. Reimbursement of occupation costs up to April 30th, 1921 was entered at 340 million gold marks by the Commission,[35] and at 437 million gold marks for the following period up to December 31st, 1922. Article 296 of the Versailles Treaty had required the German government to compensate foreign creditors possessing foreign currency claims against private German citizens: according to the Reparations Commission payments under this "clearing" agreement up to the end of November 1922 amounted to 615 million gold marks.[36]

On the German side the discharged value of Reparations up to the end of 1922 was put at 51.7 billion gold marks (cp. Table 29). Even in July 1920 at the Spa Conference the German government had tabled a calculation of Reparations paid to date totaling twenty billion gold marks.[37] The principal divergence between Allied and German estimates lay in the valuation of payments predating the London Ultimatum.[38]

Independent valuations of Germany's performance of her obligations lay between the two extremes. In France Charles Gide estimated payments up to April 1922 at between twelve and fourteen billion gold marks. In England Keynes put them at 26 billion gold marks up to the end of 1922 while the

bericht (Berlin, 1978), pp. 343–361. On this set of problems see too Hermann J. Rupieper: "Industrie und Reparationen. Einige Aspekte des Reparationsproblems 1922–24", in H. Mommsen, D. Petzina, B. Weisbrod (eds.): *Industrielles System und politische Entwicklung in der Weimarer Republik* (Düsseldorf, 1974), pp. 582–592. Idem: *The Cuno Government and Reparations 1922–1923. Politics and Economics* (The Hague, 1979).

34 Harold G. Moulton and Constantine McGuire: *Germany's Capacity to Pay. A Study of the Reparation Problem* (New York, 1923), p. 325.

35 *Ibid.*, p. 304.

36 Statistisches Reichsamt: *Deutschlands Wirtschaftslage unter den Nachwirkungen des Weltkrieges* (Berlin, 1923), p. 12.

37 E. Meier: *Handbuch*, p. 78.

38 *Ibid.*

Table 29. German reparations payments in cash and kind to August 31, 1924. Million gold marks

	German Valua-tion	Valuation by Reparations Commission
1. Liquidation of sequestrated German private property abroad (excl. in Russia, U.S.A., Brazil, Cuba)	10080	13
2. Renunciation of claims against former allies (article 260)	8600	–
3. Saar mines (capitalized on basis of prewar profitability)	1016	–
4. Public property in ceded territories	9670	2298
5. Coal and coke	2334	959
6. Coal by-products, nitrogenous products	40	40
7. Dyes and pharmaceutical products	250	88
8. Livestock	204	147
9. Agricultural machinery and equipment (article 3 of the Agreement of Jan. 16, 1919 about Prolongation of the Armistice)	21	21
10. Other deliveries in kind toward reconstruction (Appendix II, § 19 and Appendix IV)	385	385
11. Belgian works of art and the Louvain Library	16	2
12. Sea-going vessels		
a) surrendered	3426	756
b) seized (excl. ships seized in U.S.A. under Embargo Act)	1060	–
13. Non sea-going vessels	56	50
14. Railroad equipment		
a) rolling stock (article 250)	1100	827
b) equipment and stocks of materials	6	6
15. Railroads, mines and colleges in Shantung and Shanghai	95	61
16. Road haulage vehicles	59	32
17. Abandoned non-military material	5041	140
18. Private cables (maritime)	78	53
19. War materials (scrap value)	52	52
20. Prewar Reich and state debt assignable to ceded territories	675	26
21. Forced exactions during the occupation of the Ruhr		
a) in kind	820	27 (a and b)
b) in cash	550	
22. Cash payments under the London Payments Plan	1700	1700
23. Rhineland customs, 1921	3	3
24. U.K. reparation levy under the Reparations Recovery Act	373	373
25. Other cash payments (mainly to France relative to municipal obligations, pensions and social insurance in Alsace-Lorraine)	51	8
26. Railroad rolling stock under article 371	697	–
27. Clearing-house payments in settlement of private claims	617	–
28. Work done by German prisoners of war (475,000 between Armistice and March 1, 1920, after deduction of 300 mill. Rm. for food and accommodation)	1200	–
29. Surrender of German Fleet	1338	–
30. Harbor materials (compensation relative to Scapa Flow)	80	–
	51693	8067

Source: Jens Jessen: "Reparationen", p. 90.

Americans Moulton and McGuire put them at 25.8 billion gold marks up to the same terminus.[39]

So much for the range of estimates of the value of what was actually paid. In their entirety, whether paid in cash or kind, these sums were a charge on the budget of the Reich.[40] Were they so large as to be destabilizing? Could the Reich have met them out of ordinary revenue (taxation plus the operating surpluses of Reich enterprises) or was the use of inflationary methods to meet them inevitable? A standard by which to answer this question is afforded by a comparison of the ratio *after the war* between the Reparations annuity and national income with the ratio *before* the war between the burden of taxation and national income.

German national income between 1919 and 1923, expressed in 1913 prices, may be estimated as follows:[41]

1919	34.9 bn. marks	1922	40.3 bn. marks
1920	35.9 bn. marks	1923	34.9 bn. marks
1921	38.8 bn. marks		

Postwar prices however were not the same as they had been in 1913 even in gold currency countries. Thus it would be misleading to compare these national income estimates with a gold mark value of Reparations usually arrived at by converting marks to dollars at the current exchange rate. To express German national income in terms of the current purchasing power of gold or the dollar, the above estimates must be multiplied up by some estimate of change in purchasing power. As an indicator of the reduced purchasing power of the dollar relative to 1913 we use the annual average of the U.S. wholesale price index with base 1913 = 100:[42]

1919	198.3	1922	138.6
1920	221.1	1923	144.2
1921	139.7		

[39] H. G. Moulton and C. E. McGuire: *Germany's Capacity to Pay*, pp. 350 ff.

[40] This question is conceptually distinct from the so-called "transfer problem". The best survey of the "transfer problem" is provided by Gottfried Haberler: *The Theory of International Trade with its Applications to Commercial Policy* (London, 1936), pp. 63 ff. (German original, 1933). Cp. also Fritz Machlup: "The Transfer Problem: Theme and Four Variations", in F. Machlup: *International Monetary Economics* (London, 1966), pp. 374 ff. (German original, 1963).

[41] The series has been extrapolated from Hoffmann's estimate for 1913 with the aid of Henning's index reproduced in Table 40 of the present volume. Cp. W. G. Hoffmann *et al.*: *Das Wachstum der deutschen Wirtschaft seit der Mitte des 19. Jahrhunderts* (Berlin, 1965), p. 509.

[42] Ben J. Wattenberg: *The Statistical History of the United States. From Colonial Times to the Present* (New York, 1976), p. 199.

Multiplying the estimates of postwar national income in 1913 prices by this price index (divided by 100), we obtain estimates of postwar German national income in terms of the current purchasing power of the dollar, or gold:

1919	69.2 bn. current gold marks	1922	55.9 bn. current gold marks
1920	79.4 bn. current gold marks	1923	50.3 bn. current gold marks
1921	54.2 bn. current gold marks		

In now comparing Reparations demands and payments against these last estimates of postwar national income I assume that the exigencies of postwar reconstruction excluded the possibility of the demands being met by decumulation of assets – that they had to be met out of current income. On this assumption the annuity of eight billion gold marks demanded by the French Finance Minister Klotz in the spring of 1919 – and partially incorporated in the Peace Treaty stipulation that Germany pay twenty billion gold marks by May 1st, 1921 – would have removed 11.6% of German national income in 1919, 10.1% in 1920, 14.8% in 1921 and 14.3% in 1922. The reduction of the required annuity to three billion gold marks by the London Ultimatum was only partly the outcome of a more realistic perception of Germany's capacity to pay. To a great extent it did no more than recognize the deflation of world prices that had already taken place: the real relief it afforded the German economy was far less than the apparent. Three billion gold marks would still have represented 5.5% of German national income in 1921, 5.4% in 1922 and 6.0% in 1923.

Such was the relative burden implied by the demands. The burden implied by the payments actually made in cash and kind varies according to the widely divergent estimates of these payments. Between 1919 and 1922 Germany paid at least the eight billions with which she was credited by the Reparations Commission – probably considerably more, though the German estimate of fifty-one billions is doubtless an exaggeration. The independent and unconnected estimates by Keynes and by Moulton and McGuire – twenty-six billions – are probably nearer the truth. In current gold marks aggregate German national income in the four years 1919–22 was 258.7 billions according to the above estimates. Actual payments then ranged between 3.1% and 21.8% of this but were most likely (following the Keynes or Moulton/McGuire estimates) about 10%.

A different calculation supports this last conclusion. A. Jessen calculated for each of the postwar years the gold mark value of the yield to the Reich from the printing of money;[43] his estimates will be found in Table 30. Since he

[43] Arnd Jessen: *Finanzen, Defizit und Notenpresse 1914–1922* (Berlin, 1923), p. 50.

also states the proportion which this formed each year of aggregate Reich expenditure, we are able to calculate the gold mark value of this latter aggregate[44] (see Table 30, column 3). From the Reich budgetary statistics we can discover the proportion of aggregate Reich expenditures represented each year by payments in fulfillment of the terms of the Armistice and the Versailles Treaty: applying these proportions to the gold mark estimates of aggregate Reich expenditures just derived, we gain an estimate of the gold mark value of the Reich's current payments on Reparations account: 4.9 billions in 1919, falling to 2.1 billions in 1920, once the initial thrust of Allied demands and expropriations (involving the compensation of the former German owners by the Reich) was past. With the London Ultimatum of May 1921 the gold mark value of payments began to rise again: 2.8 billions in that year and 3.4 billions in 1922. Deliveries in kind and compensation to German citizens for sequestrations including those of former years probably figured more largely in this last payment than current cash payments, for which moratoria were requested and granted in 1922.

Table 30. Yield of "inflation tax" compared with expenditures in compliance with the Peace Treaty

	1. Yield from the printing of money ("Inflation tax") bn. gold marks	2. Column 1 as a % of aggregate Reich expenditures	3. Aggregate Reich expenditures bn. gold marks	4. Expenditures under the Peace Treaty as % of aggregate expenditures	5. in bn. gold marks
1919	5.95	62	9.60	51.4	4.9
1920	6.24	53	11.77	17.6	2.1
1921	3.73	43	8.67	32.7	2.8
1922	2.13	43	4.95	69.0	3.4
	18.1		35.0		13.2

Sources: Column 1: A. Jessen: *Finanzen, Defizit und Notenpresse 1914–22* (Berlin, 1923), p. 50.
Column 2: *Ibid.*, p. 47.
Column 3: Inferred from cols. 1 and 2.
Column 4: F. Hesse: *Die deutsche Wirtschaftslage von 1914–1923* (Jena, 1938), p. 422.
Column 5: Calculated from cols. 3 and 4.

[44] Monthly data can be found in *Deutschlands Wirtschaft, Währung und Finanzen* (Berlin, 1924), pp. 30ff.

Adding these gold mark estimates of the Reich's payments under the Peace Treaty together for the four years 1919–22, we get an estimate of 13.2 billions. The difference between this and the 26 billions calculated by Keynes and Moulton/McGuire lies partly in the value of sequestrated property belonging to the Reich itself. Public property in ceded territories was valued at five billion gold marks for example, the state-owned Saar mines at 650 millions, military and non-military equipment at 1.4 billions: naturally the Reich did not compensate itself but insofar as the assets had been income-earning, their surrender did diminish current revenues to the exchequer. In addition, the Reich did not compensate its own citizens uniformly and fully for the ten billion gold marks worth of private assets in foreign countries which had been confiscated and liquidated.[45] Thus the estimates in Table 30 are congruent with those of Keynes and Moulton and McGuire, and Haller's judgment,[46] that during the inflation the Reich required sums equivalent to ten percent of national income to meet its Reparations obligations, may be regarded as relatively secure.

An instructive comparison may be drawn between the burden of Reparations payments during the inflation and the corresponding burden during the years after 1924 when the Dawes Plan had reduced the annuity. Table 31 shows annual Reparations payments between 1925–31 as a percentage of national income in the same year: according to this the "burden" increased from 1.8% in 1925 to 3.2% in 1929, the first year in which the "full" Dawes Plan annuity of 2.5 billion gold marks was payable. It is well known that the transfer of these sums was only achieved as long as capital was flowing into Germany at a still greater rate. Once this inflow dried up with the onset of world depression and capital began to flow out instead, the proportion of national income employed as Reparations fell substantially; and in 1931 the Allies recognized Germany's incapacity to pay by granting the Hoover moratorium. Not only did the smaller post-1924 annuities place no immediate net burden on the German economy (because of the capital inflow): they also placed a very much smaller direct burden on the Reich exchequer because of the stipulations governing their collection. Under the Dawes Plan the major part of the reichsmark value of the annuities was collected through specially devised levies on the revenues of the German Railroads and on German business, whose existing indebtedness had been much reduced by the infla-

[45] The amounts are the estimates of H. G. Moulton and C. E. McGuire: *Germany's Capacity to Pay*, pp. 350ff.

[46] Heinz Haller: "Die Rolle der Staatsfinanzen für den Inflationsprozess", in Deutsche Bundesbank (ed.): *Währung und Wirtschaft in Deutschland 1876–1975* (Frankfurt/M. 1976), p. 138.

tion. These earmarked revenues were collected under Allied supervision and only the residue of the sum payable formed a direct charge on the Reich.[47] In any case, after 1923 the Reich was not burdened by the cost of servicing its wartime and postwar debt, except for the limited obligations arising out of the 1925 Revaluation Law. If, then, we accept the conclusion of the Allied "experts" – that Germany would not be able, even under the more favorable conditions obtaining between 1925 and 1929, to collect and transfer more than 1.8%–3.2% of her national income as Reparations, then the requirement that before 1923 actual Reparations payments (let alone Allied demands) be made without prejudice to currency stability – i.e. be raised out of taxation – must be regarded as incapable of fulfillment.

Table 31. Reparations payments as a proportion of German national income, and the German capital account balance with abroad 1925–32

	1. Reparations payments bn. reichsmarks	2. National income bn. reichsmarks	3. Column 1 as % of column 2	4. Recorded capital transactions with abroad plus balance-of-payments residual (+ = capital import – = capital export) bn. reichsmarks
1925	1.06	57.4	1.8	+3.13
1926	1.19	60.1	2.0	+0.60
1927	1.58	67.3	2.3	+3.79
1928	2.00	72.4	2.8	+4.12
1929	2.34	72.3	3.2	+2.31
1930	1.71	66.2	2.6	+0.49
1931	0.99	53.8	1.8	–2.69
1932	0.16	42.6	0.4	–0.51

Sources: Columns 1 and 4: Ausschuss zur Untersuchung der Erzeugungs- und Absatzbedingungen der deutschen Wirtschaft: *Die deutsche Zahlungsbilanz* (Berlin, 1930), p. 167. Statistisches Reichsamt: *Die deutsche Zahlungsbilanz 1924–33. Sonderheft 14 zu Wirtschaft und Statistik* (Berlin, 1934). Länderrat des Amerikanischen Besatzungsgebietes: *Statistisches Handbuch von Deutschland 1928–1944* (Munich, 1949), pp. 602–603.

Column 2: Statistisches Bundesamt: *Bevölkerung und Wirtschaft 1872–1972* (Stuttgart, 1972), p. 260.

[47] C. Bergmann: *History*, p. 132ff.

Another way of judging the burden of these unilateral transfers during the early postwar years is to compare the burden of taxation before the war. Including taxes levied by all levels of government it had amounted to eleven or twelve percent of national income.[48] This was the proportion of national income which the Reich had to annex between 1919 and 1923 simply to make its Reparations payments, and this in a period when the republic and its various governments had to endure the distrust of considerable sections of the domestic population, and when its credit worthiness was mistrusted by domestic and potential foreign investors, particularly in the U.S.A. Wealthy industrial states at the present day are unable to achieve the United Nation's target rate of public development aid to the third world: 0.7 % of national income inclusive of repayable loan assistance (in 1984 the Federal Republic could achieve only 0.45 %).[49] Yet this objective is deemed morally justifiable and worthy of endeavor by large sections of the population. In this light, a government attempting to raise through taxation an incomparably larger proportion of the national income of a much less affluent country must surely have been signing its own political death warrant, especially when the end in view was to effect a foreign transfer regarded from the outset as beyond fulfillment, unjust and indeed morally reprehensible by almost the entire population whatever its political color. In this situation, threatened by Allied sanctions on the one hand and by disintegration of the Reich on the other, no German government could have complied with Reparations demands in any way other than resort to the printing of money. Bendixen had advised this course of action in 1919, outlining the following rationale: "The same citizen who would react to tax exactions on this scale with complaints of victimization at the hands of authorities hostile to property will accept the doubling of prices without demur if he be spared new tax demands, even though the government's monetary policy is manifestly to blame. Only in taxation do people discern the arbitrary incursions of the state; the movement of prices, on the other hand, seems to them sometimes the outcome of traders' sordid machinations, more often a dispensation which, like frost and hail, mankind

---

[48] H. Haller: "Rolle", p. 139. American historians who conclude that Germany could have paid the Reparations demanded had she possessed the will to do so neglect this consideration, as also (in my view) the effects of uncertainty about the future level of Reparations; thus their conclusion is unconvincing. See e.g. Sally Marks: "Reparations Reconsidered: A Reminder", *Central European History*, 11 (1978), pp. 231–255. Stephen A. Schuker: "Frankreich und die Weimarer Republik", in M. Stürmer (ed.): *Die Weimarer Republik. Belagerte Civitas* (Königstein/Ts., 1980), pp. 93–112.

[49] According to information by the *Bundesministerium für wirtschaftliche Zusammenarbeit*, Bonn.

must simply accept. The stateman's opportunity lies in appreciating this mental disposition."[50]

Under other circumstances foreign long-term capital could have been attracted as a means of moderating the tax burden on German citizens; it should be remembered however that during the early Weimar years German bonds could not be floated in foreign centers. Contrary to American demands, the Versailles Treaty contained no final statement of Germany's total liability on Reparations account. The prolonged uncertainty about this liability made it hard for potential foreign lenders to Germany to assess her credit worthiness, that is, her ability to repay loans. This circumscribed budgetary possibilities; it also reduced Germany to the expedient of selling a depreciating currency to finance the Reparations-induced balance of payments deficit,[51] and this state of affairs would continue until Reparations became regulated in a manner more acceptable to potential investors (i.e. better adapted to Germany's capacity to pay). Walther Rathenau said that there were three ways of financing Germany's balance of payments deficit:[52] sale of the nation's assets, flotation of large foreign loans, or sale of the national currency. The first could damage the future performance of the economy and in any case subjected aspects of private economic activity to foreign control; the third would undermine monetary stability. By refusing initially to fix Germany's aggregate Reparations liability, then pitching it far in excess of her capacity to pay, the creditor governments had lost the immediate opportunity of utilizing Germany's international credit potential to effect a smoother transfer of the annuities.

Besides the objective and quantifiable relations we have been considering, Germany's capacity to pay was also constrained by subjective factors. The indefiniteness of the Reparations burden affected German attitudes and willingness to comply with the demands made of her. In 1919 W. Prion put the matter as follows: "If the German economy should ever regain its breath, the Allied Commission has the right to re-examine Germany's capacity to pay and raise the final Reparations liability beyond the sum which at present it has cautiously left unfinalized. It will not be difficult for the Commission to interpret the Wilsonian compensation paragraphs in such a way as to extract from Germany her last spare – or even indispensable – mark. Reparations are the noose in which the Commission holds the German economy, by which it can at any time prevent or delay its recovery and impede the repair of its fiscal and

50 Friedrich Bendixen: *Kriegsanleihen und Finanznot. Zwei finanzpolitische Vorschläge* (Jena, 1919), p. 9.

51 Cp. pp. 281 ff. *infra*.

52 Walther Rathenau: *Cannes und Genua. Vier Reden zum Reparationsproblem* (Berlin, 1922), p. 11.

monetary systems."[53] In the absence of an immediate and clear definition of German obligations it would "prove permanently impossible to accustom the German people again to the habits of hard work, when they know that for an unlimited future foreign economies will be the beneficiaries of their labor."[54] Writing in the late 1940s, but with no less engagement Roy Harrod described thus the psychological constraints upon the payment of Reparations: "If Britain had had to raise her exports, not in order to achieve balance and regain her fair prospects in the world, but in order to meet a levy imposed by victors, would it have been psychologically possible for her to make the tremendous effort which she has done in the last three years?" Referring to the Reparations problem following the First World War he continued: "It remains doubtful what the Allies could have extracted even had they embarked on the heroic task of total occupation of Germany. We lack experience of what civilised white men will do under the lash. It must be remembered that the proposed surpluses represent greater output per head than backward people ever produce at all."[55]

5.2. The Credit Policies of the Reichsbank

As early as the war itself, but especially in the years that followed, controversy raged in German academic and political circles over two theories of the inflation. Proponents of the "balance of payments theory" regarded the passivity of the German external balance, specifically the current balance, as the chief cause of the currency depreciation; proponents of the "quantity theory" blamed the continuous expansion of the money supply required to finance the Reich's budget deficits, for the same phenomenon.[1] Analysts from that day to this have generally inferred from the Reichsbank's public utterances that it

[53] Willi Prion: *Inflation und Geldentwertung. Finanzielle Massnahmen zum Abbau der Preise. Gutachten erstattet dem Reichsfinanzministerium* (Berlin, 1919), p. 123.

[54] *Ibid.*

[55] R.F. Harrod: *Life*, p. 279.

[1] An exhaustive treatment of the subject, taking account of the differences of opinion within the two theoretical camps, is Howard S. Ellis: *German Monetary Theory 1905–1933* (Cambridge, Mass., 1937). Cp. Karl W. Hardach: "Zur zeitgenössischen Debatte der Nationalökonomen über die Ursachen der deutschen Nachkriegsinflation", in Hans Mommsen *et al.* (eds.): *Industrielles System und politische Entwicklung in der Weimarer Republik* (Düsseldorf, 1974), pp. 368–375.

held the former theory,[2] but confidential memoranda prepared by the Bank for the government and President of the Reich undermine this assertion.[3]

The first part of this section of the chapter will describe the leading characteristics of the two theories and the weaknesses for which they were criticized. The second part will examine the arguments which the Reichsbank used in its dealings with the public on the one hand and with the government on the other, and thus obtain a more differentiated picture of its theoretical position. Finally the wisdom of the Reichsbank's discount policy will be discussed.

Critical exposition of the balance of payments and quantity theories

Central to both theoretical and political debate during the inflation[4] was the question whether after suspension of the gold standard the money supply

---

[2] Otto Veit: *Grundriss der Währungspolitik* (Frankfurt, 3rd edn. 1969), p. 520. Wolfram Fischer: *Deutsche Wirtschaftspolitik 1918–1945* (Opladen, 3rd edn. 1968), pp. 22ff. L. Albert Hahn: *Fünfzig Jahre zwischen Inflation und Deflation* (Tübingen, 1963), pp. 16ff. C. Bresciani-Turroni: *The Economics of Inflation. A Study of Currency Depreciation in Postwar Germany* (London, 1937), p. 42. Gert von Eynern: *Die Reichsbank. Probleme des deutschen Zentralnoteninstituts in geschichtlicher Darstellung* (Jena, 1928), p. 71. Walter Eucken: *Kritische Betrachtungen zum deutschen Geldproblem* (Jena, 1923), pp. 5–6. Viscount D'Abernon: "German Currency: its Collapse and Recovery 1920–1926", in his *An Ambassador of Peace. Pages from the Diary of Viscount D'Abernon* (London, 3 vols. 1929–30), vol. 2, pp. 314–320.

Alfred Lansburgh ("Die Politik der Reichsbank und die Reichsschatzanweisungen nach dem Kriege", in *Schriften des Vereins für Socialpolitik, Bd. 166 II* (1924), pp. 36–37) concedes that, in its 1920 Annual Report (published May 1921), the Reichsbank for the first time gave adequate public expression to the central role of excessive monetary expansion in the process of "increasing depreciation of the currency and exchange rate", but he criticizes the Bank for apparently having failed to speak against the government's fiscal policies or to refuse to discount further Reich treasury paper.

[3] I base my assertions on documents in the files of the Reich chancellery (Reichskanzlei) and of the Reich Finance Ministry (Reichsfinanzministerium) located in the Bundesarchiv, Koblenz – in *Bestände* R 43 I and R2 respectively. Doubtless only a small part of the correspondence between Reichsbank and government during the postwar years is preserved here. Voluminous Reichsbank records are extant in the German Democratic Republic (cp. Kurt Metschies: "Der Bestand 'Deutsche Reichsbank', Volkswirtschaftliche und Statistische Abteilung, im Deutschen Zentralarchiv Potsdam, Historische Abteilung I", *Jahrbuch für Wirtschaftsgeschichte*, 1968, III, pp. 387–391). But they refer mainly to other matters.

[4] A very clear definition of the two positions comes out in the fascinating debates between representatives of the "balance of payments" and "quantity" theories of the German currency depreciation in the *Verhandlungen der Sozialisierungskommission über die Reparationsfragen, Bd. I* (Berlin, 1921), pp. 147–162, Sitzung (i.e. meeting) of July 13, 1921. Cp. Karsten Laursen and Jørgen Pedersen: *The German Inflation 1918–1923* (Amsterdam, 1964), pp. 30–41: "Debate on the causes of the German inflation."

played an active or a passive role in the depreciation of the mark exchange rate (and hence in the rising domestic price level.) In other words: was the rise in the quantity of money a cause or a consequence of the currency depreciation? A century previously in England this question had lain at the heart of the so called bullion controversy.[5] Walter Eucken – himself a supporter of the quantity theory – employed the following diagrams to expound the explanatory sequences implied by the application of the two theories to the German case.[6] The arrows indicate causal relations.

Balance of payments theory

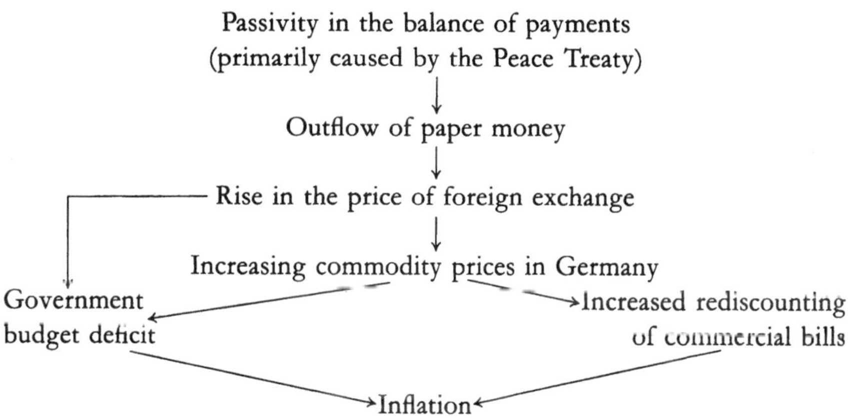

Note. It should be observed that Eucken, conforming to etymology and contemporary usage, employed "inflation" to mean "enlargement of the quantity of money" (with the possible consequence of rising prices) and not the rising price level itself.

---

[5] That controversy hinged upon alternative explanations of the depreciation of sterling against metallic currencies and against bullion itself during the years 1797–1821 (when the pound was inconvertible). See Jacob Viner: *Studies in the Theory of International Trade* (New York and London, 1937), pp. 119–209. James Angell: *The Theory of International Prices* (Cambridge, Mass., 1926). Albrecht Forstmann: *Die Grundlagen der Aussenwirtschaftstheorie* (Berlin, 1956), pp. 238–253. This controversy is to be distinguished from that between the "currency" and "banking" schools, who disagreed regarding the best methods of short-run monetary control, in the face of variations in the demand for money on the part of the economy, rather than of the state. But both sides accepted the need for convertibility as a limit on the possibilities of money creation. Cp. J. Viner: *Studies*, p. 223. Also, Friedrich Hoffmann: *Kritische Dogmengeschichte der Geldwerttheorien* (Leipzig, 1907), pp. 101–146. Charles Rist: *History of Monetary and Credit Theory from John Law to the Present Day* (New York, 1940), pp. 203–229. The views of the "banking school", which advocated a more elastic response of the money supply to short run variations in the demand for money, commanded virtually unanimous acceptance among German theorists and monetary practitioners. Cp. Herbert Patschan: "Die Entwicklung der Bankingtheorie in Deutschland. Ein dogmenkritischer Beitrag" (Dissertation, Freiburg, 1929).

[6] W. Eucken: *Kritische Betrachtungen zum deutschen Geldproblem* (Jena, 1923), pp. 8, 38.

Quantity Theory

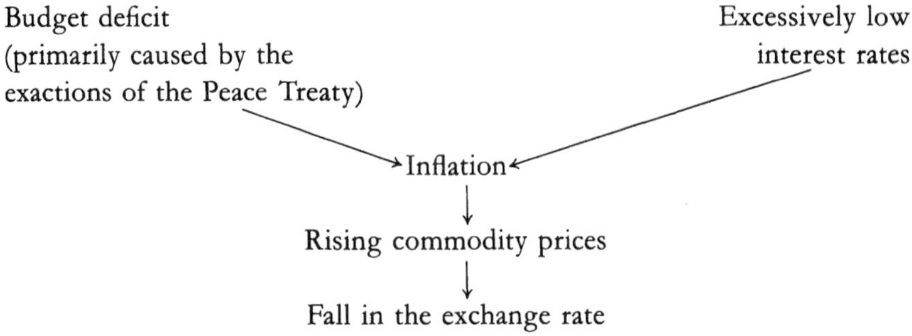

Balance of payments theorists[7] started from consideration of processes in the real economy – in the spheres of production and distribution of goods and services. They viewed the exchange rate, certainly, as the price that clears the market in which foreign exchange is traded against the domestic currency. But they laid stress on factors, affecting the supply of and demand for foreign exchange, whose elasticity in respect of exchange rate movements was small,

[7] Detailed expositions of the "balance of payments" theory can be found in the works of its principal proponents: Moritz Julius Bonn: *Die Stabilisierung der Mark* (Berlin, 1922), and Karl Helfferich: "Aussenhandel und Valutaschwankungen", *Schmollers Jahrbuch*, 21 (1897), pp. 353–409, and in his *magnum opus*, *Das Geld* (Leipzig, 6th edn. 1923), pp. 644ff. Assessments of this dazzling personality can be found in John G. Williamson: *Karl Helfferich 1872–1924, Economist, Financier, Politician* (Princeton, 1971), and in Claus-Dieter Krohn: "Helfferich contra Hilferding. Konservative Geldpolitik und die sozialen Folgen der deutschen Inflation 1918–1923", *Vierteljahrschrift für Sozial- und Wirtschaftsgeschichte*, 62 (1975), pp. 62–92.
Bonn and Helfferich were both, significantly, involved in practical economic policy – just like the proponents of the "balance of payments" theory in the English bullion controversy. Helfferich was Reich Secretary of the Treasury for part of the war, and subsequently a German Nationalist deputy in the Reichstag; Bonn was an advisor to the government on financial matters. The dominating influence of the "balance of payments" theory on the arguments employed against the Allies by postwar German governments can be seen in Walther Rathenau: *Cannes und Genua. Vier Reden zum Reparationsproblem* (Berlin, 1922), pp. 10ff., 35, as also in Statistisches Reichsamt: *Deutschlands Wirtschaftslage unter den Nachwirkungen des Weltkrieges* (Berlin, 1923), pp. 22ff. Peter Czada ("Ursachen und Folgen der grossen Inflation", in Harald Winkel (ed.): *Finanz- und wirtschaftspolitische Fragen der Zwischenkriegszeit. Schriften des Vereins für Socialpolitik, N. F. Bd. 73* (Berlin, 1973), p. 10) denied the "scientific validity" of the "balance of payments" theory, but it cannot be so easily dismissed, particularly in view of increasing evidence in real economic life of those inelasticities which the theory presupposes. Czada is correct however to state that this theory was adopted by German politicians primarily because it legitimated the economic policies actually being pursued. Yet even the Allies acted upon this theory when they acknowledged the need for a so-called "transfer protection clause" under the Dawes Plan arrangements for Reparations payments.

being related to rather rigid requirements of the real economy. If excess demand for foreign exchange develops, its price in marks rises, and this induces adjustment to some extent in the current account balance, but more especially on capital account, as it induces capital imports, thus restoring equilibrium on the foreign exchange market.

Among the real factors determining the merchandise balance, the following were typically emphasized. Full utilization of German industrial capacity required a certain throughput of raw materials, while the population required a certain supply of foodstuffs. Both – so far as domestic supplies were not available – could be obtained only by importing in quantities determined thus independently of price. This implied a certain predetermined demand for foreign exchange which, depending on export opportunities, might not always be matched by export earnings. Thus during the First World War the German balance of trade was necessarily passive; traditional export markets had been lost but German demand for foodstuff and raw material imports was undiminished. After the war the cession of territories rich in raw materials, together with the commodity deliveries on Reparations account created additional import requirements and hence additional demand for foreign exchange. On top of this, cash payments of Reparations and interest charges on foreign currency debts generated yet further demands for foreign exchange. All these foreign currency requirements had to be satisfied on the foreign exchange market, whatever the cost in domestic currency.

This increased postwar demand for foreign currency was met by a diminution of the traditional sources supplying it. The Versailles Treaty placed disadvantageous conditions on German trade.[8] Traditional foreign currency earners such as the merchant marine and German capital investments abroad had been expropriated. International financial markets refused to place long term German loans. The gap that had now opened up between the demand for and supply of foreign exchange could be closed only as long as foreigners could be continuously induced to supply it in exchange for German paper money (bank notes, bank deposits, mark-denominated bonds, other book credits) – in other words, only insofar as a short term capital inflow could be generated. These short credits however hung like a Damocles' sword over the German currency. In the measure that foreigners lost confidence in the future stability of the mark and began to demand foreign exchange for their mark balances, a rise in the mark price of foreign exchange, hence of imported

---

[8] Under it Germany was obligated to extend "most favored nation" treatment unilaterally to her trading partners, and to permit duty-free imports from the ceded territories (Alsace-Lorraine and the Saar). Tariff autonomy was not to be restored until 1925.

goods, would follow: this would be passed on in domestic costs of production and ultimately affect the entire German price level. The prices of the goods and services purchased by the Reich would increase as would the paper-mark equivalent of given Reparations outlays; thus the Reich deficit would widen as would its recourse to the money-creating powers of the Reichsbank. In the same manner the private sector would seek larger credits from the commercial banks who in turn would want to increase their discounting at the Reichsbank. The Reichsbank would be compelled to accede to the credit demands of the state and the commercial banks; otherwise it would prevent the government from the discharge of its responsibilities and permit the disruption of economic activity. In this way, "balance of payments" theorists argued, the increase in the money supply was a consequence and not a cause of the fall in the exchange rate and of the rise in domestic prices. They viewed the function of the central bank as an ancillary one, namely, to furnish a predetermined level of real "requirements" for goods and services with the necessary purchasing power, and then subsequently with more purchasing power once prices had risen.

A central bank acting on these principles however would be nullifying certain of the normal functions of price formation in markets – the indication of relative scarcities, for example, and consequently the redirecting of factors of production to areas of bottleneck; also the controlling of aggregate demand.

Balance of payments theorists justified their viewpoint with the argument that the greater part of the demand for foreign exchange was price-inelastic. They regarded as illusory the belief that by reducing the quantity of domestic money one could bring about a lower price level, thus choking off imports and stimulating exports. "Our economy possesses nothing like the degree of elasticity presupposed by such theories," was M. J. Bonn's argument against the "quantity theory" of the inflation.[9] Balance of payments theorists left space for consideration of the effects of institutional peculiarities such as wage and price rigidities which the increasing strength of trade union organization and, particularly in Germany, of monopolies and cartels introduced into productive relations in the twentieth century. Trade barriers, by which the Reparations creditors defended their home markets against the very exports that Reparations in the long run made ineluctable, represented a further element of inelasticity. Inflexibilities like these would have diverted the effects of a contractionary monetary policy from the monetary sphere (prices) to the real sphere

[9] In *Verhandlungen der Sozialisierungskommission über die Reparationsfrage, Bd. III: Stabilisierung der Währung* (Berlin, 1922), Sitzung (i.e. meeting) vom 10. März 1922, p. 13.

(production, capacity utilization, employment). Furthermore, in a democratic state such inelasticities and the associated consequences of contractionary monetary policy for the real economy acquire added significance by the fact that government majorities become endangered when the purchasing power correlative to a given economic and social requirement in respect of growth, full employment and living standards is not made available. These considerations suggest that any attempt to improve the external balance and stabilize the exchange rate through deflationary economic adjustments would have been prohibitively costly in both economic and political terms.

Fundamental to the balance of payments theorists' approach was the concept of a "requirement" (*Bedarf*) for purchasing power on the part of both the state and the private sector, to enable them to discharge certain tasks in the spheres of production and distribution of goods and services. We can regard this concept as an umbrella term for certain goals of economic policy which today would be explicitly listed alongside price and exchange rate stability: the "real" goals of growth and full employment. The idea of "requirement" indicates that balance of payments theorists assigned a high priority to these goals and were unwilling to sacrifice them as a means of achieving goals such as price and exchange rate stability by means of deflationary monetary policies. We may conclude, then, that by employing this concept and the theory of inflation which hinged on it they were expressing a preference in the trade-off between these partially conflicting policy goals.

Contrariwise, proponents of the quantity theory[10] concentrated on the consequences of money supply changes for the price level, to the neglect of its outworkings in the real sphere of production. They denied the existence of "rigid requirements" and blamed the currency depreciation solely on the creation of excess purchasing power. "To assume the contrary, one must postulate that prices will rise in a country simply because of the numbers of

[10] Among the chief proponents of the "quantity" theory of the German inflation was, besides Eucken, the Swede Gustav Cassel. See his works *The Theory of Social Economy* (London, 2 vols. 1923) (first German edn. 1918), *Money and Foreign Exchange after 1914* (London, 1922; German edn. 1925), and many others. Furthermore: Ludwig Mises: *Theorie des Geldes und der Umlaufsmittel* (Munich, 1912); idem: "Die geldtheoretische Seite des Stabilisierungsproblems", in *Schriften des Vereins für Socialpolitik, Bd. 164 III* (Munich, 1923). Karl Schlesinger: *Die Veränderungen des Geldwertes im Kriege* (Vienna, 1916). Alfred Lansburgh: "Die Politik der Reichsbank und die Reichsschatzanweisungen nach dem Kriege", in *Schriften des Vereins für Socialpolitik, Bd. 166 II* (Munich, 1924), pp. 1–54. Ludwig Pohle: *Das Problem der Valutaentwertung* (Dresden, 1919); idem: *Geldentwertung, Valutafrage und Währungsreform* (Leipzig, 1920). L. Albert Hahn: "Handelsbilanz, Zahlungsbilanz, Valuta, Güterpreise", *Archiv für Sozialwissenschaft und Sozialpolitik*, 48 (1920/21), pp. 596–614; idem: *Geld und Kredit* (Tübingen, 1924). For other adherents of this view, see H. S. Ellis: *Monetary Theory*, pp. 237 ff.

needy people who live there. In reality, prices would rise in such a country only when the needy had first been furnished with the purchasing power to make them solvent."[11] Passivity of the external trade balance and depreciating exchange rates were thus not the cause of excessive purchasing-power creation and rising domestic prices. Stabilization must begin by shutting down the domestic sources of inflation: by eliminating the budget deficits – or at least the Reichsbank's financing of them, and by raising interest rates to choke off private demands for central bank credit. The supply of money to the economy controls the degree to which real "requirements" – in principle infinite – express themselves in actual ability to purchase goods; thereby it controls the price level, the demand for foreign currency and imports, the condition of the external balance and the exchange rate.

Quantity theorists postulated a generally elastic economy possessing a readily adaptable productive structure. For them – as for classical economists such as Say or Ricardo – the effects of varying the quantity of money upon the utilization of productive capacity, hence employment, growth and real incomes were not perceived as a problem. By a species of unidimensional analysis they reduced the question of economic stabilization to its monetary aspects without consideration of the social costs arising out of its repercussions in the productive sphere. By implying that the costs of a policy of "monetary stabilization by hook or by crook" did not outweigh the advantages flowing from its success, they expressed their own particular preference in the trade-off between partially conflicting policy goals – the priority they assigned to price and exchange rate stability.

Subscription, then, to one or other theory of the currency depreciation was not independent of the individual and social scale of values[12] ranking the

[11] Albert Hahn in a lecture delivered in 1924, "Unsere Währungslage im Lichte der Geldtheorie", cited according to his book, *Fünfzig Jahre*, p. 18.

[12] In his book, *The Structure of Scientific Revolutions* (Chicago, 2nd edn. enlarged 1970), pp. 199–200, Thomas S. Kuhn had the following to say about the importance of values in the competition between alternative theories. "Debates over theory-choice cannot be cast in a form that fully resembles logical or mathematical proof... That debate is about premises, and its recourse is to persuasion as a prelude to the possibility of proof. Nothing about that relatively familiar thesis implies either that there are no good reasons for being persuaded... What it should suggest, however, is that such reasons function as values and that they can thus be differently applied, individually and collectively, by men who concur in honoring them. If two men disagree, for example, about the relative fruitfulness of their theories, or if they agree about that but disagree about the relative importance of fruitfulness, and, say, scope in reaching a choice, neither can be convicted of a mistake, nor is either being unscientific. There is no neutral algorithm for theory-choice, no systematic decision procedure which, properly applied, must lead each individual in the group to the same decision."

importance of currency stabilization amongst the tasks of economic policy. Balance of payments theorists acknowledged a wider sphere of policy objectives and constraints than quantity theorists did. They discussed conflicts between objectives and as a result subordinated price and currency stability to objectives relating to "real" magnitudes.

Which theory did the Reichsbank hold?

During the First World War the published annual reports of the Reichsbank attributed the fall in the mark exchange rate to wartime constraints on German trade and other international transactions. Of the balance of payments elements constituting the supply of foreign exchange, the German export of goods "was severely impaired, the high seas shipping business paralyzed, and a large part of German claims on foreign debtors blocked along with our foreign investments. Meanwhile a certain level of imports of foodstuffs and raw materials has proven unavoidable."[13] The Bank traced the increasing circulation of money to a "requirement" (*Bedarf*) arising out of the more extensive geographic area now served by the mark, to the increased employment and speculative hoarding of cash and – last but not least – to the "general rise in prices."[14]

With this analysis the Reichsbank was expressing subscription to the "balance of payments" theory. During the years of the postwar inflation its published reports stood by the explanation that the currency depreciation was the consequence of the factors just described, plus Reparations. Among the components of the aggregate "requirement" for purchasing power, they now emphasized rising prices and wages, the black market, the export of marks as payment for imports and as capital fleeing Germany. To an increasing degree they also stressed the undesirable but unavoidable expansion of the Reich's floating debt occasioned by its Reparations outlays – especially after the imposition of the London payments plan.[15]

In these Reports the Reichsbank certainly conveyed the impression that it regarded the effects of the Reparations and external trade policies of foreign governments on the German balance of payments as the primary cause of

---

13 *Verwaltungsbericht* (i.e. Annual Report) 1915, p. 4.

14 *Verwaltungsbericht*, 1916, p. 9.

15 *Verwaltungsbericht*, 1919, pp. 3–4; also Reports for the following years. On Reichsbank policy in the postwar years, cp. Heinz Habedank, *Die Reichsbank in der Weimarer Republik. Zur Rolle der Zentralbank in der Politik des deutschen Imperialismus 1919–1933* (Berlin-East, 1981).

inflation, and that it did not believe domestic economic policy to have the power to counter these effects. In its confidential correspondence with the government however, Reichsbank theorizing wore a different aspect. In these documents its argumentation and policy recommendations appealed to the quantity theory. The chief threat to currency stability was diagnosed as domestic in origin: the fiscal policy of the Reich. A letter to the chancellor of the Reich some months before the end of the war drew his attention to the dangers that the Reich's floating debt (which it estimated at between fifty and sixty billion marks) posed for the stability of the currency. The Bank emphatically urged the Reich not to permit the floating debt to increase further, and to take steps in its postwar fiscal policy to reduce this debt as rapidly as possible. Apart from expenditure cuts, "the speedy securing of a revenue base strong enough to provide for all expenditures arising out of interest charges on the debt, payment of pensions to the wounded and dependants of the fallen, as well as all other requirements of the Reich"[16] would be the most essential step. The Bank punctured any hopes that in the event of victory reparations from the vanquished could pay off the floating debt. "Should such compensation be realized, it would at best pay off only a modest part of that fifty to sixty billion marks."

After the war the Reichsbank's practice was to present its annual report to the President of the Reich *via* the chancellor, enclosing along with it a confidential accompanying report. This accompanying report was supposed to summarize the main points of the published report, to explain them further, and "in certain circumstances to amplify them with information which, for paramount reasons of policy, could not very well be included in a report designed for publication."[17] The Reichsbank also used these reports as vehicles for its policy recommendations to the government. The first of them dates from March 31st, 1919;[18] it reveals that the Reichsbank traced the mark's depreciation on the foreign exchanges on the one hand to the uncertain political situation at home and abroad but on the other hand also to the growth of the Reich's floating debt and the associated "continuous increase in the circulation of paper means of payment." Fiscal reform and the renunciation by the Reich of central bank credit financing were designated the "essential preconditions" for the restoration of a healthy economy and currency.

---

16 Bundesarchiv Koblenz (hereafter BA), R2/1894. Letter from the Reichsbankdirektorium to the chancellor of the Reich of July 29, 1918.

17 BA R 43 I/638 Bd. I Blatt (i.e. sheet) 25. Letter from the Reichsbankdirektorium to the chancellor, of March 30, 1919.

18 BA R 43 I/638, Bd. I, Blatt 26 ff. Letter from the Reichsbankdirektorium to the President of the Reich, of March 31, 1919.

The Reichsbank's attitude to the government's fiscal policy was not altered by the signing (on June 28th, 1919) of the Versailles Treaty, whose terms the Bank's published report described as "incapable of fulfillment" (*unerfüllbar*).[19] In two almost imploring letters of July 1919 the Reichsbank gave clearest expression to its quantity-theoretic assessment of the currency depreciation,[20] pinpointing the growth of the floating debt as the cause of the increased circulation of money and this in turn as the cause of "the already serious external depreciation of German currency." The Bank renewed its appeal to the government for expenditure economies and tax reform, so that the government of the Reich might be financed without recourse to the printing presses. The floating debt already incurred should be consolidated by funding operations and reduced by special taxes. The Reichsbank conjoined these proposals with a plain threat to suspend in future the unlimited discounting of the Reich treasury bills. In reality however this threat was more or less an empty one: given the subordination of the Reichsbank to the government of the Reich, until the passing of the Reichsbank Autonomy Law of May 1922, both sides must have been well aware that in practice the Bank was not in a position to back its words with deeds.

In the confidential report sent to the chancellor and President of the Reich in April 1920[21] along with the published report for 1919, "the perpetual increase in the circulation of paper money" occasioned by the deficitary budgeting of the Reich was once more set forth as the principal cause of the mark's internal and external depreciation. Fiscal measures to balance the budget and reduce the floating debt were again recommended as the precondition of improvement in currency conditions.

Certain major changes of emphasis in the Reichsbank's attitude can be discerned for the first time in 1921, prompted, apparently, by the ongoing tug of war over the execution of the terms of the Peace Treaty. The Treaty had deferred the definite fixing of Germany's aggregate Reparations liability until May 1st, 1921 – at the latest; when the German government showed recalcitrance over the demands made by the Allies at the London negotiations of March 1921, sanctions were threatened, and at the end of the month French troops occupied the Rhine ports of Düsseldorf, Duisburg and Ruhrort. The Allies proceeded to fix German liability unilaterally, compelling the Reich

---

19 *Verwaltungsbericht*, 1919, p. 3.

20 BA R 43 I/2391 and R 2/1894. Letters from the Reichsbankdirektorium to the Reich Finance Minister, of July 1st and 14th, 1919.

21 BA R 43 I/638 Bd. 1. Letter from the Reichsbankdirektorium to the President of the Reich, of April 6, 1920.

under threat of occupation of the Ruhr to accede to the so-called London Ultimatum of May 5th, 1921. The aggregate liability of 132 billion gold marks and, more immediately significant, the annuity of at least three billion gold marks (two billions cash plus 26% of the value of exports) have already been discussed. It was at this time, too, that Polish insurgents occupied much of the industrial district of Upper Silesia and shortly thereafter an Allied commission decided to partition the province (in spite of a plebiscite showing an overall majority in favor of Germany) and detach part of it from the Reich.[22]

Already on January 24th, 1921 Rudolf Havenstein, at that time President of the Reichsbank, had made clear in discussions about Reparations at the Foreign Office that he regarded "the payment of three billions per annum as an impossibility:"[23] this was before the above-mentioned Allied violations of German economic space. Under such circumstances Allied demands patently could not fail to influence the advice which the Reichsbank was giving to the government about financial policy. Thus, in a confidential letter of May 21st, 1921 to the President and government of the Reich, the Bank repeated its "strong reservations" about the rapid increase of the floating debt, but stated that it could no longer envisage any concrete possibility of stabilizing the currency situation. Instead, the Bank reformulated its "preconditions" for stabilization,[24] adding to the requirement that the printing of money cease the further requirements that the trade balance improve and liability under Reparations be curtailed. These remarks signify the partial adoption of the balance

---

[22] Cp. Helmut Heiber; *Die Republik von Weimar* (Munich, 4th edn. 1969), pp. 93–94.

[23] BA R 2/3216. The vehemence of German opposition to such Reparations demands may have been reinforced by the opinion of leading non-German financial experts that they would result in either impossible or at least very damaging transfer problems. E.g. J. M. Keynes: *The Economic Consequences of the Peace* (London, 1919), and idem: *The Revision of the Treaty* (London, 1922). John M. Williams: "German Foreign Trade and the Reparation Payments", *Quarterly Journal of Economics*, 36 (1922), pp. 488 ff. H. G. Moulton and C. E. McGuire: *Germany's Capacity to Pay. A Study of the Reparation Problem* (New York, 1923). A further impediment to the transfer of Reparations emerged in 1921 in the conjuncture of high economic activity in Germany with depression abroad – whereas successful transfer really needed the converse. The question whether Reparations represented an impossible burden on the German economy, incapable of collection and transfer even with Germany's cooperation, seems less relevant to me than Schumpeter's simple observation (regarding the more moderate payments under the Dawes Plan), namely, that "the Dawes tribute was *morally* inacceptable [*sic*] to Germany, and economically inacceptable to the recipient countries", and that "it is perfectly clear that, looked at as a business proposition, the Dawes tribute would have been nothing else but a 'commission' paid by Germany for the industrial conquest of the better half of the world". Joseph A. Schumpeter: *Business Cycles. A Theoretical, Historical and Statistical Analysis of the Capitalist Process* (New York, 2 vols. 1939), vol. 2, p. 704, n. 1.

[24] BA R 43 I/638 Bd. 1, Blatt 171–175.

of payments theory by the Reichsbank as the basis even of its private advice. Simultaneously, the first public statement by the Bank that deficitary fiscal policy was a principal cause of the currency depreciation appeared in its annual report for 1920, published on May 14th, 1921. The report added however that these deficits were "inevitable... on account of the severe deterioration in the Reich's financial situation."[25] Thus the public pronouncements of the Reichsbank were to some extent shifting in the direction of quantity theory. Significantly, no differences of substance can be detected between the Reichsbank's public and private assessments of economic and monetary developments from this point on, between its published annual reports and its confidential correspondence with the government. In 1922 both the published and the confidential report cite control of the floating debt as the key to controlling the inflation. But, the reports continued, not until Reparations obligations had been reduced to a level consonant with the taxable capacity of the population would the Reich be in a position to renounce this "extremely injurious mode of financing."[26] The Reichsbank, in other words, discerned an inseparable connection between the solution of the currency problem and the abatement of Reparations, and it held to this viewpoint throughout the hyperinflationary period. On May 30th, 1923, in a letter about the preconditions for stabilization addressed to the President of the Reich, the Bank stated that "only the actual realization of a revision of the Treaty of Versailles, or the very definite prospect of such a revision, would make it possible to stabilize the balance of payments and to restore equilibrium to the Reich budget."[27]

It is pointless to debate whether the Reichsbank deliberately stimulated inflation in the period from 1921, or merely accepted it. The fact is that, following the above-described events of that year, it abandoned its opposition to the Reich's inflationary fiscal policy. Two institutional changes of the same year confirm the point.

(i) The amendment made on May 9th, 1921 to the Reichsbank Law suspended until December 31st, 1923 the requirement that it hold bullion (and other authorized) reserves to the value of one third of its note issue.[28] This stipulation had only been eased, not revoked in 1914. This amendment followed consultations between the government and the Bank and clearly signifies that both sides had now come to terms with continued inflation.

(ii) From June 1st, 1921 the Reichsbank was willing to purchase gold coins

---

[25] *Verwaltungsbericht*, 1920, p. 3.

[26] *Verwaltungsbericht*, 1921, p. 5. Similarly, BA R 43 I/638, Bd. 1, Blatt, 222–223.

[27] BA R 43 I/638. Bd. 1, Blatt 269–270.

[28] *Die Reichsbank 1901–1925* (Berlin, n.d.), pp. 99–100.

from the general population at a premium over their face value. "[I]t for the first time, officially recognized the inflation."[29]

The Reichsbank Autonomy Law of May 26th, 1922 was the condition laid down by the Allies for granting the Reparations moratorium proposed at the Cannes Conference in January of the same year. It strengthened the Reichsbank's position against the government and theoretically at least gave it the power to curb the rate of monetary expansion even against the government's wishes.[30] But the Bank made no use of its newly acquired power. On the contrary, it began discounting private commercial bills in increasing quantities alongside the treasury bills of the Reich,[31] thus opening the floodgates of monetary expansion still more widely, in the interests of its traditional clients – private business. Even in August 1923, at the high point of the inflation, the Bank was acceding to the credit demands of the state, although it expected "a massive new acceleration in the inflation, exceeding by

---

29 Hjalmar Schacht: *The Stabilization of the Mark* (London, 1927) p. 49 (German original 1926).

30 This is what the Allies had hoped for when at the Cannes Conference they insisted on Reichsbank autonomy as a precondition of granting a Reparations moratorium. Cp. *Akten der Reichskanzlei. Weimarer Republik. Die Kabinette Wirth I und II*, p. LVII and Dokument Nr. 214. The Autonomy Law was put into effect by the "Decree concerning the Alteration of the Reichsbank Statute", of July 24, 1922. *Reichsgesetzblatt* 1922, II, p. 683. Cp. also Hjalmar Schacht: *Die Reichsgesetzgebung über Münz- und Notenbankwesen* (Berlin, 1926). In public discussions of the autonomy question in Germany authors took seemingly paradoxical positions. Karl Helfferich ("Die Autonomie der Reichsbank", *Bank-Archiv*, 21 (1921/22), pp. 215–217), a conservative nationalist, deplored that the autonomy was not the result of a voluntary action by the German legislative authorities, but of "the execution of a dictate" by the Allies. He nevertheless approved of the change arguing that in the new republican-parliamentary system the Reichsbank needed protection from interference by partisan and non-expert governments. In contrast, Kurt Singer ("Die Autonomie der Reichsbank", *Wirtschaftsdienst*, 7 (1922), pp. 734–735), rather a liberal internationalist, opposed the autonomy as being alien to the German tradition. A member of the Reichsbankdirektorium, K. Friedrich, conceded later that the Reichsbank had always regarded its credits to the Reich as the main source of the inflation. It was "under heaviest pressure from most important political circumstances" that the Bank decided against a stop of its credits to the Reich after it had acquired autonomy. There was also the danger that in case of need the Reich would issue its own paper money or would suspend the Autonomy Law and force the Reichsbank to continue discounting the treasury bills. Karl Friedrich: "Vom alten zum neuen Bankgesetz", *Bank-Archiv*, 23 (1923/24), p. 342. It is noteworthy that the autonomy complied with the wishes of the Reichsbank, as its president Havenstein had demanded and won the support of the Governor of the Bank of England, M. Norman, for strengthening the Reichsbank's position vis-à-vis the German government in a new Banking Law, when they had met in London in October 1921. Richard S. Sayers: *The Bank of England 1891–1944, vol. 1* (Cambridge UK, 1976), pp. 175–176.

31 Cp. the data in Frank D. Graham: *Exchange, Prices and Production in Hyper-Inflation. Germany 1920–1923* (New York, 1930), pp. 61 ff.

far what has been experienced hitherto" to be the consequence, for the Bank could not "be deaf to the conviction that necessities of state were involved and must be satisfied."[32]

This chronological account of the Reichsbank's statements regarding the processes of inflation may be summarized as follows. Neither during nor after the war did the Bank subscribe to monocausal views of the matter.[33] This stance enabled it to adjust the weights it attached to a number of causal factors

---

[32] BA R 43 I/632, Letter from the Reichsbankdirektorium to the Minister of Finance, of August 23, 1923. During the same month, however, the Reichsbank defied the government and threatened to discontinue the discounting of treasury bills by the end of the year. H. Schacht: *Stabilization*, p. 53. K. Friedrich: "Vom alten zum neuen Bankgesetz", p. 342.

[33] P. Czada ("Ursachen", p. 11) likewise, after reviewing the various explanatory approaches of modern theories of inflation, proposes that "one should *a priori* avoid monocausal explanations of the events". Cp. also Chi-Yuen Wu: *An Outline of International Price Theories* (London, 1939), p. 267: "... [C]auses and effects are, as already indicated, often confused and reciprocal... causal sequence should further be distinguished from actual sequence. In the real world the actual course is governed by various causes." The following might be added: The aim of theory-construction is to make it possible to isolate, among the confusing multiplicity of influences acting in the real world, those factors which exerted a decisive influence on the development of the phenomenon under study. In the social sciences theories have the task of explaining social structures and processes, but they also serve as instruments of ideological conflict between social groups which wish to influence these structures and processes in their own interest. The power of one theory, as against another, to command acceptance, rests therefore less on the superiority of its logical construction than on a value judgment about the importance of the matter requiring explanation and about the scale of social priorities by which events are partitioned into the classes of "cause" or "effect", and by which possible explanatory factors are either deemed independent explanatory variables on the one hand, or relegated to the "ceteris paribus" category on the other. Among those events and factors which are viewed as "consequences" or impounded in the "ceteris paribus" category, will be all those which, it is held, should remain outside the sphere of direct political manipulation. The actual selection of explanatory variables is thus the expression of a choice regarding those areas in which political attempts to influence social structures and processes should be undertaken – this choice reflecting not so much an assessment of the absolute efficacy of the means proposed in achieving the end sought, as a belief that the means proposed can achieve that end without conflicting with social interests which the theory's advocates consider sacrosanct. The controversy between "balance of payments" and "quantity" theorists of the inflation seems to me a classic exemplification of these propositions. It had less to do with the ascertainment of absolute truth than with divergent evaluations of the social costs associated with the courses of political action each theory pointed to. Kindleberger has recently argued along these lines and has suggested a structural theory of inflation that takes into account social and political factors. According to him the balance-of-payments and the quantity theories can be brought under the umbrella of the structural view. "There is no need for mono-causality... It is possible that all three schools have a part of the truth." Charles P. Kindleberger: "A Structural View of the German Inflation", in G.D. Feldman *et al.* (eds.): *The Experience of Inflation. International and Comparative Studies* (Berlin/New York, 1984), pp. 10–33, esp. p. 26.

according to the audience it was addressing and also according to the circumstances of the day, yet without sacrificing the substantial consistency of its assessments. From 1918, at the latest, leading figures at the Bank believed that the growth of the money supply triggered off by the growing quantities of Reich short-term paper in its portfolio was the principal cause of inflation: they subscribed primarily to the quantity theory. Up to 1921 their confidential reports to the government were urging the abandonment of the Reich's inflationary budget practices, sometimes even under threat of refusing further credit. The Bank's public statements, on the other hand, were principally informed until the London Ultimatum by elements of the balance of payments explanation. After this event even the Bank's published reports rated the expansion of the floating debt as the main reason for the monetary expansion, but regarded it as "unavoidable" given the Allies' Reparations policy. This line was followed from now on both publicly and privately with few divergences and was not affected by the passing, under Allied pressure, of the Autonomy Law in May 1922.

I conclude this subsection by considering two questions posed by the foregoing account of the Reichsbank's varying stances between 1918 and 1923 on the inflation problem.

Firstly, what accounts for the difference between the Reichsbank's public and private analyses of inflation in the years 1918 to 1920?

Secondly, what was the rationale, in terms of economic policy, of the shift after the London Ultimatum in the Bank's attitude toward the Reich's fiscal policy?

On the first question my answer, in brief, runs as follows. When those responsible for economic policy offer public explanations for economic events, these explanations are not merely *statements about* the events: they are always intended also as *means of influencing* their further development. A bank of issue, for example, influences the public's expectations about future developments by the opinions it gives public voice to: these expectations in turn affect the concrete economic actions of economic agents and this affects the economy's actual development path. A premature emphasis on the domestic causes of inflation in the public statements of the Reichsbank could have intensified the erosion of confidence in the currency and its future stability. Domestic and foreign demand for mark balances depended however on the degree to which this confidence was maintained; in the short run, given an unchanged fiscal deficit and rate of monetary expansion, it was the decisive determinant of the price level. By employing a "balance of payments" approach to the explanation of inflation in postwar Germany the Bank effectively forged a link between the value of the mark and the attitude of the Allies toward the Reparations issue. As long as hopes could be kept alive that Reparations demands might moderate and thus relief be brought to the German balance of payments, public stress on the balance of payments explanation could help at least to stabilize, perhaps even to stimulate, the demand for money.

Thus the Reichsbank's public commitment to the "balance of payments" analysis of inflation may be interpreted as an attempt to act, against the upward pressure on prices, from the side of the demand for money; the Bank's simultaneous private commitment to a "quantity theory" explanation when dealing with the government may express a parallel attempt to act against inflation from the side of the supply of money.

And now the second question, regarding the rationale, as a matter of economic policy, of the Reichsbank's change of stance over inflation in 1921. As I have already argued, the decision whether or not to apply the available policy instruments to the task of stabilizing the currency must always involve a consideration of the costs and the benefits: the costs of swinging an inflationary economy on to a course of price stability are met not least in the "real"sphere, by sacrifices of growth and employment. In an economy whose markets are penetrated by price inelasticities these costs, as already explained, will be so much the higher. It seems however that until the London Payments Plan was announced in May 1921 the Reichsbank regarded the costs of stabilizing the currency by fiscal deflation as lower than the benefits of achieving it. In formulating this judgment the Bank must have made some guess about the likely annual Reparations burden in the future; presumably it was working with an annual figure well below the three billion gold marks or so actually demanded by the Plan.

The relationship between the degree of deflation required to stabilize exchange rates, and the level of unilateral transfers to abroad has already been discussed: higher transfers require that larger surpluses on goods and services account be generated in order to finance them and this in turn necessitates still severer downward pressure on domestic prices. The falling international price level in 1921 meant an increase in the real transfer requiring to be financed under the gold-mark denominated demands of the London Plan. Allied demands during 1921 patently affected the Reichsbank's estimation of the costs of a stabilization policy, and in the eyes even of so conservative an institution as a bank of issue the sacrifices of growth and employment came to exceed the benefits expected from price stability. In its judgment, costs of this magnitude could mean nothing less than "the end of all economic management and order in the state."[34] Hindsight enables us to compare the devastating economic,

[34] Cp. *Verwaltungsbericht*, 1921, p. 4.

social and political costs of the German deflation of 1929–32 with the immediate consequences of hyperinflation: the comparison suggests that the Reichsbank's change of stance reflected a thoroughly sound assessment of the situation.

The discount policy of the Reichsbank

In this subsection I wish to take issue with the quantity theorists' chief criticism of Reichsbank policy during the inflation, namely, that the Bank had pursued a faulty discount policy.[1] They alleged that if the discount rate had been raised more promptly, the proportion of Reich treasury bills taken up outside the Bank itself would have been greater, and hence the inflationary impetus flowing from the Reich's deficits toward money supply growth would have been smaller. Instead, the Bank pegged its discount rate at five percent until the summer of 1922 and raised it hesitantly thereafter: not until August 1923 did discount rate reach ninety percent (cp. Table 23). Apart from this, they alleged, higher discount rates would have attracted additional capital from abroad, thus helping to stabilize the exchange rate.

In what follows I shall examine these two allegations. The further question, whether the Reichsbank's decision to increase its rediscounting of private commercial bills after July 1922 intensified the inflationary process, will be left out of consideration.

Our first task is to investigate the allegation that by raising discount rate the Reichsbank could have forced a larger proportion of its treasury bill holdings on to the private market, thus reducing its rate of monetization of the Reich's deficits. Alfred Lansburgh based his criticism of Reichsbank policy on this allegation, yet he conceded that the state's demand for credit would always be interest-inelastic, and that, given the existing scarcity of capital, the private sector's demand for credit was probably interest-inelastic too.[2] Thus the efficacy of the discount rate tool would largely depend on the interest-elasticity of the supply of credit – on the market's willingness, at higher rates of interest, to

---

[1] Cp. Julius Hirsch: *Die deutsche Währungsfrage* (Jena, 1924), pp. 14ff. Walter Eucken: *Kritische Betrachtungen zum deutschen Geldproblem* (Jena, 1923), p. 62. C. Bresciani-Turroni: *The Economics of Inflation. A Study of Currency Depreciation in Post-War Germany* (London, 1937), pp. 75–79. Gert von Eynern: *Die Reichsbank. Probleme des deutschen Zentralnoteninstituts in geschichtlicher Darstellung* (Jena, 1928), pp. 78–79.

[2] Alfred Lansburgh: "Die Politik der Reichsbank und die Reichsschatzanweisungen nach dem Kriege", in *Schriften des Vereins für Socialpolitik, Bd. 166 II* (Munich, 1924), pp. 40–45.

absorb greater quantities of short paper; and Lansburgh thought this elasticity would be high enough for discount policy to work.[3]

This investigation will concentrate on the demand-side: on the immediate effect of higher discount rates on the Reich's demand for short term accommodation. A numerical illustration will show that, far from reducing this demand, higher interest rates actually increase it. The further consequences of dearer credit on macroeconomic activity, employment and maybe the domestic political climate will not be pursued here.

The following analysis is predicated upon the assumption – shared by the Reich, the Reichsbank and Lansburgh himself – that the Reich's fiscal deficit was incapable of reduction in real terms: that, measured at constant prices, neither expenditure economies nor increases in tax yields could be achieved. In the budget forecasts for 1919 and 1920 the cost of debt servicing represented more than fifty percent of the Reich's ordinary expenditure.[4] At that time funded War Loan stock amounted to about one hundred billion marks, bearing interest at five percent. The floating debt came to an additional fifty-five billion marks at the beginning of 1919, and reached eighty-six billions at the end of it (cp. Table 20); the annual rate of interest on the short-term treasury paper that made up this revolving credit was likewise five percent – the official discount rate – whether payable to the Reichsbank or to private holders. The fiscal deficit requiring to be financed by expansion of this floating debt exceeded fifty percent of aggregate Reich expenditure in all years of the postwar inflation.[5]

The following severely simplified numerical example may thus be viewed as an approximation of the actual Reich budget in 1919 or 1920. For simplicity's sake it will be assumed that the floating debt consisted entirely of interest-bearing treasury certificates.

---

[3] *Ibid.*, p. 42.

[4] Arnd Jessen: *Finanzen, Defizit und Notenpresse 1914–1922* (Berlin, 1923), Tafel (i.e. Table) 5.

[5] *Deutschlands Wirtschaft, Währung und Finanzen. Im Auftrage der Reichsregierung den von der Reparationskommission eingesetzten Sachverständigenausschüssen übergeben* (Berlin, 1924), p. 30. Peter-Christian Witt: "Tax Policies, Tax Assessment and Inflation: Toward a Sociology of Public Finances in the German Inflation 1914–1923", in Nathan Schmukler and Edward Marcus (eds.): *Inflation Through the Ages: Economic, Social, Psychological and Historical Aspects* (New York, 1983), pp. 464–465. Detailed statistical information on the structure of the Reich Government budget has been gathered by Steven B. Webb: "Government Revenue and Spending in Germany, 1919–1923", in G. D. Feldman *et al.* (eds.): *The Adaption to Inflation* (Berlin/New York, 1986).

(1) Revenues		Expenditures	
Ordinary revenues	100	Interest payments	
Increase in the		on War Loan (5%)	50
floating debt	100	on the floating	
		debt (5%)	50
		Other expenditures	100
	200		200

The question is, how do alternative Reichsbank discount policies affect the proportionate size of the Reich's deficit? For the second example, (2a), I shall assume that the Reichsbank carries on with its five percent "cheap money" policy and that, in the year following that represented in example (1) above, the price level has risen on average by one hundred percent. Assuming then that in this second year the volume of the Reich's ordinary revenues and its expenditures other than debt charges did not alter in *real* terms, the structure would appear as follows.

(2a) Revenues		Expenditures	
Ordinary revenues	200	Interest payments	
Increase in the		on War Loan (5%)	50
floating debt	105	on the floating	
		debt (5%)	55
		Other expenditures	200
	305		305

But if the Reichsbank instituted a "dear money" policy for the second year, and succeeded thereby in reducing the rate of price increase, the structure of the budget would wear a very different appearance. Assume that discount rate was increased to fifteen percent and that in the second year prices were on average only ten percent higher than in the first. The volume of ordinary revenue and expenditure other than debt charges remains constant in real terms. Then the outcome is shown in example (2b).

At first sight this result may appear paradoxical. The deficit requiring to be financed by expansion of the floating debt is larger in current prices, and very much larger in real terms, in the example where prices rise little (2b) than in the example where they rise much (2a). The paradox is a direct consequence of the difference in the discount rates. In example (2a) the debt-financed deficit is a

(2b) Revenues		Expenditures	
Ordinary revenues	110	Interest payments	
Increase in the		on War Loan (5%)	50
floating debt	215	on the floating	
		debt (15%)	165
		Other expenditures	110
	325		325

little higher (at current prices) than in the previous year – 105 as against 100 – because of the need to pay interest at 5% on the increase of 100 in the floating debt incurred during the earlier year; the rate of interest paid on the existing floating debt does not change. In example (2b) both the additional floating debt incurred during the preceding year and the entire floating debt already contracted by the start of that year must bear interest at the higher discount rate of 15%. This is because the floating debt consists of revolving credits which need to be recontracted at the new higher interest rate when they fall due.

Supposing, then, that a restrictive Reichsbank credit policy had worked quite rapidly on the rate of price inflation, the above examples show that it would have tended to raise rather than reduce the Reich's real demand for short-term credit. Only if the interest elasticity of the private sector's willingness to supply such credit had outweighed this effect would these additional credit requirements of the state have been met on the open market. Lansburgh's supposition that this was a realistic prospect must be considered very doubtful. After the end of the war the Reich's credit rating with private investors was very poor. During 1919 five percent War Loan stood on average at eighty percent of par on the stock market,[6] implying a yield to maturity (over an average remaining term of seven years) of more than nine percent; occasional support actions prevented this yield from rising even higher. By contrast mortgage credit banks were still successfully floating 4% mortgage bonds, and business firms were still successfully floating 4½% or 5% bonds up to 1922.[7]

A "dear money" policy could have depressed the market price of long-dated Reich debt severely. It is unlikely that this would have stimulated the readiness of private money and capital market investors to lend to the Reich.

[6] *Statistisches Jahrbuch f.d. Deutsche Reich*, 41 (1920), p. 116.

[7] A. Lansburgh: "Politik", p. 41. Cp. also p. 127 *supra*.

Private investors would expect currency stabilization, by increasing the real burden of debt charges, to aggravate the difficulty of meeting the expenditures of the Reich in a non-inflationary manner, and hence to increase the risk of state bankruptcy.

Much more plausible is the assumption that, if the objective of policy was to keep as low as possible the deficit requiring short-term financing, then low discount rates were necessary to its success. If the gap between the Reich's expenditure including debt charges and its tax revenue could not be closed, then the Reichsbank could hope for no more from its monetary policy than a relative stabilization of the price level: insofar as the success of such a policy depended on confidence in the currency, and confidence was in turn influenced by the size of the budget deficit, then an increase in discount rate and thus in the budget deficit could only have accentuated the loss of confidence and flight from the currency.

Would a higher discount rate however have attracted additional capital from abroad, thus helping to stabilize the exchange rate? This was the second contention of the quantity theorists. The belief that this effect would be forthcoming reflects the way discount policy operated in nineteenth century England, in the era when it had been elevated to the Bank of England's chief instrument of monetary management. The peculiar efficacy of discount policy rested however on special preconditions, as the most able monetary theorists had always perceived. In 1913 the young Keynes observed, ".... [T] he bank rate policy of the Bank of England is successful because by indirect means it causes the Money Market to reduce its short-period loans to foreign countries, and thus to turn the balance of immediate indebtedness in our favour. This indirect policy is less feasible in countries where the Money Market is already a borrower rather than a lender in the international market. In such countries a rise in the bank rate cannot be relied on to produce the desired effect with due rapidity."[8]

Schumpeter remarked as follows on the special English situation before the First World War: "Management of the international component, however, was so successful only because there was the powerful wall of short and semi-liquid claims on foreign debtors that sheltered the English structure."[9] He

---

[8] J. M. Keynes: *Indian Currency and Finance. The Collected Writings of J. M. K., ed. E. Johnson and D. E. Moggridge, vol. I* (London, 1971), p. 18 (original edn. 1913). Cp. Ralph G. Hawtrey: *The Art of Central Banking* (London, 1932), p. 410: "It is therefore a great mistake to rely upon attracting foreign balances by means of a high bank rate as a feature of monetary policy, except as a purely temporary expedient."

[9] Joseph A. Schumpeter: *Business Cycles. A Theoretical, Historical and Statistical Analysis of the Capitalist Process* (New York, 2 vols. 1939), vol. 2, p. 673.

estimated that in 1909 these immediately mobilizable claims stood at between one hundred and fifty and two hundred million pounds at least. For 1914 E.V. Morgan estimated them at three hundred and fifty million pounds.[10] On this basis Schumpeter proceeded to argue, "Similarly, a cyclical increase in bank rate had not only restrictive but also relieving effects and incidentally... turned unfavourable exchanges, as a rule with the utmost ease. Hence we cannot be surprised to find that a general belief in the effectiveness of bank rate grew up among bankers and economists which, without this short capital structure, it would be difficult to understand. It is more astonishing that so many people failed to see the dependence of that effectiveness on the historically unique technical position of the London money market and instead tried to explain it by a perfectly general – and unrealistic – theory. This theory... greatly overstressed the influences which bank rate can exert on foreign exchanges and gold movements through successive effects on volume of domestic transactions, volume of deposits, price level and incomes, balance of international and commodity trade."[11]

After the war and during the inflation Germany's position was the converse of this. Before 1914, indeed, Germany had occupied a net creditor position toward the rest of the world. In scale it had not been comparable to the English, and her net long asset position had dominated her net short position; nevertheless it was quite pronounced. The McKenna Committee estimated that at the outbreak of war German overseas assets had been worth about twenty-eight billion marks, of which twenty billions had consisted of portfolio investments, four or five billions of direct investments and three or four billions of short-term credits.[12] Foreign claims against Germany had been small: foreign deposits, whether by foreign central or commercial banks, at German banks were put at about one billion marks,[13] claims arising out of the financing of foreign trade at about the same.[14] The value of foreign portfolio and direct investments in German long-term assets has not yet been estimated

---

[10] E. Victor Morgan: *Studies in British Financial Policy 1914–1925* (London, 1952), p. 3.

[11] J. A. Schumpeter: *Business Cycles*, vol. 2., pp. 673–4.

[12] Reparation Commission: *The Report of the Second Committee of Experts*, reprinted as appendix B of Harold G. Moulton: *The Reparation Plan. An Interpretation of the Reports of the Expert Committees Appointed by the Reparations Commission. November 30, 1923* (New York, 1924), p. 176. Also, Allied Powers (1919–) Reparation Commission, "Documents Collected by the Second Committee of Experts: flight of German capital" (Paris, 1924) p. 7a (unpublished, in the Hoover Institution on War, Revolution and Peace, Stanford, California).

[13] Arthur J. Bloomfield: *Short-term Capital Movements under the Pre-1914 Gold Standard. Princeton Studies in International Finance, No. 11* (Princeton, 1963), p. 78.

[14] Hoover Institution..., Allied Powers (1919–)..., p. 305.

to my knowledge, but must have been relatively small: Helfferich, for example, in the course of his investigation of German national wealth and specifically of the value of German assets in other countries, did not take this offsetting item into consideration.[15]

Thus, as things stood before 1914, Johann Plenge's demand that the authorities employ discount policy to exert stricter control over the money market[16] had some justification, even in relation to the regulation of capital transactions with abroad. Wartime import surpluses totaling about fifteen billion gold marks had to be financed however by selling a large portion of Germany's claims on abroad – insofar as these had not already been sequestrated. According to the McKenna Committee, Germany forfeited 16.1 billion gold marks' worth of assets in other countries through sequestration measures;[17] further confiscations came at the end of the war with the Peace Treaty. At the same time Germany's short-term indebtedness to abroad was increasing: for the war years Glasenapp, Vice-president of the Reichsbank, estimated the increase at seven or eight billion gold marks.[18] In summary, one can conclude that by the end of the war Germany had lost her net creditor position toward the rest of the world. This was true even before Reparations are taken into account.

Germany's commercial debts to abroad increased yet further between 1919 and 1923. Import surpluses totalling between 6.3 and 7.3 billion gold marks, and cash payments on Reparations account of 2.6 billion marks (according to the McKenna Committee estimates) had to be financed. Doubtless there was also a flight of German capital out of the mark into stable foreign currencies which must also be taken into account: the same Committee put this sum, by the end of 1923, at 6.75 billion gold marks.[19] However the net balance of ownership of short-term *mark* denominated assets probably showed a constant deficit towards abroad and in these circumstances the conditions for using discount policy to stabilize the exchange rate were not sufficiently met. In any case, until the mark was pegged against gold or stable foreign currencies, "there could be no question of regulating the exchange rate by discount policy

---

[15] Karl Helfferich: *Deutschlands Volkswohlstand 1888–1913* (Berlin, 6th edn. 1915), p. 111.

[16] Johann Plenge: *Von der Diskontpolitik zur Herrschaft über den Geldmarkt* (Berlin, 1913), esp. pp. 351–352.

[17] *The Report of the Second Committee of Experts*, as reprinted in H.G. Moulton: *The Reparation Plan*, p. 301.

[18] Otto von Glasenapp: "Germany's Balance of Payments with Other Countries", in the *Manchester Guardian Commercial Supplement: Reconstruction in Europe*, April 20, 1922, pp. 28–29.

[19] *The Report of the Second Committee of Experts*, as reprinted in H.G. Moulton: *The Reparation Plan*, p. 295.

directly, as long as speculative gains or losses from exchange rate movements far exceeded international interest rate differentials."[20]

Havenstein's policy was later defended by Hjalmar Schacht, his successor as President of the Reichsbank. Despite his own expert employment of discount policy in the preservation of currency stability after the mark exchange rate had been pegged to gold in the summer of 1924, Schacht wrote concerning the applicability of such a policy during the inflation itself, "To put up the discount rate, as the Bank was recommended by many to do, would not in the circumstances have helped to master the inflation. For the rapid day-to-day depreciation of the mark, putting up the discount rate was far too slow a remedy. It would have been necessary ultimately to put it up to a figure which, when applied to the whole complex of business transactions of the country – many long-term interest charges were based on the Reichsbank discount rate – would have involved as much injury to large classes as the inflation itself. Moreover the demands on the Reichsbank from private quarters were minimal in comparison with the demands of the Reich, and to the Reich the level of the discount rate was ultimately a matter of indifference, since in the last resort it was only living on the note printing press."[21]

In April 1924, a critical month for the survival of the new post-stabilization currency, Schacht himself did not meet the crisis by raising discount rate but rather by rationing credit. He justified his course of action in the following terms. Discount rate could operate as a tool of monetary control, and particularly as a means of attracting foreign short capital, only in "normal conditions. The powerful political factors which have been operating during the post-war period have changed the position, and it is a matter of experience that under present conditions changes in bank rates have far less effect on the international movements of capital than was the case before the war. The attraction of the interest rate is no longer the only factor. Political apprehensions and allowance for currency risks today play a far larger part than was formerly the case. Moreover, in Germany at this period, before the restoration of stability in foreign political relations, the disproportion between the supply and demand of capital was so clamant that no interest rate could have produced any sort of reasonable relation between the two."[22]

Thus there were good grounds for the Reichsbank's refusal to raise discount rate before July 1922 and for accommodating it hesitantly to the high

---

[20] Ludwig Bente: "Die deutsche Währungspolitik von 1914–1924", *Weltwirtschaftliches Archiv*, 23 (1926), p. 136⁺.

[21] H. H. G. Schacht: *The Stabilization of the Mark* (London, 1927), p. 73 (German original, 1926).

[22] *Ibid.*, p. 160.

money market rates thereafter. If we bear in mind the fiscal situation of the Reich, we may justifiably conclude that the reticence of discount policy was a moderating and not an intensifying force in the inflationary process.[23]

[23] Even without investigating the effects on the external balance, W. Schmitt came to the conclusion in his contemporary study, that "Discount policy, without simultaneous exaction of higher taxes and the utmost effort to balance the budget, would of course be entirely ineffectual in the long run". See Wilhelm Schmitt: "Die Diskontpolitik der Reichsbank während der Inflation" (Dissertation, Freiburg, 1926), p. 67. W. Guderjahn, in a study published in the same year, assessed the likely effects on capital imports of raising discount rate in the following terms: "The Reichsbank would not be able to attract capital from abroad by raising discount rate and hence could not by this means improve the strength of the currency. 'External discount policy' was thus wholly paralyzed." Walter Guderjahn: "Ursachen und Wirkungen der Inflation in Deutschland unter besonderer Berücksichtigung des Zinsfusses" (Dissertation, Frankfurt, 1926), p. 43.

Chapter 6
Other Explanatory Factors

6.1. The Short-run Determinants of Production

It now remains to investigate the factors influencing the other elements of the "equation of exchange" set out on p. 98 – the real national income (Table 40), i. e. domestic productive activity plus current account balance, and the velocity of circulation of money or demand for money balances. To take the real supply of goods available to satisfy monetary demand on the goods market first. (The supply of services is disregarded, because statistical information is lacking.) This section of the chapter will consider the political forces that were acting on the size of that supply in this period.

War affected production in a twofold manner.

Firstly, industrial production fell continuously during the war years as a result of problems with the supply of raw materials , shortage of manpower and deterioration of productive equipment in the absence of adequate replacement investment (Table 32 and Diagram 4). Agricultural production was subject to similar constraints; it suffered a dramatic drop in 1917 (followed by the "turnip winter"), recovering slightly in 1918 (Table 33).

Secondly, the war involved a blockade of German foreign trade which not only made it difficult to export but also impeded the imports of the foodstuffs and raw materials on which the German economy so largely depended.[1] The blockade outlasted the war; it was not lifted until the Versailles Treaty was ratified in the summer of 1919.[2] Exports were reduced more sharply than imports, and an import surplus opened up totaling about fifteen billion gold

[1] Even before the war three-quarters of German merchandise imports consisted of primary products. Cp. Statistisches Bundesamt: *Bevölkerung und Wirtschaft 1872–1972* (Stuttgart, 1972), p. 193.

[2] Erich Eyck: *A History of the Weimar Republic* (Cambridge, Mass., 2 vols. 1962–4), vol. 1, p. 89. (Swiss original, 1954). In detail: Suda L. Bane and Ralph H. Lutz (eds.): *The Blockade of Germany after the Armistice 1918–1919. Selected Documents of the Supreme Economic Council, American Relief Agency and Other Wartime Organizations* (London, 1942), esp. pp. 552 ff. A. C. Bell: *The Blockade of Germany 1914–1918* (London, 1961), p. 709.

Table 32. Growth of German industrial production 1913–31. Index 1928 = 100

1913	88	1923	46
1914	73	1924	69
1915	59	1925	81
1916	56	1926	78
1917	55	1927	98
1918	50	1928	100
1919	37	1929	101
1920	54	1930	89
1921	65	1931	72
1922	70		

Sources: Rolf Wagenführ: *Die Industriewirtschaft. Entwicklungstendenzen der deutschen und internationalen Industrieproduktion 1860 bis 1932. Vierteljahrshefte zur Konjunkturforschung, Sonderheft 31* (Berlin, 1933), pp. 22, 28, 56. For the war years: Statistisches Bundesamt: *Bevölkerung und Wirtschaft 1872–1972* (Stuttgart, 1972), p. 176. Since Wagenführ (p. 24) suggests that Germany lost about 10% of her industrial capacity in the territorial cessions imposed by the Peace Treaty, the index values for 1913–18 have each been reduced by this percentage to facilitate comparability with the postwar data.

Table 33. German grain production 1910–31 (Quantities harvested of rye, wheat, barley and oats). Million tons

1910	25.2	1921	16.7
1911	25.8	1922	12.8
1912	28.0	1923	18.0
1913	30.3	1924	16.2
1914	26.6	1925	19.5
1915	21.5	1926	17.8
1916	21.8	1927	19.2
1917	14.9	1928	22.7
1918	17.2	1929	22.1
1919	14.4	1930	20.0
1920	13.9	1931	20.1

Source: Statistisches Bundesamt: *Bevölkerung und Wirtschaft, p. 161.*

marks for the war years[3] and about five billions for 1919.[4] Thus in macroeconomic terms the behavior of the foreign trade balance tended to enlarge the domestic supply of saleable goods. But it also tended to disrupt and hence to reduce the rate of domestic production, and this effect probably outweighed the supply-increasing effect of the trade balance's swing towards passivity.

[3] Statistisches Reichsamt: *Deutschlands Wirtschaftslage unter den Nachwirkungen des Weltkrieges* (Berlin, 1923), p. 22.

[4] F. Hesse: *Die deutsche Wirtschaftslage von 1914 bis 1923. Krieg, Geldblähe und Wechsellagen* (Jena, 1938), pp. 472–473.

Diagram 4. Growth of German industrial production 1913–31 (Semi-logarithmic scale). 1928 = 100
Source: Table 32.

German industrial production fell to a record low directly after the war ended (Diagram 4), and political relations with the outside world were largely to blame. To the effects on production of continuing blockade were added the further effects of loss of territory, hence of industrial capacity, through the Armistice and Peace Treaty, and the transport bottlenecks created by the surrender of the merchant marine and twenty percent of railroad rolling stock.[5] Political events within Germany also contributed to the decline: both the introduction of the eight hour day and the high incidence of strike activity had a considerable impact on production, while the political struggle among the groupings supporting the 1918 revolution, and between these groupings and the forces on the right sometimes reached civil war proportions. Output per worker and per man-hour dropped to a record low in 1919.[6] The revolutionary period came to an end however in the spring of 1920 with the failure

[5] Figures from Statistisches Reichsamt: *Deutschlands Wirtschaftslage*, p. 10. The difficulties caused by reconversion to peace conditions to economic activity in the town of Barmen have been examined by Jürgen Reulecke: *Die wirtschaftliche Entwicklung der Stadt Barmen von 1910 bis 1925* (Neustadt an der Aisch, 1973), pp. 111–123.

[6] *International Labor Office: Enquête sur la Production. Rapport Général, Tome II, 2* (Paris, 1924), pp. 1017 ff. On the effects of industrial conflict on e.g. the Berlin electrical engineering industry, see Peter Czada: *Die Berliner Elektroindustrie in der Weimarer Zeit* (Berlin, 1969), pp. 169–172.

of the Kapp putsch on the one hand and the suppression of the "red army" in the Ruhr on the other. The political situation relaxed and industrial production recovered rapidly, reaching a peak in 1922. Political disturbances caused it to drop sharply again in 1923. The occupation of the Ruhr and Germany's response to this – passive resistance – knocked the heart, so to speak, out of the German productive machine, with inevitable repercussions on the level of productive activity elsewhere in Germany. Scarcity of goods, then, played some part in the collapse of the mark in 1923 as it had, alongside the fiscal practice of the Reich, in 1919.

Agricultural output also remained relatively low during the early postwar years, as is reflected in the data on grain production (Table 33). Wartime exhaustion of the soil was the principal reason for this decline,[7] and the supply of fertilizer was not sufficient to remedy the problem for some time thereafter. Annual variations were mainly caused by climatic forces. Low levels of agricultural output, however caused, were a factor acting from the side of production to maintain a larger inflationary gap than otherwise would have been the case. The poor harvest of 1922 may even have been partly responsible for the contemporaneous slide into hyperinflation: the larger foodstuffs imports which it made necessary must have added to the downwards pressure on the exchange rate.[8]

6.2. Factors Affecting the Demand for Money

The last element of the "equation of exchange" to be investigated is the velocity of circulation of money, or its correlate, the demand for real cash balances; changes in one are inversely proportional to changes in the other. What factors determine this demand?

Equilibrium models proceed from the assumption that the market for money clears continuously, so that the actual quantity of money always repre-

---

[7] Frank D. Graham: *Exchange, Prices and Production in Hyper-Inflation: Germany, 1920–1923* (New York, 1967), p. 286 (original edn. 1930). Cp. Rudolf Bertold: "Die Entwicklung der deutschen Agrarproduktion und der Ernährungswirtschaft zwischen 1907 und 1925", *Jahrbuch für Wirtschaftsgeschichte*, 1974 IV, pp. 83–111.

[8] Harvest failures also played an important part in the bullion controversy regarding the causes of early nineteenth century British currency depreciation Cp. Frank W. Fetter: *The Development of British Monetary Orthodoxy 1797–1875* (Cambridge, Mass., 1965), pp. 26ff. Jacob Viner: *Studies in the Theory of International Trade* (New York, 1937), p. 138.

sents the intersection between the functions governing the demand for and the supply of money. The demand for money depends, among other things, on the level of prices, but the relationship between the two is not proportional. The relationship between the observable stock of money (i.e. the quantity of money demanded and supplied) and the price level expresses the demand for real balances, but this demand undergoes large variation, especially in periods of rapid currency depreciation. Neo-quantity theorists explain this variation by reference to changes in real income and wealth and, above all in circumstances of inflation, by reference to changes in the yield expected from holding money compared with the yield expected from holding other kinds of assets. Expectations regarding future change in the purchasing power of money constitute, along with the interest rate, a principal determinant of the (opportunity-) costs or benefits expected from the holding of cash assets. When currency depreciation is intense, they become the decisive determinant.[1]

Cagan assumes that expectations about future price change are formulated adaptively on the basis of past experience. On this argument expectations surrender their autonomous influence on the demand for money; they are reduced to a variable dependent on actual past price change, hence past monetary policy.

Currency history however amply proves that sudden short-run reversals of expectations do occur in ways not mechanically traceable to past price experience, but rather, for example, to events in the political sphere.[2] Especially in periods when the political and economic situation is unstable, the assumption of a stable adaptive expectations function is inadmissible. Cagan himself conceded that abrupt expectational shifts occur even during hyperinflations, par-

---

[1] P. Cagan: "The Monetary Dynamics of Hyperinflation", in Milton Friedman (ed.): *Studies in the Quantity Theory of Money* (Chicago, 1956), p. 31.

[2] This has been a factor in the espousal of the "rational expectations" hypothesis by much of the more recent literature in monetary theory. Cp. T. J. Sargent and N. Wallace: "Rational Expectations and the Dynamics of Hyperinflation", *International Economic Review*, 14 (1973), pp. 328–350. The extent of monetary theorists' preoccupation, particularly in the U.S.A., with the evidence yielded by the German hyperinflation about the formulation of expectations can be seen in the following recent articles: Jacob A. Frenkel: "The Forward Exchange Rate, Expectations and the Demand for Money: the German Hyperinflation", *American Economic Review*, 67 (1977), pp. 653–670; idem: "Further Evidence on Expectations and the Demand for Money during the German Hyperinflation", *Journal of Monetary Economics*, 5 (1979), pp. 81–96. Andrew Abel *et al.*: "Money Demand during Hyperinflation", *Journal of Monetary Economics*, 5 (1979), pp. 97–104. Michael K. Salemi: "Adaptive Expectations, Rational Expectations and Money Demand in Hyperinflation Germany", *Journal of Monetary Economics*, 5 (1979), pp. 593–604.

ticularly at their commencement and at their termination. These shifts are "incapable of prediction by economic variables, even though we may be certain such shifts will eventually occur under the circumstances." And so Cagan restricted the predictive power of his expectational variables to the statement that, "when the shifts are absent, expectations of price change depend closely on past events."[3] In my view Cagan's attempt, to prove the stability of the demand-for-money function even during hyperinflations, founders on this concession, if the postulate of a shift in the expectations function is required to explain something so central as the transition from inflation to hyperinflation.[4] The apparently close fit of his demand-for-money functions against the data – reflected in the high correlation coefficients which Cagan himself regarded as confirmation of his theory – is in my view explained simply by the fact that the variance in his regressions is dominated by the strong changes in the trend values of his variables. Inflations and hyperinflations, by definition and experience, are periods of rapid trend increases in prices on the one side, and a declining trend in the demand for real money balances (i.e. rising trend in the velocity of circulation) on the other; to have this confirmed adds little to our knowledge.[5]

When the real supply of goods is constant, changes in the price-deflated quantity of money reflect changes in the velocity of circulation. This condition was not satisfied during the early postwar years, since the rate of production and hence the real supply of goods was subject to sharp variation – for example the sharp falls of industrial output in 1919 and 1923 (Diagram 4). This must be borne in mind in seeking to infer changes in the demand for real money balances during those years. But in 1921 and 1922, both years during which the rate of price inflation shifted sharply upwards, industrial production was developing relatively smoothly. Agricultural output did fall drastically in 1922; nevertheless changes in production were proportionately smaller than changes in the demand for real cash balances.

---

[3] P. Cagan: "Monetary Dynamics", p. 77. For criticism of Cagan see above all Rodney L. Jacobs: "A Difficulty with Monetarist Models of Hyperinflation", *Economic Inquiry*, 13 (1975), pp. 337–360.

[4] Ragnar Nurkse: *The Course and Control of Inflation. A Review of Monetary Experience in Europe after World War I. League of Nations Publication 1946 II A 6* (Geneva, 1946), p. 7. The importance of expectations (or "confidence") in the determination of the demand for real money balances (or velocity of circulation of money), and thus of the price level, was already remarked by D'Abernon, British Ambassador in Berlin during the inflation, and also a trained economist. See Viscount D'Abernon: "German Currency: its Collapse and Recovery 1920–1926", *Journal of the Royal Statistical Society*, 90 (1927), pp. 36–37.

[5] On the relation between the demand for real balances and velocity of circulation, see pp. 13 and 99 *supra*.

Table 34 contains an index of the level of real balances $\left(\frac{M}{P}\right)$ as the basis of our study of the demand for money. The index was formed by dividing estimates of the quantity of money by estimates of the price level. Complete monthly estimates of the quantity of money (M_1, M_2, M_3) are not available, so the monetary base (coin, bank notes, deposits at the Reichsbank) was employed as the numerator. The rate of expansion of the monetary base exceeded that of the money supply during the inflation, in virtue of the progressive substitution of central bank money for the forms of money other banks could create (cp. Table 18). Table 34 therefore understates the decline in the demand for real balances during the postwar inflation; the degree of bias is not great however since even in 1920 the monetary base already stood in a 2 : 3 relationship with the deposits at credit institutions (cp. Table 18). Our index needs to be capable of detecting abrupt changes in the quantity of money rather than the actual level, and for this purpose knowledge of movements of the monetary base is sufficient.

Table 34. The real value of the monetary base 1919–23*. 1913 = 1

	1919	1920	1921	1922	1923
Jan.	2.67	0.772	0.978	0.600	0.147
Feb.	2.59	0.588	1.052	0.564	0.136
March	2.81	0.680	1.206	0.476	0.238
April	2.76	0.749	1.145	0.427	0.298
May	2.50	0.802	1.090	0.451	0.250
June	2.73	0.987	1.147	0.461	0.210
July	2.29	0.948	1.068	0.360	0.143
Aug.	1.82	0.905	0.795	0.239	0.199
Sept.	1.67	0.952	0.827	0.229	
Oct.	1.47	0.967	0.714	0.164	
Nov.	1.24	0.934	0.586	0.130	
Dec.	1.25	1.074	0.665	0.184	

Sources: Tables 11 and 1.

* The deflation of the nominal values was undertaken with the aid of the wholesale price index which relates to average prices over the month, whereas nominal monetary base data relate to the stock at the end of the month. Real values, particularly for the hyperinflationary period will tend thus to be overestimated. Abrupt changes in the level of real cash balance holding will nevertheless be clearly discernible, as e.g. in mid-1922 at the start of the hyperinflation.

The selection of an appropriate price index is more problematical. A national product deflator, which would reflect the prices of all goods and services is not available. Cost-of-living indexes (Tables 4, 8 and 9) reflect change in only a subset of all prices in the economy and, in view of the disproportionate representation of administered prices in the underlying "baskets", in a subset which may not fully reflect market forces. The wholesale price index also reflects only a subset of all market prices, but it seems the most suitable of those available (Table 1). It probably reacted more sharply to market forces than any other index.

Government price controls limit the informational content during the war years of all the available price indexes; change in real balances will therefore be studied for the postwar years only. Other considerations also speak against the attempt to push the investigation back into the war years: for example the relative increase in cash settlements owing to the growing importance of the black market, and the extension of the geographical area served by the mark currency owing to its introduction into occupied territories (e.g. Belgium in 1916).[6] As a result, changes in the real quantity of money at that time reflected institutional changes as well as expectation-induced changes in the demand for real cash balances.

Diagram 5. Monthly movements in the real value of the monetary base 1919–22 (Semilogarithmic scale). 1913 = 1
Source: Table 34.

[6] *Die Reichsbank 1901–1925* (Berlin, n.d.), pp. 53–54.

Diagram 5 reveals that at the start of 1919 real balances were very high by comparison with before the war: about three times as high as in 1913. This is partly to be explained by the factors pointed to by the Reichsbank itself during the war as grounds for expanding the note issue: the employment of its notes beyond the German borders, the displacement of credit money by cash and, especially, the hoarding of cash prompted by fears of bank illiquidity or wealth taxation.[7] The revolution of 1918 clearly precipitated further hoarding, for on November 15, 1918 the "Council of People's Commissars" believed itself compelled to issue an "Edict concerning the Security of Bank and Savings Bank Deposits, War Loan, and the Salaries of Public Servants" in order to forestall a run on the banks. This edict stated expressly that the expropriation of bank and savings bank deposits, holdings of money, stock market securities or other deposits was not intended by the Ebert-Haase government.[8]

The high value of real balances in the first half of 1919 is also partly to be explained as the early manifestation of foreign speculative purchases of paper marks, for this began "apparently with the armies of occupation, when the soldiers perceived the opportunities for gain in case the mark should return to par. Through the medium of letters to the folks at home, knowledge of this opportunity was soon disseminated among all classes of people."[9] Rathenau is reported to have remarked, "We were completely surprised at the discovery of this means of procuring funds abroad. After the war Germany's commercial credit in world markets was almost extinct, and we could find practically no sale for interest-bearing bonds. Then, all of a sudden, we discovered that the citizens of foreign countries who were unwilling to purchase interest-bearing bonds were nevertheless willing and anxious to buy non interest-bearing paper currency. We were thereby enabled to buy the food and raw materials required to replenish our depleted stocks."[10]

Thirdly, the high real value of cash balances during the first half of 1919 also reflects the fact of price controls, and their consequence that the quantity of money was not matched by the supply of goods to be had on the official markets. The money was to some extent employed on the black market where prices were higher, and if black market prices had been incorporated in the

---

[7] *Verwaltungsbericht der Reichsbank*, 1916, p. 9.

[8] Cp. Wilhelm Riensberg: "Die preussischen Sparkassen im Kriegs- und Revolutionsjahre 1918", *Zeitschrift des Preussischen Statistischen Landesamts*, 60 (1920), p. 139. One of the ironies of history is that by its "inflation tax" the German government had achieved everything by 1923 that it had given assurances against in this decree.

[9] Harold G. Moulton and Constantine E. McGuire: *Germany's Capacity to Pay. A Study of the Reparation Problem* (New York, 1923), pp. 85–86.

[10] *Ibid.*, p. 86.

construction of the wholesale price index, the quotient $\frac{M}{P}$, our estimate of real balances, would have been lower. The decline in the real balance index in the latter half of 1919 thus partly reflects the process of decontrol which was affecting wholesale markets in raw materials and manufactures during these months[11] but did not reach the markets for basic foodstuffs or the retail stage of distribution until later.[12]

But the decline in real balances after the middle of 1919 is, lastly, also to be explained as the expression of a collapse of confidence precipitated by the imposing of the Reparations burden on Germany. Bresciani-Turroni explained the phenomenon in the following way: "Probably the signing of the treaty provoked a psychological crisis in certain German circles, lack of confidence in the future of Germany dominated the German mind and was manifested – for the first time in the history of the mark – in a 'flight from the mark', i.e. in a demand for foreign exchange."[13]

Essentially the fall in the value of real balances from mid–1919 reflects the movement of the denominator of $\frac{M}{P}$ – prices. This came to a halt in the spring of 1920 as conflict between domestic political factions diminished, increasing imports improved living conditions, industrial production began to grow and, in March 1920, the Erzberger tax reforms were enacted. "[I]t seemed that a certain faith in the mark was again established among the German population."[14] Confidence and optimistic expectations about the future value of the mark remained dominant until the London Ultimatum of May 1921. Prices remained broadly stable, despite the continued growth of the nominal quantity of money (Tables 11, 1). The value of real balances showed an upward trend.

The Reparations schedule dictated in London was regarded as beyond the German capacity to pay not merely in Germany itself but also by Germany's potential creditors abroad.[15] The payment of the first billion gold marks, due

---

[11] The products of the iron and steel industry had already been decontrolled in January 1919. Cp. Hans Schieck: "Der Kampf um die deutsche Wirtschaftspolitik nach dem Novembersturz 1918" (Dissertation, Heidelberg, 1958), p. 233. Reichsbank foreign currency controls were lifted in September 1919. Cp. Rudolf Kühne: *Die Devisenzwangswirtschaft im Deutschen Reich während der Jahre 1916 bis 1926. Eine währungspolitische Reminiszenz* (Frankfurt, 1970), p. 13.

[12] Cp. Table 24.

[13] C. Bresciani-Turroni: *The Economics of Inflation. A Study of Currency Depreciation in Post-War Germany* (London, 1937), p. 54.

[14] *Ibid.*, p. 57.

[15] Cp. p. 139 *supra*.

by October 1921, induced a severe fall in the mark exchange rate and unsettled confidence in the currency, particularly in German business circles. Rapid currency depreciation and fall in the value of real balances followed.

Foreigners, by contrast, retained their confidence in the future value of the mark rather longer than the Germans themselves.[16] Paper marks in the form of bank notes and mark deposits continued to be purchased abroad into the year 1922. But during that year foreign confidence in the mark collapsed as well. Whereas up to the middle of 1922 foreigners were generally counting on a recovery of the mark, the markets thereafter were dominated by transactors moving out of marks or refusing to enter into new mark engagements. This shift in non-German mark expectations may be traced primarily to two events in the political sphere that dashed hopes of a peaceful resolution of the Reparations question, hence of a mark revival:

Firstly, the publication on June 10, 1922 of the report of the Bankers' Committee chaired by J. P. Morgan which the Reparations Commission had appointed. It recommended the postponement of long-term lending to Germany until after a revision of the Reparations schedule. Professional operators in the currency markets, particularly, read this as a sign not to count on a speedy recovery of the mark.

Secondly, the murder of Rathenau on June 22, 1922. This generated disquiet even among the speculating public in foreign countries about Germany's domestic political stability and consequently about the future of the mark (cp. pp. 290 ff.).

When non-Germans joined domestic citizens in the flight from the mark, it triggered off the hyperinflationary phase in the depreciation of the currency: this is usually dated in the summer of 1922.[17] The demand for real balances began to decline precipitously (Diagram 5) and this, together with the more rapid growth of the nominal money supply, caused the rate of price increase to accelerate. P. Beusch emphasized the political factors behind the transition to hyperinflation with this assessment of the situation in the summer of 1922. "If,

[16] Friedrich Hesse: *Die deutsche Wirtschaftslage von 1914 bis 1923* (Jena, 1938), p. 354, noted: "The speculative expectations are not unambiguous. On the German side, they undoubtedly reckon with a depreciation of the mark, abroad, however, with an appreciation." Michael A. Heilperin: *Postwar European Inflations, World War I. A Study of Selected Cases* (New York: National Bureau of Economic Research, unpublished manuscript, 1945), p. 94, observed: "Bearish speculation against the mark started earliest in Germany itself, while the outside world still maintained a belief in the eventual rehabilitation of the currency."

[17] P. Cagan: "Monetary Dynamics", p. 26, designates August 1922 the month when hyperinflation (= more than 50% monthly price increase) began. However, the turning point in price movements can already be detected in July. Cp. Table 1 of the present work.

in spite of all, a new act in the tragedy of the mark was about to begin in the coming months [i.e. after June 1922] the fault lay not so much in the realms of economics and finance as in those of domestic and foreign politics."[18]

In the early months of 1923 the value of real balances recovered a little in connection with the stabilization action promoted by the Reichsbank between February and April as a response to the occupation of the Ruhr. In any case real cash balances had reached the minimum limit dictated by the fact that wages had to be paid in cash. The frequency of wage payments increased of course during the hyperinflation until for some it occurred daily,[19] but with this the ultimate limit was reached.

6.3. Conclusion: Ranking the Reasons for the Inflation

In this chapter and the last, the inflation, i.e. the price increase, has been "factorized" into the three other elements of the "equation of exchange" – the money supply (chapter 5) and the real supply of goods and the velocity of circulation (the present chapter). The political forces causing changes in the behavior of these factors have been examined. In this concluding section I wish to "weight" the contributions of each of these factors and of the political forces behind them, to price change.

There can be no doubt that the growth in the quantity of money – principally caused by the budget deficits of the Reich – represented "at least an essential *condition* without which the general rise in prices could not have gone far."[20] The political grounds of the budget deficit must therefore bear the chief responsibility for the inflation, at least in the long run. Rising expenditures were the active agents creating the deficits – war expenditures between 1914 and November 1918, thereafter Reparations, but also welfare and employment expenditures. Defeat, then, was the event in the international political arena which determined the subsequent course of the inflation; the revolution of November 1918 was the corresponding domestic political event because of its budgetary implications: parties came to power that were concerned to

[18] Paul Beusch: *Währungszerfall und Währungsstabilisierung* (Berlin, 1928), p. 2.

[19] Gerhard Bry: *Wages in Germany 1871–1945* (Princeton, 1960), p. 224.

[20] R. Nurkse: *Course and Control*, p. 17.

promote social reforms and a more equitable distribution of income and wealth.

Tax revenues lagged far behind expenditures. Between 1914 and 1918 this was on account of the weak position of the Reich relative to the states in the fiscal structure; between 1918 and 1923 it was a consequence of the political weakness of the republican governments which prevented their capitalizing on their centralization of the tax system by pushing through the severe taxation measures necessary to avoid inflation.

Other factors dominated the short-run behavior of the price level however, namely real supply of goods and the demand for real cash balances, and their determinants.

During 1919 and 1923 political circumstances at home and abroad disrupted production sufficiently to add substantially to the pressure on prices, whereas the growth of production in the intervening years tended rather to ease it.

The velocity of circulation of money, changing in inverse relation to the demand for real money balances, appears to have been the most variable of the factors determining the rate of price increase. It is principally a function of expectations about the future value of the currency. The main influence on the state of these expectations was exerted by political events. In the closing years of the war, particularly, the mark exchange rate reflected movements in the military situation and the anticipated political consequences of possible victory or defeat. The manner has already been described in which after 1918 external political factors such as the Reparations question and its relation to Germany's credit-standing abroad, and domestic political factors such as the 1918 Revolution and the consequent faction fighting between supporters and opponents of the republic, affected the state of confidence and the demand for real cash balances. The importance of expectations and confidence in the currency to the course of the inflation is registered in the fact that between spring 1920 and May 1921 the price level scarcely changed despite considerable expansion of the money supply. The demand for money was rising as a "stabilization of confidence" took place. Nor can the commencement of the hyperinflationary phase be explained unless the importance of the collapse of this confidence is appreciated.

Part Three
The Effects of the Inflation

Chapter 7
Employment, Fluctuations, Growth

7.1. The Domestic Economy

Towards the end of 1912 the last prewar business cycle reached its peak. Recovering from the world-wide effects of the 1907 U.S. financial crisis,[1] the international economy had entered a long upswing, but this came to an end in the international tensions and threat of general hostilities accompanying the outbreak of the first Balkan War in October 1912. In Germany as elsewhere panic selling occurred on the stock market, loans were called in and the hoarding of cash jumped up; as a result, "1913 was dominated by shortage of capital and incipient overproduction."[2] From the conjuncture of his cyclical indicators Friedrich Hesse deduced "that before the war the German economy was showing signs of stagnation."[3] This was principally a result of the threat of war, and it is at least possible that a pacific policy designed to remove that threat could have revived the economy, as may be concluded from the following assessment. "German conditions weaken in almost exact proportion to the increase in international political tensions. Slight signs of trade revival... appeared at the start of 1914 and again in May, but they are immediately extinguished again by political events."[4]

When war broke out, its initial effect on economic activity was severe. War brought administrative measures in its train which greatly disrupted business dealings, and it induced uncertainty about the future which brought private investment activity almost to a standstill. "People could see the difficulties and could not tell how everything would turn out. The whole affair seemed like a devastating body-blow at the economic organism and at economic links with

---

[1] Joseph A. Schumpeter: *Business Cycles. A Theoretical, Historical and Statistical Analysis of the Capitalist Process* (New York, 2 vols. 1939), vol. 1, pp. 425ff.

[2] Arthur Spiethoff: *Die wirtschaftlichen Wechsellagen. Aufschwung, Krise, Stockung* (Tübingen, 2 Bde. 1955), Bd. 1, p. 139.

[3] Friedrich Hesse: *Die deutsche Wirtschaftslage von 1914 bis 1923. Krieg, Geldblähe und Wechsellagen* (Jena, 1938), p. 13. Cp. Reinhard Spree: *Wachstumstrends und Konjunkturzyklen in der deutschen Wirtschaft von 1820 bis 1913* (Göttingen, 1978), esp. the figure on p. 107 showing the sharp break in the trade cycle in 1913.

[4] F. Hesse: *Deutsche Wirtschaftslage*, p. 13.

other countries; vast amounts of manpower had suddenly been abstracted from their normal occupations, and managers and foremen removed from their posts. On top of this came the dislocating effects of the troop mobilization on the means of transport. All this caused the spirit of enterprise to flag."[5] This account leaves unmentioned the liquidity squeeze of the first few weeks of the war, described earlier in the present work,[6] and the dampening effect of the resultant dearness of credit on the private sector's propensity to invest.

The result was a sharp drop in productive activity which is reflected particularly in labor market statistics (Table 35). Unemployment among trade unionists jumped from 2.9% in July 1914 to 22.4% in August; not until the middle of 1915 did it again fall below the July 1914 figure. These figures even underestimate the reduction in employment due to the call-up of much of the labor force. In any case, the government found the actual unemployment problem sufficiently menacing to cause it, amid its war efforts, to introduce measures simply to create work: the schedule of public buildings' construction was advanced and emergency relief works were opened up. A Central Agency for Job Opportunities (*Reichsstelle für Arbeitsvermittlung*)[7] was established to improve the flow of information on the labor market, thus assisting mobility.

More efficient intermediation between jobs and workers was so much the more important in view of the peculiar distribution of job opportunities in the reviving economy, even in the private sector. It served as a supply-side lubricant of the transition to a war economy, complementing the demand-side lubricant of inflationary financing. Export-dependent and consumer-goods industries would be forced to reckon with thin business for the war's duration, whereas war-related industries could count on high and rising demand for their products: these differences would be reflected in the demand for labor. As early as autumn 1914 the demands of war production were causing manpower shortages in the engineering and metals industries, but building and textile workers were suffering severe unemployment.[8] Inflation eased the

---

[5] *Ibid.*, p. 22.

[6] Cp. pp. 64–65 *supra*.

[7] F. Hesse: *Deutsche Wirtschaftslage*, p. 24.

[8] Detailed statistics will be found in the *Reichsarbeitsblatt* 1913/1914 and subsequent years. On the structural change in the economy during the inflation cp. Wolfram Fischer: "Bergbau, Industrie und Handwerk 1914–1970", in H. Aubin and W. Zorn (eds.): *Handbuch der deutschen Wirtschafts- und Sozialgeschichte* (Stuttgart, 2 Bde. 1971–76), Bd. 2 (1976), pp. 796ff; also Wolfram Fischer and Peter Czada: "Wandlungen in der deutschen Industriestruktur im 20. Jahrhundert. Ein statistisch-deskriptiver Ansatz", in Gerhard A. Ritter (ed.): *Entstehung und Wandel der modernen Gesellschaft. Festschrift für Hans Rosenberg zum 65. Geburtstag* (Berlin, 1970), pp. 116ff.

economic transformation and particularly the transfer of labor, because it created an environment where price and hence wage increases in the war industries, rather than price and hence wage cuts in the purely civilian industries, opened up the differentials necessary to attract labor to the former. Price increases caused real wages to deteriorate in all industries during the war, but money wage increases made the deterioration smaller in the war-related than in the civilian industries.[9]

Table 35. Unemployment among members of trade unions 1914–23 (%)

	1914	1915	1916	1917	1918	1919	1920	1921	1922	1923
January	4.7	6.5	2.6	1.7	0.9	6.6	3.4	4.5	3.3	4.2
February	3.7	5.1	2.8	1.6	0.8	6.0	2.9	4.7	2.7	5.2
March	2.8	3.3	2.2	1.3	0.9	3.9	1.9	3.7	1.1	5.6
April	2.8	2.9	2.3	1.0	0.8	5.2	1.9	3.9	0.9	7.0
May	2.8	2.9	2.5	1.0	0.8	3.8	2.7	3.7	0.7	6.2
June	2.5	2.5	2.5	0.9	0.8	2.5	4.0	3.0	0.6	4.1
July	2.9	2.7	2.4	0.8	0.7	3.1	6.0	2.6	0.6.	3.5
August	22.4	2.6	2.2	0.8	0.7	3.1	5.9	2.2	0.7	6.3
September	15.7	2.6	2.1	0.8	0.8	2.2	4.5	1.4	0.8	9.9
October	10.9	2.5	2.0	0.7	0.7	2.6	4.2	1.2	1.4	19.1
November	8.2	2.5	1.7	0.7	1.8	2.9	3.9	1.4	2.0	23.4
December	7.2	2.6	1.6	0.9	5.1	2.9	4.1	1.6	2.8	28.2

Source: Reichsarbeitsblatt, 1913/14 and subsequent vols. They are brought together in F. Hesse: *Deutsche Wirtschaftslage*, pp. 478ff.

Liquidity problems did not affect the flow of orders to manufacturing except during the first weeks of the war, for inflationary war financing eliminated them. The Reich, particularly, paid little attention to price in its ordering of military equipment; its access to the note printing presses removed the necessity of doing so. Helfferich described a buyer's panic among the various Army purchasing agencies as they sought to outbid each other;[10] profiteering with its undesirable redistributional implications was doubtless the consequence. Be that as it may, this "money doesn't matter" attitude must have stimulated production: for while Table 32 shows that production fell after war broke out (owing to the economic dislocation already described), and while it remained below the prewar level, the rate of decline was moderate between 1915 and 1918, and least between 1916 and 1917, following the initiation of the inflationary Hindenburg program. The output-exciting effects of

[9] Statistics in Gerhard Bry: *Wages in Germany 1871–1945* (Princeton, 1960), p. 211. Cp. also Jürgen Kocka: *Klassengesellschaft im Krieg 1914–1918* (Göttingen, 1973), p. 18.

[10] Karl Helfferich: *Der Weltkrieg* (Berlin, 3 Bde. 1919), Bd. 2, p. 134.

deficit-financed state purchases are most clearly reflected on the labor market. Unemployment among trade unionists was below one percent from mid – 1917 to the end of the war, and the fact, that from 1917 Sickness Insurance statistics revealed more female than male employees, reflects the intensified civilian mobilization of people marginal to the labor force.[11]

Inflationary financing, especially during the second half of the war, may thus have prevented a sharper fall in output as a whole. The ample supplies of liquidity with which it nourished the economy may also have substantially eased the required restructuring of production. How extensive this wartime restructuring was, may be deduced from Tables 36 and 37. Production in the war industries remained above the average for industry as a whole throughout the war, in the case of non-ferrous metals even exceeding the 1913 level. But in the purely civilian industries output dropped much more than the average, and in the case of housebuilding virtually ceased altogether. The structure of profits[12] and wages[13] shifted correspondingly, so that labor and capital were attracted to the war industries rather than to the others (cp. Table 37). By 1918 employment in the war industries was some 10% greater than it had been in 1913, that in the "mixed" industries some 37% smaller, and that in the purely civilian industries no less than 59% smaller. Overtime was worked above all in the war industries whereas the authorities even decreed short-time working in certain civilian industries.[14] Thus the balance of labor inputs measured in man-hours tipped even more sharply towards the war industries than Table 37, measured in persons, suggests.

When the war ended unemployment rose very sharply at first, mainly owing to military demobilization. The unemployment percentages in Table 35 do not fully reflect this, because most ex-soldiers seeking employment were initially not members of trade unions. The most important labor union organization, the *Freie Gewerkschaften*, grew from 1.5 million members in the third quarter of 1918 to 7.3 million members in the fourth quarter of 1919.[15] Production now dropped well below that of the closing stages of the war, the index for 1919 as

[11] Statistics in F. Hesse: *Deutsche Wirtschaftslage*, pp. 478 ff.; and, in greater detail, in the *Reichsarbeitsblatt*, 1913/14 and subsequent years.

[12] Statistics in Rolf Wagenführ: *Die Industriewirtschaft. Entwicklungstendenzen der deutschen und internationalen Industrieproduktion 1860 bis 1932. Vierteljahrshefte zur Konjunkturforschung, Sonderheft 31* (Berlin, 1933), p. 23.

[13] Statistics in G. Bry: *Wages*, p. 211.

[14] Jürgen Kuczynski: *Die Geschichte der Lage der Arbeiter unter dem Kapitalismus, Bd. 4: Darstellung der Lage der Arbeiter in Deutschland von 1900 bis 1917/18* (Berlin-East, 1967), pp. 390–391.

[15] Heinrich A. Winkler: *Von der Revolution zur Stabilisierung. Arbeiter und Arbeiterbewegung in der Weimarer Republik 1918 bis 1924*, Berlin 1984, p. 275.

Tables 36. Indexes of production in important sectors and branches of industry, 1913–18. 1913 = 100

Branch of industry	1913	1914	1915	1916	1917	1918
War industries						
Mining	100	84	78	86	90	83
Iron and steel	100	78	68	81	83	53
Non-ferrous metals	100	89	72	113	155	234
Civilian industries						
Housebuilding	100	68	30	10	4	4
Building materials	100	88	69	59	58	35
Merchant ships	100	73	65	75	61	42
'Mixed' industries						
Textiles	100	87	65	27	22	17
Alcohol, tobacco	100	92	88	84	67	63
All industries	100	83	67	64	62	57

Source: R. Wagenführ: *Industriewirtschaft*, p. 23.

Table 37. The relative importance of sectors of industry according to the occupational statistics of the Social Insurance, 1913–18. 1913 = 100

Sector of industry	1913	1914	1915	1916	1917	1918
War industries	100	88	78	89	103	110
Civilian industries	100	91	53	46	43	41
'Mixed' industries	100	91	77	69	63	63

Source: R. Wagenführ: *Industriewirtschaft*, p. 23.

a whole standing about one quarter below that for 1918.[16] The end to the purchasing of war matériel was the reason: the economy now faced a restructuring process as drastic as that faced in 1914; only in the reverse direction.

The government made deliberate efforts to counteract this drop in production and investment activity, as well as to facilitate the required restructuring, by means of its demobilization measures and the stepping up of railroad and postal and other investment programs.[17] The inflationary means used to fi-

[16] Cp. Table 32 *supra*.

[17] On this see some statistics in *Deutschlands Wirtschaft, Währung und Finanzen. Im Auftrage der Reichsregierung den von der Reparationskommission eingesetzten Sachverständigenausschüssen übergeben* (Berlin, 1924), pp. 100ff. On the demobilization, see above all Gerald D. Feldman: "Wirtschafts- und sozialpolitische Probleme der deutschen Demobilmachung 1918/19", in Hans Mommsen *et al.* (eds.): *Industrielles System und politische Entwicklung in der Weimarer Republik* (Düsseldorf, 1974), pp. 618–636. Hans Schieck: "Der Kampf um die deutsche Wirtschaftspolitik nach dem Novemberumsturz 1918" (Dissertation, Heidelberg, 1958).

nance these and other expenditures, such as the compensation paid to industrialists for property forfeited in ceded territories, fed the economy with additional liquidity. This factor, too, no doubt facilitated both the general recovery of industrial output after 1919 and the specific process of restructuring.

Diagram 6. Price and unemployment movements 1919–22 (Semi-logarithmic scale; monthly data)
Source: Table 35 and 1

The strong influence of currency depreciation upon the rate of economic activity in Germany[18] is demonstrated by the almost exactly inverse movements of unemployment and prices in Diagram 6 (the same could be shown for unemployment and the exchange rate). The period between the start of 1919 and spring 1920 was one both when prices were rising continuously and when unemployment was tending to fall. Thereupon the currency entered a period of "relative stabilization", and the unemployment rate jumped from 1.9% in March and April 1920 to 6% by July, not falling back below 3% until after the

[18] On this see Peter Czada: "Grosse Inflation und Wirtschaftswachstum", in H. Mommsen *et al.* (eds.): *Industrielles System*, pp. 386–395. Gustav Clausing: *Die wirtschaftlichen Wechsellagen von 1919 bis 1932* (Jena, 1933).

start of the next phase of currency depreciation in May 1921 (Table 35). In 1922, as the rate of price increase accelerated towards hyperinflation, labor scarcity, or "overemployment" predominated: the unemployment rate was generally below one percent as it had been during the inflationary conditions of the second half of the war.

An argument frequently encountered is that much of the stimulus to production from inflation was transmitted *via* exports.[19] Since the fall in the mark exchange rate was generally more rapid than the rise in German prices relative to prices abroad (cp. Table 2), the competitivity of German products on world markets was enhanced. However the domestic "multiplier" effects of this were smaller, probably, than has often been supposed. Between 1919 and 1924 German exports were substantially less by value than German imports,[20] the latter consisting mainly of primary products with low price elasticities of demand. Hence the indirect effects transmitted from inflation to production *via* the external sector were probably redistributive rather than expansionary overall: the stimulus afforded by falling exchange rates to export-orientated industries such as engineering would be offset by their retardative effects on sectors such as food, drink and tobacco whose outputs were sold at home but whose raw material inputs were to a significant extent purchased abroad. In actuality the stimulus to aggregate production from inflation was probably transmitted mainly through the fall in real interest rates which the rising prices brought about, and which animated domestic investment. This stimulus would have been efficacious even had Germany been cut off from world markets; there were already signs of its operation during the wartime Allied blockade.

International comparisons serve as a means of isolating the effects of inflation on production (Table 38). In France reconstruction policy was associated with a moderate degree of inflation and, although the hostilities on French soil had done great damage to her productive capacity, French industrial output exceeded its 1913 level from 1924 onwards. In Great Britain by contrast the 1920 level of industrial output already equaled the 1913 level, but the policy of deflation embarked on in that year permitted only a limited recovery of production thereafter from the level to which it dropped in 1921; as a result

---

19 The consensus of C. Bresciani-Turroni: *The Economics of Inflation. A Study of Currency Depreciation in Post-War Germany* (London, 1937), pp. 227–228, F. D. Graham: *Exchange, Prices and Production in Hyper-Inflation: Germany, 1920–23* (New York, reprint 1967), pp. 209 ff. and R. Wagenführ: *Industriewirtschaft*, p. 28.

20 The so-called McKenna Committee estimated the German deficit on merchandise account between 1919 and 1923 at 6.3–7.3 bn. gold marks. See p. 283 *infra*.

the 1913 level was not attained again, not even in the more prosperous years of the later 1920s. Industrial output in Germany rose steeply between 1919 and 1922, suffered a severe setback in 1923 owing to the occupation of the Ruhr and the stabilization crisis, recovered in 1924 almost to the 1922 level, and in 1927 for the first time exceeded the 1913 level.

Table 38. Indexes of industrial production in France, Great Britain and Germany, 1913, 1919–31. 1928 = 100

	France*	Great Britain	Germany*
1913	79	107	98
1919	45		37
1920	49	107	54
1921	43	73	65
1922	61	87	70
1923	69	95	46
1924	85	98	69
1925	84	93	81
1926	98	72	78
1927	86	103	98
1928	100	100	100
1929	109	106	101
1930	110	97	89
1931	98	89	72

* contemporary boundaries
Source: R. Wagenführ: *Industriewirtschaft*, p. 64.

Petzina and Abelshauser regard the 1920s as a period of "relative stagnation" in the German economy, similar to that obtaining in the U.K. at the same time; however they explicitly exclude the inflationary years up to 1922 from this characterization.[21] Inflation, according to Abelshauser, promoted capital accumulation during the early postwar years, thus "exerting a positive [influence] on a variable critical to reconstruction and growth – namely the investment ratio."[22] By inducing forced saving, it also generated the required

[21] Dietmar Petzina and Werner Abelshauser: "Zum Problem der relativen Stagnation der deutschen Wirtschaft in den zwanziger Jahren", in H. Mommsen *et al.* (eds.): *Industrielles System*, p. 64.

[22] Werner Abelshauser: "Inflation und Stabilisierung. Zum Problem ihrer makroökonomischen Auswirkungen auf die Rekonstruktion der deutschen Wirtschaft nach dem Ersten Weltkrieg", in Otto Büsch and Gerald D. Feldman (eds.): *Historische Prozesse der deutschen Inflation 1914 bis 1924. Ein Tagungsbericht* (Berlin, 1978), p. 168. See also Werner Abelshauser und Dietmar Petzina: "Krise und Rekonstruktion. Zur Interpretation der gesamtwirtschaftlichen Entwicklung Deutschlands im 20. Jahrhundert", in W. Abelshauser und D. Petzina (eds.): *Deutsche Wirt-*

investment finance. Laursen and Pedersen concluded that real investment was at least as high during the inflation as before the war.[23] Real postwar national income was certainly less than prewar, and so their conclusion implies that the investment ratio during the postwar inflation period exceeded even the 15.5% which Petzina reported for 1910–13,[24] exceeding too the approximately similar ratio that was achieved in the Federal Republic during the 1950s' reconstruction period.[25] In 1925–9, after the currency stabilization, the ratio of net investment to net national income was put at only 10.5%.[26]

Against this background we may assess the judgment of Bresciani-Turroni[27] and others that although the inflation promoted economic activity, employment and growth in the short run, the high level of capital accumulation it achieved was in fact a waste of economic resources. Investment appraisal during the inflation lacked "any secure basis for judging profitability in the long term, because relative prices were continually changing."[28] The result, in the view of these writers, was an excrescent mushrooming of fixed capacity which had to be cut back by a painful process of rationalization once

---

schaftsgeschichte im Industriezeitalter. Konjunktur, Krise, Wachstum (Königstein/Ts., 1981), pp. 62–63. For the German machine building industry this general assessment has not been found to be true in an empirical study by Dieter Lindenlaub: "Maschinenbauunternehmen in der Inflation 1919 bis 1923: Unternehmenshistorische Überlegungen zu einigen Inflationstheorien", in G. D. Feldman *et al.* (eds.): *The German Inflation Reconsidered. A Preliminary Balance* (Berlin/New York, 1982), pp. 49–106. More extensively Lindenlaub's monograph with the same title (Berlin/New York, 1985).

[23] K. Laursen and J. Pedersen: *The German Inflation 1918–1923* (Amsterdam, 1964), pp. 82–83. In his article "Wachstum und Wechsellagen 1914–1970", in H. Aubin and W. Zorn (eds.): *Handbuch*, Bd. 2, p. 701, Knut Borchardt expresses doubts concerning the thesis of a strong investment boom during the inflation. His doubts are apparently confirmed by the only direct estimates of the growth of the real capital stock between 1914 and 1923 – those of G. Gehrig: "Eine Zeitreihe für den Sachkapitalbestand 1925 bis 1938 und 1950 bis 1957", *Ifo-Studien*, 7 (1961), p. 35. This series is cumulated for these years from estimates of steel production. But in view of the loss of steel-making capacity consequent on the territorial cessions of 1919, steel production was probably abnormally low in relation to aggregate investment in these years; indeed a large part of that investment was directed to making good that lost capacity.

[24] Dietmar Petzina: *Die deutsche Wirtschaft in der Zwischenkriegszeit* (Wiesbaden, 1977), p. 177.

[25] *Ibid.*

[26] *Ibid.*

[27] C. Bresciani-Turroni: *Economics*, p. 197. He also remarks on the injurious effects of hyperinflation on labor productivity: C. Bresciani-Turroni: "The Movements of Wages in Germany during the Depreciation of the Mark and after Stabilization", *Journal of the Royal Statistical Society*, 92 (1929), p. 397. See too Ausschuss zur Untersuchung der Erzeugungs- und Absatzbedingungen der deutschen Wirtschaft, IV. Unterausschuss (Arbeitsleistung), Bde. 1–9 (Berlin, 1927–30).

[28] R. Wagenführ: *Industriewirtschaft*, p. 28.

the mark had been stabilized. The real work of reconstructing the German economy did not begin until after the 1923 stabilization.[29]

This judgment fails to recognize the double macroeconomic significance of investment activity. Not only does it add to aggregate productive capacity once it is completed; it also stimulates aggregate income and demand while it is being undertaken. The reason why the productive capacities constructed during the inflation proved unprofitable and in need of rationalization after 1924 was not simply that the basis for investment appraisal had been unsound when they had been embarked on, causing them to extend the economy's productive potential in the "wrong" direction. It was also a consequence of general demand deficiency in the post-stabilization economy, flowing from an investment ratio *at that time* which was low by comparison with the periods of normal growth before 1914 and after 1948. Thus demand deficiency not only caused much of the fixed capital stock to seem unproductive; it also left a large part of the labor supply unemployed. It cannot be blamed on the preceding inflation. "Impediments to growth were an experience common to all the major industrial countries in Europe. Tendencies toward stagnation were present in their economic structures even before 1913 and after 1918 only grew to critical proportions."[30] The inflation-induced investment boom in Germany overcame these growth constraints and eliminated the demand deficiency for a few years. That during those years the output of the investment goods industries reached a scale in relation to national income which was in line with that of the "normal" growth periods before the First and after the Second World Wars, can hardly be judged a misallocation of resources. "Structural weakness" is much rather to be discerned in the low investment activity of the later 1920s, whatever its domestic or international causes, than in the high investment activity of the earlier 1920s.

7.2. The World Economy

The fiscal policy of the German government and resultant monetary expansion did not just affect aggregate demand, output and employment within Germany's own borders. Particularly after the lifting of the Allied blockade in the summer of 1919 and the decontrol of domestic prices around that time, its

[29] C. Bresciani-Turroni: *Economics*, p. 403.

[30] D. Petzina und W. Abelshauser: "Zum Problem der relativen Stagnation", p. 75.

effects were also felt abroad. When Germany rejoined the international economy, her restocking demands for imported raw materials and other productive inputs were initially high. Thereafter, and as long as deficit financing continued to sustain the growth of industrial output, the reintegration of labor into the productive process[1] and the expansion of national income,[2] an "income effect" would cause German import demand to keep rising as well. To the extent that this resulted in growing import surpluses, the boom in Germany was raising aggregate demand in foreign countries. The increase in their exports to Germany represented an exogenous increment to aggregate demand in their own countries analogous to a domestic investment boom and with corresponding multiplier effects on their own domestic products.[3]

The cycle of economic activity in Germany, in the other major industrial belligerent states (particularly the U.S.A. and U.K.), and also in the neutral European economies ran in phase during the war. In each it was subject to the common influence of the war effort, and the huge munitions demands affected belligerent and neutral economies alike. This congruence lasted till the beginning of 1920, for up till that time the common problems of reconversion to peace production, reintegration of demobilized servicemen and satisfaction of restocking demands also dominated the several economies. The various ex-belligerent governments all rapidly removed wartime controls, thus all promoting a revival of private enterprise, to which also they all gave full scope by financing their demobilization policies out of continuing budget deficits.[4] All pegged interest rates at low levels in 1919, mainly to facilitate the cheap funding of their large internal wartime debts and to prevent price falls on existing government bonds.[5]

In the second half of 1919 particularly, a pronounced boom developed worldwide, and was attended everywhere by sharply rising prices, even in

---

[1] Cp. Table 35.

[2] Cp. Tables 32 and 40.

[3] On the underlying theory see the summary exposition in Erich Schneider: *Einführung in die Wirtschaftstheorie, Teil III: Geld, Kredit, Volkseinkommen und Beschäftigung* (Tübingen, 9th edn. 1965), pp. 303–311. Cp. Rudiger Dornbusch and Stanley Fischer: *Macroeconomics* (New York, 2nd edn. 1981), esp. pp. 680ff. Charles P. Kindleberger and Peter H. Lindert: *International Economics* (Homewood, 6th edn. 1978), pp. 349–382. More generally, Fritz Machlup: *International Trade and the National Income Multiplier* (Philadelphia, 1943).

[4] Derek H. Aldcroft: *From Versailles to Wall Street 1919–1929* (London, 1977), pp. 66ff. Particularly on the U.S.A. cp. Hal B. Lary: *The United States in the World Economy* (Washington, D.C., 1943), p. 138. For Germany, Hans Schieck: "Der Kampf um die deutsche Wirtschaftspolitik nach dem Novemberumsturz 1918" (Dissertation, Heidelberg, 1958).

[5] D.H. Aldcroft: *From Versailles*, p. 67. On the U.S.A. see Milton Friedman and Anna J. Schwartz: *A Monetary History of the United States 1867–1960* (Princeton, 1963), pp. 223ff.

"hard" currency countries such as the U. S. A.[6] Thus in Great Britain the wholesale price index jumped from 246 in May 1919 to a peak of 325 in May 1920 (1913 = 100) – a jump of nearly forty percent. Wholesale prices in the U. S. A. at their peak, also in May 1920, were some twenty-five percent above their 1919 level. The price peak in France was reached in April 1920; that month French prices stood some seventy-seven percent higher than in April 1919.[7] This boom greatly facilitated the transition to civilian production and the reintegration of labor in non-war-related occupations.

In the several countries the annual averages of industrial output (1913 = 100 in each case) rose rapidly between 1919 and 1920: from 56 to 61 in France (i. e. by about nine percent),[8] from 55.1 to 61.2 in the U. K. (about eleven percent).[9] In the U. S. A. manufacturing output in the first quarter of 1920 was almost nine percent higher than during the corresponding quarter of the year before.[10] Unemployment rates, where they are known, were similarly low: 2.4% in both 1919 and 1920 in the U. K.;[11] 1.5% and 5.2% respectively in the U. S. A., yet the rise is exclusively attributable to the fall in military employment: civilian employment continued to increase.[12]

At the end of 1919 and beginning of 1920 it began to be recognized in Britain, more ominously in the U. S. A., that the boom and its inflationary manifestations would have to be brought under control; this recognition dictated a recasting of monetary policy. In Great Britain the rate for three-monthly money had lain below 4% per annum up to October 1919; but if the weak exchange rate were not to be further weakened by capital outflows once international transactions had been liberalized, short rates would have to rise. The three-monthly rate was therefore pushed up to 6¾% by the second half of 1920.[13] Fiscal reservations about a like step finally disappeared in the U. S. A. once the budget had been stabilized. From November 1919 the Federal Reserve Board pursued a "dear money" policy with the aim of breaking domestic

[6] W. Arthur Lewis: *Economic Survey 1919–1939* (London, 1949), pp. 18–19.

[7] International Conference of Economic Services (ed.): *International Abstracts of Economic Statistics 1919–1930* (London, 1934), pp. 72, 105, 210.

[8] *Ibid.*, p. 75.

[9] Brian R. Mitchell: *European Historical Statistics 1750–1970* (London, 1975), pp. 356–357.

[10] *International Abstracts*, p. 213.

[11] B. R. Mitchell: *European Historical Statistics*, p. 168.

[12] Ben J. Wattenberg: *The Statistical History of the United States. From Colonial Times to the Present* (New York, 1976), p. 126.

[13] *International Abstracts*, p. 105. Derek H. Aldcroft: *The Inter-War Economy. Britain, 1919–1939* (London, 1970), p. 326.

inflation.[14] Three-monthly money, which in the first nine months of 1919 had cost less than 6%, averaged above 8% in 1920.

It is a moot point whether, as for example Jacques Néré[15] or Jørgen Pedersen[16] assert, the monetary measures just described, together perhaps with the deflationary swing in the U. S. and British fiscal balances, bear the sole or at least the major responsibility for breaking the world economic boom in 1920, or whether autonomous structural factors would have caused an upper turning point anyway without the policy changes;[17] but the matter cannot be discussed here. The fact is that the "dear money" policy which the U. S. A. instituted at the turn of 1919/1920 and further intensified in June 1920 powerfully aggravated the economic slide into depression. Friedman and Schwartz found that between August 1920 and February 1921 there occurred "the sharpest price decline in the period covered by our money series and perhaps also in the whole history of the United States."[18] The same point holds for output and employment in the industrial sector. Aldcroft reached similar conclusions regarding the British economy.[19]

A few figures will illustrate the intensity of the 1921 depression. Between 1920 and 1921 industrial production fell by 20% in the U. S. A.,[20] by 18.6% in the U. K.,[21] and by 11% in France.[22] Between the same two years two million jobs disappeared in the U. S. A.; unemployment reached 12% in the second of them.[23] On average 2.4% of trade union members were unemployed in Britain in 1920; 14.8% on average in 1921.[24] At the bottom of the slump, about mid-year 1921, 2.4 million insured persons in Great Britain were out of work, 22% of the total insured population.[25]

---

[14] M. Friedman and A. J. Schwartz: *Monetary History*, pp. 229–230.

[15] Jacques Néré: *La Crise de 1929* (Paris, 1967), p. 21.

[16] Jørgen Pedersen: "Some Notes on the Economic Policy of the United States during the Period 1919–1932", in H. Hegeland (ed.): *Money, Growth and Methodology. Essays in Honour of Johan Akerman* (Lund, 1961), p. 47.

[17] Cp. J. D. Pilgrim: "The Upper Turning Point of 1920. A Reappraisal", *Explorations in Economic History*, 11 (1974), pp. 271 ff. He rejects the structural hypothesis in favor of the monetary.

[18] Friedman and Schwartz: *Monetary History*, p. 232.

[19] D. H. Aldcroft: *Inter-War Economy*, p. 34.

[20] B. J. Wattenberg: *Statistical History*, p. 667.

[21] D. H. Aldcroft: *Inter-War Economy*, p. 32.

[22] *International Abstracts*, p. 65. Further internationally comparative tables of growth rates and related indicators are to be found in Angus Maddison: *Economic Growth in the West. Comparative Experience in Europe and North America* (New York, 1964), and Ingvar Svennilson: *Growth and Stagnation in the European Economy* (Geneva, 1954).

[23] Wattenberg: *Statistical History*, p. 126.

[24] Mitchell: *European Historical Statistics*, p. 168.

[25] Aldcroft: *Inter-War Economy*, p. 37.

Errors of monetary policy played a part either in initiating or at least in aggravating the slide into world depression both in 1920/21 and between 1929 and 1932. The astonishing feature of the earlier slump however, sharply distinguishing it from the later, was the speed of recovery out of it. The significance of this statement becomes clearer when we recollect that the angle of descent into the earlier slump was also far more sheer than that into the later: in the 1920/21 slump U. S. wholesale prices fell on average by 3.4% per month but by only 0.9% per month between 1929 and 1932. The corresponding monthly average rates of decline for U. S. industrial production are 2.4% and 1.5%.[26] Why then, in spite of the more virulent collapse, was the lower turning point reached so much more rapidly in the earlier slump than in the later?

In my judgment the answer to this question lies in the fact that in 1920, when many of the world's major industrial states were swinging their fiscal and monetary policies on to a deflationary course, one of them – Germany – refused to join in. In those countries currency stabilization, whether internal (as in the U. S. A.) or external (more particularly in the U. K.) was the overriding policy goal, but in Germany full employment took precedence. This is apparent from the fact that in the second half of 1920 and in 1921, public sector investment was stepped up in Germany as a work-creating measure within the framework of the so-called "productive" unemployment relief.[27] The ranking of policy goals at the time is revealed by a communication from the minister-president of Prussia to the chancellor of the Reich, proposing the extensive work creation measures that ultimately gained the approval of and financial support from the Reich government. It would be most deeply regrettable, the document comments (in the course of other remarks), "if purely financial exigencies were to prevent the creation of work opportunities for tens of thousands of workers."[28]

In January 1921 Walther Rathenau, too, speaking as a government advisor, acknowledged the utility of inflation as a prophylactic against Germany's "catching" the slump currently afflicting other industrial nations, and urged the government to act accordingly. "He was not afraid of inflation. If he might make an aside not strictly relevant to the agenda: should the depression that has attacked England with full force spread across to us, we ought to print money a bit faster and start construction works, using the employment these

---

[26] R. A. Gordon: "Cyclical Experience in the Inter-War Period. The Investment Boom of the Twenties", in National Bureau of Economic Research (ed.): *Conference on Business Cycles* (New York, 1951), p. 171. D. H. Aldcroft: *From Versailles*, p. 69.

[27] Cp. *Akten der Reichskanzlei. Weimarer Republik. Das Kabinett Fehrenbach*, Dokumente Nr. 84, 164, 184, and 215.

[28] *Ibid.*, Dokument 84, p. 219, n. 2.

create as a dam against the depression. It was incorrect when people said that printing money was bringing us to ruin."[29]

Economic conditions in Germany in 1920 and 1921 certainly presented a striking contrast to those in the other leading industrial countries. Despite the new taxes introduced under the Erzberger reforms and designed to enlarge the Reich's fiscal base,[30] expansion of the floating debt remained an important means of defraying Reich expenditure.[31] Reichsbank discount rate and private rates on the money market remained low. It is true that the general price level and the exchange rate became rather more stable between the springs of 1920 and 1921,[32] and that this, together with depression abroad, dampened foreign demand for German exports, and created difficulties for export-dependent industries. Domestic demand nevertheless remained buoyant and as a result German industrial production continued to climb – by 20.4% between 1920 and 1921, following a 46% increase between 1919 and 1920.[33] Average unemployment during 1921, at 2.8% of trade union members, was below the 1920 average of 3.8%.[34] Unemployment was in fact higher in the first half of 1921 than over the year as a whole, and at that time between 7% and 9½% of organized workers were, additionally, on short time;[35] still, by comparison with conditions in Great Britain or the U. S. A. in 1921, the German picture was a rosy one.

With steady expansion in Germany went a steady expansion of her import demand. During the 1920/21 slump Germany offered the world's suppliers the only important market that was still growing. Imperfect as they are for this period, Germany's foreign trade statistics clearly substantiate this view (Table 39). Import quantities have to be employed, since the currency instability makes import values at current prices meaningless. Some of the quantity data were converted to "gold mark values" using 1913 prices; but even the simple quantities themselves reflect changes in real import values fairly reliably, since the commodity structure was relatively invariant in this period, and not unlike

---

29 Bundesarchiv Koblenz R 2/3216. "Vermerk über eine Besprechung im Auswärtigen Amt am 24. Jan. 1921 über die Frage des sogenannten Indexschemas", p. 6. [Record of a discussion in the Foreign Office on Jan. 24, 1921 about the question of the so-called index-schedule.]

30 Karl Bräuer: *Die Neuordnung der deutschen Finanzwirtschaft und das neue Reichssteuersystem* (Stuttgart, 1920). Erwin Respondek: *Die Reichsfinanzen auf Grund der Reform von 1919/20* (Berlin, 1921). G. Strutz: "Die Reichssteuerpolitik der Nachkriegszeit", *Zeitschrift für die Gesamte Staatswissenschaft*, 78 (1924), pp. 631 ff.

31 Arnd Jessen: *Finanzen, Defizit, und Notenpresse 1914–1922* (Berlin, 1923), p. 47.

32 Cp. Tables 1,4,8 *supra*.

33 Cp. Tables 32 and 38 *supra*.

34 F. Hesse: *Die deutsche Wirtschaftslage von 1914 bis 1923* (Jena, 1938), pp. 480–481.

35 *Ibid.*, p. 481.

what it had been before the war. Since more than three quarters of the value of imports consisted of homogeneous bulk commodities with low value:weight ratios, changes in the value of imports were also reflected by changes in their quantities, measured in tons.

Table 39. German merchandise imports in 1920–23 in comparison with 1913

	in 1000 tons 1.	in mill. gold marks (1913 prices) 2.
1913	72831	11206
1920	18841	3947
I. half year	8398	
II. half year	10443	
1921	25663	5751
I. half year	11470	
II. half year	14193	
1922	45867	6310
I. half year	17157	
II. half year	28710	
1923	46573	4821

Sources: Column 1: *Statistisches Jahrbuch f. d. Deutsche Reich,* 1923, p. 189. F. Hesse: *Deutsche Wirtschaftslage*, pp. 464–465.
Column 2: *Deutschlands Wirtschaft, Währung und Finanzen* (Berlin, 1924), p. 18.
Stat. Reichsamt: *Der Auswärtige Handel Deutschlands in den Jahren 1920, 1921 und 1922 verglichen mit dem Jahre 1913. Statistik des Deutschen Reichs, Bd. 310, Heft 1* (Berlin, 1924), p. 2 (Introduction).

Monthly data on the volume of German imports in 1919 and the first seven month of 1920 can be found in *Sammlung von Aktenstücken über die Verhandlungen auf der Sachverständigenkonferenz zu Brüssel vom 16. bis 22. Dezember 1920* (Berlin, 1921), pp. 86–89, 102–104. Imports amounted to 2478000 tons in the first half and to 7446000 tons in the second half, i.e. to a total of 9924000 tons in 1919.

Table 39 indicates that import quantities, thus measured, were 36.2% greater in 1921 than in 1920. In gold mark valuation (1913 prices) the increase was as much as 45.7%. This implies that between these years imports with a high value:weight ratio were increasing faster than average. The converse was the case between 1921 and 1922: imports increased by 78.7% when measured in tons but by 10% in gold mark value.

German import movements can be traced more reliably in the external trade statistics of other countries where currency and other conditions of recording trade were more propitious. Chief among these was the U. S. A. Aggregate U. S. exports declined from $ 8.23 billions in 1920 to $ 4.49 billions in 1921, that is, by 45.4%.[36] Between 1920 and 1921 the U. S. wholesale price index (1926 = 100) dropped from 154.4 to 97.6,[37] so that at constant prices exports dropped by about 14%. At the same time however the value in current prices of U. S. exports to Germany was growing: from only $ 93 million in 1919 it leapt up to $ 311 million in 1920 and climbed further to $ 372 million in 1921. Indeed the increase by quantity in U. S. exports to Germany between 1920 and 1921 was 90%, because of the simultaneous fall in wholesale prices. The significance of the German economy for the U. S. market becomes clear when we realize that the proportion of all U. S. exports going to Germany expanded from only 1.2% in 1919 to 3.8% in 1920 and 8.3% in the slump year 1921.[38]

For particular commodities the German market was of cardinal importance to the U. S. export sector. This was connected with the complementarity between the trade structures of the two countries: primary, particularly agricultural, commodities formed up to 75% of German imports[39] and likewise a high proportion of U. S. exports. Thus of U. S. raw cotton exports totaling $ 534 millions in 1921, $ 110.9 millions or 20.8% went to Germany – more than to Great Britain.[40] In the same year Germany took more than 30% of U. S. copper exports, more than 30% of its meat exports and even 13% of its wheat and wheaten flour exports.[41] In these commodities the role of the expanding German market in sustaining the level, or mitigating the fall, of U. S. sales to abroad becomes particularly evident. Total U. S. exports of raw cotton on the one hand, and of meat and meat products on the other, scarcely changed by quantity between 1920 and 1921, but this constancy conceals a nearly exact doubling of raw cotton quantities going from the U. S. A. to Germany[42] and a 60% increase in the volume of U. S. meat and meat products

[36] B. J. Wattenberg: *Statistical History*, p. 903.

[37] *Ibid.*, p. 200.

[38] *Ibid.*, p. 903.

[39] J. W. F. Thelwall and C. J. Kavanagh: *Report on the Economic and Financial Conditions in Germany to March 1922* (London, 1922), p. 33.

[40] *Ibid.*, p. 37.

[41] Calculated from statistics for the separate countries in Department of Commerce, Bureau of Foreign and Domestic Commerce: *Trade of the United States with the World 1920–1921, Part II: Exports* (Washington, D.C., 1922), pp. 33–38. Cp. C.-L. Holtfrerich: "Amerikanischer Kapitalexport und Wiederaufbau der deutschen Wirtschaft 1919–1923 im Vergleich zu 1924–1929", *Vierteljahrschrift für Sozial- und Wirtschaftsgeschichte*, 64 (1977), pp. 497–529, esp. p. 505. Total U. S. exports of particular commodities are also reported in Wattenberg: *Statistical History*, p. 898.

[42] Dept. of Commerce, Bureau of Foreign and Domestic Commerce: *Trade*, p. 34.

exported to the same destination. Wheat was the biggest item within the U. S. export category "Bread Grains and Flour" – and the exports of it to Germany quadrupled in quantity between the two years. The quantity of U. S. copper going to Germany rose by about 150%.

The value of German exports to the U. S. A. was trifling during these years: $11, $89 and $80 million in 1919, 1920 and 1921 respectively.[43] Thus the expansion of U. S. exports to Germany translated almost totally into a net increase in U. S. aggregate demand and may thus have acted to initiate world-wide recovery. To form a quantitative estimate of the amount by which the German decision in 1920/21, not to break the inflation, raised aggregate demand in the U. S. A, one must first specify the counterfactual: the probable impact on the U. S. economy of a hypothetical German *de*flation. The German economic structure resembled the British sufficiently for us to suppose that, had Germany been afflicted by a depression as deep as that in Britain and America, U. S. exports to Germany would have fallen in the same ratio as U. S. exports to Britain. The value of U. S. exports to Britain fell from $1.83 billion in 1920 to $0,94 billion in 1921,[44] i. e. by about one half. To a hypothetical Germany in depression, then, the U. S. A. would have been able to export goods to a value of only about $155 million in 1921 (i. e. one half of the $311 millions exported thither in 1920). The difference between this counterfactual export and the $372 millions actually exported to Germany in 1921 represents the direct contribution of expansionary policies in Germany to reflation in the U. S. A.; it ignores the indirect effects of exports destined for Germany but shipped in the first instance to ports in other countries, and of the German boom on the exports of third countries, hence on *their* imports from the U. S. A. This direct contribution was thus about $220 million and represented about 0.3% of U. S. gross national product in 1921 ($69.6 billion).[45]

The same calculation may also be attempted for Great Britain – Europe's leading industrial nation besides Germany. However two obstacles must first be surmounted.

Firstly, a large proportion of all exports from the U. K. were actually re-

[43] Wattenberg: *Statistical History*, p. 906.

[44] *Ibid.*, p. 903.

[45] *Ibid.*, p. 224. I have examined the same problem in greater detail, with the aid of monthly statistics on German-American trade, in C.-L. Holtfrerich: "Die konjunkturanregenden Wirkungen der deutschen Inflation auf die US-Wirtschaft in der Weltwirtschaftskrise 1920/21", in G. D. Feldman *et al.* (eds.): *The German Inflation Reconsidered. A Preliminary Balance* (Berlin/New York, 1982), pp. 207–234.

exports: about one seventh in both 1920 and 1921.[46] And the share of re-exports in British exports to Germany was larger still: 57% in 1920 and 56% in 1921.[47] Doubtless the British economy enjoyed an indirect spin-off from the maintenance and growth of the re-export trade, but the main stimulus must have been received by the countries from which the exported commodities originated. If, then, having excluded re-exports, we can show that the quantitative effect of expansion in Germany on exports originating in the U.K. was of an order of magnitude sufficient to have assisted in starting British recovery, our argument will be so much the stronger, because we will have been neglecting the indirect impulses flowing through the re-export trade. The following calculations therefore refer to U.K. domestic exports, which U.K. overseas trade statistics show separately from re-exports.

The second obstacle is the fact that unfortunately 1921 was the year in which the geographical recording of U.K. foreign trade was accommodated to the postwar European territorial adjustments. Thus, for example, in 1921 for the first time British exports to Alsace-Lorraine are recorded under "France" and not "Germany". Germany lost about ten percent of her industrial capacity owing to the territorial losses under the Versailles Treaty,[48] and so the values of U.K. exports from and imports to Germany recorded for 1919 and 1920 have been reduced by ten percent in each case, thus rendering them comparable with those for subsequent years. With this modification, direct German-British trade during the postwar inflation may be held to have run as follows (in £ million):[49]

	U.K. exports to Germany	U.K. imports from Germany
1919	13.2	0.8
1920	19.5	26.4
1921	17.9	19.8
1922	32.1	25.9
1923	42.6	34.1

[46] Brian R. Mitchell and Phyllis Deane: *Abstract of British Historical Statistics* (Cambridge, 1962), p. 284.

[47] *Ibid.*, p. 323.

[48] Rolf Wagenführ: *Die Industriewirtschaft. Vierteljahrshefte zur Konjunkturforschung, Sonderheft 31* (Berlin, 1933), p. 24.

[49] Mitchell and Deane: *Abstract*, p. 323.

As a share of aggregate U.K. domestic exports, exports to Germany evolved as follows:[50]

1919	1.7%
1920	1.5%
1921	2.5%
1922	4.5%
1923	5.6%

These figures imply that during the early postwar years the importance of the German market to the British economy was much less both than it had been to the prewar British economy (Germany took 7.7% of total British exports in 1913), and than it currently was to the postwar U. S. economy. However this is partly a statistical illusion: in the early postwar years a great deal of British trade with Germany was channeled through the Netherlands, and this explains why in 1919 and 1920 recorded British exports to the Netherlands were twice as high as, and in 1921 and 1922 still greatly exceeded, recorded British exports to Germany.[51] Thereafter the fall in recorded British exports to the former country virtually mirrored the rise in recorded British exports to the latter.

Even so, the dimensions of growth of direct and hence recorded U.K. (domestic) exports to Germany were quite impressive. The British wholesale price index (1913 = 100) fell from 307.3 in 1920 to 197.2 in 1921;[52] thus at constant prices recorded British domestic exports to Germany rose by 43% in these two years. Using the same deflator aggregate U.K. domestic exports fell by 18% in real terms between the same two years: at current values the fall was from £1334.5 million to £703.4 million.

Let us now postulate a fiscal and monetary deflation in Germany of the same order as that in the U.K. and U. S. A. and specify its effects on U.K. domestic exports to Germany by the actual decline in U.K. exports to the U. S. A. In 1921 the current value of U.K. exports to the U. S. A. was 43% less than in the previous year – £44 million as against £77 million.[53] If in 1921 direct U.K. domestic exports to Germany had also been 43% less by value than in 1920 they would have amounted to only £10.9 million and not the £17.9 million actually recorded. The difference between the counterfactual and actual values – £7.0 million – represented the direct contribution of the German inflation

50 Total domestic exports: *Ibid.*, p. 284.

51 *Ibid.*, p. 323.

52 *Ibid.*, p. 477. *International Abstracts of Economic Statistics*, p. 100.

53 Mitchell and Deane: *Abstract*, p. 320.

toward maintaining aggregate demand in the U.K. in 1921. It represented 0.13% of U.K. gross domestic product in that year, which was valued at £5312 million.[54] If we could now add the excluded indirect effects – of Anglo-German trade *via* the Netherlands, of the repercussions on the British economy of the stimulus to the re-export trade, and of the growth of British exports to third countries, induced by the rise of their exports to Germany – we would doubtless find the support afforded by the German inflation to British economic activity in 1921 to have been considerably in excess of the figure just calculated. Consideration of the re-export trade alone would double it.

The French economy, too, benefited from the effects of the German inflation. At current values French exports to Germany increased from 1.5 billion francs in 1920 to 2.36 billion francs in 1921. This was an increase of 60% at a time when the current value of French imports from Germany fell from 2.7 billion to 2.5 billion francs.[55] Estimates of French gross national product at current prices are not available however; thus unfortunately it is not possible to quantify the relative stimulus afforded to France by the increased German import demand.

The stimulus afforded to economic activity in Germany's smaller European neighbors – the Netherlands, Belgium, Switzerland, the Scandinavian and the central and south-east European countries – by her continued growth during the slump, must have been distinctly stronger in relative terms than in the cases already considered, because of the much greater dependence of these economies upon the German economy. The quantification of this stimulus must however be deferred to a later, separate study.

Were the relative stimuli, as calculated for the U. S. and the U. K. economies strong or weak? A standard of comparison is required. In January 1967 the first stabilization program of the West German federal government was announced. Its aim – of halting the recession then in progress through demand reflation – was to be achieved by public expenditure increases of 2.5 billion DM, mainly effective in the same year.[56] The sum represented 0.5% of the Federal Republic's gross domestic product in that year. A second stabilization program of 5.3 billion DM was announced in July 1967;[57] but most of the

[54] Mitchell: *European Historical Statistics*, p. 790.

[55] Figures from *Die Wirtschaftskurve*, *1* (1922), Heft 2, p. 72.

[56] Sachverständigenrat zur Begutachtung der gesamtwirtschaftlichen Entwicklung: *Jahresgutachten 1967/68, "Stabilität im Wachstum"* (Stuttgart, 1967), p. 75.

[57] *Ibid.*, p. 80. Cp. also Alois Oberhauser: "Geld- und Kreditpolitik bei weitgehender Vollbeschäftigung und mässigem Preisanstieg (1958–1968)", in Deutsche Bundesbank (ed.): *Währung und Wirtschaft in Deutschland 1876–1975* (Frankfurt/M, 1976), p. 627.

expenditures sanctioned under it were not actually made until 1968, when economic recovery was already perceptible. Another comparison is furnished by the agreement at the July 1978 Bonn economic summit, that world economic activity be supported through co-ordinated reflationary fiscal programs amounting to one percent of the gross domestic products of the western industrial nations.[58] The effect of these programs was probably distributed over several years however, so that in any single year the relative stimulus to demand was substantially less. Thus we may conclude that if aggregate demand in the U. K. and the U. S. A. in 1921 was lifted by 0.2% or 0.3% under the impact of inflation-induced German import demand, then the stimulus afforded was entirely comparable to that of modern stabilization programs. This conclusion is fortified when we recollect that to some extent these modern programs act through tax cuts, whose initial impact on aggregate demand is reduced by the marginal propensity to save of the primary beneficiaries, whereas this primary "leakage" does not diminish the impact of exogenous expenditure increases such as additional exports.

The impact of German import demand on the world economy is not merely to be analyzed by its relation to *aggregate* demand abroad however. Its importance becomes especially evident when we relate the structural composition of German imports to the structural aspects of the depression abroad, particularly in the U. S. A. The main commodities imported by Germany – raw cotton, wheat, meat and meat products – were also the staple exports of the U. S. agricultural sector. In 1921 these commodities accounted for one third of U. S. exports overall.[59] Raw cotton, wheat and copper were among the chief staples of international commodity markets, and their prices were quoted on all the major exchanges. The U. S. A. was the world's leading supplier of all three: it accounted for more than one half of the world's copper output[60] and about half of the world's raw cotton crop.[61] It grew about one third of the world's wheat, but if we take exportable surpluses into consideration only and exclude wheat grown and consumed domestically, the share supplied by the U. S. A., together with Canada and Argentina, was much larger.[62] Thus demand and price conditions on the American markets for these commodities exerted a decisive influence on the world market for them.

---

[58] "Bonner Wirtschaftsgipfel. Treffen der Staats- und Regierungschefs am 16. und 17. 7. 1978", in Deutsche Bundesbank (ed.): *Auszüge aus Presseartikeln, Nr. 56*, 1978.

[59] Calculated from B. J. Wattenberg: *Statistical History*, pp. 898 and 903.

[60] Wladimir Woytinsky: *Die Welt in Zahlen* (Berlin, 7 Bücher, 1925–8), *4. Buch: Das Gewerbe*, p. 176.

[61] W. Woytinsky: *Die Welt in Zahlen. 3. Buch: Die Landwirtschaft*, p. 171.

[62] *Ibid.*, p. 118.

The price elasticity of demand for primary, and particularly agricultural, products is low, as also is the price elasticity of their supply at least in the short run. Thus small shifts of the demand curves for these products have large effects on their price. Cyclical variations in the demand for these products may be conceptualized as shifts of the demand curves on the price-quantity plane, and if these curves shift inwards towards the origin on world markets, the incomes of many producers, particularly in the agricultural sector, will be seriously affected by the price falls, with consequential effects on these producers' demands for industrial products. Thus a deflationary spiral can be initiated which may remain in motion for a long time. The world slump of 1929–33 is an example of this process: it was attended by mass unemployment in the industrial sector, impoverishment and distress in the agricultural, and bank collapses in the financial sector.[63] The post-1929 deflationary spiral originated in structural overproduction in the world's primary goods sector, expressing itself in falling prices and swelling unsold stocks from as early as 1925. "The abundance of credit up to the middle of 1928 helped to paper over the structural cracks... The world might have evaded the consequences of raw-material overproduction had it escaped monetary deflation. Surpluses and deflation provided the fateful mixture."[64]

Exactly the same constellation was present in 1920/21. Particularly after the dose of fiscal and monetary restriction in 1920 in the U.S.A. and U.K., the scene was set for a severe and protracted world slump of the 1929–33 type. The rapid price falls on world primary commodity markets in 1920/21 show this.[65] The fact that these price falls nevertheless came to a standstill in 1921 and that the worst of the world slump as a whole was already past in 1922[66] is in my view at least partly the outcome of the inflationary policy and boom conditions in Germany, and their repercussions on demand for major internationally traded commodities. This conclusion is not automatically inconsistent with the judgment of Hal B. Lary,[67] according to whom U.S. economic recovery was the active agent of recovery in the world at large *via* the growth of U.S. import demand in 1922.[68] Certainly this mechanism holds for countries like Australia and Japan and regions such as South America, but not for

---

[63] Cp. W. A. Lewis: *Economic Survey*, pp. 56ff.

[64] Charles P. Kindleberger: *The World in Depression* (London, 1973), p. 107.

[65] See the diagrams in *ibid.*, pp. 88–89. Cp. also League of Nations: *Economic Stability in the Post-War World. The Conditions of Prosperity after the Transition from War to Peace* (Geneva, 1945), p. 85.

[66] D.H. Aldcroft: *From Versailles to Wall Street*, p. 68.

[67] H.B. Lary: *The United States in the World Economy*, p. 149.

[68] On this see also League of Nations: *Economic Fluctuations in the United States and the United Kingdom 1918–1922* (Geneva, 1942), pp. 18–20.

Germany where the effect of inflation was to isolate economic activity from the movement of the international business cycle. Rather the reverse: increasing German demand for leading U. S. primary products in 1921 cannot have failed to make a significant contribution to U. S. economic stabilization, for it was principally directed towards U.S. agricultural staples, the export of which supplied more than one quarter of U.S. agricultural income in that year.[69]

Many writers attach cardinal significance to the deflation of agricultural and raw materials prices in explaining the development of the U. S. slump after 1929.[70] W. Arthur Lewis wrote, "The principal cause seems to have been the surprisingly rapid fall of agricultural and other raw material prices which checked confidence in recovery, and persuaded businessmen to 'wait and see' rather than to make new investments."[71] Considerable importance must therefore be attached to the effect of German import growth during 1921, in interrupting this cumulative process at a time when otherwise the demand for U. S. exports was spiraling downwards. Between 1929 and 1932 not a single industrial country was able to sustain a high level of aggregate demand, let alone generate the rapid demand growth and hence import growth achieved by the German economy in 1921. The "synchronized deflation" pursued by all of them was largely responsible for making the downswing as protracted and pronounced as it was. The comparison of the two slumps, then, fortifies the conclusion, that one of the main reasons why the earlier slump was "very much shorter"[72] than the later one, was the countercyclical impulses flowing to the world economy from fiscal and monetary expansion in Germany. Indeed it may be scarcely an exaggeration to suggest, that a depression of the severity and type experienced in the thirties would have reached the world economy already in the early twenties, had Germany not been pursuing expansion at any price – even that of a gigantic inflation – and thus acting, if not as the "locomotive" of world economic recovery, then at least as the "brake" upon further economic decline.[73]

---

69 B. J. Wattenberg: *Statistical History*, p. 887.

70 C. P. Kindleberger: *World in Depression*, pp. 105ff. Peter Temin: *Did Monetary Forces Cause the Great Depression?* (New York, 1976), pp. 146–51, 172.

71 W. A. Lewis: *Economic Survey*, p. 56.

72 D. H. Aldcroft: *From Versailles*, p. 68.

73 Not all the effects of the German inflation on economic activity abroad can be exactly quantified within the limits of this study; in their totality they probably never can be. A complex econometric model would run up against the deficiencies of the statistical information about international trade flows after the First World War. The quantitative estimation of the cyclical stimuli afforded to the world's two leading trading nations (the U. S. A. and U. K.) by the German inflation is sufficient to show however that analysis need not confine itself to summary statements such as Aldcroft's: "The main blessing was that the postwar depression was very much shorter" (*From Versailles*, p. 68); indeed the selfsame writer in another place observed that, "the initial upswing was generated by the export revival" (*Inter-War Economy*, p. 37).

Chapter 8
Distributional Effects within Germany

8.1. The Context and Contours of the Debate

The *agenda* of engaged political debate and the *explananda* of academic economic theory intersect at the question of the income distribution, and of the general laws and *ad hoc* influences governing it.[1] Because this is perennially so, Preiser believes that "even purely theoretical analysis... does not always find it easy to make a neat separation between value judgment and reality."[2] Maybe this is true, but in the following discussion I shall make the effort at least to hold empirical statement and value judgment apart – to let the "facts" arbitrate acceptably between the competing views of the subject without being automatically disbelieved by readers whose opinions differ from mine.

The attention paid by political scientists and economists to the phenomenon of inflation is a direct consequence of their great interest in matters relating to the income distribution. For "a change in the value of money, that is to say in the level of prices, is important to society only insofar as its incidence is unequal... A man's receipts and his outgoings are not all modified in one uniform proportion. Thus a change in prices and rewards, as measured in money, generally affects different classes unequally...."[3]

Economic historians of Marxian persuasion are enthusiastic defenders of the thesis that the German inflation worked to the disadvantage of the wage and salary earner, not just during the war but particularly after it. "[T]hrough redistribution of national income at the expense of the working class and others in employment, a form of imperialist primitive accumulation took

---

[1] David Ricardo: *On the Principles of Political Economy and Taxation. The Works and Correspondence of D. Ricardo, ed. P. Sraffa, vol. 1* (London, 1951), p. 5. (original edn. 1817).

[2] Erich Preiser: *Nationalökonomie heute. Eine Einführung in die Volkswirtschaftslehre* (Munich, 8th edn. 1969), p. 72.

[3] J. M. Keynes: *A Tract on Monetary Reform. The Collected Writings of J. M. Keynes, ed. E. Johnson and D. E. Moggridge, vol. IV* (London, 1971), p. 1 (original edn. 1923). The centrality of the distributional aspects to the interest shown in inflation is also evident from the space devoted to the subject in recent works of popular scholarship on the German inflation. Adam Ferguson: *When Money Dies. The Nightmare of the Weimar Collapse* (London, 1975). William Guttman and Patricia Meehan: *The Great Inflation. Germany 1919–1923* (London, 1975).

place."[4] Jürgen Kuczynski speaks of a "rapid collapse of the purchasing power of wages effected by the inflation" during the years 1918–23, in part the result of the preceding war economy but in part also "deliberately provoked by monopoly capital in Germany in order to reduce the situation of the workers."[5] Krohn argues in like fashion. He speaks of the "immiserization of the wage earners" during the inflation and asserts that after the war "the growth trends up to 1922 [worked] exclusively to the benefit of the owners of the means of production."[6] Non-Marxian historians, too, generally support the thesis that "measured by the real wage rate workers were unambiguously the losers in absolute terms during the inflation."[7] And contemporary assessments tended in the same direction. G. Kessler characterized as "fateful, [the fact] that in 1919 a definitive wage settlement was attempted so to speak in a vacuum, in other words, with no consideration of the real economic exigencies under which individual firms for the most part and the economy as a whole were forced to operate. Thereupon businesses undoubtedly had no alternative but to raise prices, and then began that ever more desperate race between price increases, wage increases and tax increases, from which the state was the first to retire exhausted (managing to limp along thereafter only with the assistance of the note printing presses). Soon after, the workers found it impossible by wage increases to keep pace with the price increases which their own actions had unleashed. The end result was, in defiance of the bulwarks erected by the winter of revolution [i. e. of 1918/19], real wages did not in fact rise: they fell even further."[8]

Most writers do concede that the process of inflation did bring about full employment, thus shielding workers from the threat of involuntary idleness in the short run at least – until the stabilization crisis of 1923/24. Beyond that, there is general acknowledgment of the benefits flowing from the introduction of the eight hour day following the Stinnes-Legien agreement, from the

---

[4] Hans Mottek *et al: Wirtschaftsgeschichte Deutschlands. Ein Grundriss, Bd. III* (Berlin-East, 2nd edn. 1975), p. 246.

[5] Jürgen Kuczynski: *Die Geschichte der Lage der Arbeiter unter dem Kapitalismus, Bd. 5* (Berlin-East, 1966), p. 150. Similarly Kurt Gossweiler: *Grossbanken, Industriemonopole, Staat. Ökonomie und Politik des staatsmonopolistischen Kapitalismus in Deutschland 1914–1932* (Berlin-East, 1971), p. 151.

[6] Claus-Dieter Krohn: *Die grosse Inflation in Deutschland 1918–1923* (Cologne, 1977), p. 35.

[7] Gerald D. Feldman: "Gegenwärtiger Forschungsstand und künftige Forschungsprobleme zur deutschen Inflation", in Otto Büsch and Gerald D. Feldman (eds.): *Historische Prozesse der deutschen Inflation. Ein Tagungsbericht* (Berlin, 1978), p. 15.

[8] Gerhard Kessler: "Die Lage der deutschen Arbeiterschaft seit 1914", in Bernhard Harms (ed.): *Strukturwandlungen der deutschen Volkswirtschaft* (Berlin, 2 vols. 1928), vol. 1, pp. 470–471.

setting up of works councils based on the Works Constitution Law, and from the fact that collective labor agreements, where concluded, were declared binding on employers.[9] This conceded, the demonstration that real wages during the war and again between 1918 and 1923 were less than they had been in 1913 is made the proof of the assertion that the inflation redistributed income from workers to employers. This is identical to the assertion that workers' real incomes would have been higher between 1918 and 1923 had policy been orientated toward price stability than they were under the inflationary policy actually being pursued. In the third section of this chapter the validity of this thesis will be examined.

8.2. Changes in National Income

Before examining changes in the distribution of income during the inflation period we should first consider the available estimates of the national income aggregate at this time.

Official estimates of German national income extend back to 1891,[1] the year in which Miquel's tax reform in Prussia finally transferred the power to levy income tax from the communes to the Prussian state. This implies that these estimates are derived from statistics of taxation, and obviously from those pertaining to direct tax yields in particular. That is to say, of the three approaches to the computation of national income (or, national product at factor cost) – the "income", "product" and "expenditure" approaches[2] – German official statistics employ the first. Estimates by W. G. Hoffmann[3] and J. H. Müller[4] extend back to the middle of the nineteenth century.

---

[9] J. Kuczynski: *Geschichte, Bd. 5*, pp. 150–161. On the Stinnes-Legien agreement see above all Gerald D. Feldman: "German Business between War and Revolution: the Origins of the Stinnes-Legien Agreement", in Gerhard A. Ritter (ed.): *Entstehung und Wandel der modernen Gesellschaft. Festschrift für Hans Rosenberg zum 65. Geburtstag* (Berlin, 1970), pp. 312–341. Hans-Hermann Hartwich: *Arbeitsmarkt, Verbände und Staat. Die öffentliche Bindung unternehmerischer Funktionen in der Weimarer Republik* (Berlin, 1967), pp. 3–22.

[1] Statistisches Reichsamt: *Das deutsche Volkseinkommen vor und nach dem Kriege. Einzelschriften zur Statistik des Deutschen Reichs, Nr. 24* (Berlin, 1932).

[2] Cp. Alfred Stobbe: *Volkswirtschaftslehre I. Volkswirtschaftliches Rechnungswesen* (Berlin, 4th edn. 1976), pp. 125ff. Wilfred Beckerman: *An Introduction to National Income Analysis* (London, 2nd edn. 1976), pp. 12–18.

[3] Walther G. Hoffmann *et al.*: *Das Wachstum der deutschen Wirtschaft seit der Mitte des 19. Jahrhunderts* (Berlin, 1965), e.g. pp. 165ff. Here national income estimates from the product, expenditure and income sides are presented.

Table 40. Indexes of real national income in Germany 1914–24; also 1903–13 and 1925–35. 1913 = 100

	Henning*	Graham	Roesler	Witt	Hoffmann
1903					72
1904					75
1905					77
1906					79
1907					82
1908					84
1909					86
1910					89
1911					92
1912					96
1913					100
1914	96	82	83	90.2	
1915	96	74	67	81.4	
1916	92	69	64	80.2	
1917	88	67	62	78.5	
1918	88	66	57	74.7	
1919	72	55		67.1	
1920	74	66		74.0	
1921	80	73		79.3	
1922	83	80		82.6	
1923	72	61		74.4	
1924	82	74		87.3	
1925					94
1926					90
1927					107
1928					109
1929					111
1930					104
1931					93
1932					85
1933					93
1934					102
1935					111

* The influence of territorial changes is eliminated in this index.

Sources: 1903–13 and 1925–35: W. G. Hoffmann *et al.*: *Wachstum*, p. 455.

1914–24: F.-W. Henning: *Das industrialisierte Deutschland 1914 bis 1972* (Paderborn, 1974), pp. 42, 47, 49, together with explanatory letters to me dated October 20 and 31, 1978. F. D. Graham: *Exchange, Prices and Production*, pp. 301, 316, as computed and cited by P. Cagan: "The Monetary Dynamics of Hyperinflation", p. 105. K. Roesler: *Die Finanzpolitik des Deutschen Reiches*, p. 154. P.-C. Witt: "Finanzpolitik und sozialer Wandel ...", p. 424.

[4] Walther G. Hoffmann and J. Heinz Müller: *Das deutsche Volkseinkommen 1851–1957* (Tübingen, 1959). This work supplies income-side estimates based on tax statistics.

Common to these standard series is the decision to leave the decade 1914–24 blank. Hoffmann and Müller write that, "on account of the inflation a calculation of national income during these years would be meaningless."[5] For calculations of national income at current prices this is unquestionably true.

Nevertheless various attempts have been made to calculate national income between 1914 and 1924, all seeking to express it at constant (1913) prices. Data presented by K. Roesler cover the war years, while the separate estimates of F.W. Henning and P.-C. Witt embrace the entire decade 1914–24. F.D. Graham's indexes of output in the several sectors of the economy have also been employed to obtain a national income series. These estimates have been juxtaposed in Table 40. Comparison of them discloses a consensus that national income declined during the war years and that the minimum level was reached immediately after it, in 1919. Thereafter the three series that continue show a recovery lasting until 1922, followed by a sharp drop during the final year of the inflation.

Despite their differing methods of calculation, then, the indexes agree in their dating of the turning points of national income movements; and thus this dating may be regarded as reliable. The indexes do not agree however about the extent to which national income levels changed from year to year. Roesler's series is based on Wagenführ's index of industrial production (cp. Table 36) and it shows sharper declines during the war years than the others. Wagenführ's index however embraces only about 55% of all industrial production,[6] and industrial production as a whole was in turn about 42% of the output of the entire economy;[7] Roesler's index can hardly be considered representative of movements of national product as a whole.

The series derived from Graham is to be preferred to Roesler's because it at least makes the attempt to reflect output movements in all three sectors of the economy. The index numbers under his name in Table 40 are simply the arithmetic means, for each year, of his index numbers of output in industry, agriculture and freight transport. More comprehensive calculations underlie the indexes by Henning and Witt. Henning employed quantity estimates of output in various branches of industry (e. g. pig iron manufacture and processing, consumption of textile raw materials – his procedure so far resembling Wagenführ's), joining to them estimates of agricultural production and of

[5] *Ibid.*, p. 4.

[6] R. Wagenführ: *Die Industriewirtschaft. Vierteljahrshefte zur Konjunkturforschung, Sonderheft 31* (Berlin, 1933), p. 47.

[7] Calculated from data in Hoffmann *et al.*: *Wachstum*, p. 453.

employment in the productive and non-productive (i. e. public sector) divisions of the tertiary sector, and thus obtaining estimates of output in the economy as a whole. In doing so he eliminated the effects of the territorial changes after 1918, making his series refer to a constant, standard Reich territory.

Each of these estimates proceeded from the product side. Witt however used taxation statistics to build up estimates from the income side. Hoffmann and Müller had already expressed reservations about the applicability of this approach to this period[8] and, given the rapid changes in the value of money, I, too, find it the least promising. Witt seeks to corroborate his results by demonstrating the agreement of calculations using the same methods on post-1925 data with the now once more available standard series.[9] This proves little, in my judgment; for the decisive determinant of reliability of a method proceeding from current-value magnitudes during the pre-1924 period is rapidity of reaction to changes in the value of money, and his post-1925 control calculations are unable to test for this.

Henning and Witt do not provide a complete account of their methods, and until they do no final evaluation of their results is possible. Their wartime estimates differ markedly; thereafter the two series are quite similar. The broader, more representative statistical base, which distinguishes both of them from the series by Roesler and that based on Graham, causes them to capture more adequately the effects of the mushrooming of the tertiary sector – of military and bureaucratic employment during the war and of commercial and clerical (e. g. bank staffs') employment thereafter. This may be the reason why Henning's and Witt's national income estimates lie uniformly above Roesler's and the one derived from Graham. But if one has to choose between Henning's and Witt's, Henning's must be preferred because of the greater reliability in this period of product-side estimates starting from real magnitudes.

Henning's data indicate that in the first two years of the war national income was only some four percent lower than in 1913, but that the intensified military exertions initiated in 1916 by the Hindenburg program enlarged this shortfall to twelve percent during 1917 and 1918. A sharp decline occurred in 1919, reducing national income to a level twenty-eight percent below that of 1913 – no doubt owing to the dislocating effects on production of reconver-

---

[8] Cp. p. 225 footnote 5.

[9] Peter-Christian Witt: "Finanzpolitik und sozialer Wandel in Krieg und Inflation 1918–1924.", in Hans Mommsen *et al.* (eds.): *Industrielles System und politische Entwicklung in der Weimarer Republik* (Düsseldorf, 1974), p. 40.

sion to a peacetime economy, of the social innovations of the revolution (the eight hour day) and of the strike activity, whether politically or economically motivated, of that year. The 1919 decline was particularly severe in industry, as the index of industrial output reveals (Table 32). 1920–22 were years of recovery – 1921 especially. National income rose steadily and in 1922 was only seventeen percent less than in 1913; however in 1923, the year of the occupation of the Ruhr, it was reduced to the level of 1919 again.

The subsequent history can be pursued with the aid of Hoffmann's calculations. Not until 1927 was the 1913 real national income level exceeded and the pre-depression peak was reached in 1928 and 1929 at some nine and eleven percent respectively above the 1913 figure. The ensuing depression reduced real national income at its trough in 1932 to the level of 1922, the postwar inflation-period peak.

This completes our study of the evidence about change in real national income aggregates. I turn now to consider how it was distributed – whether between classes (wage and salary earners, owners of real capital, owners of financial assets), or within classes (employed relative to unemployed, skilled relative to unskilled). Aggregate real income levels were approximately the same in 1922 and 1932 but the inflation in progress in the former year and the deflation that ruled during the latter caused two quite different distributions of this aggregate.

8.3. Changes in Real Wages

Wage statistics: their origins and reliability

A brief discussion of the sources and evolution of German official wage statistics forms a necessary preface to an assessment of their quality during the inflation. In 1925 O. von Zwiedineck-Südenhorst surveyed the field thus:[1]

(i) Up till recently official statistical agencies had shown little interest in it.

(ii) Non-official investigations, particularly those by workers' organizations, dominated the field both in respect of the scope of their inquiries and of volume of publication.

---

[1] Otto von Zwiedineck-Südenhorst: "Lohnstatistik", article in the *Handwörterbuch der Staatswissenschaften* (Jena, 6 Bde. 1921–5) Bd. 6 (1925), p. 387. On the historical development of official wage statistics in Germany see the excellent survey in *Die Lohn- und Gehaltserhebung vom Februar 1920. Statistik des Deutschen Reichs, Bd. 293* (Berlin, 1921), pp. 11⁺–19⁺.

(iii) Quite a large amount of wage-statistical material was yielded incidentally by data collected for other purposes – for example by the Social Insurance Funds and tax authorities and through registration of collective labor agreements.

(iv) Most of the material was fairly local in its coverage.

The following commentary may be offered on these four points, taking them in reverse order.

The local, decentralized nature of wage statistics reflects the federal structure of the German state, of its administrative organs and of its worker and employer organizations; centralization began only with the founding of the Weimar Republic. Decentralized collection and processing enhanced the descriptive power and accuracy of the data but makes it harder to draw macroeconomic conclusions about wage movements.

The incidental origins of much of the material (see point (iii) above) also impairs its usefulness in certain respects. The income data which the official sickness, accident, old age and invalidity insurance schemes collected in order to assess contributions was not collected on a uniform basis. Workers were often credited with an average earnings level customary to their locality and not with their actual individual incomes. Overtime earnings and piece-rate bonuses were often disregarded, while upper limits on the graduation of contributions meant that higher earnings levels often went unrecorded. Contributions were calculated against earnings per day, so that changes in hours worked were not noted. This last defect is shared by records of the tax authorities, since income tax assessment was based on income over the entire year. And when the value of money is subject to rapid alteration as in the period we are considering, annual data are practically unusable as a basis for calculating the purchasing power of income.

Collective labor agreements (*Tarifverträge*) covered a growing proportion of the labor force after the First World War[2] and the statistics they generated offer wage information differentiated by sex, age, occupation, position and qualification. Collective agreements also regulated hours worked. Their weakness as a source of wage data lies however in the fact that the wages negotiated under them were in practice minimum wages: wages actually earned could be substantially greater, particularly under piece rates.

The wage data collected privately by workers' (also employers') organizations – referred to in Zwiedineck-Südenhorst's second point – are more

[2] *Die Tarifverträge im Deutschen Reich. Reichsarbeitsblatt, Sonderheft 48* (Berlin, 1928). In 1913 1.4 million workers were covered by collective agreements; in 1919 6.0 and in 1922 as many as 14.3 millions. Cp. Dietmar Petzina: *Die deutsche Wirtschaft in der Zwischenkriegszeit* (Wiesbaden, 1977), p. 88.

satisfactory than the foregoing as regards coverage and method of collection. Usually however the aim of collecting them was to support the position of one or other party to wage negotiations, and so they may suffer from selectivity and bias in their method of calculation.

Given the deficiencies of the various incidental and non-official sources, cardinal significance attaches to the development of purpose-designed official wage statistics, exhibiting the required degree of differentiation, free from suspicion of bias, and able to collect and process the information on which an adequate objective account of wage conditions could be based; and with this we reach the first point of Zwiedineck-Südenhorst's summary. Statistical offices at three different levels of government engaged in the collecting and processing of wage data – those of the municipalities, of the federal states and of the Reich; and there was only partial collaboration between the levels. Of these, the coverage and quality of the investigations conducted by the municipalities and federal states (especially Saxony and Baden) were vastly superior to the statistics of the Reich.[3] Prior to the First World War the activities of the Reich in this field had been confined to the regular reporting of a small range of wage information in the *Reichsarbeitsblatt* (founded in 1903): miners' wages in the chief colliery districts as reported by the official Mining Administration, and wages and working hours of civilian workers in Naval and Military establishments.

In 1902 the Imperial Statistical Office had set up a Section for Labor Statistics. In 1907 the Office sought the permission of the Reich Interior Office to process wage particulars from collective labor agreements, thus generating a reliable statistical base to be placed at the disposal of those seeking to resolve industrial conflicts or negotiate new agreements. The Reich Interior Office handled this request dilatorily, and by the First World War the hoped-for "Archive of Collective Agreements" (*Tarifarchiv*) had not yet materialized.

The war led to its further postponement. However it also led to increased state intervention in and control of the economy, particularly after the passing of the so-called Auxiliary Service Law of 1916, and this made the need for reliable information about pay so much the more obvious, not least to the authorities charged with managing the economy. Besides this, "the enormous growth of business profits on the one side, and the catastrophic decline in the general standard of living on the other, boded a crisis and made some regulation of working conditions a matter of urgency – so much the more so as the employers seemed oblivious to the dangers."[4] On September 30, 1916 the

[3] Bibliography in O. von Zwiedineck-Südenhorst: "Lohnstatistik", p. 395.

[4] *Ibid.*, p. 390.

Imperial Statistical Office instituted its own sample investigation of wages, by issuing a circular to those industrial associations already participating in the regular monthly reporting on the state of the labor market for the *Reichsarbeitsblatt.* The investigations related to average daily earnings during the last weeks of March and September, and information covering the period from March 1914 to March 1919, when the last survey was conducted, was collected from about three hundred and seventy plants. The surveys left a good deal to be desired however: information was collected neither about workers' qualifications, nor about overtime which assumed considerable proportions particularly during the second half of the war. Estimates rather than exact replies were often supplied and no account was taken of purchasing power disparities between regions.

Notable advances were achieved by the workers during the 1918 revolution and early postwar years: working hours were reduced, collective agreements rendered binding, and works councils set up on the basis of the Works Constitution Law. Unemployment relief was introduced and in any case unemployment remained low.[5] When agreement was reached in the "Central Working Community (*Zentralarbeitsgemeinschaft*) of the Commercial and Industrial Employers and Employees of Germany" to implement the eight hour day with corresponding legislation following, the stipulation was added that earnings reductions on the grounds of the reduction in hours were not permissible. In February 1920 the government conducted a Wage and Salary Investigation, not least to check up on the observance of this stipulation. It was the most detailed and comprehensive investigation to have been conducted up to that point, and distinguished wages by occupation and qualification of worker, system of wage payment, hours worked, social situation and many other statistical desiderata. But it remained the only such investigation during the inflation period, because its main object, namely the ascertainment of information concerning the real wage level, could not be realized on account of the great variability of wages and prices. "The results of this ambitious statistical inquiry shared the fate of all investigations of monetary quantities in that period: owing to the pace of currency depreciation they rapidly became meaningless."[6] As a result, the contours of wage change during the postwar infla-

[5] "Denkschrift über die seit dem 9. November 1918 auf dem Gebiete der Sozialpolitik getroffenen Massnahmen", in *Verhandlungen der Verfassungsgebenden Deutschen Nationalversammlung, Bd. 335* (Berlin, 1920), Drucksache Nr. 215. Cp. also Ludwig Preller: *Sozialpolitik in der Weimarer Republik* (Stuttgart, 1949). Jürgen Kuczynski: *Die Geschichte der Lage der Arbeiter unter dem Kapitalismus, Bd. 5* (Berlin-East, 1966), p. 160.

[6] Statistisches Bundesamt: *Bevölkerung und Wirtschaft 1872–1972* (Stuttgart, 1972), p. 39.

tion have to be inferred from evidence about the incomes of a number of specific occupational categories whose earnings were continuously reported and may reasonably be thought representative of general earnings' change.

Wage statistics: findings

The pace of currency depreciation was the overriding determinant of change in money wages and salaries both during the 1914–18 and the 1918–23 periods. In the long run, therefore their trend was upward; and in the short run their angle of ascent was accommodated, more or less closely, to the various phases in the movement of prices.[7] This "more or less" was the factor that determined the movements of workers' *real* incomes and thus the living standards of the greater part of the population.

Besides the relationship between money wage change and price change it is also of interest to investigate changes in the wage structure – in the relation of money wages to each other. Workers' aggregate living standards are affected by changes in this structure: lower-paid workers generally have a higher propensity to consume than higher-paid workers, so that a compression or expansion of wage and salary differentials may raise or lower the average consumption of workers as a whole.

How, then, did both the average level and the structure of wages and salaries change in real terms during the inflation? The first general statement that may be made is that workers' real weekly wages lay consistently below their 1913 levels both during the war and in the postwar inflation period. Secondly: in both periods the structure of wage differentials became severely compressed. But while the validity of these general statements is scarcely contestable, attempts to quantify them are greatly impeded by the "index number problem" – a problem affecting real wage comparisons even in periods of monetary stability but much more so in times of monetary collapse (cp. pp. 25 ff.).

A variety of real wage indexes can be devised for the period 1914–23, depending on the price index employed to deflate money wage earnings; they all agree however in showing an initial decline after 1913. Thus Calwer's price index (average of the cost in two hundred towns of the standard food ration of a German marine) increased by 129% between 1913 and 1918, the Reich Statistical Office's cost-of-living index (regularly calculated from February

[7] Karl Bräuer: *Die Anpassung der Löhne und Gehälter an die Lebenshaltungskosten mit besonderer Rücksicht auf die deutschen und englischen Verhältnisse* (Dresden, 1922).

1920 but estimated retrospectively for the preceding years) by 213%, and the wholesale price index by 117% (see Tables 1,4,9). By comparison, an inquiry by the Bavarian State Statistical Office concluded that between June 1914 and October 1918 the hourly money wage earnings of skilled workers in Bavarian industry had risen by 104% and of unskilled by 120%.[8] Having completed his own comprehensive statistical investigation of wartime real wage change, P. Quante's summary assessment ran as follows: "... for all [workers], rising prices and the widespread wage reductions in the early stages of the war soon meant a severe fall in real wages: this occurred, at the latest, by the end of the first year of the war. The decline was rectified, if at all, not before the summer of 1917; after this time and until the end of the war certain categories of workers had some success in regaining their peacetime living standards."[9]

The details in Table 41 offer a rough guide to the real income changes experienced by various groups of workers during and after the war. The money wage data underlying it have been uniformly deflated by the Reich Statistical Office's cost-of-living index. The series confirm that real income levels reached a minimum in 1917 and recovered quite steeply thereafter until 1919. The 1919 level could not be sustained in the years following: even so, the real wages of unskilled railway workers for example, which in 1919 had exceeded their 1913 level by 20%, more or less equaled it in 1921 and fell short of it in 1920 and 1922 by only about 11% and 12½% respectively. It was only in 1923 that a shortfall of about 30% against 1913 was registered.

In 1923 skilled railway workers' real wages were 50% percent below their 1913 level. Especially from the second half of the war their real wages experienced more severe declines relative to 1913 than those of unskilled railway workers, and this experience was shared by the other better-paid workers in the Table – printers and Ruhr miners. During the years 1919–22 skilled railwaymen averaged a real wage some 25% below that of 1913 and printers some 35%. Even Ruhr miners, despite their key role in economic reconstruction, could average no more than about 80% of their 1913 real wage. The sharper reduction of skilled than of unskilled real earnings implies a compression of wage differentials during the inflation. Bresciani-Turroni's estimates of skill differentials are reproduced in Table 42.

The compression of the differentials among salary earners can be seen in Table 43.[10]

---

8 Gerhard Bry: *Wages in Germany 1871–1945* (Princeton, 1960), p. 433.

9 Peter Quante: "Lohnpolitik und Lohnentwicklung im Kriege", *Zeitschrift des Preussischen Statistischen Landesamts*, 59 (1919), p. 370.

10 In this connection see too "Die Wirkungen der Geldentwertung auf die Gehälter der Beamten und Staatsangestellten in den Jahren 1919 bis 1923", *Hamburger Statistische Monatsberichte*, 1923,

Table 41. Indexes of average real weekly wages of railway workers, printers and Ruhr miners as per collective agreements 1913–23. 1913 = 100

Year and month	Railway workers Skilled	Railway workers Unskilled	Printers	Hewers and Haulers in the Ruhr
1914	97.2	97.2	97.2	93.3
1915	79.7	80.8	77.3	81.3
1916	69.2	73.8	60.6	74.4
1917	63.9	74.2	49.4	62.7
1918	83.3	99.8	54.1	63.7
1919	92.2	119.8	72.3	82.4
1920				
Jan.	67.2	89.8	61.0	80.0
Feb.	59.0	78.9	53.6	70.2
March	52.3	69.9	47.5	62.7
April	64.0	87.5	43.5	69.3
May	60.5	82.7	55.1	66.4
June	70.5	93.5	61.1	72.6
July	71.7	95.1	66.1	74.4
Aug.	74.7	99.0	69.4	84.6
Sept.	75.3	99.8	69.9	85.9
Oct.	71.3	94.6	66.3	91.6
Nov.	68.3	90.6	69.1	88.4
Dec.	66.0	87.5	66.7	85.3
Average	66.7	89.1	60.8	77.6
1921				
Jan.	71.9	96.3	65.5	84.4
Feb.	73.9	98.9	71.2	87.3
March	74.5	99.7	71.7	88.0
April	75.2	100.7	72.4	92.2
May	75.7	101.4	72.9	95.9
June	72.7	97.3	69.9	92.9
July	67.3	90.1	64.8	86.5
Aug.	73.6	99.8	63.1	81.9
Sept.	70.2	95.1	65.4	89.9
Oct.	90.3	121.1	69.1	82.2
Nov.	77.6	104.1	63.8	97.5
Dec.	71.5	95.9	76.6	90.5
Average	74.5	100.0	68.9	89.1

Table 41. (continued)

Year and month	Railway workers Skilled	Unskilled	Printers	Hewers and Haulers in the Ruhr
1922				
Jan.	69.3	93.5	72.0	83.1
Feb.	58.6	79.0	67.9	78.8
March	49.4	66.7	60.3	76.3
April	61.8	84.6	63.3	73.8
May	75.3	102.0	72.2	80.7
June	78.4	106.8	74.1	75.7
July	70.9	96.5	65.5	69.5
Aug.	66.3	91.0	51.9	59.1
Sept.	83.4	114.4	55.6	75.6
Oct.	53.3	73.5	50.3	51.6
Nov.	48.5	66.9	44.4	52.6
Dec.	55.0	76.2	53.1	62.2
Average	64.2	87.6	60.9	69.9
1923				
Jan.	44.2	61.1	42.8	47.7
Feb.	48.0	66.4	46.3	75.6
March	59.6	82.4	74.6	86.2
April	55.2	76.3	71.7	79.9
May	51.9	71.6	59.2	69.6
June	55.5	77.0	55.9	70.8
July	42.9	59.4	36.6	47.6
Aug.	53.7	74.3	66.7	78.5
Sept.	51.8	71.5	38.5	74.7
Oct.	44.1	60.8	35.7	81.2
Nov.	46.4	62.0	54.0	55.7
Dec.	58.0	66.0	67.9	73.3
Average	50.9	69.1	54.2	70.1

Source: Statistisches Reichsamt: *Zahlen zur Geldentwertung*, p. 41. G. Bry: *Wages*, p. 210.

Both Tables indicate that this compression of differentials took place in two stages:

(i) during the second half of the war and particularly in 1916/17, suggesting the influence in some manner of the contemporaneous intensification of the war effort under the "Hindenburg program", and

pp. 77–80. Andreas Kunz: "Verteilungskampf oder Interessenkonsensus? Einkommensentwicklung und Sozialverhalten von Arbeitnehmergruppen in der Inflationszeit 1914 bis 1924", in G. D. Feldman *et al.* (eds.): *The German Inflation Reconsidered. A Preliminary Balance* (Berlin/New York, 1982), pp. 347–384.

Table 42. Wages of skilled workers as percentage of wages of unskilled 1913–23

1913	145.8
1914	145.9
1915	143.8
1916	136.2
1917	125.6
1918	121.8
1919	112.2
1920	109.2
1921	108.5
1922	106.8
1923 (Jan.–Oct.)	105.5

Source: C. Bresciani-Turroni: *The Economics of Inflation,* p. 313.

Table 43. Real monthly salaries of typical categories of Reich civil servants in cities 1913–23. 1913 = 100

		Civil Servants	
	Higher	Middle-ranking	Lower
1913	100	100	100
1914	97.2	97.2	97.2
1915	77.3	77.3	77.3
1916	58.9	58.9	58.9
1917	42.9	48.6	53.6
1918	46.8	55.0	69.6
1919	40.2	54.8	89.3
1920	31.7	44.0	71.3
1921	39.3	52.2	82.3
1922	35.6	46.4	72.9
1923	38.0	49.5	69.9

Source: Statistisches Reichsamt: *Zahlen zur Geldentwertung,* p. 43.G. Bry: *Wages,* p. 230.

(ii) during the first year after the war. Probably this was the result not only of the demands of workers' organizations and left-wing political groups for a more egalitarian income distribution, but also of the distressed economic conditions of the time. In such circumstances the securing of a subsistence wage was the workers' first priority, and employers were placed under a moral obligation to adjust the earnings of lower-paid workers – the unskilled and women – more completely to the fall in the value of money than the earnings of the better paid – skilled workers, salaried employees and officials.

A further factor in the reduction of wage differentials after the war was the rapid unionization of the unskilled, particularly in 1919. This, together with the great extension of the system of collective agreements effected a relative improvement in their bargaining position.[11] It has also been suggested that the smaller rate of urban immigration from the countryside after the war reduced the supply of unskilled labor while the full employment of the 1920–22 boom years raised the demand for it, both by comparison with the prewar situation.[12]

Wage differentials between men and women and between old and young workers were also compressed during the course of the inflation. During the war however differentials did widen between wages in war-related and civilian industries,[13] and there is some indication that inter-industrial differentials remained high to the end of the inflation.[14]

It must not be forgotten that the compression of differentials during and after the war was not a peculiarly German phenomenon; it can be observed in other countries too with relatively stable currencies.[15]

Narrowing the perspective now from the general trends to the details of wage movements, we are again confronted by problems of evidence and the lack of any general investigation of the question after the Reich Statistical Office's specially sanctioned[16] Inquiry of February 1920.[17] Month-by-month wage movements must – as before – be inferred from data relating to individual occupational categories. On the other hand, the commencement of the Reich Statistical Office's cost-of-living index in February 1920 did improve the basis for calculating monthly real wage movements; its more comprehensive underlying basket of goods, more detailed regional basis and the account taken of black market prices make it a more reliable deflator than any other

---

11 C. Bresciani-Turroni: *The Economics of Inflation. A Study of Currency Depreciation in Post-War Germany* (London, 1937) p. 313. Idem: "The Movements of Real Wages in Germany during the Depreciation of the Mark and after Stabilization", *Journal of the Royal Statistical Society*, 92 (1929), pp. 375, 392. On the role of the trade unions during the postwar inflation see more generally Heinrich Potthoff: *Gewerkschaften und Politik zwischen Revolution und Inflation* (Düsseldorf, 1979). H. A. Winkler: *Von der Revolution zur Stabilisierung* (Berlin, 1984).

12 Rudolf Meerwarth: "Zur neuesten Entwicklung der Löhne", *Zeitschrift des Preussischen Statistischen Landesamts*, 62 (1922), p. 336.

13 G. Bry: *Wages*, p. 207.

14 *Ibid.*, p. 219.

15 International Labor Office: *Fluctuations des salaires dans différents pays de 1914 à 1921* (Geneva, 1922), *Wage Changes in Various Countries 1914 to 1925* (Geneva, 1926), *Workers' Standard of Life in Countries with Depreciated Currency* (Geneva, 1925). J. H. Richardson: "Some Aspects of Recent Wage Movements and Tendencies in Various Countries", *International Labour Review*, 17 (1928), pp. 179–203.

16 I. e. by Decree of the Reich Labor Minister dated March 9, 1920. Cp. *Reichsgesetzblatt*, 1920, p. 309.

17 *Die Lohn- und Gehaltserhebung*. Cp. A. Aghte: "Lohnsteigerungen 1913 bis 1920", *Wirtschaft und Statistik*, 1 (1921), pp. 81–84.

index.[18] Gradual decontrol in the retail sector from about the same time also facilitates the task of reconstructing short-run real wage change.

Let us start from consideration of the findings of the Reich Wage and Salary Inquiry of February 1920, already several times referred to. The Inquiry investigated the pay received by 1.6 million wage earners and 227 thousand salary earners employed in 11,697 workplaces in all parts of the country.[19] Numerous occupational categories in fourteen branches of industry were encompassed. For each occupational group and workplace it sought information on the number of workers, their sex, their average hourly wage rate and their average total income during the four weeks of February, with hourly and piece rates separately listed. Especial interest attaches for our purposes to income data relating to branches of industry for which comparable prewar information is also available. Building, leather manufacture, woodworking, textiles, clothing, iron and non-ferrous metals are industries in this category, as were salary earners in all the investigated branches. The relevant comparisons are presented in Table 44.

Table 44. The level of money wages and salaries in various industries (Reich average). February 1920 compared with 1913/14 (= 1)

	Hourly wages	Four-weekly earnings
Construction	5.5–6.1	n. a.
Leather	6.0–7.0	n. a.
Woodworking	6.4–7.3	5.1–6.2
Textiles	7.3–9.3	5.5–7.1
Clothing	5.5–7.9	n. a.
Iron and other metals	5.6–8.0	n. a.
Salaried employees	–	4.6–4.7

Sources: Statistisches Reichsamt: *Die Lohn- und Gehaltserhebung vom Februar 1920. Statistik des Deutschen Reichs, Bd. 293* (Berlin, 1921), pp. 21, 25, 26, 32, 33, 36, 46. A. Aghte: "Lohnsteigerungen", pp. 82–84.

The first thing to be observed from this Table is the far smaller increase of salaries in money terms (standing in February 1920 at 4.6 or 4.7 times the 1913/14 level) than of wages. This conclusion is not dependent on a comparison of four-weekly salaries with hourly wage rates: it holds for the comparison with four-weekly wage earnings too, as indicated by the relevant indexes for woodworking and textiles. Confining now our attention to wages, we can observe secondly the much greater increase of hourly than of four-

[18] Cp. Bry: *Wages*, pp. 209, 440ff. Also see pp. 28ff. *supra.*

[19] *Die Lohn- und Gehaltserhebung*, p. 19⁺.

weekly earnings, reflecting the shorter hours worked after the war than before it. Thirdly, the Table expresses the compression of skill differentials: in every case the lower limit to the range of index values refers to skilled workers and the upper limit to the unskilled, or women.

The implications of the Table for real earnings may be deduced from the fact that in February 1920 the Reich Statistical Office's cost-of-living index stood at 8.5 times its 1913/14 level where the basket included food, heating and lighting, accommodation and clothing, and at 7.0 for the same basket excluding clothing. Thus the average real wage of all workers investigated and for whom the comparison can be made declined unambiguously between the outbreak of war and February 1920. The fall of real daily and monthly earnings was large, that of hourly not so great. It is possible to express real wages in February 1920 as a percentage of their prewar level by application of the formula

$$\frac{\text{Wage index}}{\text{Cost-of-living index}} \cdot 100$$

using as the wage index the figures in Table 44 and two alternative cost-of-living indexes, namely the Reich Statistical Office's indexes inclusive and exclusive of clothing. An argument can be made for excluding clothing on the grounds that this class of expenditure, unlike the others, can be postponed in periods of real hardship; still the index including clothing cost yields a much more accurate deflator of money income movements. The real reasons for appending estimates of real income change using the deflator that excludes clothing are twofold: firstly between February 1920 and March 1922 the Reich Statistical Office published only the index excluding clothing, and so this was the index on which most contemporary discussion was based; and secondly, in order to illustrate the effects of variation in the basket of goods on the calculation of real income change. Table 45 reproduces the results of this exercise.

Comprehensive as the Wage and Salary Inquiry was, it pertains to a single month only. The representativeness of evidence pertaining to February 1920 for real income conditions during the whole postwar inflationary period may be gauged from the behavior of the available real wage time series. Four such monthly series, beginning in January 1920 and pertaining to skilled and unskilled employees of the Reich (railway workers), hewers and haulers in the Ruhr, and printers, have already been presented in Table 41. They refer to the real values of the wages negotiated under collective labor agreements, including the similarly negotiated cost-of-living supplements. Inspection shows that the first few months of 1920 represented a low point in real wage movements,

Table 45. Real income levels in various industries (Reich average) February 1920 as percentage of 1913/14

	Deflated using the cost-of-living index including clothing		excluding clothing	
	Hourly wages	Four-weekly earnings	Hourly wages	Four-weekly earnings
Construction	65–72	n. a.	79–87	n. a.
Leather	71–82	n. a.	86–100	n. a.
Woodworking	75–86	60–73	91–104	73–89
Textiles	86–109	65–84	104–132	79–101
Clothing	65–93	n. a.	79–113	n. a.
Iron and other metals	66–94	n. a.	80–114	n. a.
Salaried employees	–	54–55	–	66–67

Sources: Tables 44 and 4.

close to the wartime minimum of 1917, and that not until the final phase of the inflation, during 1922/23, were equally low or lower wages again recorded.

Diagram 7 confirms this conclusion. In it are depicted the findings of the comprehensive statistical Inquiries undertaken by the State Statistical Office of the City of Hamburg into wages paid in the principal industries and services in the city.[20] They were published on a monthly basis between January 1921 and August 1922 and compared with the corresponding data for April 1, 1920 and July 1, 1914. The subject of these Inquiries was the wage rates and cost-of-living supplements negotiated by collective agreement, however, and not actual earnings as investigated by the Reich's Inquiry of February 1920. Thus the resultant series must be taken to reflect minimum wages; they will not, for example, reflect overtime earnings and these, owing to the reduction of the standard day to eight hours, gained a certain, if limited, importance in the boom period of 1921 and 1922 (cp. p. 244).

---

20 *Der Wert der Gehälter und Löhne in Hamburg. Statistische Mitteilungen über den hamburgischen Staat, ed. H. Sköllin, Nr. 13* (Hamburg, 1922). Cp. the data on the real wages of skilled and unskilled in various industries in Rudolf Wissell: "Die Lebenshaltung der deutschen Arbeiterschaft seit dem Kriege", in *Deutschland. Jahrbuch für das deutsche Volk, ed. W. Külz, Bd. 1* (Leipzig, 1927), pp. 164–172, esp. Tables 1 and 2. These show a minimum at February 1920; not until 1923 were lower values recorded. Similarly, for February/March 1920, see the monthly real wage series in Margarete Soecknick: *Die Entwicklung der Reallöhne in der Nachkriegszeit, dargestellt an typischen Thüringer Industrien* (Jena, 1927). Cp. too Internationaler Gewerkschaftsbund, Amsterdam (ed.): *Die Lage der Arbeiterschaft in Deutschland* (Berlin, 1923).

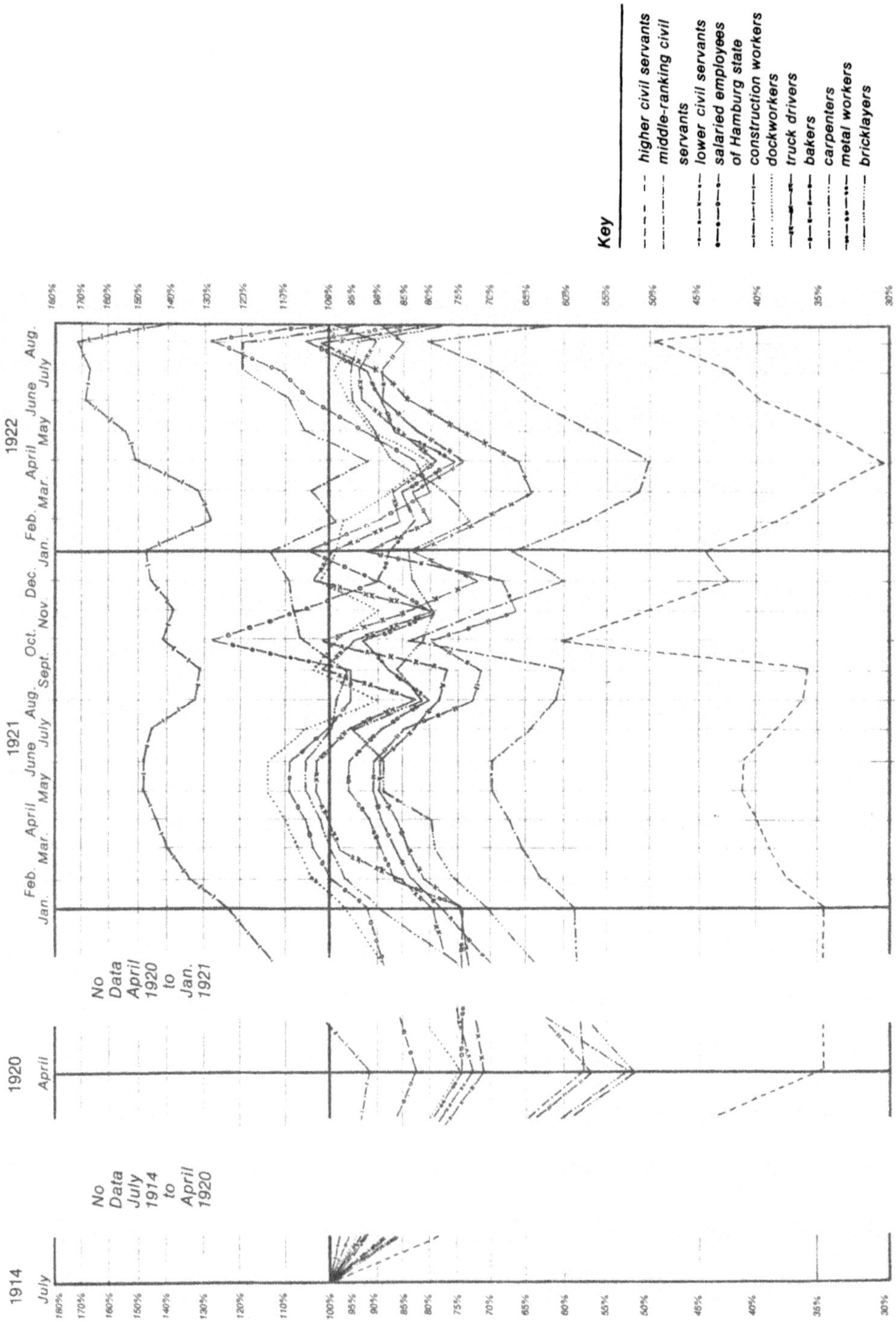

Diagram 7. Changes in real wages and salaries (hourly rates), as per collective agreements, 1920–22 as percentage of July 1914 (Semi-logarithmic scale)
Note: The data pertain to the first day of each month indicated.
Source: Der Wert der Gehälter und Löhne in Hamburg (Hamburg, 1922).

Collectively agreed wage rates were also often substantially exceeded when payment was by piece-rate.[21] "Workers income levels, particularly those of the unskilled, often turn out to be much higher than the [collectively agreed] wage rates would imply."[22] In Diagram 7 it is the hourly paid workers in the various occupational categories whose "tariff" wage rates are depicted. It confirms that by comparison with 1921 and parts of 1922, real hourly wage levels were especially low in the spring of 1920.

After the war the *Frankfurter Zeitung* investigated the collectively agreed wage rates of a wide variety of occupations in the Frankfurt region, publishing its findings on a regular basis.[23] On the problems presented by this kind of statistic in general, and by pre- and postwar wage comparisons in particular, it offered the following observations.

"1. The collectively agreed wages of manual workers – the group that chiefly concerns us – are increasingly supplemented again by *piece-rate bonuses*. These differ greatly however between occupations and localities, and according to results produced and state of trade.

"2. The increasing cost of living has caused the conventional wage, dependent on work done, to be supplemented by a *social wage*, varying according to family considerations – and this to no small extent in many a trade and many a locality. There are cases where wage earners with large families receive as "social supplement" up to forty percent of the value of their basic wage. The Berlin metal and engineering industry is a good example of this, while in other places "social wages" play only a modest role.

"3. Present-day wages cannot without further ado be compared with peace-time [i. e. prewar] wages even where apparently comparable data exist: the current working week is only forty-six or forty-eight hours but was much longer before the war.

"4. Furthermore, wage statistics calculated upon hourly rates presuppose some "normal" number of hours worked, but this presupposition is not always satisfied. *Overtime* is encountered in times of boom; short-time working is the lot of many workers during recession.

"5. Finally it must be borne in mind that a not insignificant number of workers has to get by without the help of collective labor agreements or

---

[21] Hildegard Heuer: "Die Entwicklung der Metallarbeiterreallöhne auf den Kieler Werften in der Zeit vom 1.4.1920 bis 30.10.23" (Dissertation, Kiel, 1929), *passim*. She compares hourly and piecework rates in the Kiel shipyards.

[22] *Der Wert der Gehälter*, p. 22.

[23] *Die Wirtschaftskurve*, 1 (1922) and subsequent volumes.

Public Servants' Remuneration Laws,[24] and often gets by very badly. In mind are categories of workers who are formally self-employed, such as seamstresses and private tutors, but also artists, freelance writers and certain theater personnel. Such groups cannot go unremarked for precisely among them do we find those members of the labor force whom the rising cost of living has most badly affected."[25]

Wage series for twenty-nine occupational categories in the Frankfurt region were combined into a composite index with a base of 1914 = 1; this index is shown in Table 46. The money wage index in the first column had to be deflated by the national cost-of-living index of the Reich Statistical Office since the corresponding regional index for Frankfurt was not available to a 1913 base. The Frankfurt "dearness statistic" can however be compared with the corresponding Reich average:[26] the two exhibit similar rates of change even though their levels show some significant differences.

Table 46 indicates that the real value of collectively agreed hourly wages could be sustained at above the prewar levels during the second half of 1920 and throughout 1921. Only in 1922 and 1923 did they fall, at times, under the prewar levels. However the variability of real wages was also of course much greater in this last pair of years than it had been before the war, owing to rapidly accelerating inflation. The series' maxima and minima occur in months closely agreeing with those of the Hamburg indexes of real hourly wages depicted in Diagram 7 during the period for which they are concurrent. The Hamburg series ceased in August 1922, but the correspondence just noted encourages us to believe that the movement of real wages shown by the Frankfurt index during the final phase of the inflation is representative of real wage movements at this time in other regions too. However it must be noted that the drop in the collectively agreed *hourly* rates during the last quarter of 1922 and in 1923, as shown by the Frankfurt index, is far less severe than that of the collectively agreed weekly rates shown in Table 41; this is true whether we measure the "drop" against prewar data or against real wage levels in the immediately preceding period. The real value of the collectively agreed weekly wages of skilled railway workers for example was 16.1% less in the second half of 1922 than it had been in the second half of 1921, and 30.1% less in the first

24 The concept of *Beamte* (civil servant, public official) in German is a wide one embracing not only clerical but also manual workers in public sector employment, including the railways.

25 *Die Wirtschaftskurve*, 1 (1922), Heft 2, p. 30.

26 Cp. *Vierteljahrshefte zur Statistik des Deutschen Reichs*, 29–32 (1920–1923), *passim*. On the "dearness statistic", see pp. 28–29 *supra*.

Table 46. Indexes of the money and real hourly wage rates of 29 categories of workers in Frankfurt and district, as per collective agreements, 1920–23 (1914 = 100)*

	Money wages	Cost of living	Real wages		Money wages	Cost of living	Real wages
	(1)	(2)	(3)		(1)	(2)	(3)
				1922			
				Jan.	23.60	20.41	1.156
1920				Feb.	25.46	24.49	1.040
Jan.	6.32			March	28.30	28.97	0.977
July	11.25	10.65	1.056	April	33.10	34.36	0.963
				May	42.35	38.03	1.114
Sept.	11.44	10.15	1.127	June	50.55	41.47	1.219
Oct.	11.76	10.71	1.098	July	60.50	53.92	1.112
Nov.	12.01	11.18	1.074	Aug.	93.14	77.65	1.199
Dec.	12.07	11.58	1.042	Sept.	154.4	133.2	1.159
1921				Oct.	213.1	220.7	0.966
Jan.	11.90	11.79	1.009	Nov.	333.1	446.1	0.747
				Dec.	586.7	685.1	0.856
May	13.84	11.20	1.236				
				1923			
July	14.16	12.50	1.133	Jan.	1140	1120	1.018
Aug.	14.60	13.33	1.095	Feb.	2366	2643	0.895
Sept.	16.68	13.74	1.214	March	3365	2854	1.179
Oct.	17.25	15.04	1.147	April	3613	2954	1.223
Nov.	19.33	17.75	1.089	May	4150	3816	1.088
Dec.	22.37	19.28	1.160	June	7082	7650	0.926

* For the cost-of-living index 1913/14 = 1. Since wages and prices were fairly stable in 1913–1914, this should not greatly affect the accuracy of the base of the real wage index (col. 3). However the fact that the money wage data refer to the beginning of the month but the cost of living index is an average for the month may bias the real wage index downwards in times of rising prices. On this problem, see C. Bresciani-Turroni: "Movements of Wages", pp. 381–382, the literature there cited and the attempts to quantify this bias.

Sources: Column 1: *Die Wirtschaftskurve*, 1–3 (1922–24), *passim.*
Column 2: Cp. Table 4
Column 3: Column 1 divided by column 2.

half of 1923. For unskilled railway workers the corresponding declines were 14.5% and 28.2%. On the other hand, the real value of collectively agreed hourly rates in the Frankfurt district was only 11.7% less in the second half of 1922 than in the second half of 1921, and 7.5% less in the first half of 1923.[27] Thus the deterioration of workers' real income levels after the middle of

27 Calculated from Table 46.

1922[28] seems to flow principally from a diminution of "wage drift" – that is, of the gap between actual and collectively agreed wages, as well as from a reduction in hours worked. The postulate of appreciable "wage drift" up to the summer of 1922 is rendered plausible by the excess demand in the labor market up to that point, which began to ebb away thereafter (cp. Table 35). Short-time working was certainly on the increase in the second half of 1922, suggesting a more general decline in hours worked, and this became intensified owing to the occupation of the Ruhr in January 1923.[29]

In evaluating this array of information about workers' real incomes particular attention must be paid to the fact that at the end of the war trade unions had succeeded in achieving a long standing demand: the eight hour day. A ten hour day had previously been the norm – coupled with considerable overtime especially during the war[30] – so that the fall in the length of the normal working week from 1919 was substantial. In 1913 one third of industrial workers covered by collective agreement had worked an agreed working week of between fifty-two and fifty-four hours. One quarter had worked between fifty-four and fifty-eight hours while almost thirty percent had worked between fifty-eight and sixty hours. Between 1919 and 1922 the collectively agreed working week was forty-eight hours for more than eighty percent of all workers covered by such agreements; most of the rest worked shorter hours.[31] It may therefore be assumed that the early postwar working week, as laid down in collective labor agreements, was some fifteen percent shorter on average than it had been before the war. However the average hours actually worked may have been more than twenty percent below the 1913 average: overtime had normally added eight percent to the standard working week before the war and sometimes up to twenty percent during it; but little overtime was worked in the years following it.[32] This, as already

[28] The *Statistische Jahrbücher f. d. Deutsche Reich*, esp. 42 (1921/22) and 43 (1923), contain data about the development of weekly earnings of various types of workers as per collective agreements. The deterioration of real income in the second half of 1922 and in 1923 is clearly discernible.

[29] Internationaler Gewerkschaftsbund: *Lage der Arbeiterschaft*, p. 113. Friedrich Hesse: *Die deutsche Wirtschaftslage von 1914 bis 1923. Krieg, Geldblähe und Wechsellagen* (Jena, 1938), p. 481.

[30] Cp. "Zusammensetzung und Löhne der Arbeiterschaft sowie die Arbeitszeit während des Krieges", *Reichsarbeitsblatt*, 17 (1919), pp. 618–623. Cp. too *Arbeitszeit, Lohn und Verdienst in Nürnberger Gewerben 1904–1919. Beilage zu den Statistischen Monatsberichten der Stadt Nürnberg vom Mai 1920* (Nuremberg, 1920). Robert R. Kuczynski: *Postwar Labor Conditions in Germany. Bulletin of the U.S. Bureau of Labor Statistics, No. 380* (Washington, D.C., 1925), p. 121.

[31] R. R. Kuczynski: *Postwar Labor Conditions*, pp. 98, 101.

[32] These particulars derive from a large Berlin electrical engineering plant: Kuczynski: *Labor*, p. 121.

mentioned, is the explanation for the greater shortfall, against 1913, of weekly than of hourly real wages in the years 1919–23.

It can be shown that there was a more pronounced decline in the hours worked by unskilled than by skilled workers:[33] compared with 1913 the decline for the unskilled amounted to about twenty percent, for the skilled about twelve percent. This difference partly reflects the fact that unskilled laborers had worked longer than skilled men in 1913, and also the fact that a greater proportion of ancillary than of skilled employment was regulated by collective labor agreements between 1919 and 1923, and hence observed the eight hour day more rigidly.

These considerations indicate that at least twelve percent of the decline in skilled workers' real incomes between pre- and postwar years occurred because fewer hours were being worked. This part of the decline cannot be considered an impoverishment of their living standards but rather an enrichment of the "basket of goods" worker households could consume, by the corresponding increase of leisure. No meaningful comparison of pre- and postwar real income levels can be made that does not take change in the length of the working week into account. If in Table 41 the index values of skilled workers' weekly wages are raised by fourteen percent for the postwar period and the values for the unskilled by twenty-five percent, a truer comparison with the corresponding 1913 values will be afforded. This done, it still turns out that skilled workers' real incomes were lower between 1919 and 1923 than in 1913 (skilled railway workers in 1919 excepted), but the dimensions of the decline appear less dramatic. Unskilled workers' real incomes, thus adjusted, were greater between 1919 and 1922 than in 1913, sometimes considerably so, and only fell short of the 1913 level in 1923.

This finding tallies with contemporary assessments. For example in an article which he wrote at the end of 1921 W. Morgenroth observed, that the "deterioration of living standards [among parts of the middle class] is considerably greater than among the broad mass of the working classes, of whom some have suffered only a small deterioration, and others none at all."[34] Eulenburg, too, noted that during the postwar period "labor at first benefited from the inflation. This must be strongly emphasized."[35] This is especially true if we

---

[33] Calculated from particulars on real hourly and weekly wages of skilled and unskilled workers combined into a weighted average for eight branches of industry. See G. Bry: *Wages*, pp. 453–454.

[34] Wilhelm Morgenroth: "Indexziffern", article in the *Handwörterbuch der Staatswissenschaften*, Bd. 5, pp. 403–404.

[35] F. Eulenburg: "Die sozialen Wirkungen der Währungsverhältnisse", *Jahrbücher für Nationalökonomie und Statistik*, 122 (1924), p. 781. A similar contemporary assessment will be found in

compare real wage movements with real national income movements over the same period (Table 40). For "one should not try to understand the place of a class in society by reference to what it was formerly, but always by reference to its relation to the whole."[36]

The following overall judgment of real wage change between 1914 and 1923 may now be offered. All categories of workers suffered substantial real income losses between the outbreak of war and 1917, their relative losses exceeding the decline of real national income as a whole (Tables 40, 41). Quante formulated the matter thus: "For all workers real wages declined appreciably between the middle of 1915 and the middle of 1917. For most workers this decline lasted for the duration of the war and there were only a small number for whom the prewar levels were maintained. For a very few an actual improvement over prewar levels is ascertainable."[37] After the war, and up till about the middle of 1922 – apart from a sharp dip at the beginning of 1920 – the real wage level was higher than it had been during the second half of the war. For the shorter period between spring 1920 and summer 1921 when prices and exchange rates were tending to stabilize, the real wage rates of the less skilled categories of workers were touching their prewar levels in weekly terms and sometimes substantially exceeding them in hourly terms, given the reduction in the working week. On the other hand, skilled workers' weekly wages were in some cases very much below prewar levels: 25%–35% less in the case of skilled employees of Reich enterprises, 30%–40% less in the case of printers. The experience of public officials was similar: at lower grades salaries were some 15–30% less in real terms than before the war and in the middle grades some 50% less.[38] But these categories, too, benefited from the fact that the working week was at least twelve percent shorter than before the war. Shorter hours represented a welfare gain: this was the rationale of the long trade union campaign for the eight hour day. In November 1918 it was at

Leo Stern (ed.), *Die Auswirkung der grossen sozialistischen Oktoberrevolution auf Deutschland, Bd. 4* (Berlin-East, 1959), p. 1697.

36 F. Eulenburg: "Soziale Wirkungen", p. 776. This consideration is not taken into account by the International Federation of Trade Union's Study, *Die Lage der Arbeiterschaft* (see footnote 20 above). Much of this study rests on a simple comparison of the movements of money wages and retail prices since 1914 – deducing from this an immiserization of the working class during the inflation. The fact that rents on dwellings scarcely increased is mentioned, but the purchasing power thereby released for spending on the disproportionately more expensive consumer goods is neglected.

37 P. Quante: "Lohnpolitik", p. 370. Cp. Jürgen Kocka: *Klassengesellschaft im Krieg 1914–1918* (Göttingen, 1973), pp. 12–21.

38 Statistisches Reichsamt: *Zahlen zur Geldentwertung in Deutschland 1914 bis 1923* (Berlin, 1925), pp. 41, 43. See footnote 24 above, p. 242.

length achieved and workers' welfare losses in the subsequent period were less than the above-stated percentage weekly real income shortfalls by the percentage reductions in the working week.

These conclusions permit an inference about the share of national income going to wages and salaries. If the proportionate decline of average real wage and salary levels between 1913 and 1919–22 was smaller than the corresponding decline of real national income, and the rate of employment was as high or higher in the later period than in the earlier, then labor's share must also have been at least as high in 1919–22 as in 1913. Indeed it may well have been higher, particularly for the more poorly paid workers. The thesis, that the inflation worked to the disadvantage of wage and salary earners,[39] is thus left without foundation – at least for the period before the summer of 1922, before the onset of hyperinflation.

The situation changed however in the second half of 1922. From then on the gap between current and prewar real wage and salary levels tended to be much larger than during the immediately preceding period;[40] this is the reality underlying the horror-images of hyperinflation.[41] Bry states that, "during the last phases of the crisis [real wages lay] pitifully below the real wages that prevailed before the outbreak of World War I."[42] I agree with this judgment. However I cannot accept his judgment regarding the preceding period, between the springs of 1920 and 1922, that real wages lay "substantially below"[43] the prewar levels.[44] Bry pays insufficient attention to the implications of shor-

---

[39] Cp. pp. 221–223 *supra*.

[40] This can also be deduced from the fact that wages' share in the selling price of products of various industries declined steeply from the second half of 1922, as data collected by the *Frankfurter Zeitung* show. Cp. *Die Wirtschaftskurve*, 2 (1923), Heft 3, pp. 37 ff. On the final phase of the inflation see too the carefully constructed real wage estimates of R. Meerwarth: "Zur neuesten Entwicklung", esp. p. 340.

[41] Especially Fritz K. Ringer (ed.): *The German Inflation of 1923* (New York, 1969). See too the documents in Herbert Michaelis and Ernst Schraepler (ed.): *Ursachen und Folgen. Vom deutschen Zusammenbruch 1918 und 1945 bis zur staatlichen Neuordnung Deutschlands in der Gegenwart*, Bd. 5 (Berlin, 1960).

[42] G. Bry: *Wages*, p. 233.

[43] *Ibid.*

[44] Bresciani-Turroni, in his "Movements of Wages", p. 392, expresses himself cautiously as regards real wages in 1920 and 1921, accepting the view of the International Labor Office, that the workers' income position had improved in those years and that the decline had not set in till 1922–1923 (I. L. O, *Workers' Standard of Life*). Cp. also the data in R. Wissell: "Lebenshaltung", Tabellen (i. e. Tables) 1 and 2 on pp. 166–167. Further, M. Soecknick: *Entwicklung*, Tabellen 2,7 and 10, and Hermann Knecht: "Die Entwicklung der Löhne und Gehälter der Münchener Arbeiter- und Beamtenschaft in der Kriegs- und Nachkriegszeit bis Ende 1923" (Dissertation, Erlangen, 1925). See also the methodologically very refined case study by Merith Niehuss:

ter working hours. If the workers themselves strove for and gained this reduction, one cannot then complain on their behalf that unaltered hourly rates yielded lower weekly earnings. No doubt hopes were disappointed that hourly rates would *increase*. But if national income falls because shorter hours are not offset by higher productivity, it cannot be made to "go round" twice in order to give everyone the same personal income as before. Reduction of working hours can be viewed as a way of spending income. If workers themselves bring it about, then it reflects the desire to apply some income formerly earned to the purchase of leisure. At unchanged hourly wage rates it no more represents a "loss of income" than would the purchase of a radio, but rather a voluntary decision about how to spend income, reflecting the preference of those who brought it to pass.

It may however be argued that inflation did add another kind of cost to income-earning. *Uncertainty* about future income increased, as a result of the extreme variability of real wages,[45] which in turn arose from the irregular pace of cost-of-living increases and the rather fitful accommodation of money wages to it. The measurement of the welfare costs of such uncertainty is far from easy. Arguably, however, they were entirely "psychic", whereas the real and material effects of uncertainty on the wage-earners' living standards were actually positive. Uncertainty made *carpe diem* the soundest maxim: a foreshortening affected the time-horizon within which people planned their expenditures. The incessant price rises likewise weakened the propensity to save. Even where current income levels left scope for saving, past experience indicated the unwisdom of acquiring monetary assets; to spend income quickly and wholly on consumer goods seemed the wiser course. Inflation may thus have tended to inhibit voluntary saving, and thus to raise levels of consumption and standards of living.

Statistics of consumption: problems

The particular difficulties besetting the calculation of real incomes during periods of severe monetary instability have by now received ample discussion. In the actual period of our study, the changing importance of price controls and rationing meant that commodity scarcities were not fully reflected in

---

Arbeiterschaft in Krieg und Inflation. Soziale Schichtung und Lage der Arbeiter in Augsburg und Linz 1910 bis 1925 (Berlin/New York, 1985).

45 This variability was particularly pronounced during the hyperinflation. Cp. Soecknick: *Entwicklung*, Tabellen (i.e. Tables), 2,7 and 10.

rising prices, and in any case the cost-of-living index is not an entirely satisfactory income deflator if our object is to ascertain the *level* of living standards. Hence statistics of consumption supply a useful check on the validity of the inferences we have drawn from the real income estimates; to the extent that they deal with the consumption of basic necessities, they also yield additional direct information about living standards.

The study of consumption can be pursued at the "macro" or at the "micro" level – from aggregate consumption statistics reduced to a per capita basis, or from the findings of household expenditure surveys. Changes in the macroeconomic consumption of everyday foods, both absolute and proportionate, may be studied in order to draw inferences about changes through time in average living standards. A general decline in quantities consumed, for example, or the substitution of lower quality foods for higher (e.g. canned meat or fish for beef, carbohydrates such as farinaceous foods for protein such as meat) would imply a worsening of living standards.

Such "macro" statistics as are available, comparing average per capita foodstuffs consumption in Germany in 1920–23 with that of 1913, are presented in Table 47. They indicate that consumption levels – whether of proteins or of carbohydrates – were generally lower in the later period. Consumption of imported fruits had dropped dramatically, but that of cocoa – also imported – shows a surprising increase; consumption of salt was also higher than in 1913. Up to 1921 the interpretation of these statistics is complicated by the concurrent operation of controlled, grey and black markets in many basic foods:[1] consumption supplied from the second and third markets slipped through the official statistical net. The promise of better profits was attracting increasing supplies to the black market, while reluctance to exchange goods for depreciating currency was encouraging barter transactions on the so-called "grey" market. Thus the 1920 and 1921 data, at least, understate consumption.

The "micro" approach to consumption involves the study of the budgetary practices of a sample of representative households over successive periods. From changes in the relative distribution of household expenditure among separate commodities or commodity classes, and from changes in the actual quantities purchased of the separate commodities, inferences may be drawn about changes in living standards. Where changes in the structure of expenditure are discovered Engel's Law may be invoked to interpret them; this much

---

[1] Potatoes and meat were not decontrolled, for example, till the autumn of 1920. Cp. pp. 87 ff. *supra*. See also Hans Feierabend: *Die volkswirtschaftlichen Bedingungen und die Entwicklung des Fleischverbrauchs in Deutschland seit Beginn des Weltkriegs* (Berlin, 1928).

Table 47. Per capita consumption of various commodities in Germany 1920–23. 1913 = 100*

	1920	1921	1922	1923
Potatoes	–	47	80	62
Rice	81	132	66	69
Meat	–	–	61	54
Herring	223	75	60	91
Imported fruit	29	21	19	16
Sugar	72	88	109	103
Salt	121	117	163	122
Cocoa	96	161	177	104
Coffee	27	50	24	25
Beer	37	53	50	44
Distilled spirits	25	36	71	43
Cotton	37	53	59	41

* Not all of the data cover exactly the calendar year; see source.

Source: G. Bry: *Wages*, p. 233.

verified "law" states that the proportion of household expenditure laid out on food is higher, the lower the household's real income level or the level of satisfaction of its needs.

Household expenditure surveys of this type will yield valid inferences about changes in the living standards of an entire nation, or large social group within the nation, only if the consumption habits of the sample selected for the survey are representative of those of the population for which the information is sought. Within every country, household income and household patterns of expenditure vary widely according to social and economic status and family situation. This implies that investigations of household budgets will yield meaningful results only when the sample investigated is drawn from a fairly homogeneous social group; furthermore that the conclusions reached about levels and changes of real income and consumption apply to that group only. Acting on this principle, the Imperial Statistical Office restricted its 1907 investigation of household budgets to low-income, mainly working-class families.[2] The budgets of a sample of households of metal workers, investigated at about the same time by the Metal Workers' Union, exhibited a rather similar structure.[3] During the war the Committee for Consumer Interests (KAKI: *Kriegsausschuß für Konsumenteninteressen*) collected the budgets of a

[2] *Erhebung von Wirtschaftsrechnungen minderbemittelter Familien im Deutschen Reich. 2. Sonderheft zum Reichsarbeitsblatt* (Berlin, 1909).

[3] Vorstand des Deutschen Metallarbeiterverbandes: *320 Haushaltsrechnungen von Metallarbeitern* (Stuttgart, 1909).

group of low-income families; and these are thus quite comparable with the two aforementioned prewar surveys made during 1907/08.[4]

Middle-class households will exhibit quite a different structure of expenditure. The *Frankfurter Zeitung* sought to document the lower level of living standards after the war than before it from case studies of three such households – all of a highly educated type, and gaining their income from salaried employment or professional fees. Three could hardly constitute a representative sample; still, the expenditure changes documented offer perhaps a rough guide to the experience of this particular type of middle-class household. Our discussion of real wage movements has already indicated that this type of household suffered far more severely than most from the inflation; its experiences are certainly not representative of those of the mass of wage and salary earners. Unfortunately however surveys of working-class household expenditure do not exist for the postwar inflationary period.

A second problem, specially concerning the interpretation of household surveys from whatever class between 1914 and 1924, is created by rent control. Before the war rent accounted for some twenty percent of total household expenditure; as the inflation proceeded however this percentage declined towards zero (Tables 4 and 8). At an otherwise constant standard of living this would necessarily cause the shares of other expenditures in the total to increase. Part of the proportionate increase shown by expenditure on food and drink during and after the war is to be attributed to this effect, rather than to a decline in living standards. Engel's Law interprets the structure of expenditure in terms of living standards only on the presupposition that supply and demand on the relevant markets are unconstrained by non-market forces.

Statistics of consumption: findings

Turning first to the household budgets collected by the War Committee for Consumer Interests (KAKI), we compare the expenditure patterns they reveal with those disclosed by the two surveys from 1907/08. As already stated, these two prewar surveys yield very similar results, and so in Table 48 only one of them – that of the Imperial Statistical Office – is reproduced.

[4] Waldemar Zimmermann: "Die Veränderung der Einkommens- und Lebensverhältnisse der Arbeiter durch den Krieg", in Rudolf Meerwarth *et al.*: *Die Einwirkung des Kriegs auf Bevölkerungsbewegung, Einkommen und Lebenshaltung in Deutschland* (Stuttgart, 1932), pp. 431 ff. On the findings of the KAKI expenditure surveys see too Götz Briefs *et al.*: *Die Hauswirtschaft im Kriege* (Berlin, 1917) and R. E. May: "Die deutsche Volksernährung gemessen am tatsächlichen Konsum grosser Konsumentenkreise", *Schmollers Jahrbuch*, 41 (1917), pp. 153–232.

Table 49 shows the findings of the wartime KAKI investigation. It shows the average distribution of the expenditure of households at various income levels taken together, and also of working-class households separately.

Table 48. The structure of expenditure of households of workers in typical income groups, 1907

Expenditure on	Annual income (marks) 1200–1600	1600–2000	2000–2500	1907 average
	%	%	%	%
Food, drink and tobacco	54.9	51.7	50.2	52.3
Clothing, linen	9.4	11.0	12.0	10.8
Rent, household costs	16.8	17.7	17.0	17.2
Heating and lighting	4.9	4.3	3.8	4.3
Other outlays	14.0	15.3	17.0	15.4

Source: Kaiserliches Statistisches Amt: *Erhebungen von Wirtschaftsrechnungen minderbemittelter Familien im Deutschen Reich. 2. Sonderheft zum Reichsarbeitsblatt* (Berlin, 1909). Cited according to W. Zimmermann: "Veränderung", p. 317.

Table 49. The structure of expenditure of households in various income groups and of workers' households, 1916, 1917, 1918: April each year

	Average of all income categories 1916	1917	1918	Workers' households 1917	1918
	%	%	%	%	%
Food, drink and tobacco	52.1	51.0	48.0	59.8	53.5
Clothing, shoes, repairs	7.6	9.9	16.8	10.1	14.4
Rent	10.7	11.3	8.3	8.1	6.8
Heating and lighting	3.6	5.4	5.4	5.5	5.5
Other outlays	26.0	22.4	21.5	16.5	19.8

Source: Reichsarbeitsblatt, 15 (1917), pp. 145–156 and 188ff. Also: *Beiträge zur Kenntnis der Lebenshaltung im dritten (vierten) Kriegsjahr. Sonderheft 17 (21) zum Reichsarbeitsblatt* (Berlin, 1917, 1919). Cited according to Zimmermann: "Veränderung", pp. 436–437.

What conclusions may be drawn from the two Tables? Confining our attention for the moment to the 1907 data in the first Table, we can clearly discern the action of Engel's Law across the different income levels: the share of expenditure going on food and drink is the greatest (54.9%) in the lowest income group, and least (50.2%) in the highest. As income rises, so do the shares of expenditure devoted to clothing and to the residual category, "other outlays" – mainly services such as education and recreation, insurance, transport. The share of expenditure going on heating and lighting tends to fall as we move up the income groups; that on rent remains roughly constant.

Thus it ought to be possible to draw conclusions about change in real income levels from intertemporal comparison between the structures of expenditure in 1907 and in the later years of the war. The average findings for all workers' households in Table 48 (fourth column) and the separately shown findings for workers' households in Table 49 (fourth and fifth columns) are probably the most directly comparable data in the two Tables. From this comparison it appears that the outlays on food and drink formed a considerably higher proportion of total expenditure in 1917 than in 1907 – 60% against 52.3%. In 1917 the share spent on heating and lighting (5.5%) was distinctly higher than in 1907 (4.3%). Both these comparisons suggest a depression in workers' households' living standards in 1917. However the behavior of the shares of expenditure accounted for by clothing and "other outlays" does not appear to support this simple conclusion; both were very little smaller in 1917 than in 1907. The resolution of this puzzle lies in the fall of the share of expenditure going on rent – from 17.2% in 1907 to 8.1% in 1917 – owing to the twin forces of the "rent freeze" (*Mietstop*) and inflation-induced increases in money wages. Thus outlays on food and on heating and lighting could claim greater shares of total expenditure in 1917 without eating into the shares spent on "clothing" and "other outlays".

No such clear picture emerges when we compare the expenditure structure in 1918 with that of 1907. The share of expenditure accounted for by heating and lighting was considerably greater in the later year; that claimed by food was however only slightly larger. These increases might suggest a more depressed standard of living in 1918 than in 1907, but the 4-percentage-point increases in the shares spent on clothing and on "other outlays" contradicts this conclusion. Only rent occupied a smaller share in 1918 than in 1907, for reasons already stated.

Comparison of the years 1917 and 1918 leaves little doubt that the standard of living was higher in the later year. Certainly the percentage share spent on heating and lighting did not change, but that spent on food fell substantially; the shares spent on clothing and "other outlays" rose by 4.3 and 3.3 percentage points respectively. These three comparisons speak unambiguously for an improvement in living standards – a finding which supports what we had already concluded from the real income series in Table 41.

Do comparisons made with prewar budget surveys done in 1907 really reflect the relation between wartime and *immediate* prewar living standards – i.e. those of 1913 or 1913/14? It is safe to assume that the living standards of wage and salary earners improved considerably between 1907 and 1913; at 1913 prices national income was 40.0 billion marks in the former year and 48.5 billion marks in the latter.[5] Zimmermann concluded after examination of prewar data on wages, prices and aggregate consumption: "It can certainly be shown that during the last two decades before the war the average member of the population had increasing scope to widen his diet in the direction of the more expensive foodstuffs, as well as of alcohol and tobacco... This consists with the fact emphasized above, that wage increases were running ahead of the rises in food prices."[6]

Before the war there were no state controls on prices, production or consumption. It is reasonable therefore to postulate that between 1907 and 1913 the composition of the expenditure of the lower income categories of workers came to resemble that displayed in 1907 by the highest income category. This implies that a more accurate comparison of working-class living standards in 1917 and 1913 is achieved if we compare the last two columns of Table 49 with the third column in Table 48; this comparison will tend to strengthen the impression that real income was lower in the later year.

In Table 50 the focus of attention shifts from the structures of consumer expenditure to the physical quantities consumed. Average consumption of foodstuffs making up more than half of total household expenditure is shown for the wartime (KAKI) survey – itemizing all three years – and for the two prewar surveys. The final column shows per capita consumption levels in the entire population implied by macroeconomic consumption data.

Abstracting for the moment from the fact that the wartime KAKI survey was biased heavily towards low-income families and hence not representative of consumption in the population as a whole, let us firstly observe the differences between the findings of this survey (columns 1–3) and the per capita quantities implied by the aggregative data for 1912/13 (column 6). The comparison suggests that the consumption of meat was smaller in the second half of the war – less than half as great as in 1912/13; and by bringing fish into the comparison we do not greatly change it. Less milk was consumed during the war; slightly more eggs in 1916 but not thereafter; likewise for fats. Consumption of fruit and vegetables declined by between one quarter and one third – and these were the chief sources of vitamins. Consumption of carbohydrates did not increase in the proportion that consumption of other foods had fallen. Sugar consumption was lower than in 1912/13, that of bakery products, pasta and other cereals much the same, while potato consumption, which had been at the prewar level in 1916, fell by one third in 1917 owing to the bad harvest and, after a good harvest, jumped to one third above the prewar level in 1918.

---

[5] W. G. Hoffmann *et al.*: *Das Wachstum der deutschen Wirtschaft seit der Mitte des 19. Jahrhunderts* (Berlin, 1965), p. 455. Cp. Table 40 *supra*.

[6] W. Zimmermann: "Veränderung", p. 328.

Table 50. Average per capita consumption of various foodstuffs 1916–18 compared with prewar. Grams per month

	KAKI budget surveys (all households)			Official survey of working class families	320 households of metal workers	Average per capita consumption in Germany
	1916	1917	1918	1907/08	1908	1912/13
	1	2	3	4	5	6
1. Bread	8304	8407	8956		13155 (1.–2.)	11010 (1.–3.)
2. Other bakery products	466	199	417			
3. Flour, pasta and other cereals	1445	2005	1592		1100	
4. Potatoes	16793	10934	21806	7666	10590	16380
5a. Butter	862 (5a.–5b.)	539 (5a.–5b.)	368	1116 (5a.–5b.)	525 (5a.–5b.)	750 (5a.–5b.)
5b. Fats, margarine, oils			289			
6a. Meat	1524 (6a.–6b.)	1941 (6a.–6b.)	1030	2291 (6a.–7.)	2064 (6a.–7.)	4020 (6a.–7.)
6b. Sausage, ham			439			
7. Canned meat	377	42	244			
8. Fish, smoked foods	857	404	776			690 (8.–9.)
9. Canned fish	–	–	–			
10. Eggs	12* (= 600 g)	7*	8*	340	425	510
11. Milk	8 Ltr. (= 9870 g)	7.7 Ltr.	9 Ltr.	10560	9580	13813
12. Cheese, cottage cheese	363	334	396	360		
13. Vegetables, fruit, dried vegetables	1703	2413	2860			10740 (13.–14.)
14. Canned vegetables and fruit	870	440	809			
15. Fruit purée, jam, artificial honey	890	622	1532			
16. Sugar	1184	897	843			1410
17. Coffee	226	90	241			
18. Substitute coffees	345	400	429			

* no. of eggs

Source: W. Zimmermann: "Veränderung", pp. 448–451.

Overall, then, there appears to have been a clear decline in the average quantities of foods consumed. The most serious falls were registered in the vitamin-supplying vegetables and fruit, and in proteins, while carbohydrates consumption showed no unambiguous decline. Thus the nutritional balance tipped towards the more basic carbohydrates.

Acknowledging now the need for homogeneity in the household groups presupposed by the comparison, let us compare the KAKI findings (columns

1–3) with the findings of the 1907/08 budget surveys (columns 4–5). This comparison will modify but not overturn the conclusions already reached. The fall in meat consumption appears smaller, and the consumption of eggs, milk and cheese did not greatly change. Declines registered against "fats", "bread" and "other bakery products" are obviously counterbalanced by increases against "pasta and other cereals", and above all by the rise in potato consumption (twice as high in 1916, thrice in 1918). Against this modification of the evidence of decline of working-class living standards between 1907/08 and 1916/18 must however be set the fact of their continuous improvement between 1908 and 1913. In view of this it cannot be doubted that physical consumption did fall between 1913 and the second half of the war and this, together with changes in the structure of food consumption, substantiates the proposition that wage and salary earners' real incomes fell during the war. The declines suffered by families with above-average incomes were probably even greater.

Comparing the three war years with each other, the quantities in Table 50 clearly indicate that 1917 was the worst year and that already by 1918 consumption had recovered again to a remarkable extent. This finding, too, corroborates the real income estimates in Table 41.

As already stated, there exist only three isolated examples of postwar household budget investigations and these are at best typical of the expenditure habits of certain middle-class households in big cities. One case study analyzes the household accounts pertaining to a civil servant's family of six plus a maid – seven in all. After one son had married during the war the number of persons was usually five or six and settled at five from December 1921 when a maid could no longer be afforded and a daily help was substituted. In 1913/14 about half the household's income had been derived from the husband's employment (annual salary 6319.96 marks – i. e. a higher civil servant) and about one third from the wife's career (annual earnings 3448.38 marks); the remainder was income from capital. During the inflationary years of 1920 and 1921 the husband still contributed about one half of household earnings, but the wife now only ten percent. The remainder was interest income, secondary earnings of the husband, contributions from the children's earnings, and realization of assets.[7]

[7] Henriette Fürth: *Der Haushalt vor und nach dem Kriege. Dargestellt an Hand eines mittelbürgerlichen Budgets* (Jena, 1922), pp. 16ff. Some further household budgets for similar families are evaluated in Adolf Günther: "Die Folgen des Krieges für Einkommen und Lebenshaltung der mittleren Volksschichten Deutschlands", in R. Meerwarth *et al.*: *Einwirkung*, pp. 210ff.

Table 51. The structure of expenditure of a higher civil servant's household 1913/14–1923. (%)

	1913/ 1914	1920	1921	1922	1922				1923		
					1.	2.	3. Quarter	4.	1.	2. Quarter	3.
I. Victuals	27	49	44	49	40	33	45	52	66	58	56
II. Household requirements	10	14	16	13	16	15	11	13	20	10	23
III. Other outlays	63	37	40	38	44	52	44	35	14	32	21

Source: H. Fürth: "Haushaltsrechnungen", *Die Wirtschaftskurve*, 1 (1922), 2 (1923), *passim*.

With this background let us examine the differences between this household's pre- and postwar expenditure patterns. Table 51 shows the proportionate division of its expenditure between victuals, household requirements and "other outlays". Rent and clothing fall under "other outlays", but heating, lighting, laundering, etc. under "household requirements."[8] The increased proportion of total expenditure laid out on victuals after the war is unmistakable, reflecting an inverse movement of living standards for this household. Food accounted for 27% of expenditure in 1913/14, but almost 50% in 1920. The situation clearly eased in 1921 as the share fell to 44%, but in 1922 it climbed again to 49%. The quarterly analyses reveal that a rapid deterioration set in with the onset of hyperinflation in the second half of 1922. A peak was reached in the first quarter of 1923 when victuals claimed no less than 66% of expenditure. These were the months when the Ruhr was occupied and the passive resistance commenced. The share going on food fell back after this but remained higher than in the preceding years till the end of the inflation.

Table 52 supplies the corresponding analysis of quantities consumed. Here the degree of impoverishment of consumption standards in this civil servant's household can be observed. The consumption of higher quality foodstuffs such as meat, butter, eggs, milk and wheat bread was much smaller between 1920–23 than in 1913/14 and it is not evident that consumption of inferior foodstuffs increased by an offsetting amount; however details of the consumption of flour, potatoes and pod vegetables – important "inferior" foodstuffs – are lacking for the last two years of the inflation. Only fats and rye bread were clearly used in greater quantities after the war than before it, but even the consumption of these declined sharply after peaks in 1920 and 1921 respec-

[8] H. Fürth: "Haushaltsrechnungen", *Die Wirtschaftskurve*, 1 (1922), Heft 2, p. 26.

Table 52. Per capita consumption of various foodstuffs in the household of a higher civil servant 1913/14 and 1920–23. Grams, liters or no. of eggs per day

	1913/ 1914	1920	1921	1922	1923	1922 1. Quart.	2. Quart.	3. Quart.	4. Quart.	1923 1. Quart.	2. Quart.	3. Quart.	4. Quart.
Rye bread	175	330	243	254	206	201	241	295	277	131	209	230	256
Wheat bread	115	8	41	32	36	46	54	13	13	63	61	8	10.5
Meat	130	75	105	77	66	114	47	74	72	73	82	57	51.3
Sausage, ham	17	18	17	30	13	26	43	21	30	19	9.5	15	8.9
Fats	9	19	43	36	29	34	39	41	30	39	31	27	19
Butter	32.5	8	9	11	10	9	13	7	16	17	15	7	1.5
Eggs	1.4	0.4	0.7	0.75	0.41	0.35	1.4	1.03	0.2	0.3	0.9	0.28	0.16
Milk	0.4	0.075	0.063	0.067	0.092	0.064	0.076	0.027	0.1	0.059	0.15	0.114	0.047
Sugar	63	69	56	48	24	41	70	36	46	47	29	17	2
Flour, etc.	89	105	43			10							
Pod vegetables	13	20	12			10							
Potatoes	300	980	328										
Fruit	375	282	123			48	78	152					

Source: H. Fürth: *Der Haushalt vor und nach dem Krieg*, pp. 32–33; also *Die Wirtschaftskurve*, 1–3 (1922–1924), *passim*.

tively. In conclusion: the quantities consumed in the household of this high official well illustrate the deterioration in the living standards of the particular section of the middle classes, to which it belonged, during the postwar years, with further intensification of the distress clearly visible in 1922 and 1923.

The second case study relates to the household (three adults) of a Berlin doctor residing in one unchanged dwelling in an unchanged manner before, during and after the war. It was supposed to represent the experience of the professional middle class without independent means.[9] The published Tables for this household present only index numbers showing change in total money expenditure and certain of its subdivisions (food, heating and lighting, rent); the series is a continuous one however, running on a half-yearly basis between 1912 and the end of 1920 and on a quarterly basis thereafter to the middle of 1922 (see Table 53). It can be seen that expenditure on food increased more than expenditure as a whole, expenditure on rent less, while the increase of expenditure on heating and lighting was sometimes more, sometimes less, but on average about the same as the increase of the total.

The text of the study makes the following observations about the structure of the household's expenditure in this case. "Before the war it used to be reckoned, as is well known, that the middle classes spent one third of their income on food and drink and about one sixth on rent. In our case study the corresponding proportions were 32.1 and 13 pCt; the fact that the percentage for rent is lower is fortuitous... The artificial influencing of prices during the war has the effect that the share of all expenditures other than food declines quite substantially as a proportion of the total. Particularly in the years 1918 and 1919 outlays on food rise above one half of total expenditures... These outlays in fact fall to about one third in the first half of 1921 but reach 40.6 and 44 pCt. during the last two quarters [i.e. the first half of 1922], thus approaching again the levels of the last year of the war and the revolution... High as the expenditure on heating may be, its share of total expenditure remains remarkably constant at 1¼ to 1½ times the peacetime [i.e. prewar] share... Rent has fallen from a peacetime 13 pCt. to 1.6 pCt. during the last two quarters."[10]

1918 and 1919 were thus the worst years of this household's real income experience, when foodstuffs' share of total expenditure climbed above the fifty percent mark. Improvement followed, and after a period when it remained relatively stable (and thus real income too according to this indicator) foodstuffs' share dropped to prewar proportions in the first half of 1921. But de-

---

[9] Hans Hirschstein: "Haushaltsrechnungen", *Die Wirtschaftskurve*, 1 (1922), Heft 3 pp. 25–29.
[10] *Ibid.*, pp. 28–29.

Table 53. Indexes of the money expenditure of the household of a Berlin doctor 1912–22. 1912–14 = 100

		Food-stuffs	Heating and lighting	Rent	Total expenditure
I Half	1912	93.7	136.5	94.3	86.8
II Half	1912	86.8	61.2	94.3	103.5
I Half	1913	105.5	139.8	94.3	99.7
II Half	1913	101.6	87.2	103.6	112.5
I Half	1914	112.5	74.5	113.1	107.2
Average		100	100	100	100
II Half	1914	112.1	72.0	113.1	105.2
I Half	1915	110.6	78.7	113.1	105.5
II Half	1915	–	–	–	–
I Half	1916	–	–	–	–
II Half	1916	165.6	81.1	113.1	124.1
I Half	1917	192.1	110.9	113.1	136.6
II Half	1917	216.5	197.9	113.1	164.1
I Half	1918	258.7	100.0	113.1	162.1
II Half	1918	407.5	218.0	113.1	265.0
I Half	1919	393.6	216.8	113.1	239.8
II Half	1919	531.0	473.6	132.5	340.6
I Half	1920	693.6	388.5	152.9	457.0
II Half	1920	1000.1	954.0	154.0	773.0
I Quarter	1921	1132.1	1628.0	158.4	979.6
II Quarter	1921	987.8	260.8	317.0	976.4
III Quarter	1921	868.2	1619.0	173.6	1082.0
IV Quarter	1921	1332.4	815.0	407.8	1035.6
I Quarter	1922	1830.0	1754.0	173.6	1478.8
II Quarter	1922	2734.0	2278.0	445.2	2049.0

Source: H. Hirschstein: "Haushaltsrechnungen", *Die Wirtschaftskurve,* 1 (1922), Heft 3, p. 26.

terioration set in again particularly during the first half of 1922. It can thus be concluded that in the case of this household the periods when real income was most depressed coincided with those when price rises were most rapid.

Shifts in the composition of expenditure during and after the war may be traced in the case of the third household also. Once again this was a middle-class household consisting in this case of three adults – two women with middle ranking salaried employments and their housemaid. In 1913/14 the household enjoyed an annual income of about 4800 marks.[11] The division of its expenditure among rent, food, heating and lighting, and "other outlays" is given in Table 54.

[11] *Die Wirtschaftskurve,* 2 (1923), Heft 1, p. 28.

Table 54. The structure of the expenditure of a three-person household (middle-ranking salaried employees) 1912/13–1923

	Rent	Food	Heating and Lighting	Other outlays
	%	%	%	%
1912/13	30.2	30.3	4.8	34.7
1913/14	27.1	30.7	6.8	35.4
1914/15	22.4	34.2	4.7	38.7
1915/16	21.4	42.5	4.4	32.0
1916/17	18.1	48.6	2.1	31.2
1917/18	17.7	42.7	5.5	34.1
1918/19	13.1	55.5	4.9	26.5
1919/20	6.8	58.1	11.6	23.5
1920/21	4.3	47.8	8.8	39.1
1921/22	2.3	59.3	10.8	27.6
I quarter 1922	3.8	55.2	4.3	36.7
II quarter 1922	2.6	47.2	21.5	28.7
III quarter 1922	1.2	69.3	9.3	20.2
IV quarter 1922	0.4	64.7	15.7	19.2
I quarter 1923	0.55 (0.2)[1]	53.6	13.1	32.75
II quarter 1923	4.6 (0.3)	35.7	6.1	53.6
III quarter 1923	0.2 (0.2)	91.6	3.6	4.6

[1] The percentage in parentheses is the share of "net" rent.
Source: Die Wirtschaftskurve, 2 (1923), Heft 1, p. 29; Heft 4, p. 21.

In this Table too the rising share of expenditure on food during the war and reaching a preliminary peak in the years 1918/19 and 1919/20 betrays the decline of real income. The situation eased in 1920/21 – the year of relative stabilization – but in the following year, and especially in the second half of 1922 when hyperinflation had begun, the share spent on food jumped dramatically, touching nearly 70%. Things eased again in the first half of 1923 but in the third quarter of the year a catastrophic 91.6% of all expenditure went on food.

The range of household expenditure surveys described in this section offer a far from complete and reliable account of the changes in living standards experienced at this time by the various strata of the German population. Best attested is the assertion that even the lower income groups had to suffer a distinct reduction of their living standards in the second half of the war. As far as the postwar period is concerned, the three individual case studies will support the impression of substantial deterioration in the living standards of the urban professional and salaried middle classes. For this class the most pronounced deterioration occurred in two periods, the first of which ran from 1918 to the spring of 1920 – i. e. from the last year of the war to the ending of the revolutionary unrest – and the second of which commenced with the onset of hyperinflation. Between these two periods, and particularly during 1921 their material situation showed some improvement.

In the parts they illuminate, the household expenditure surveys thus confirm the findings of the real income calculations. The most serious gap in the evidence is the lack of surveys of low-paid and unskilled working-class households during the postwar period – a group far more numerous than the middle classes represented by the three case studies we possess. Evidence was presented earlier in the chapter that the real incomes of the unskilled may even have exceeded prewar levels during parts of the postwar inflation, and it would have been particularly desirable to check this conclusion in view of its incompatibility with the prevalent interpretation of the postwar inflation as a period of general impoverishment. Perhaps however the fact, that where household expenditure surveys exist they corroborate the direct real income calculations, may encourage us to credit the evidence of these calculations in respect of social groups and periods for which independent corroboration is not available.

Statistics of health

Statistics relating to the health of the population during the inflation can also serve as indicators of nutritional change and hence of real income changes during the period. The Reich Health Office produced reports on general health in its *Veröffentlichungen des Reichsgesundheitsamts*, and published a good deal of statistical material.[12] The most salient evidence was summed up in a memorandum of October 1923 whose title may be translated, "On the health of the German People as of the period from the beginning of January to the end of September 1923."[13] According to this memorandum mortality in general and infant mortality in particular declined during the postwar years – even in 1923 – and lay considerably below prewar levels. This fact does not suggest general nutritional deterioration. The memorandum itself explains the discrepancy between the improvement shown in the statistics and the prevalent

12 Evaluated in Franz Bumm (ed.): *Deutschlands Gesundheitsverhältnisse unter dem Einfluss des Weltkrieges* (Stuttgart, 1928).

13 "Über den Gesundheitszustand des Deutschen Volkes nach dem Stande von Anfang Januar bis Ende September 1923": to be found in Arthur N. Young Papers, Archives of the Hoover Institution, Stanford, California Box 2. The following quotations are taken from this memorandum.

complaints about the poor state of postwar health in the following manner. "During the war and postwar period a weeding-out of the population was taking place. Many of its more sickly and infirm members, who under normal conditions would have survived for longer, have suffered premature deaths. The consequence is that death can no longer reap the same harvest as formerly... Mortality among infants... has however been lower throughout the entire postwar period than in earlier years. Infants, as already remarked in several places, fared much better than the rest of the population in the years following 1914. The increase in voluntary welfare activity and the fact of the Reich maternity benefit greatly contributed to this, and the old rule, that in times of hardship and high prices mothers are more likely to suckle their babies, was once again verified, thus ensuring infants of the best nourishment of all". Fertility had also declined, and this further reduced infant mortality, "since experience shows that the care taken in the nursing and management of infants and children increases, the fewer there are of them in the family."

But in the same context it was also observed, "that in 1920 and 1921 the standard of nutrition improved, and this led to an improvement in the health of the population". Following this however, and coincident with the start of the hyperinflation, "a renewed and progressive deterioration took place in the standards of nutrition and clothing". Only the wealthy few and the rural population was exempt from the "horrifying and universally evident under-nourishment"; the general population was forced to cut back its consumption of fats and proteins and substitute cereal-based foods. The dietary deterioration was particularly injurious to children. Fat deficiency, so the memorandum continued, lowers resistance to illness while protein deficiency retards their growth and development. "Present conditions are having an effect on nutrition not unlike those observed during the war, although the reasons for the crisis differ inasmuch as during the blockade the food was not available for money to buy whereas now the food is available but the population lacks the money to buy it". This last remark of course reflects the difference between controlled markets whose prices are held down, as in the second half of the war and to a lessening degree up to 1921, and the uncontrolled markets of 1923 where scarcities were fully reflected in prices.

A particularly clear portrayal of the effect of nutrition on public health is afforded by statistics of tuberculosis. The memorandum describes the wartime and postwar history of the disease as follows. "The campaign against this most deadly of infectious diseases had so far succeeded in driving it back that in Germany in 1913 there were only 14.33 fatalities per ten thousand inhabitants. During the war its incidence increased by 72.6% in urban areas and by 55.5% in the Reich as a whole. Happily however a rapid decline took place after the war, almost regaining the limit reached before it. A big-city minimum of 14.9 tuberculosis fatalities per ten thousand inhabitants was achieved in 1921, but this rose to 15.9 in 1922." The incidence rose yet further in 1923 as the quarterly statistics in Table 55 show.

Table 55. Fatalities from tuberculosis per 10000 inhabitants in 46 German cities, 1921–23

	I Quarter	II Quarter	III Quarter	IV Quarter	Entire year cases	Entire year incidence
1921	18.1	15.8	12.2	13.5	22438	14.9
1922	18.2	18.0	13.1	14.4	26123	15.9
1923	20.8	19.1			22329 (= I. + II. Qu.)	

Source: Memorandum des Reichsgesundheitsamts vom Oktober, 1923, in Arthur N. Young Papers, Hoover Institution, Stanford, Box 2, pp. 9, 10.

Deaths from tuberculosis were distinctly higher in the second quarter of 1922 than in the same quarter of 1921. The long winter bore some responsibility for this; however the rate showed a year-on-year increase for the rest of 1922 and this must reflect the general worsening of health conditions associated with deteriorating nutrition and falling real incomes. Exact statistics of the numbers who contracted tuberculosis do not exist, but the memorandum of the Reich Health Office reported, "that a continuous increase in admissions to tuberculosis clinics has been detected throughout the Reich since 1922 and is still in progress". Admissions in Berlin for the year 1922/23 were for example as much as 29% above those for the preceding twelve months.

The degree of malnutrition and consequent deterioration of health in big cities in 1923 may be judged from the following account by Professor Czerny, Director of the Berlin University Clinic, dated April 24, 1923. "My children's clinic is currently filled to overflowing with serious cases of tuberculosis of the lung, a condition normally encountered rather seldom among children... Only during the war and on account of the poor nutrition at that time have we previously observed a similar increase in tuberculosis cases." In 1923, Czerny continued, milk and sugar were particularly deficient, children being fed with farinaceous foods instead. In Leipzig, Hamburg, Breslau, Cologne and Frankfurt/Main the same situation could be observed. The deterioration during the course of 1923 itself can be deduced from the fact that in Berlin as many tuberculous children had already been admitted to the Empress Auguste-Viktoria Hospital for Combating Mortality in Infants and Young Children between April and September 1923 as had been admitted during the entire twelve months from April 1922 to March 1923. This evidence is doubtless typical of developments in big cities specifically; as already stated, mortality declined in the Reich as a whole in 1923, as did infant mortality in particular. Mortality in the countryside must then have fallen still faster than the Reich average to compensate for the increase in urban tuberculosis fatalities – an indication of the fact that the hyperinflationary hardships of 1923 were borne primarily by the urban population.

Famine oedema, scurvy, pellagra and other diseases associated with malnutrition were also increasingly evident in 1923. The memorandum concludes by observing that behavior and public morality had deteriorated *pari passu* with the physical condition of the people. "As a result, cases of the most serious crimes such as murder, robbery, burglary and theft increase from week to week."

All in all this stocktaking of the nation's health during the inflation supports the conclusions about workers' real incomes yielded by the real income calculations. Conditions were worst during the second half of the war and in 1923 – once the hyperinflation had caused real incomes to fall again from the relatively high levels enjoyed during 1920 and 1921.

8.4. The Distribution of National Income

Changes in the value of money derive their politically explosive potential from their impact on the income distribution.[1] In the present section this impact will be studied under two aspects.

[1] Thus particularly in the 1970s a consequence of the acceleration of inflation in the western world was a spate of studies dealing with the distributional effects of its (more moderate) modern manifestations. As regards Germany, see Manfred Ziercke: *Die redistributiven Wirkungen von Inflationen* (Göttingen, 1970). Horst Georg Koblitz: *Einkommensverteilung und Inflation in kurzfristiger Analyse* (Berlin, 1971). Ulrich Schrage: *Einkommensverteilung und Inflation* (Bamberg, 1973). Hans-Dieter Frey: *Auswirkungen von Preissteigerungen auf die Verteilung des Einkommens und des Vermögens* (Tübingen, 1975). Wolfgang J. Mückl und Richard Hauser: *Die Wirkungen der Inflation auf die Einkommens- und Vermögensverteilung. Zwei Literaturstudien* (Göttingen, 1975). Bernd Goerzig: *Die Verteilungswirkungen der Inflation auf den privaten und öffentlichen Sektor. Ermittlung von Inflationswirkungen nach alternativen Berechnungsansätzen* (Göttingen, 1975). For a survey of the field see Heinrich Hoelzer and Josef van Almsick: "Der Einfluss der Inflation auf die Verteilung von Einkommen und Vermögen", *Wirtschaftswissenschaftliches Studium*, 5 (1976), pp. 351–356.

(i) The functional distribution of income. This is its distribution among the various factors of production as "recompense" for their contribution towards generating it.

(ii) The personal distribution of income. This indicates the proportions received by households categorized according to level of income.

Deficiencies of data compel us to infer distributional changes during the decade 1914–24 from comparison of its structure before the war (1913) and after the stabilization (from 1925 on).[2] In the interim many factors were affecting the income distribution: the changed role of the trade union movement, changes in the tax system, the increasing importance of state transfer payments, changes in Germany's external economic relations, and so on. Nevertheless the inflation may be credited with the primary responsibility for the distributional changes that occurred. Indeed it may be stated that the latent purpose of inflation is always to effect such a redistribution of income and wealth from creditors as will make it possible either for the state or for particular private interests, which under stable prices would not possess the requisite means, to realize a desired rate of consumption or investment spending.

The functional distribution of income

Bourgeois economists[3] as well as Marxian theorists habitually reduce industrial societies to only two classes – "capitalists" and "workers". Wage and salary earners – the main constituents of the latter class – are perhaps sufficiently alike in their supplier status on the market for labor, and in the particular contractual forms of the employments from which they derive their incomes, to be considered as a unit, despite the vast income differentials that divide them. However I question whether a study of the distributional conse-

[2] Statistisches Reichsamt: *Das deutsche Volkseinkommen vor und nach dem Kriege. Einzelschriften zur Statistik des Deutschen Reichs, Nr. 24* (Berlin, 1932).

[3] Neoclassical textbooks also normally decompose national income into only wages and profits. E.g. Ernst Helmstätter: *Wirtschaftstheorie, Bd. 2* (Munich, 1976), pp. 227–240. Cp. C.E. Ferguson: *The Neoclassical Theory of Production and Distribution* (Cambridge, 1969), pp. 215ff. More generally on the theory of distribution, see Martin Bronfenbrenner: *Income Distribution Theory* (London, 1971). Official West German statistics, too, divide national income in the first instance into two categories only: Income out of paid employment (*Einkommen aus unselbständiger Arbeit*), and Income out of business enterprise and capital (*Einkommen aus Unternehmertätigkeit und Vermögen*). See e.g. Sachverständigenrat zur Begutachtung der gesamtwirtschaftlichen Entwicklung: *Jahresgutachten 1977/78*, Tabelle (i.e. Table) 16.

quences of inflation can best be pursued by likewise lumping together every kind of capitalist into a single class. Indeed a large part of this process of redistribution is transacted between two different groups of capitalists; in the interests of the analysis, then, a distinction is highly desirable.[4]

On the one side there are the "enterprise capitalists" ("active", or "real capitalists"): those capitalists who possess and manage the use of real productive equipment and undertake investment not only out of their own but also out of borrowed capital. Generally speaking, then, these own real assets and owe money. On the labor market they demand the labor power of and owe wages to the workers. On the financial markets they demand credit and owe interest and this distinguishes them from the other group of capitalists – the owners of financial assets.

This other group of capitalists – the "rentier class" ("money", or "passive capitalists") is correspondingly defined by its creditor status on the financial markets. Owners of real estate who receive their incomes out of the letting and leasing of their property should perhaps also be assigned to this class, since their incomes take the form of money claims rather rigidly fixed in the short term by contract or regulation, and not readily adjustable when the value of money changes.

During the epoch of "high capitalism" in the late nineteenth and early twentieth centuries the rentier class became increasingly numerous and distinct, so that it became possible to assign individuals in the wealthier classes to one or other of the two categories of capitalists.[5]

The significance of this division of the capitalist class at once becomes apparent when we consider the evidence in Table 56 about the functional distribution of income in 1913 and in 1925–31. Whereas income from paid employment is combined under a single heading – "wages and salaries" – income from enterprise and wealth-holding is divided into four categories, two of which relate to profits from business enterprise – in agriculture/forestry and in trade/industry respectively – and two of which relate to rentier income – from "letting and leasing" and from "financial assets" (quoted securities, shares in private companies, private mortgages, savings deposits, etc.).

"Enterprise capitalists'" share of national income after the inflation was not greatly different from what it had been in 1913; the fall in the share going to agricultural enterprise is an expression rather of the long-term decline of the

[4] Thus, too, J. M. Keynes: *A Tract on Monetary Reform. The Collected Writings of J. M. K., ed. E. Johnson and D. E. Moggridge, vol. IV* (London, 1971), pp. 4ff. (original edn. 1923).

[5] *Ibid.*, p. 5.

Table 56. Data on the functional distribution of German national income 1913 and 1925–31 (%)

Income Source	1913	1913	1925	1926	1927	1928	1929	1930	1931
	Prewar boundaries	Postwar boundaries of Reich							
1	2	3	4	5	6	7	8	9	10
Agriculture and forestry	13.0	12.5	9.5	9.3	8.4	7.7	7.6	7.4	8.2
Trade and industry	19.7	20.1	18.2	17.3	17.0	16.2	15.5	14.2	13.2
Wages and salaries	45.3	45.3	56.3	55.5	54.9	56.5	56.6	56.4	57.9
Financial assets	12.4	12.5	2.0	2.5	3.0	3.7	4.2	4.6	5.3
Letting and Leasing	2.0	2.0	0.9	1.0	1.1	1.1	1.1	1.3	1.6
Pensions and other transfers	3.0	3.0	9.2	11.4	10.5	11.2	12.0	14.3	17.6
Total private income	95.4	95.4	96.1	97.0	94.9	96.4	97.0	98.2	103.8
Plus									
Undistributed profits of companies	2.6	2.6	1.5	1.4	1.9	1.7	1.2	0.6	−1.8
Revenues of public enterprises	2.4	2.4	2.4	3.3	3.4	3.3	3.2	3.3	1.7
Employers contributions to social insurance	1.2	1.1	2.1	2.6	2.7	3.0	3.2	3.4	3.9
Taxes not included in private income	0.2	0.2	4.3	4.2	4.9	4.0	4.7	5.7	6.6
Minus									
Double counting arising out of government transfers	1.8	1.7	6.4	8.5	7.8	8.4	9.3	11.2	14.2
National income	100.0	100.0	100.0	100.0	100.0	100.0	100.0	100.0	100.0

Source: Statistisches Reichsamt: *Das deutsche Volkseinkommen vor und nach dem Kriege*, p. 84.

primary sector and a characteristic of industrial economies *per se*. The share going to "rentiers" however dropped dramatically – from 15% in 1913 to about 3% in 1925 and 1926. During the inflation itself rentiers' share was probably even smaller owing to the operation of rent control and the rapid depreciation of all fixed value monetary claims.[6] During the high employment

[6] In "Die sozialen Wirkungen der Währungsverhältnisse", *Jahrbücher für Nationalökonomie und Statistik*, 122 (1924), p. 755, F. Eulenburg values the aggregate of monetary assets in Germany in 1913 at 150–160 bn. marks. This corresponds roughly with the estimate of Adolf Günther on p. 168 of "Die Folgen des Krieges für Einkommen und Lebenshaltung der mittleren Volksschichten Deutschlands", in Rudolf Meerwarth *et al.*: *Die Einwirkung des Krieges auf Bevölkerungsbewegung, Einkommen und Lebenshaltung in Deutschland* (Stuttgart, 1932) – and with

years 1920–22 profits' (i.e. the "real capitalists'") share of national income was probably somewhat greater than in 1925–26 and the share going to wages and salaries somewhat smaller; this cyclical phenomenon does not touch the fact that the real losers from the process of redistribution were not the workers (who right up to the present day are recipients of only a small fraction of total unearned income)[7] but the recipients of rentier incomes. This explains the judgment of that knowledgeable contemporary, M. J. Bonn: businessmen had invented, in inflation, "a capitalist variant of communist expropriation. They robbed not their class enemies, but the broad mass of their own supporters."[8]

Paid employees formed about the same proportion of the working population in 1925 as in 1907.[9] Thus an enlarged share of wages and salaries in national income in the later period also implies a rise in the ratio of the average per capita income of paid employees to the average per capita income of the active population as a whole. On this view wage and salary earners may be regarded as the most unambiguous beneficiaries of the redistribution that attended the inflation.[10] "Real" capitalists almost maintained their share, and rentiers – i.e. recipients of unearned incomes – were the greatest losers. These consequences are perhaps also registered in the higher participation rates after the stabilization: 51.3% of the population was actively in the labor force in

---

that of Richard Hauser: "Zur Währungsfrage", *Bank-Archiv*, 18 (1918/19), p. 197. Hauser estimates the domestic currency bond stock for the prewar period at about 60 bn. marks, the mortgage bond stock at 40 bn. marks. These aggregates, which were substantially increased by the Reich's wartime bond flotations, were devalued (in real terms) by the inflation, as were the incomes they yielded.

7 In 1972 only 5.8% of the gross income of the households of those in paid employment (*Arbeitnehmer*) in West Germany was derived from the category "Business Enterprise and Capital". For the household income of those in self-employment (*Selbständige Haushalte*) the proportion was 86.3%. Cp. Sachverständigenrat zur Begutachtung der gesamtwirtschaftlichen Entwicklung: *Jahresgutachten 1977/78*, Tabelle (Table) 16. Before, during and after the First World War income from capital probably formed an insignificant part of the income of working-class households, given the lower level of economic development and hence the lower propensity to save on the part of the mass of income earners. This is confirmed by Georg Gradnauer and Robert Schmidt: *Die deutsche Volkswirtschaft. Eine Einführung* (Berlin, 1921), p. 151.

8 Moritz Julius Bonn: *Wandering Scholar* (New York, 1948), p. 278.

9 Statistisches Bundesamt: *Bevölkerung und Wirtschaft 1872–1972* (Stuttgart, 1972), p. 142. Between 1907 and 1925 salaried staffs and public officials increased from 10.3% to 17.3% of the occupied population, while wage earners declined from 54.9% to 49.2%.

10 However the increase in wages' share cannot be entirely attributed to the inflation; the same phenomenon was to be observed in Great Britain, a country with a falling postwar price level. See Phyllis Deane and W. A. Cole: *British Economic Growth 1688–1959. Trends and Structure* (Cambridge, 1964), pp. 241–258. A. L. Bowley and J. Stamp: *The National Income 1924. A Comparative Study of the Income of the United Kingdom in 1911 and 1924* (Oxford, 1927).

1925 as against 45.5% in 1907.[11] Elements in the population which before the war had lived from income for which they had not worked, such as the yield on capital, now had to take up gainful activity.[12]

Table 56 also discloses the substantial increase in the share of national income represented by transfer payments from the state. This comes to light in the two lines, "Pensions and other transfers", and "Double counting arising out of government transfers". The share of incomes received as state pensions and benefits rose from 3% in 1913 to 9.2% in 1925. It is chiefly connected with the expansion of the "welfare state"[13] particularly after the end of the war: war pensions, unemployment relief and other welfare benefits.[14] This expansion, too, benefited workers and others without wealth, rather than the "capitalist class". How far inflation itself aided the expansion of social expenditure in early Weimar years hardly admits of an exact answer. It may be premised however that the influence was positive: inflation acts as a tax source which even the weakest governments can always exploit.[15] Past and present experience shows that deflationary policy, by contrast, is always associated with measures of public economizing precisely in the fields of social expenditure – as the later history of the Weimar Republic, both after 1923 and particularly between 1929 and 1932 abundantly demonstrates.

According, therefore, to the data on the functional distribution of income, wage and salary earners benefited the most from the distributional effects of the inflation after the war. They shared the benefits in part with the business class, the "real capitalists", with whose employer associations their own trade unions collaborated in the "Central Working Community" (*Zentralarbeitsgemeinschaft*); the gains were made chiefly at the expense of the rentier class. Wage and salary earners' households generally belonged to the lower income categories, whereas rentier households – whether entirely dependent on unearned income or using it to supplement income from gainful activity[16] – were

---

[11] Statistisches Bundesamt: *Bevölkerung und Wirtschaft*, p. 140

[12] Cp. F. Eulenburg: "Soziale Wirkungen", pp. 757–758.

[13] On this see the forthcoming study by Peter-Christian Witt: *Die Finanz- und Wirtschaftspolitik des Deutschen Reiches 1918–1924. Wohlfahrtsstaat und Demokratie am Anfang der Weimarer Republik*, cited in Jens Flemming *et al.*: "Sozialverhalten und politische Reaktionen von Gruppen und Institutionen im Inflationsprozess. Anmerkungen zum Forschungsstand", in Otto Büsch and G. D. Feldman (eds.): *Historische Prozesse der deutschen Inflation. Ein Tagungsbericht* (Berlin, 1978), p. 261.

[14] Statistisches Reichsamt: *Das deutsche Volkseinkommen*, p. 81.

[15] J. M. Keynes: *Tract*, p. 37.

[16] This was usual for example for the households of military officers, professors and (higher) civil servants before the First World War. The results of this inquiry into the social conditions of the working class are confirmed by Werner Abelshauser: "Verelendung der Handarbeiter? Zur

most commonly found in the upper income groups. The functional redistribution effected by the inflation must thus have implied a more egalitarian distribution of personal income. To this we now turn.

The personal distribution of income and wealth

Table 57 supplies information about the personal distribution of income – that is, its distribution among households classified by size of income – in 1913, 1926 and 1928. It is based on tax statistics. The purchasing power of money was lower in the latter two years than in the first, and to take account of this the income boundaries by which households are classified differ in the two periods.[17] In making comparisons the fact of the 1926 recession[18] must be borne in mind – a recession more pronounced than that of 1913. In 1928 the level of economic activity was more comparable with that of 1913 and, for the purpose of ascertaining fundamental shifts in the distribution, comparison of these two years will be best. Table 58 sets out the relative change in the individual income classes between these two years.

The considerable and complementary shifts in the two lowest income categories between 1913 and 1928 are at first striking: a large proportion of income earners and national income have slid down into the bottom class. This is at least in part attributable to the fact that the number of persons liable to taxation was increased after the war. On the other hand, the boundary of the lowest class was pitched too high in 1913, relative to its placement in 1926 and 1928: a limit of 800 rather than 900 marks would have matched the postwar 1200 marks better, given the change in the purchasing power of money.[19] The graduations are dictated however by the principles of assessment governing the underlying tax statistics and so cannot be remedied. Considering both the two lowest income categories together we see that, both before the war and

---

sozialen Lage der deutschen Arbeiter in der grossen Inflation der frühen zwanziger Jahre", in Hans Mommsen and Winfried Schulze (eds.): *Vom Elend der Handarbeit. Probleme historischer Unterschichtenforschung* (Stuttgart, 1981), pp. 445–476.

[17] For a criticism of the comparison, see Statistisches Reichsamt: *Das deutsche Volkseinkommen*, p. 129.

[18] On the 1926 slump see F. Blaich: *Die Wirtschaftskrise 1925/6 und die Reichsregierung. Von der Erwerbslosenfürsorge zur Konjunkturpolitik* (Kallmünz, 1977). Dieter Hertz-Eichenrode: *Wirtschaftskrise und Arbeitsbeschaffung. Konjunkturpolitik 1925/26 und die Grundlagen der Krisenpolitik Brünings* (Frankfurt/M., 1982) Carl T. Schmidt: *German Business Cycles 1924–33. Publications of the N.B.E.R. No. 25* (New York, 1934) pp. 35ff.

[19] *Das deutsche Volkseinkommen*, p. 108.

Table 57. The stratification of personal income in Germany 1913, 1926, 1928

Income categories		1913		1926		1928	
1913	1926, 1928	No. of taxpayers	Uncorrected incomes	No. of taxpayers	Uncorrected incomes	No. of taxpayers	Uncorrected incomes
1	2	3	4	5	6	7	8
marks	reichsmarks	%	%	%	%	%	%
to 900	to 1200	47.6	22.5	64.0	34.4	57.8	29.1
above 900 to 2100	above 1200 to 3000	42.7	37.2	28.2	32.3	31.8	32.6
above 2100 to 3300	above 3000 to 5000	5.3	10.4	4.9	12.6	6.4	14.0
above 3300 to 5500	above 5000 to 8000	2.4	7.0	1.8	7.2	2.5	8.9
above 5500 to 8500	above 8000 to 12000	0.9	3.9	0.6	3.7	0.8	4.5
above 8500 to 10500	above 12000 to 16000	0.27	1.7	0.21	2.0	0.28	2.2
above 10500 to 16500	above 16000 to 25000	0.37	3.1	0.18	2.3	0.23	2.6
above 16500 to 30500	above 25000 to 50000	0.25	3.5	0.10	2.3	0.13	2.6
above 30500 to 70000	above 50000 to 100000	0.13	3.8	0.03	1.4	0.04	1.6
above 70000	above 100000	0.06	6.9	0.01	1.8	0.02	1.9
	Total	100.0	100.0	100.0	100.0	100.0	100.0

Source: Statistisches Reichsamt: *Das deutsche Volkseinkommen vor und nach dem Kriege*, p. 108.

Table 58. Changes in the stratification of personal income in Germany. 1928 as % of 1913

Income categories		No. of taxpayers	Uncorrected incomes
1923	1928		
marks	reichsmarks	%	%
to 900	to 1200	+61	+24
above 900 to 2100	above 1200 to 3000	− 1	−16
above 2100 to 3300	above 3000 to 5000	+60	+28
above 3300 to 5500	above 5000 to 8000	+34	+21
above 5500 to 8500	above 8000 to 12000	+18	+10
above 8500 to 10500	above 12000 to 16000	+35	+24
above 10500 to 16500	above 16000 to 25000	−17	−19
above 16500 to 30500	above 25000 to 50000	−28	−28
above 30500 to 70000	above 50000 to 100000	−60	−61
above 70000	above 100000	−65	−73
	Total	+33	− 4

Source: as for Table 57.

after, they contain about ninety percent of income recipients liable to taxation and about sixty percent of aggregate taxable income. The slightly higher percentages for 1926 may well be connected with the recession of that year, since recessions commonly affect high incomes relatively more severely than low ones.

It is immediately observable from Table 58 particularly that it was not the middle incomes which were affected the most severely by the postwar redistributive processes; in fact it was exclusively the upper income groups and specifically all four income classes receiving in excess of sixteen thousand marks per annum. Such high incomes derive almost exclusively from business enterprise and ownership of wealth; here, then, we find the counterpart of the decline in rentier income which Table 56 disclosed as an effect of the inflation. Where members of middle income groups derived income from financial assets, the inflation must have caused them losses also. But for these groups as a whole, increases in income from other sources must have more than offset losses from capital income, for they emerged from the inflation attracting a larger share of national income overall. The old argument that the middle classes were the principal victims of the inflation[20] is thus not merely open to

20 *Die Verelendung des Mittelstandes. Heft 106 der Beiträge zur Statistik Bayerns* (Munich, 1925). This work confined its detailed investigation of the middle classes (*Mittelstand*) to officials (*Beamte*), salaried employees and professional people – i.e. to groups whom the inflation indeed impoverished. According to Robert Michels: *Umschichtungen in den herrschenden Klassen nach dem*

the objection that it is insufficiently differentiated;[21] at this level of aggregation it is simply false, for on the contrary, according to Tables 57 and 58 the middle income groups constitute the only categories which the inflationary process enlarged. The chief victims – contrary to the impression which Bresciani-Turroni seeks to convey[22] – were the highest income recipients. Their losses have less to do with the introduction by the Erzberger reforms of a tax system tailored to the individual capacity to pay – a tailoring which the inflation nullified in the short run anyway – than with the confiscatory implications of inflation for the owners of money capital.

Thus inflation brought about a more equitable personal income distribution in Germany.[23] Available measures of the degree of personal income

---

Kriege (Stuttgart, 1934), p. 106, the effects of the inflation were not purely negative on either the "old" middle class (i.e. the more prosperous self-employed, farmers, masters of small businesses, etc.) or the "new" middle class (i.e. salary earners). F. Eulenburg states in his "Soziale Wirkungen", p. 756, that the annihilation of money values affected primarily "the broad stratum of the middle class", yet he does not unqualifiedly regard the middle class as a whole as losers from the inflation. In *Die Umschichtung der europäischen Vermögen* (Berlin, 1925), esp. p. 40, Richard Lewinsohn reaches a similarly ambivalent verdict. "Whether a destruction of the middle class really occurred in Germany, as is constantly asserted and was apparently the case, must be considered at least doubtful. Doubtless the old (urban) middle class was annihilated by the currency depreciation, but in its place thousands have newly gained wealth, and possess today the salient characteristics of the middle class." Heinrich August Winkler essentially adopts this cautious assessment in his *Mittelstand, Demokratie und Nationalsozialismus. Die politische Entwicklung von Handwerk und Kleinhandel in der Weimarer Republik* (Cologne, 1972), pp. 28–29. In *The German Inflation 1918–1923* (Amsterdam, 1964), p. 121, K. Laursen and J. Pedersen express a more decided opinion. "It has been argued in retrospect that the 'middle class' was made to suffer inequitably by the inflation, that in fact it was exterminated, leaving the field to the 'high finance' and the proletariat, and that this was the real cause behind the emergence and development of nazism. In our view this is an altogether erroneous diagnosis. The term 'middle class' is vague. But if by the term is understood 'middle sized' farmers and small and middle sized business enterprises, the converse is nearer the truth." This opinion is entirely supported by evidence of the data presented here on the more equitable distribution of the German national income after the inflation.

21 On the differentiating of the concept of "middle class" (*Mittelstand*) see above all Theodor Geiger: *Die soziale Schichtung des deutschen Volkes. Soziographischer Versuch auf statistischer Grundlage* (Darmstadt, 1967), esp. pp. 106 ff. (original edn. 1932). Geiger emphasizes the importance of "mentality" as a subjective element of the "feeling of belonging" to a particular class, in contrast to objective criteria such as level of income. Cp. too A. Günther: "Die Folgen des Krieges", esp. pp. 224 ff. where quite an elaborate differentiation of the middle class is undertaken.

22 C. Bresciani-Turroni: *The Economics of Inflation. A Study of Currency Depreciation in Post-War Germany* (London, 1937), pp. 290 ff.

23 Thus the opinion, "The inequality of the distribution of income increased greatly between 1919 and 1923" (J. Flemming *et al.*: "Sozialverhalten", p. 258), is, in my view, untenable.

inequality confirm this. For the Reich as a whole, W. G. Hoffmann estimated the Pareto coefficient α at 1.50 in 1913, at 1.98 in 1926 and at 1.89 in 1928;[24] an increase in this coefficient indicates an increase of equality. For Prussia, where two thirds of the German population lived and two thirds of the national income was generated, statistics of direct taxation permit the calculation of the Pareto coefficient back to 1850. Between the middle of the nineteenth century and 1900 it fell from 1.88 to 1.44: income inequality increased. Between 1900 and 1913 the coefficient was approximately constant. Grumbach attributes this constancy to the increasing power of the trade unions, expansion of social insurance and more progressive taxation – changes which affect primarily income from capital and retard the growth of profits and the accumulation of wealth.[25] The growth and distribution of wealth are the primary determinants of income distribution: "besides these factors all others appear to be of secondary significance."[26]

The coefficient dropped very sharply during the war, reaching a minimum of 1.35 in 1918. The increase in inequality thereby indicated may be attributed to war profiteering and the effect of this on the concentration of wealthholding. But between 1925 and 1929 the Pareto coefficient was at a much higher level than even in 1913 – between 1.73 and 1.88. Thus in the intervening period some dramatic process of income and wealth redistribution must have occurred, undoing in a few years most of the concentrative effects of the previous seventy years of industrialization.

Grumbach himself, in order to explain this phenomenon, calls attention to his finding that the distribution of financial wealth was less equal than the distribution of wealth as a whole.[27] Thus an annihilation of financial values

---

[24] W. G. Hoffmann *et al.*: *Das Wachstum der deutschen Wirtschaft seit der Mitte des 19. Jahrhunderts* (Berlin, 1965), p. 515. They reproduce the findings of Franz Grumbach: "Statistische Untersuchungen über die Entwicklung der Einkommensverteilung in Deutschland" (Dissertation, Münster, 1957), p. 29, where the methods of calculating, and the reservations about, the Pareto coefficient as a measure of the equality of the income distribution are expounded. Cp. also Angelos Angelopoulos, *Die Einkommensverteilung im Lichte der Einkommensteuerstatistik* (Leipzig, 1931), esp. pp. 119–123; he compares the distribution in 1914 and 1926 and reaches the same conclusions as those expressed here. On methods of measurement and their problems, see the more recent studies of Albert Jeck: *Wachstum und Verteilung des Volkseinkommens. Untersuchungen und Materialien zur Einkommensverteilung in Deutschland 1870–1913* (Tübingen, 1970). J. Heinz Müller und Siegfried Geisenberger: *Die Einkommensstruktur in verschiedenen deutschen Ländern 1874–1913* (Berlin, 1972). Cp. more generally, M. Bronfenbrenner: *Income Distribution Theory*, pp. 43ff.

[25] F. Grumbach: "Statistische Untersuchungen", p. 92.

[26] *Ibid.*, p. 89.

[27] Ibid., pp. 95–96.

would tend to promote greater equality in the distribution of the income derived from wealthholding and hence in the distribution of all incomes.

If, furthermore, the annihilation of financial assets is associated with a reduction of the aggregate value of all assets, there will be a yet stronger tendency toward income equality. Income from capital of whatever kind, like the distribution of asset-holding itself, is less equally distributed than the national income as a whole; if the proportion of national income which is derived as income from capital declines, the overall distribution of national income will become more equal.

Tables 59 and 60 show that the two effects did indeed combine during the inflation. Table 59 indicates that at December 31, 1923, taxable wealth was more equally distributed than it had been ten years earlier.[28] The two lowest wealth classes virtually doubled their share of aggregate wealth and the middle categories – encompassing wealth held in fortunes between thirty thousand and one hundred thousand marks – also enlarged their share of the total. But the categories above these and embracing the largest fortunes diminished relative to the aggregate, and the proportionate decline was larger, the higher the category. See Table 60.[29]

Table 60 also indicates that over this ten year period the aggregate value of wealth declined by 61.2%.[30] This is much in excess of the 25–30% fall in real national income between 1913 and 1923 suggested by Table 40, and so we may conclude that income from capital did indeed become a smaller proportion of national income.[31] Greater equality in the distribution of national income would follow from this – as already argued.

---

28 On the problem of the comparability of the pre- and postwar wealth distribution data, see Statistisches Reichsamt: *Die deutsche Vermögensbesteuerung vor und nach dem Kriege. Statistik des Deutschen Reichs, Bd. 337* (Berlin, 1927), p. 204. The main point is that the regulations governing the valuation of assets did not tally. "Even so, a comparison is not valueless".

29 A "Lorenz curve" of the distribution of wealth-holding in excess of 10,000 marks can readily be calculated for the data in Table 59: it too indicates greater equality in 1923 than in 1913.

30 In "Volksvermögen, Volkseinkommen und Steuerlast einst und jetzt", *Weltpolitik und Weltwirtschaft*, 1 (1925), Heft 1, pp. 11 ff, K. Helfferich reached a similar estimate of the proportionate decline of German national wealth between 1913 and the end of the inflation – namely from 310 bn. to 150 bn. marks. He offers an interesting analysis of the losses: 50 bn. on account of wartime deterioration of real assets (= neglect of repair and replacement investment), 30 bn. through loss of assets abroad, 25 bn. owing to losses in ceded territories, 10 bn. in equipment surrendered under the terms of the Armistice and Peace Treaty, and 50 bn. in the form of diminished profitability of capital employed in business enterprise, reflected in reduction of equity values. Cp. Wilhelm Winkler: "Volksvermögen", article in the *Handwörterbuch der Staatswissenschaften* (Jena, 8 Bde. 1921–9), Bd. 8 (1928), p. 775.

31 Cp. Table 56 *supra*.

Table 59. The stratification of wealthholding (above 10000 gold marks) by individuals in Germany according to the *Vermögensteuer* (Wealth Tax) statistics, 12.31.1913 and 12.31.1923. % of total

Wealth category in gold marks	December 31, 1913 No. of taxpayers %	Net wealth %	December 31, 1923 No. of taxpayers %	Net wealth %
above 10000 to 20000	34.20	7.38	47.489	14.87
above 20000 to 30000	20.36	7.36	19.397	10.45
above 30000 to 50000	19.49	11.03	15.683	13.30
above 50000 to 100000	14.65	14.88	10.595	16.09
above 100000 to 500000	9.78	27.90	6.092	25.61
above 500000 to 1000000	0.94	9.48	0.494	7.40
above 1000000 to 3000000	0.48	11.14	0.214	7.29
above 3000000 to 10000000	0.09	6.47	0.033	3.46
above 10000000	0.01	4.36	0.003	1.53
Total above 10000	100.00	100.00	100.00	100.00

Source: Statistisches Reichsamt: *Die deutsche Vermögensbesteuerung vor und nach dem Kriege. Statistik des Deutschen Reichs, Bd. 337* (Berlin, 1927), p. 206.

Table 60. Changes in the stratification of wealthholding in Germany. 12.31.1923 as % reduction on 12.31.1913

Wealth category in gold marks	No. of taxpayers	Net Wealth
above 10000 to 20000	−18.9	−21.7
above 20000 to 30000	−44.4	−44.9
above 30000 to 50000	−53.0	−53.2
above 50000 to 100000	−57.8	−58.0
above 100000 to 500000	−63.6	−64.4
above 500000 to 1000000	−69.4	−69.7
above 1000000 to 3000000	−73.8	−74.6
above 3000000 to 10000000	−78.5	−79.2
above 10000000	−85.3	−86.4
Total above 10000	−41.6	−61.2

Source: as for Table 59.

An illuminating overall perspective on the effects of the inflation on domestic income and wealth distribution is afforded by a comparison with the Old Testament prescriptions for the "year of Jubilee."[32] This "year of rest" was to recur every fifty years and in it debts were to be cancelled, rural (not urban) land sold or mortgaged during the intervening forty-nine years to be restored

[32] Old Testament, Leviticus 25.

to its original owners, and Israelite slaves and bondservants to be set free. Concentrations of income and wealth were thus reversed in a rhythmically recurring process. Mortgaged property was disencumbered, and laborers released from their subordination. They could of course fall into bondage again, but the more diligent among them obtained the chance of a fresh start. Original relationships and distributive structures were reconstituted and the economic struggle to increase income and amass wealth could begin again.

The German inflation happened about fifty years after the founding of the second empire. Monetary claims and liabilities have greater implications for the distribution of wealth and power in industrial than in pre-industrial societies, and, in the monetary sphere, the inflation acted like a "year of Jubilee". Its economic and social consequences were somewhat similar. The cards were dealt out afresh: the capitalist contest for power, profit and property could be recommenced – not of course from the beginning entirely, since the ownership of real property had not been touched, but at any rate under altered starting conditions.

Chapter 9
Inflation and the International Distribution of Income

9.1. Preliminary Observations

In discussions of the distributive effects of inflations in general and of the German inflation after the First World War in particular, attention generally centers on the redistribution of income and wealth within the country experiencing the inflation.[1] Underlying this preoccupation is, in economic terms, the theoretical model of the closed economy. In this model the high rates of investment and of economic growth during the postwar inflationary years[2] appear as the result of a process of domestic redistribution in which consumers, including besides rentiers the broad mass of wage and salary earners, suffered. The following quotation from Emil Lederer is characteristic of this viewpoint. "During the entire [postwar inflation] period, the [real] wage level stood far below the prewar wage level. Per capita production declined, but not as fast as [real] wages. If we assume an average reduction in real wages of no more than five hundred [gold] marks per wage and salary earner [per annum] ... then we obtain a figure of six or seven billion gold marks per annum, or a total of between twenty-four and twenty-eight billion gold marks, as the sum which industry accumulated in unpaid wages. This sum, plus the aggregate value of the savings deposits which the inflation had annihilated... (estimated at about fifty billion marks), plus also the unpaid taxes, supplied, without the help of foreign loans, the funds for the astonishingly rapid reconstruction of the German economy."[3]

---

[1] Cp. the recent works on the distributional effects of the inflation cited in note 1, p. 265 *supra*. Also Franz Eulenburg: "Die sozialen Wirkungen der Währungsverhältnisse", *Jahrbücher für Nationalökonomie und Statistik*, 122 (1924), pp. 748–794.

[2] Cp. Tables 32, 40, and Diagram 4.

[3] Emil Lederer: "Umschichtung der Einkommen und des Bedarfs", in Bernhard Harms (ed.): *Strukturwandlungen der deutschen Volkswirtschaft* (Berlin, 2 Bde. 2nd edn. 1929), Bd. 1, p. 52 (original edn. 1928). See also Julius Hirsch: "Wandlungen im Aufbau der deutschen Industrie" in the same work, Bd. 1, p. 201, "... the inherent sense of the inflation as an economic occurrence was the reduction of consumption for the benefit of the renewal and reconstruction of

On this view, then, the inflation was primarily a problem of *domestic* politics. But this understanding does not square with the simple fact that even contemporary political debate about the inflation revolved round arguments about its *international* causes and consequences. Even at the time the inflation was primarily viewed either as a means of influencing, or as the outcome of, events in the international arena.

The official German viewpoint has already been described.[4] It followed the balance-of-payments theory of the inflation and asserted that the currency depreciation was caused by the deficit in Germany's current account balance. This deficit arose on the passive side out of the large imports made necessary by Germany's shortage of raw materials; Reparations payments constituted a further important item on this side. On the active side, so the argument went, exports were able to earn only a meager quantity of foreign exchange, owing especially to the trade discrimination practiced against Germany by foreign governments. Until foreign markets for German exports were re-opened (most-favored-nation treatment restored), Reparations demands reduced, and long-term foreign loans made available to Germany, thereby restoring proper balance-of-payments equilibrium, the depreciation of the currency would inevitably follow from the workings of supply and demand on the foreign exchange market.

The French had a different view. They argued that the German government knowingly and deliberately pursued an inflationary policy with the aim of evading its Reparations obligations. But both French and Germans agreed that circumstances in, or considerations respecting, the international arena determined the inflationary outcome.

This agreement suggests the utility of performing an analytical "dissection" of the inflationary process that will expose its international "dimension". The model of a "closed" economy conceals this dimension; our "scalpel" will be the model of an "open" economy. What it lays bare will enable us to answer two questions. Firstly, what were the effects of the inflation on the distribution of income and wealth between the German economy as a whole and the rest of the world? In other words, what part did foreign countries play

---

productive equipment". Similarly, Fritz Sternberg: *Der Niedergang des deutschen Kapitalismus* (Berlin, 1932), p. 183.

[4] See p. 156 *supra*. Also Walther Rathenau: *Cannes und Genua* (Berlin, 1922), pp. 10ff. and p. 35. See also the government memoranda: *Deutschlands wirtschaftliche Leistungsfähigkeit*, and *Denkschrift über die Zahlungsfähigkeit Deutschlands für die Wiedergutmachung* (both Berlin, 1920); or the government memorandum of March 1923: *Deutschlands Wirtschaftslage unter den Nachwirkungen des Weltkrieges* (Berlin, 1923), pp. 21–24. See too Hermann Bente: "Die deutsche Währungspolitik von 1914 bis 1924", *Weltwirtschaftliches Archiv*, 23 (1926), I, p. 135+.

in raising the capital to finance Germany's high investment and facilitate her rapid growth during the early postwar years? Secondly, what light does the answer to this question shed upon the degree to which economic policy in postwar Germany was rationally pursued, given the goals it set itself and the constraints under which it acted?

9.2. Methods of Calculation and Findings

The boundary between those who gain and those who lose from the redistributive effects of changes in the value of money is the boundary between debtors and creditors. Considering an economy as a closed system, gains and losses from inflation can be predicated of particular social and occupational groups according to the side of this line on which their members typically stand. In like manner, the nation as a whole will gain or lose from the process of inflation in the measure that it is a net debtor or creditor *in its own currency* to abroad.

Germany lay on the debtor side of this international economic boundary. Even in the period 1914–1918, but especially between 1919 and 1922, foreign countries accumulated substantial paper-mark claims on Germany, thereby granting credit or, put differently, exporting capital to Germany. This was how Germany financed her large external current account deficits of those years. "Foreign credits of the usual kind... could not be obtained [by Germany] on any large scale", was the contemporary observation of M. J. Bonn. "The necessary funds have been furnished chiefly by all kinds of speculation in marks."[5]

Germany became a mark-currency debtor to abroad. In addition, her own claims on foreign countries had either been sold during the war to finance imports or confiscated by enemy governments. Unlike the better-known import of capital by Germany after 1924, the capital influx of the inflation period was exclusively of a short-term nature; it consisted predominantly of foreign speculation in the mark made in the expectation of a recovery of its value on the foreign exchange markets. In as much as such expectations found expression in a premium on the mark in the *forward* exchange market, this speculation also induced exchange-risk-covered foreign investments in the German money market, attracted by the high rate of return (domestic interest

[5] Moritz Julius Bonn: *The Stabilization of the Mark* (Chicago, 1922), p. 29.

rate plus swap rate).[6] A further difference between the pre-1923 and the post-1924 capital inflows was that currency depreciation practically converted the pre-1923 flows into unilateral capital transfers. Because the statistical information was inadequate,[7] this international effect of the inflation was often overlooked. Gustav Stolper, for example, wrote, "During the inflation period, Germany indeed discharged her reparation obligations out of her own resources, without the crutch of foreign capital."[8] In reality, foreign capital was flowing into Germany in significant amounts.

Two different methods may be used to estimate the extent of Germany's foreign indebtedness – more particularly her mark-denominated indebtedness – in this period.

(i). The indirect method: estimating it as the residual of all other items in the balance of payments. The balance of payments is constructed according to the principles of double entry bookkeeping, so that to every plus or minus item in the current balance there corresponds a minus or plus item in the capital balance.[9] Gold and foreign exchange movements and the residual balancing

---

[6] By "swap rate" is meant the difference between the forward and spot market rates of exchange on an annual basis and expressed as a percentage of the spot. See pp. 74 *supra* and 292 *infra*.

[7] Cp. Fritz Schmidt: *Internationaler Zahlungsverkehr und Wechselkurse* (Leipzig, 1922), pp. 28, 393. Schmidt was already remarking on the almost total dearth of statistical information about short-term foreign credits to Germany. The difficulties and limits, but also some possible ways of estimating these data are exemplified in Arthur I. Bloomfield: *Short-term Capital Movements under the Pre-1914 Gold Standard* (Princeton, 1963). At least for the years 1914 until 1934, (after which, following the world economic crisis, statistical reporting of short-term international capital flows was improved) the remark of Jacob Viner (*Studies in the Theory of International Trade* (New York, 1937), p. 407) holds good: "International short-term lending still awaits its historian".

[8] Gustav Stolper, Karl Häuser and Knut Borchardt: *The German Economy 1870 to the Present* (New York, 1967), p. 98.

[9] Fritz Machlup distinguishes three concepts of the balance of payments which are often confused, in "Three Concepts of the Balance of Payments", in his *International Payments, Debts and Gold* (New York, 2nd edn. 1976), pp. 69ff. (original edn. 1964. The London, 1966, edition was entitled *International Monetary Economics*). The three concepts are:

1. The market balance, as a model of a given situation on the foreign exchange market in respect of the effective supply and demand schedules on that market. This is an *ex ante* concept chiefly used for the analysis of the effects which changes in the exchange rate might have on the amounts of foreign exchange effectively demanded and supplied.

2. The program balance as a statement of sources and uses of foreign exchange, expected or planned, over a given future period, based on the nation's capital and consumption requirements, and as a program of meeting an excess of requirements over resources by recourse to foreign finance expected or sought. This is also an *ex ante* concept for use, not in the analysis of an actual supply-demand constellation and its possible influences on the exchange rate (as in case 1), but rather for use in planning, forecasting or negotiating, with major emphasis not on

item are entered under capital account; they too represent (for the most part) changes in the asset position of the domestic economy relative to abroad.[10]

Quantifying Germany's considerable trade deficit between 1919 and 1922 is not an easy matter owing to the difficulty of ascertaining correct gold-mark valuations of the trade flows. Estimates vary from 4.5 to 11 billion gold marks.[11] To this were added the 2.6 billion gold marks' worth of cash Reparations payments.[12] A small surplus may have been earned on invisible account during those years (chiefly from tourism) but it was very small: the sum of the trade deficit plus Reparations represents the order of magnitude of the current account deficit as a whole (cp. Table 61).

---

what is effectively demanded but on what is felt to be desirable with reference to some accepted standards.

3. The accounting balance as a record of all transactions, real and financial, which have taken place over a past period of one or more years, between a country's residents and residents of other countries, the record being kept in the form of double-entry bookkeeping with each credit entry being balanced by an offsetting debit entry and vice versa. This is an *ex post* concept based on statistical information and estimates, and is used chiefly for the description and conceptual classification of past developments. This balance "necessarily balances" (p. 82); a net surplus or deficit on the directly recorded transactions must be exactly matched by a counter-entry of opposite sign in the "residual" category. Deficits or surpluses can appear only in sub-balances (e. g. the merchandise, services, basic or foreign exchange and gold balances) which of course are so selected as to throw light on the state of the "market" or "program" balances.

[10] The definitional and causal relations between the various forms of international capital movements on the one side and of cross-border flows of goods and services (particularly goods) on the other are dealt with by Fritz Machlup: "Capital Movements and the Trade Balance", in idem: *International Payments*, pp. 447–464.

[11] R. Pilotti, a member of the Guarantee Committee of the Reparations Commission in Berlin, estimated in a memorandum (Berlin Document 3062) of January 19, 1924, that the total deficit on the German trade balance between 1919 and 1923 was 4.5–6.5 bn. gold marks. Cp. Leonard P. Ayres Papers, Library of Congress, Manuscript Division, Washington, D. C., Box 2, Folder: "Documents, Memos, Report re Germany's Fiscal Positions, January-March 1924". Also in Archives of the Hoover Institution, Stanford, California, Henry M. Robinson Papers, Box 16; and in Archives Nationales, Paris, Commission de Réparation, Comité de Garanties, Fond AJ 6, 806. The German government put the deficit in the years 1919–22 alone at 11 bn. gold marks. Cp. *Deutschlands Wirtschaftslage unter den Nachwirkungen des Weltkrieges*, p. 23. The McKenna Committee finally estimated the deficit at 6.3–7.3 bn. gold marks for the postwar inflation years. See p. 203 footnote 20, *supra* and p. 285 footnote 15 *infra*.

[12] According to the calculations of the Reparations Commission, Germany paid the following sums between the Armistice and December 31, 1922: cash Reparations payments – 1.7 bn. gold marks, "clearing house" payments in settlement of prewar international private claims – 0.6 bn. gold marks, the portion of total occupation costs (0.63 bn. gold marks) which was transferred abroad – 0.3 bn. gold marks. These sums totaled 2.6 bn. gold marks. Cp. R. Pilotti as cited in the preceding footnote. This figure was used in the calculations of the McKenna Committee.

To this must be added the gold-mark value of German capital exports during those years, and then we have the total which had to be financed by the sale to abroad of real assets, the sale to abroad of long- and short-term foreign-currency denominated debt instruments, and the sale to abroad of paper marks and other short-term mark claims. If the sale to abroad of real assets and foreign-currency denominated claims can be quantified, then the sale to abroad of paper mark claims can be inferred from the balance of payments as a residual. See Table 61.

Table 61. The structure of the German balance of payments 1919–23

Credits i.e. foreign currency receipts		*Debits* i.e. foreign currency outlays
II. Export surplus in the invisible balance		I. Import surplus on merchandise balance III. Cash payments on Reparations account
Net capital imports	=	Current account deficit
V. Import of capital to Germany 1. against the sale of real assets or foreign-currency denominated debt to abroad: a) gold and foreign exchange b) real estate c) common stocks d) foreign-currency denominated bonds e) short-term foreign-currency denominated debt. 2. against the sale of domestic-currency denominated debt to abroad: a) fixed interest mark bonds b) German banknotes c) mark deposits at German banks d) other short term mark debt		IV. Export of capital from Germany

This method does not promise reliable results. Not only is the statistical information about categories I, II and V.1 of the scheme in Table 61 deficient; direct estimates of category IV – capital exports – are virtually unobtainable; it would be difficult even to make an informed guess. A direct investigation would require access to the books of all foreign bankers and brokers through whom Germans and their foreign agents placed their investments. It may be doubted whether a world-wide search on this scale would ever be practicable, but in any case the undertaking would fail against the intransigence of banks' refusal to reveal the secrets of their relations with their clients; even in the 1920s attempts by official agencies to gain information from bank sources on this matter failed.

(ii) The second method of estimating Germany's mark indebtedness to abroad in this period is to proceed directly – to try to assemble direct information on the various ways in which foreigners could acquire mark-denominated assets – by buying German domestic securities, by buying German banknotes, and by making mark deposits in German banks.

F.D. Graham used the first, or indirect method.[13] He reckoned that by accumulating paper claims foreigners transferred capital to Germany to the amount of 15.7 billion gold marks over the period 1914–22 as a whole. J.M. Keynes and K. Singer employed the second, or direct, method, and estimated the unrequited resource transfer into Germany between 1919 and 1922 at between eight and ten billion gold marks.[14] Their calculations had to make do with rather scanty and unreliable data. However the McKenna Committee in collaboration with official German agencies made extensive inquiries into the matter and in the end put a figure of 7.6–8.7 billion gold marks on Germany's gains from the sale of mark-denominated bank balances and banknotes to foreigners.[15]

The McKenna Committee used the second, or *direct* method of estimating this sum, as part of its procedure for obtaining an *indirect* estimate of the quantity which it had really been set up to ascertain – the value of Germany's capital assets abroad. It had been established by the Reparations Commission

[13] Frank D. Graham: *Exchange, Prices and Production in Hyper-Inflation: Germany, 1920–23* (Princeton, 1930), pp. 255–259.

[14] J.M. Keynes: "Speculation in the Mark and Germany's Balances Abroad", in *Reconstruction in Europe. Manchester Guardian Commercial Supplement* of September 28, 1922, pp. 480–482. Reprinted in *The Collected Writings of J. M. Keynes, ed. E. Johnson and D.E. Moggridge, vol. XVIII* (London, 1978), pp. 47ff. esp. p. 53. Kurt Singer: "Die deutsche Auslandsverschuldung", *Wirtschaftsdienst*, July 27, 1922, pp. 660–661. Both estimates were cited and evaluated in Harold G. Moulton and Constantine E. McGuire: *Germany's Capacity to Pay. A Study of the Reparation Problem* (New York, 1923), pp. 80–85, 295–302.

[15] "The Report of the Second Committee of Experts", in *Reports of the Expert Committees appointed by the Reparations Commission* (London, 1924), pp. 135–6; reprinted in Harold G. Moulton: *The Reparation Plan. An Interpretation of the Reports of the Expert Committees...* (New York, 1924), pp. 304–5. The McKenna Committee had been set up in order to investigate the widespread rumors (particularly in France) of enormous amounts of German capital abroad. The various methods by which German firms had supposedly transferred capital abroad had been the subject of tendentious discussion in e. g. L. Wulfsohn and G. Wernle, *L'Évasion des Capitaux Allemands* (Paris, 1923).

in 1924, alongside the Dawes Committee, with the special task of quantifying the amount of German capital which had "fled" the country during the inflation, and to make proposals for utilizing these sums in payment of Reparations. The Committee took as its starting point an estimate of the aggregate value of German wealth abroad just before the outbreak of war, and with the aid of a staff of experts sought to employ balance-of-payments analysis to estimate the additions to and subtractions from that stock up to the end of 1923. In effect it prepared a detailed classification of the items falling under the headings I, II, III and V of the scheme in Table 61, sought to quantify them, and hence infer IV as a residual, obtaining by this indirect route an estimate of Germany's wealth abroad at the end of the inflation.

Among the most careful investigations commissioned by the Committee was an examination of the accounts of eight leading Berlin banks[16] undertaken by a London firm of accountants – that is, of the Deutsche Bank, Dresdner Bank, Disconto-Gesellschaft, Darmstädter und Nationalbank, Berliner Handelsgesellschaft, Commerz- und Privatbank, Mitteldeutsche Creditbank, and Mendelssohn and Co. The object was to obtain exact evidence about the development of foreigners' net mark credit balances – that is, their mark deposits with, net of their mark indebtedness to, German banks. From the data they collected they calculated the extent to which foreigners had suffered creditor losses from the depreciation of the mark, the counter-value of which had benefited the German economy. They estimated these losses at between seven and eight billion gold marks. More than one million foreigners, so it was discovered, had held accounts at German banks during the course of the five years since the war. This indicates the breadth of mark speculation on the part of the foreign business community during those years.

The following method served as a basis for the calculation of these foreign losses. For seven of the eight banks it was possible to determine the net mark balances in foreigners' accounts at the end of each month from December 31, 1918 to June 30, 1923. Each of these aggregated net paper-mark balances was then valued in gold marks using two different exchange rates: the average mark-dollar exchange rate for the same month and the equivalent average for the following month. When the value of the mark fell on the foreign ex-

[16] A copy of the 21-page auditors' report can be found in the Leonard P. Ayres Papers, Box 1, Folder "Rep. Committee – Report". Another copy is in Archives Nationales, Paris, Commission de Réparation, Fond AJ 6, 393. Unfortunately the statistical appendixes of the report are missing in both locations. Ayres was consulted as an "expert" by both the Dawes and McKenna Committees and was involved in the auditing of the German banks. The following remarks, insofar as they go beyond the published report of the McKenna Committee, are based on this document.

changes between the two months, the difference between the two gold-mark values was counted as a loss to foreigners from holding mark bank balances; when the value of the mark rose, the difference was counted as a gain. The monthly outcomes were then cumulated and added to the gold-mark value of foreigners' bank accounts on June 30, 1923 – which last item entered the sum as a loss, in view of the utter collapse of the mark in the months following (this gold-mark value of the June 30, 1923 balances was in any case negligible). It was assumed that the seven audited banks handled approximately 72% of the foreign currency business of all German banks. From this, the loss on foreigners' bank balances in all banks in Germany was estimated at between seven and eight billion gold marks.

According to data from the Deutsche Bank, which accounted for about thirty percent of foreign currency business in Germany (more than any other bank), citizens of foreign countries held mark balances, thus participating in this loss-making short-term capital export to Germany, in descending size of national share, as follows:

1. U.S.A.	4. Italy	7. Switzerland
2. Spain	5. Holland	8. Greece
3. Austria	6. Poland	9. Great Britain

Thus the United States bore the lion's share of the losses. The American financial expert, Leonard P. Ayres, who was a consultant to the Dawes and McKenna Committees and had been involved in the auditing of the German banks, estimated the U.S. loss at $770 million (= about 3.2 billion gold marks).[17] This represented little less than half of the total estimated gains to Germany from the depreciation of foreigners' mark bank balances.

What share of total bank deposits was accounted for by foreigners' bank balances during those years? In the accounts of the audited banks the experts found information on this matter as follows (the percentages refer to the end of each year: cp. Table 62):[18]

1918:	20%	1921:	36%
1919:	35%	1922:	11%
1920:	36%	1923:	2%

[17] Leonard P. Ayres: "The Works of the Dawes and McKenna Committees", in the *Cleveland Trust Monthly*, 5 (1924), no. 5, May, p. 6. A copy of the article is filed in Leonard P. Ayres Papers, Box 8.

[18] Allied Powers (1919-) Reparation Commission, Documents collected by the Second Committee of Experts: flight of German capital. Paris, 1924. (= unpublished material in Hoover Institution, Stanford, California) pp. 134s, 134k. Also in National Archives, Washington, D.C., Records of the Department of State, Decimal File. Record Group 59, Case 462.00 R 296, Sub Number 225. And in Archives Nationales, Paris, Commission de Réparation, Fond AJ 6, 395.

From this it is evident that foreigners possessed a significant and increasing share in bank deposits in the early years of the inflation. The share in 1919–21 was about the same as in 1929, when foreigners held some 38% of the value of deposits in German joint stock banks.[19] K. E. Born pointed out in his discussion of the 1931 banking crisis that the significance of foreigners' bank deposits is underestimated by their relative share. Their withdrawal increased the demand for foreign exchange, and this represented a loss of primary liquidity for the banking system as a whole, inducing a super-proportionate reduction in credit *via* the money multiplier. In contrast most domestic depositors were also debtors of their banks. They could therefore influence the banks' liquidity only by altering the banks' net liability position towards them, or by changing the maturity structure of their bank assets relative to that of their bank liabilities.

Table 62. Deposits at German banks 1918–1923

	Deposits at the seven Berlin great banks					Deposits at all German banks	
	Total deposits		Of which foreigners' deposits			Foreigners' deposits	
	Papermark value (bn.)	Gold mark* value (bn.)	%+	Papermark value (bn.)	Gold mark* value (bn.)	Papermark value (bn.)	Gold mark* value (bn.)
Dec. 31, 1913	(5.1)	(5.1)					
Dec. 31, 1918	19.7	9.8	20	3.9	2.0	5.4	2.8
Dec. 31, 1919	39.1	3.3	35	13.7	1.2	19.0	1.7
Dec. 31, 1920	62.6	3.6	36	22.5	1.3	31.3	1.8
Dec. 31, 1921	115.6	2.6	36	41.6	0.9	57.8	1.3
Dec. 31, 1922	1618.2	0.9	11	178.0	0.1	247.2	0.14
Dec. 31, 1923	$1.1 \cdot 10^{12}$	1.1	2	$22 \cdot 10^{9}$	0.02	$30.6 \cdot 10^{9}$	0.03

* Papermark values deflated by current dollar exchange rate.

+ Cp. footnote 18.

Sources: Deposits at the seven Berlin great banks: P. B. Whale: *Joint Stock Banking in Germany* (London, 1930), p. 216.

Foreigners' deposits at all German banks: a grossing up of the figures in columns 4 and 5 in a 100 : 72 ratio, corresponding to the evidence of the document cited in footnote 16, that the seven banks had a 72% share of all foreign currency business.

[19] Karl Eric Born: *Die deutsche Bankenkrise 1931. Finanzen und Politik* (Munich, 1967), p. 20. When domestic citizens withdraw deposits in order to transfer them abroad the effect is of course the same. On this whole question see the useful contribution by F. Machlup: "Die Theorie der Kapitalflucht", *Weltwirtschaftliches Archiv*, 36 (1932), pp. 512–529.

The data in Table 62 show that in 1922 foreigners' willingness to hold mark bank balances declined more sharply than German willingness. This set the scene for the acute liquidity crisis of the first half of 1922, about which there was much complaint.[20] Such crises generally lead to bank and business collapses, but in 1922 this outcome was avoided, because the lost liquidity could be replenished from other sources, namely from the Reichsbank which, beginning in July 1922, increased the supply of central bank money by stepping up its discounting of private bills.[21]

This evidence suggests that the destabilizing shift from inflation into hyperinflation during 1922 was connected with the increasing reluctance of foreign depositors to take up further creditor positions in marks – in other words, with the cessation of the capital imports which the German economy had been able thus to obtain until that year. The flight abroad of German business capital, as it seems to me, played only a secondary role. German firms were compelled, as ever, to retain a minimum of cash balances in marks for the conduct of their everyday operations. Moreover Germans were subject to foreign exchange controls and to the legislation on capital flight. Both of these could of course be evaded, but they circumscribed the ability of Germans, relative to that of citizens of other countries, to transfer liquid funds abroad.[22]

Unfortunately the monthly data concerning foreigners' balances in German banks, from which the turning point in foreigners' investment behavior could have been more exactly determined, could not be found. Contemporary observers, however, noted the change. W. Eucken wrote, "In contrast to the earlier postwar years, only small amounts of German money in fact came into foreign hands in 1922 owing to the decreasing readiness of foreigners to accept it."[23] Discussing foreigners' deposits, Friedrich Hesse pointed out that

---

20 *Die Wirtschaftskurve*, 1 (1922), Heft 2, p. 58. On the details of the 1922 liquidity crises, see pp. 66 ff. *supra*.

21 *Verwaltungsbericht der Reichsbank*, 1922.

22 The "Law concerning Trade with Foreign Means of Payment" [Gesetz über den "Handel mit ausländischen Zahlungsmitteln"] of February, 3, 1922, re-established Reichsbank control over the foreign currency market. Such control had already been exercised during the second half of the war. Control was further tightened by the government's "Decree concerning Speculation with Foreign Means of Payment" [Verordnung über die Spekulation mit ausländischen Zahlungsmitteln] of October 12, 1922. Cp. Rudolf Kühne: *Die Devisenzwangswirtschaft im Deutschen Reich während der Jahre 1916 bis 1926. Eine währungspolitische Reminiszenz* (Frankfurt/M., 1970), pp. 21–22.

23 Walter Eucken: *Kritische Betrachtungen zum deutschen Geldproblem* (Jena, 1923), p. 15. Cp. pp. 20–22, 57, 65 of the same work.

"from the middle of 1922 on... foreigners did not accept any more German marks."[24]

The turning point in Germany's capital balance in 1922 is to be explained by the following political developments which changed expectations about the future value of the German currency.

(i) The change of government in France in January 1922 from Briand to Poincaré, portending a change from compromise to confrontation in French Reparations policy.

(ii) The failure of the Genoa Conference in April.

(iii) The report, on June 10,1922, of the international bankers' committee set up by the Reparations Commission and chaired by J. P. Morgan, that long-term lending to Germany should be postponed until the current Reparations schedule had been revised.[25] This indicated particularly to the professionals on the foreign exchange markets not to count on a speedy recovery of the mark.

(iv) The murder of Rathenau on June 22 1922, raising doubts among the speculating public abroad about Germany's domestic political stability and, consequently, raising anxiety about the future value of the mark.[26]

---

[24] Friedrich Hesse: *Die deutsche Wirtschaftslage von 1914 bis 1923. Krieg, Geldblähe und Wechsellagen* (Jena, 1938), p. 367. Statistics by the Reichsbank on the monthly in- and outflow of foreign exchange 1920 to March 1922 show that especially in the second half of 1921 and also in the first quarter of 1922 the Reichsbank was able to procure large amounts of foreign exchange by selling marks abroad. Cp. Zentrales Staatsarchiv (GDR) Potsdam, 25.01 Reichsbank, 6435; Blatt 115.

[25] Cp. the detailed report by Carl Bergmann, state secretary (ie. chief civil servant) in the Foreign Office, to the cabinet on June 13, 1923, printed in *Akten der Reichskanzlei. Weimarer Republik. Die Kabinette Wirth I und II*, Dokument Nr. 291. The cabinet, and particularly Rathenau, surmised that the report of the Morgan Committee would have this effect on the mark exchange rate, as the discussion shows. Cp. *ibid.*, pp. 870–871. Rudolf Havenstein, President of the Reichsbank, subsequently regarded this report as the major cause of the mark's depreciation after the middle of 1922. Cp. *ibid.*, Dokument Nr. 378.

[26] The effect of both the above mentioned June events on the external value of the mark is emphasized by Carl Bergmann: *The History of Reparations* (London, 1927), p. 139. Other contemporary observers, however, have pointed out that, besides the change in expectations, new regulations by the German government demanding the invoicing of German exports in foreign currency played a role in reducing the foreign demand for marks on the spot and forward foreign exchange markets. Cp. F. Hesse: *Deutsche Wirtschaftslage*, p. 194. Paul Wallich: "Der Bedarf an fremden Devisen per spätere Termine", *Bank-Archiv*, 22 (1922/23), p. 1. Statistics of the Reparations Commission reveal an increase during 1922 in the proportion of German exports invoiced in foreign currencies, as a percentage of total exports. Cp. Archives Nationales, Paris, Commission de Réparation, Fond AJ 6, 494, 561. Also Public Record Office, London, T 160, 111.

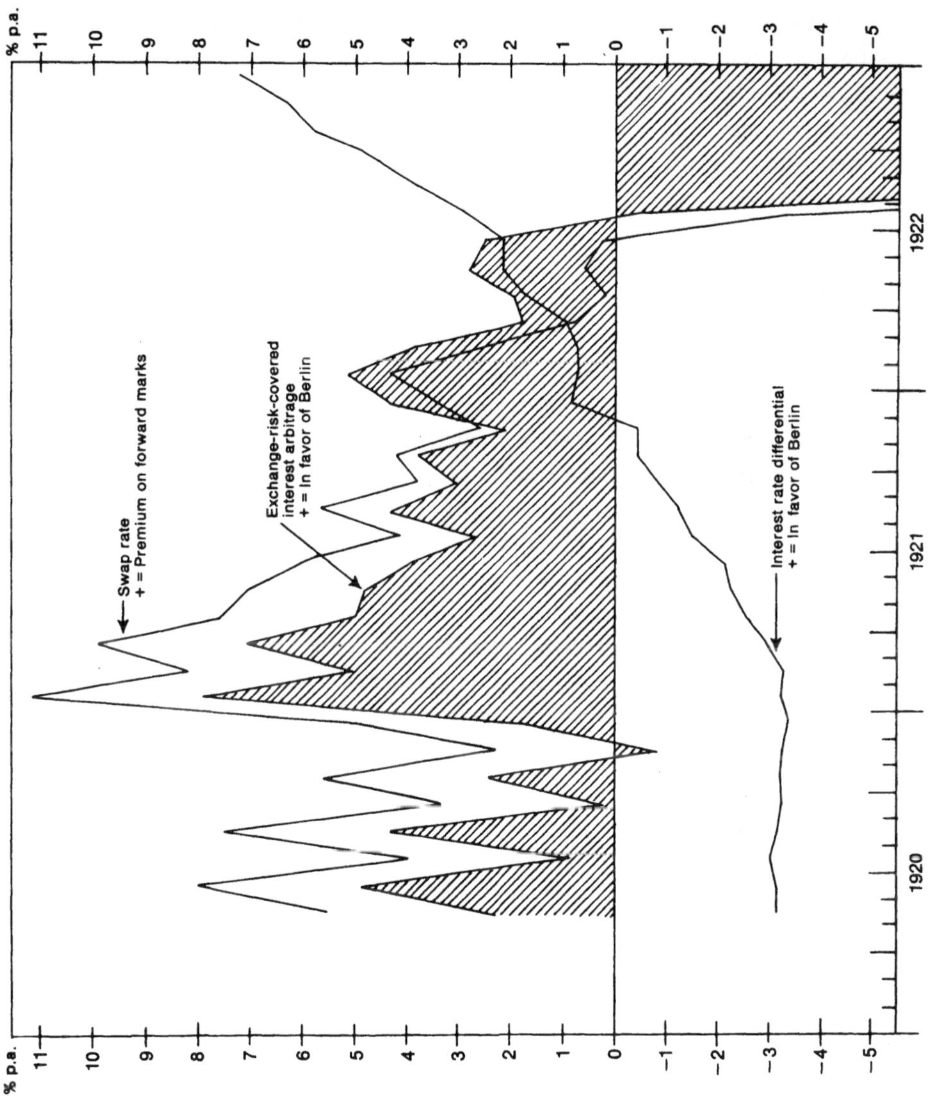

Diagram 8. Covered interest arbitrage between London and Berlin, 1920–22

Sources: Swap rate: calculated from forward mark quotations in London. Cp. p. 292 of text, footnote 28.

Interest rates, German. *Privatdiskont* on the Berlin money market: *Statistisches Jahrbuch für das Deutsche Reich*, 43 (1923), p. 269. United Kingdom. Discount rate on three month bank bills: *Statistical Abstract for the United Kingdom 1913–29* (London, 1931), p. 205.

There is however an indicator that allows us to determine more precisely when foreigners withdrew from the German money market: the forward exchange rate. This reflects expectations about the future valuation of a currency in times of fluctuating exchange rates.[27] The percentage difference between the spot and the forward exchange rate of a currency on a yearly basis (the so-called swap rate), added to the domestic money market interest rate, determines the yield of exchange-risk-covered foreign investments in the domestic money market. Data concerning the forward exchange rate of the mark, namely the quotations in London, exist on a monthly basis from May 1920,[28] and on a weekly basis after December 1920, a year after the Reichsbank became legally empowered to deal on this market.[29] The forward exchange rate of the mark remained considerably above the spot rate until early in 1922. From April until June 1922 the forward rate was more or less the same as the spot rate. In the last week of June 1922 the forward rate for the first time was quoted at a discount from the spot rate, and from then on discounts persisted for the duration of the inflation period. The relatively high premia for forward marks until early 1922 indicate that until that time expectations of a future strengthening of the mark dominated among those trading on foreign exchange markets. Between March and June 1922, by contrast, uncertainty predominated. Finally in the last week of June 1922 bear expectations prevailed, and continued to do so until the end of the inflation (cp. Diagram 8).[30]

---

27 A clear and detailed treatment of the theoretical side of this problem is provided by Herbert G. Grubel: *Forward Exchange, Speculation and International Flow of Capital* (Stanford, 1966). An introductory chapter will be found in Richard E. Caves and Ronald W. Jones: *World Trade and Payments. An Introduction* (Boston, 1973), pp. 498–521. See too Charles P. Kindleberger: "Speculation and Forward Exchange", in his *Europe and the Dollar* (Cambridge, Mass., 1966), pp. 271–289.

28 Monthly data for May to December 1920, in J. M. Keynes: "The Forward Market in Foreign Exchange", *Reconstruction in Europe. Manchester Guardian Commercial Supplement*, April 20, 1922, pp. 11–15. Weekly data from January 1921 in Paul Einzig: *The Theory of Forward Exchange* (London, 1937), pp. 449–455.

29 In December 1919 the Reichsbank was authorized to participate in the forward exchange market. In the first half of 1920 also some private banks started to offer forward exchange contracts to their clients. The possibilities for such business were enlarged by a change of the "Börsengesetz" on December 23, 1920. Cp. *Reichsgesetzblatt*, 1919, p. 2119 ("Gesetz vom 16. Dezember 1919 betreffend Änderung des Bankgesetzes vom 14. März 1875, Artikel VI"). *Die Reichsbank 1901–1925* (Berlin, n. d.), pp. 95–96. Joachim Vogel: *Das Devisentermingeschäft* (Berlin, 1924), pp. 7, 27. Eugen Jacobsen: "Die Wiedereinführung des Terminhandels und das Börsengesetz", *Bank-Archiv*, 20 (1920/21), p. 129.

30 The decisive change in expectations in mid-1922 was also noted by Walter Guderjahn: "Ursachen und Wirkungen der Inflation in Deutschland unter besonderer Berücksichtigung des Zinsfusses" (Diss., Frankfurt/M., 1926), p. 29: "The forward exchange rates in London provide

The impact on foreigners' German bank balances of this turn-round in expectations is evident. As long as bull expectations produced a forward premium for the mark, there was a large incentive for foreign banks, precisely when they were not willing to run exchange risks, to invest in the German money market – that is, to transfer funds to German banks. When foreigners covered the funds they transferred against exchange risk by sale of marks in the forward market, they, firstly, earned interest on their German bank deposit; but until spring 1922 this interest was lower than in other major financial centers. A further profit from the transfer resulted however from the premium on forward marks received by the foreign depositor when his investment in Germany fell due for reconversion into his own currency – that is, from the fact that the foreign depositor got back a greater value of his own currency than he had had to lay out to buy marks in the first place. As long as this annualized percentage difference between the spot and forward exchange rate of the mark (the swap rate), plus the earned domestic German interest rate, yielded a higher return in Berlin than equivalent investments did in non-German money markets, foreign investments in the German money market paid off.

But after the mark's forward exchange premium had disappeared and ultimately been reversed into a forward discount, the incentive for foreigners to invest in the German money market also disappeared. The rise in German domestic interest rates was not sufficient to create an equivalent incentive.

Obviously the losses from the depreciation of the mark were not absorbed by the foreigners who held the exchange-risk covered marks. Deposits by foreign banks at German banks would normally be so covered, for this is standard bank practice. Nevertheless these investments must receive full consideration in calculating the losses which foreigners sustained from the depreciation of the mark. Some persons had taken up the counter-position to these banks in the forward market – that is, had bought the forward marks which the foreign banks were selling in connection with the exchange-risk coverage of their mark deposits. These were the losers. Most likely they were the foreign importers of German goods or simply foreign speculators in German marks.

Information of comparable accuracy to that on foreigners' bank balances is not available about the other forms of German paper-mark indebtedness to abroad – for example about the export of bank notes and of mark-denominated securities or about the direct borrowing abroad (in marks) by

---

a clue to speculators' expectations. They show that the foreign bull speculation [concerning the mark] lasted until mid-1922".

German firms. The McKenna Committee estimated the German gains from the postwar accumulation of Reichsbank notes in foreign hands at between only six and seven hundred million gold marks and the gain from the sale of mark securities and real estate together at only 1.5 billion gold marks.[31] However I have uncovered relatively reliable estimates of the value of German mark-denominated bonds sold between 1919 and 1923 in the U. S. A. alone, amounting to $ 300 million (i. e. 1.25 billion gold marks).[32] Albert Janssen, the Belgian member of the McKenna Committee who did the preparatory work for the Committee's estimation of Germany's inflation-period export of securities, was of the view that even three billion gold marks, the sum estimated under this head by Moulton and McGuire,[33] was too low.[34]

It seems to me that the German gains from the export of Reichsbank notes were also greatly underestimated by the McKenna Committee. For example, estimates of the proportion of Reichsbank notes in foreign possession during 1919–20 ran at nearly fifty percent of the total circulation: fifteen billion marks out of thirty billion in June 1919,[35] and twenty-five billion out of fifty-four billion in June 1920.[36] In those years the holdings of German bank notes in foreign hands seem to have been possibly even somewhat greater in value than foreigners' deposits in German banks (cp. Table 62).

It appears that the politics of Reparations induced the McKenna Committee

31 "The Report of the Second Committee of Experts", as reprinted in Moulton: *Reparation Plan*, pp. 305–6.

32 Carl-Ludwig Holtfrerich: "Amerikanischer Kapitalexport und Wiederaufbau der deutschen Wirtschaft 1919–1923 im Vergleich zu 1924–1929", *Vierteljahrschrift für Sozial- und Wirtschaftsgeschichte*, 64 (1977), pp. 519–520.

33 Moulton and McGuire: *Germany's Capacity*, pp. 89–90. They rely on an estimate by Robert R. Kuczynski.

34 Allied Powers (1919-): Reparation Commission, "Documents collected by the Second Committee of Experts: flight of German capital", p. 161.

35 League of Nations: *Currencies after the War: A Survey of Conditions in Various Countries* (London, 1920), p. 51.

36 Letter from Reichsbank Direktorium to the Reich Foreign Minister, dated June 28, 1920, with background documents for the conference at Spa, in: Politisches Archiv des Auswärtigen Amts, Bonn, Abt. W. Rep., Akten betreffend Verhandlungen zur Ausführung des Friedensvertrages in Spa 9125, Kent Catalogue 242450-242595, on microfilm, National Archives, Washington, D.C., T 120, Reel 3462. In December 1920 the German government estimated the foreign holdings of short- and long-term mark-denominated securities at a minimum of 25 billion marks, those of German banknotes and credit claims together at a minimum of 70 billion. Paper money holdings – according to this estimate – were less than half of this sum, credit claims the major portion; the considerably larger part of these claims was denominated not in foreign exchange, but in marks. *Sammlung von Aktenstücken über die Verhandlungen auf der Sachverständigenkonferenz zu Brüssel vom 16. bis 22. Dezember 1920* (Berlin, 1921), p. 193.

to underestimate the actual gains Germany derived from these positions. Leonard P. Ayres, who attested the reliability of the results of the auditing exercise on German banks, nevertheless supported this view in his assessment of the final findings of the Committee. "This is in no sense a statistical, economic or financial finding. It is the result of numberless compromises between the conflicting claims of the English and Americans on the one side, and the Latins [France, Belgium, Italy,] on the other... The final figures simply represent the result agreed upon, so as to have some result, after neither side would concede anything more."[37] According to my own estimates, Germany gained at least fifteen billion gold marks at the expense of foreigners from the postwar inflationary process.

In contrast to their experience in lending to Germany after 1924 under conditions of monetary stability, Germany's pre-1923 creditors saw their accumulated mark claims dwindle away, as German prices escalated and the external value of the mark plummeted. As long as foreigners were willing to invest funds in marks, they helped to stabilize the German currency. This was the case from February 1920 to May 1921, the period when the mark was fairly stable on the foreign exchanges despite a nearly fifty percent growth of the high-powered money stock.[38] But as soon as pessimism overtook foreigners' expectations of the mark's future value, they began to refuse to transfer further funds into mark assets and to terminate existing mark engagements. Thus their own actions began to cause or to reinforce the very depreciation from which they wished to escape. In this way transactions, originally conceived as international capital transfers which left claims for repayment in the hands of the creditors, were transformed into unilateral transfers in favor of Germany – in fact into free foreign aid toward the reconstruction of the German economy.

Taking into account only the seven or eight billion gold marks (i.e. $1.7 to $1.9 billion) which Germany is estimated to have gained from foreign deposits in German banks between the end of the war and 1923,[39] we have a sum which even in nominal terms exceeded the $1.5 billion received by West Germany after the Second World War under the Marshall Plan.[40] In fact prices were higher after the Second World War than after the First; in real terms,

[37] Leonard P. Ayres Papers, Journal of L.P. Ayres. Economic Advisor. Dawes Plan Committee 1924, p. 96.

[38] C. Bresciani-Turroni: *The Economics of Inflation. A Study of Currency Depreciation in Post-War Germany* (London, 1937), p. 30. Cp. Tables 1 and 11 *supra*.

[39] "The Report of the Second Committee of Experts", reprinted in Moulton: *Reparation Plan*, pp. 304–5.

[40] G. Stolper *et al.*: *The German Economy*, p. 238.

then, the excess is still greater. Total American aid to Germany between 1946 and 1953, including the so-called GARIOA shipments of foodstuffs and raw materials, amounted to $ 3.6 billion.[41] But if the rise in prices is taken into account, this sum is not much greater than the amount that Germany gained from the depreciation of foreign balances in German banks after the First World War. Another comparison: the much better-known inflow of capital to Germany from the sale of bonds abroad between 1924 and 1929[42] was about equal to the foreigners' losses on their German bank balances during the postwar inflation. And, to reiterate, the 1924–29 flow was only lent by foreigners; the value of the 1918–23 deposits was entirely lost to them.

Finally, we can obtain a perspective on Germany's gains from foreign purchases of mark claims by comparing them with Germany's unilateral transfers *to* abroad – her Reparations obligations. Between 1919 and 1923 Germany transferred 2.6 billion gold marks in cash to the Allies (cp. footnote 12 p. 283). This was only one third of what foreigners lost through the depreciation of their German bank balances. Including deliveries in kind and all other transfers, the Allies credited Germany with payments under the Versailles Treaty until the beginning of 1924 of about eight billion gold marks – almost exactly the value of the contrary unilateral transfer to Germany through the depreciation of these balances.[43] Keynes was correct then when as early as 1922 he wrote, "By this means Germany has already had her much-discussed international loan, and on the easiest terms imaginable – as for interest, most of it bears none; and as for capital, only such proportion is repayable as Germany may herself decide when she comes to fix the value of the paper mark."[44]

---

41 Horst Mendershausen: *Two Postwar Recoveries of the German Economy* (Amsterdam, 1955), p. 105.

42 *Ibid.*, p. 105. Also, Ausschuss zur Untersuchung der Erzeugungs- und Absatzbedingungen der deutschen Wirtschaft: *Die deutsche Zahlungsbilanz* (Berlin, 1930), p. 138.

43 According to data on German payments under the Versailles Treaty in Moulton and McGuire, *Germany's Capacity*, p. 64, the Reparations Commission credited Germany, up to January 31, 1923, with the following totals:

Cash payments from Germany	1.7 bn.	gold marks
Cash from other sources credited to Germany	0.1 bn.	gold marks
Deliveries in kind	3.6 bn.	gold marks
Public property in ceded territories	2.6 bn.	gold marks
Total	8.0 bn.	gold marks

All German payments to France and Belgium, the principal recipients, ceased after the occupation of the Ruhr in January 1923. Cp. Carl Bergmann: *History*, p. 178.

44 J. M. Keynes: "Speculation in the Mark and Germany's Balances Abroad", as reprinted in *The Collected Writings of J. M. Keynes, vol. XVIII*, p. 50.

9.3. A Cost-Benefit Evaluation

The real costs to the German economy arising out of this short-term capital inflow were a function of the way the external value of the mark developed. If the currency had been stabilized at a time when foreign holdings of paper-mark claims were still significant in real terms – for example at the beginning or the middle of 1921 – then the German balance of payments would have been burdened in the future by the interest and amortization on these holdings, in addition to Reparations.[45]

Various early plans for stabilizing the mark provided for the conversion of Germany's private foreign short-term debts into long-term foreign bonds.[46] An early stabilization attempt without such a consolidation of these short debts would most likely have ended in failure, had it been undertaken when these debts were still significant in real terms. This was pointed out by M. J. Bonn for example during the Socialization Commission's deliberations on the Reparations issue in March 1922, when it came to discuss the possibilities for stabilizing the German currency: "On the day that the German government... annouces its intention that... the dollar shall neither rise above 200 marks nor fall below 198 marks, the whole business is at an end. For, at that moment when everybody knows that the mark can rise no further, the many billions (people speak of 70 billions; nobody has counted them), invested by foreigners in mark balances in the hopes that the price of the dollar would fall and that of the mark rise substantially, will be thrown on the market and cause such a *deroute* as no organization on earth could contain."[47]

---

[45] For example Germany paid 1.26 bn. reichsmarks in 1929 as interest alone to foreign countries for the foreign credits she had received, mainly since 1924. This amounted to about 50% of the Reparations payments during the same year. Cp. Rolf Wagenführ: *Die Industriewirtschaft. Vierteljahrshefte zur Konjunkturforschung, Sonderheft 31* (Berlin, 1933), p. 32.

[46] The Reichsbank pointed this out continually. In 1919 for example it suggested that the paper-mark notes held in Belgium and northern France as a result of German wartime occupation of those territories (approx. 8 bn. marks) be converted into a long-term mark loan. See letter from the Reichsbank Direktorium to the Reich Finance Minister, dated July 1, 1919, in Bundesarchiv, Koblenz, R 2/1894. Foreign loans were also envisaged in the stabilization plans of the Reich Economic Ministry in the summer of 1922 and in the November 1922 report of the financial experts whom the German government had invited to Germany to study the situation on the spot. See Paul Beusch: *Währungszerfall und Währungsstabilisierung* (Berlin, 1928), pp. 12–19.

[47] *Verhandlungen der Sozialisierungskommission über die Reparationsfragen, Bd. III (Stabilisierung der Währung)*, Sitzung [i.e. meeting] of March 10, 1922 (Berlin, 1922), p. 4.

By rejecting an early stabilization and by allowing the depreciation of the mark to run its course, Germany was able to eliminate her private mark debts to foreigners and thereby to relieve her economy of considerable obligations. At the same time the currency depreciation worked in the political sphere to convince the Allies of the need to reduce German Reparations payments, that is, it worked to moderate the public debts owed by the German state to foreign governments as well. Gustav Büscher pointed this out when he wrote: "The German saw that each new plunge of the mark reinforced worldwide belief that Germany was unable to pay its Reparations debts as demanded. The depreciation of the mark, the bankruptcy of the state, was the only weapon of which the Allies had been unable to deprive him."[48]

Considered as a form of taxation,[49] inflation was in practice the only way in which the German government could involve foreigners, namely those who had accumulated credit positions in marks, in financing a good part of its own expenditure and of German private investment too. From this viewpoint Germany's inflationary policy may under the circumstances be judged a thoroughly rational strategy, at least as long as the benefits from the depreciation of foreigners' mark claims were not thought to be outweighed by the inflation's domestic social costs. In terms of foreign policy the inflation served the "national interest."[50]

But it is not easy to decide how far the "inflation strategy" represented a freely-made choice by the German government, and how far the makers of German economic policy found themselves pushed into the inflationary whirlpool by the pressures of external economic problems and by the threat to domestic political stability posed by unemployment.

Roland W. Boyden, the U.S. government's "unofficial observer" at the Reparations Commission, assessed the German situation in November 1921 as follows: "One hears a good deal of a conspiracy on Germany's part to force revision [of the Versailles Treaty] by allowing herself to drift into voluntary

---

48 Gustav Büscher: *Die Inflation und ihre Lehren* (Zürich, 1926), pp. 60–61. Hugo Stinnes and Walther Rathenau also viewed inflation in 1922 as a weapon of German foreign policy. Cp. Peter Wulf: *Hugo Stinnes. Wirtschaft und Politik 1918–1924* (Stuttgart, 1979), p. 470.

49 League of Nations: *Report of the International Financial Conference of Brussels 1920* (Geneva, 1920), p. 8, "Inflation is in fact an unscientific and ill-adjusted method of taxation." For a more detailed treatment, with attempts at calculating the amounts yielded by the "inflation tax" in various countries of the time, see J. M. Keynes: "Inflation as a Method of Taxation", in *Reconstruction in Europe. Manchester Guardian Commercial Supplement* of July 27, 1922, pp. 268–9. Also in J. M. Keynes: *A Tract on Monetary Reform. The Collected Writings of J. M. Keynes, ed. E. Johnson and D. E. Moggridge,* vol. IV (London, 1971), pp. 37–60 (original edn. 1923, pp. 41–62).

50 A standard treatment of this concept is Hans J. Morgenthau: *Politics among Nations. The Struggle for Power and Peace* (New York, 3rd edn. 1960), chapter 1.

bankruptcy. Perhaps there are a few Germans who would regard this as sound policy, but I see not the least indication that it is either a national or a governmental policy. In fact, I got rather a definite impression when I was in Berlin that everybody there who had any sense regarded the fall of the mark as a calamity, even if it and accompanying conditions did lead to revision. But the fact is that the important causes which have led to the fall of the mark are obvious, and there is no need of searching for a cause so far-fetched as a definite German conspiracy to this end."[51]

The inflationary development was of course foreseen by the German government early on as a consequence of, or reaction to, the terms of the Versailles Treaty. Commenting on the Allied peace conditions on May 29, 1919, the German government argued, "The placing of German government loans, either at home or abroad, in any large amounts will not be possible in the near future; any compensation, therefore, will be possible only by means of a large issue of paper money. The serious inflation that has already developed would increase without check if the proposed conditions of peace were to be carried out... Monetary instability, however, would not affect Germany alone, but all exporting countries; for Germany, with the continuous depreciation of her currency, would be an element of disturbance, incessantly throwing her products on to the market at ruinous prices."[52]

This statement can be interpreted equally well either as a covert diplomatic threat on Germany's part or as an expression of the destitution of her financial policies. The future of the mark certainly depended not only on the extent of the Reparations debt, but also on taxation policy within Germany – a matter the statement leaves unmentioned. Still, the higher the Reparations demands, the higher taxes had to be to ensure currency stability. Currency stability at all costs is just as naive a strategy in the economic sphere as victory at all costs in the military sphere.

The costs of a rigorous fiscal policy in postwar Germany would have been borne almost exclusively within the country, and we know from the experience of Great Britain and the U. S. A. during the 1920–21 slump what these costs would have been: unemployment, interrupted growth, foregone consumption on the part of the broad mass of the population. The benefits would have accrued however to domestic savers, pension recipients and rentiers – to the extent that these did not also necessarily bear the brunt of the rigorous

[51] Letter from Roland W. Boyden in Paris to his brother Albert A. Boyden in New York, dated November 22, 1921, one day after the return of the Reparations Commission from Berlin, in Frank W. Taussig Papers HuG 4823.4, Harvard University Archives, Cambridge, Mass. Also in James A. Logan Papers, Archives of the Hoover Institution, Stanford, California.

[52] C. Bergmann: *History*, pp. 19–20.

taxation. Private creditors abroad would have benefited by the smaller depreciation of their mark credits, and Germany's foreign governmental creditors would have benefited by the smaller reduction, or even the enlargement, of the Reparations annuities. Until Germany's total Reparations liability was fixed, and as long as she continued to declare the demands made of her "unfulfillable" – as long, then, as these demands were still the subject of negotiation – the German government had to reckon with the likelihood that the Allies would bump up their next Reparations demand by the degree to which German domestic economic and fiscal measures had shown success in the meantime. Inflation offered the opportunity to effect a different distribution of the costs and benefits between German and foreign citizens: the benefits were registered as jobs, growth, and higher real incomes and consumer purchasing power – benefits which accrued to the broad mass of the domestic population. The costs of the policy fell to no small degree on foreigners: the depreciation of foreigners' mark balances and the gradual lessening of the Reparations exactions upon a government which, surrounded by a prospering economy, could present the appearance of financial exhaustion and plead its inability to mend matters.

Chapter 10
Ending and Mending: Stabilization and Revaluation

10.1. Stabilization

After the failure of the Kapp Putsch in March and the suppression of the "red army" in the Ruhr in April 1920, the postwar revolutionary period came to a close[1] and German currency conditions entered a period of greater stability. This lasted until May 1921, when the forcing of the London Ultimatum upon the German government subjected the German state's powers of survival to an external test as injurious to the currency as the internecine domestic conflicts of the revolutionary period. Between these two storms was the lull lasting from April 1920 to May 1921; in this period, in spite of a few wobbles, prices and the exchange rate were generally steady (see Tables 1, 4, 8), but this steadiness rested on gathering confidence and not on an alteration of fiscal and monetary policy. Confidence must have been causing the demand for money to rise: this is clear from the fact that the Reich's deficits had not disappeared and the growth of the monetary base had scarcely slackened (cp. Table 11 and Diagram 3).

People simply "began to think that currency conditions were stabilizing"[2] and this climate of expectation proved self-fulfilling even in the absence of any switch of policy. But in fact currency stabilization – in the sense of thoroughgoing policies to stop the domestic price rises and to restore a fixed, freely convertible gold parity – was not even under consideration at this time. Rather the contrary: this was the period when the more stable exchange rate had eliminated the export advantage hitherto gained by German industry

---

[1] Wolfgang J. Mommsen: "Die deutsche Revolution 1918–1920. Politische Revolution und soziale Protestbewegung", *Geschichte und Gesellschaft*, 4 (1978), pp. 362–391.

[2] Gerald D. Feldman: "Gegenwärtiger Forschungsstand und künftige Forschungsprobleme zur deutschen Inflation", in O. Büsch and G. D. Feldman (eds.): *Historische Prozesse der deutschen Inflation. Ein Tagungsbericht* (Berlin, 1978), p. 13. Cp. also G. D. Feldman: "The Political Economy of Germany's Relative Stabilization During the 1920/21 World Depression", in G. D. Feldman *et al.* (eds.): *The German Inflation Reconsidered. A Preliminary Balance* (Berlin/New York, 1982), pp. 180–206.

from the more rapid external than internal currency depreciation and when, as if this was not enough, the slump abroad was acting anyway to depress world demand for German exports. To prevent the high unemployment then affecting the U.K. and the U.S.A. from spreading to Germany, the government was being advised rather to print more money than less.[3] Allied governments of course had contrariwise a great interest in German currency stabilization; *they* looked for the "solidifying of an equilibrium between German domestic and world market prices."[4] British industry wanted "the competitive advantage on world markets which the fall in the mark was giving to German industry to be curtailed" by a currency stabilization. Unemployment averaged 16.9% in Britain in 1921, reaching 23.4% in May,[5] the month of the London Ultimatum. The renewal of German "currency dumping", commencing after that month, thus represented a particularly irksome aggravation of the trouble, and it is not surprising that at the Cannes Conference in January 1922 the Allies made their granting of a Reparations moratorium chiefly conditional upon a halt to the printing of money and a stabilizing of the exchange rate. Supplementary tax measures and expenditure economies were demanded as the means of balancing the Reich's budget; it was further required that the Reichsbank be made autonomous, in the hope of stiffening its resistance to the Reich's demands for credit.[6]

The German side accepted these conditions. The required fiscal measures were undertaken and the Reichsbank Law of 1875 was amended to make the "Reichsbank administration" responsible no longer to the chancellor but to the Bank's Board of Directors (*Reichsbankdirektorium*) instead. And in fact, following the great "tax compromise" of spring 1922, it did prove possible to meet a large part of Reich expenditure out of ordinary tax revenue. Beusch described this development as follows: the new tax sources, made available to the Reich between 1919 and 1921 under the Erzberger reforms, had already increased "the revenues of the Reich during fiscal year 1921 to the extent that they sufficed to cover ordinary expenditures except for those incurred under the Peace Treaty. By the beginning of 1922 revenues had increased not merely in nominal but even in gold mark values while on the other side there had been

---

3 Walther Rathenau in the Foreign Office. See "Vermerk über eine Besprechung im Auswärtigen Amt am 24. Januar 1921." [Record of a discussion in the Foreign Office on January 24, 1921], p. 6. Bundesarchiv Koblenz R 2/3216. Cp. pp. 210–1 *supra*.

4 Karl Helfferich: "Die Autonomie der Reichsbank", *Bank-Archiv*, 21 (1921/22), p. 215 (April 1, 1922).

5 *British Labour Statistics. Historical Abstract 1886–1968* (London, 1971), p. 306.

6 On the Allied demands at the Cannes Conference, see Carl Bergmann: *The History of Reparations* (London, 1927), pp. 115ff.

strict expenditure economies. In the first quarter of the new fiscal year (April–June 1922) Germany was able to finance not only its entire ordinary and extraordinary expenditure out of taxation, but even to apply a considerable sum from the same source to meeting Reparations charges."[7]

At the same time a compulsory loan was imposed upon business – likewise at the insistence of the Allies. However the business circles affected managed to secure the concession that it could be subscribed in paper marks rather than in foreign exchange as originally intended. Under these terms the loan could not act to stabilize the currency as the Allies had wished: it did not yield to the Reich foreign currency for effecting the Reparations transfers, or obviate the need to acquire that currency by dumping marks on the foreign exchanges. Nor could a mark-denominated compulsory loan even exert a contractionary effect on liquidity and the money supply within Germany: as long as the Loan Bureaux continued to exist and to accept goverment loan stock as the main form of collateral against which they would lend cash, such stock constituted part of the *liquid* assets of the individual or firm possessing it. In periods when virtually the entire new loan stock was pledged at the Loan Bureaux, and hence the major part of its aggregate value was to be found in the form of *Darlehnskassenscheine* (Loan Bureau Certificates) among the cash in circulation or at the Reichsbank, the money supply increased almost in the proportion that the transfer of purchasing power to the state through new loan subscriptions acted initially to reduce it. One may conjecture that this was the state of affairs during the "credit crisis" of 1922.[8]

Even so, the contracting tendency of the budget deficit in the spring of 1922 did help to restrict the economy's liquidity base and retard monetary expansion. For a few weeks the pace of exchange rate depreciation slackened, and one can almost speak of a stabilization. On the Berlin foreign exchange market the dollar exchange rate averaged 284.19 marks in March, 291.00 in April, 290.11 in May and, on June 9, 289.25.[9] Then the rate broke, and depreciation turned into hyperinflation – a transition to be attributed to collapse in demand for the mark. In the period following the renewal of currency depreciation after May 1921 German business had increasingly calculated prices, made out invoices, discharged its payments and even held its cash in "hard" foreign currency. This raised the domestic demand for foreign exchange and reduced

[7] Paul Beusch: *Währungszerfall und Währungsstabilisierung* (Berlin, 1928), p. 1.

[8] Cp. pp. 66ff. *supra*. Also *Akten der Reichskanzlei. Weimarer Republik. Die Kabinette Wirth I und II*, Dokument Nr. 378, p. 1108.

[9] Statistisches Reichsamt: *Zahlen zur Geldentwertung in Deutschland 1914 bis 1923* (Berlin, 1925), pp. 6, 9.

the domestic demand for marks. As long however as the falling mark exchange rate had continued to induce foreign, and mainly speculative, purchases of marks, the domestic demand for foreign exchange could be satisfied without precipitating a catastrophic collapse in the mark's external value. But once foreigners lost confidence in the mark's future and reduced their mark purchases, the hyperinflation commenced. For a considerable section of the German business community however, currency stabilization had already taken place – i. e. for all those whose business operations were already being conducted on a foreign currency standard. They may still have made and accepted payment in marks – but invariably at the exchange rate ruling that day, and any surplus mark balances were spent or converted into hard currency as quickly as possible.[10] Only in retail transactions and in the payment of wages and salaries did the mark retain its monetary functions somewhat longer. And even in these spheres the onset of hyperinflation increased the demand for foreign moneys, particularly for U. S. (dollar), British (sterling), Dutch (guilder) and Swiss (franc) banknotes. Value-maintaining emergency moneys and debt instruments denominated in quantities of commodities (rye, coal, etc.) came into circulation;[11] once the hyperinflation was under way virtually nobody still reckoned in marks except the government itself and other public bodies. This all adds up to the statement that stabilization on a foreign currency standard had already taken place in wide areas of the economy before the official stabilization measures commenced. Beusch for example provides the information that in August 1923 an estimated two to three billion gold marks' worth of foreign moneys was circulating in Germany. "If this is so, then the value of foreign currencies employed in transactions within Germany was almost ten times as great as the value of the paper-mark circulation."[12]

From the beginning of the hyperinflation in mid-1922, proposals for a mark stabilization proliferated, both from the side of the German government and from the Allies. On June 10 the mark rate broke when the bankers' committee set up by the Reparations Commission and chaired by J. P. Morgan made

[10] Friedrich Hesse: *Die deutsche Wirtschaftslage von 1914 bis 1923. Krieg, Geldblähe und Wechsellagen* (Jena, 1938), p. 399. Gerald D. Feldman: *Iron and Steel in the German Inflation 1916–1923* (Princeton, 1977), pp. 293–294. Rudolf Dalberg: *Deutsche Währungs- und Kreditpolitik 1923–1926* (Berlin, 1926), pp. 16ff.

[11] Quantitative estimates are to be found in Alfred Lansburgh: "Banken. Die Notenbanken in der Zeit des wirtschaftlichen Aufbaues", article in the *Handwörterbuch der Staatswissenschaften, Ergänzungsband* (Jena, 1929), p. 43. See too W. D. Preyer: *Roggenpapiere und Roggensteuern* (Jena, 1923).

[12] P. Beusch: *Währungszerfall*, p. 8.

public its refusal to recommend long-term foreign lending to Germany until her Reparations liabilities had been adjusted to her capacity to pay. Thereupon a flood of Allied plans for stabilizing the mark streamed forth. Generally these proposed to improve Germany's prospects for borrowing abroad by reducing or suspending Reparations charges. Even the Poincaré government in France, "hawkish" though it was on the Reparations issue, came up with a plan to trade a reduction in German liability from the 132 billion marks fixed in the London Ultimatum to 50 billions, in return for a cancellation of interallied debts; it further recommended that the reduced Reparations liability be paid off mainly through international loans.[13] This was pretty close to the orders of magnitude at which both the European Allies and Germany would have been willing to settle the matter. All such plans foundered however on the intransigence of the main war debt creditor. "It appeared... that there was not the slightest inclination in America to make such a surrender."[14]

And so interest focused on other plans in which the 132 billion gold mark liability would remain officially in force but the payments' schedule would be reformulated, particularly with the aid of moratoria and stabilization loans. Having watched the mark's plunge on the foreign exchanges during the weeks following June 10, 1922 and observed a fruitless stabilization action by the Reichsbank during that month and the next,[15] the German government petitioned the Reparations Commission on July 12 for a moratorium on cash Reparations payments for the rest of that year, and throughout 1923 and 1924. The desired postponement was gained for 1922 because Belgium, the only creditor with cash payments still outstanding for that year, agreed to accept six monthly Reich treasury bills in payment. Sir John Bradbury, British representative on the Reparations Commission, proposed a similar scheme for cash payments due during 1923 and 1924, but possessing considerably longer term implications. He proposed that the German government should make its payments in the form of treasury certificates with a five year term. The Allied governments should place these on the market, adding their own guarantee to them. In this way Germany would defer its 1923 and 1924 Reparations payments for five years. In the meantime Germany should return to the gold standard. The Reichsbank should apply one half of its one billion gold marks' worth of gold reserves to stabilizing the mark at a rate of four thousand to the

[13] C. Bergmann: *History*, p. 149. Cp. pp. 144–5 *supra*.
[14] Bergmann: *History*, p. 149.
[15] Hjalmar H. G. Schacht: *The Stabilization of the Mark* (London, 1927), p. 53 (original German edn. 1926).

dollar, and use the other half as collateral against which to obtain trade credits from abroad.[16] French opposition meant that this plan, too, came to nothing.

Eventually, at the beginning of November 1922 the Reparations Commission itself came to Berlin for a week for an on-the-spot investigation of the situation. At the same time a group of international financial experts was meeting in Berlin at the invitation of the German government which desired it to devise currency stabilization proposals.[17] The group consisted of Brand, Cassel, Jenks, Keynes, Vissering, Dubois and Kamenka and they shared the view of the German, British and American governments that stabilization would prove impossible without at least temporary respite for Germany from the Treaty charges. Beyond this, the group's views diverged. An Anglo-Saxon subgroup consisting of Brand, Cassel, Jenks and Keynes submitted a report expressing the opinion that Germany could and must stabilize on the basis of resolute fiscal and monetary action of her own; the advice tendered by Vissering, Dubois and Kamenka held that credit from abroad would additionally be necessary for successful stabilization. The latter view coincided with the view which the German government itself expressed in its stabilization proposals forwarded to the Reparations Commission on November 4, 1922: "For the support of the mark Germany's collaboration with the capital resources of the outside world will be required." And in the same communication the government reiterated its *ceterum censeo*: "An effective and permanent stabilization of the mark will be possible only after a definite settlement of the reparation problem conforming with Germany's capacity."[18]

Little is gained in my view by seeking objective answers to the questions whether or not stabilization was achievable without an external Loan, whether or not it was achievable without reduction of Reparations payments. In actuality the mark was stabilized initially in 1923 without foreign credit, proving that this was no indispensable precondition. And maybe the Reparations demands were more "fulfillable" – i.e. capable of transfer without damage to the stability of the currency – than the actual record of payment suggests. The decisive question however is: at what cost to the economy? Reparations transfers under stable currency conditions, but in the absence of equivalent capital imports, might well be achievable only at the cost of a double deflation: the raising of the required sums within Germany would

[16] Bergmann: *History*, pp. 150–151.

[17] K. B. Netzband and H. P. Widmaier: *Währungs- und Finanzpolitik der Ära Luther 1923–1925* (Basel, 1964), p. 13.

[18] Bergmann: *History*, p. 152 Auswärtiges Amt: *Das Gutachten der internationalen Sachverständigen über die Stabilisierung* (Berlin, 1922).

necessarily involve the restriction of other expenditure – i. e. consumption and investment, but if this failed to reduce imports sufficiently the transfer would still be "undereffected" and additional deflation would be required. The cost, then, of Reparations payments under currency stability might well be considered economically and politically intolerable.[19] On the other hand, Reparations payments against simultaneous and equivalent capital imports imposed no immediate net burden on the economy.

On the German side the Reparations demands enunciated at Versailles and finalized in London were viewed as morally and hence politically unacceptable because the economic costs of complying with them were thought to be out of all proportion with Germany's share of responsibility for the outbreak of the war and for the damage done during it.[20] On the other hand, the advantages afforded by currency depreciation to German industry in its competitive struggle for world markets with other industrial countries, particularly Great Britain, were not unrecognized. The interest of other countries in German stabilization was continually being brought home to her.[21] If Germany was to make efforts herself in this direction, she would exact a price from the outside world: the reduction of Reparations demands and the extension of international credit. In the short run this would relieve the transfer problem just described; in the long run it would "privatize" Reparations – i. e. replace debts owed to foreign governments by debts contracted to private foreign creditors on international capital markets. The whole Reparations issue would become depoliticized; the discussion would be removed from the floodlights of the political stage where it inflamed the emotions of the masses in the countries concerned, thereby narrowing politicians' room for maneuver in their search for a reasonable solution to the problem.

Thus Germany had something to offer that the Allies desired: a determined recasting of her fiscal and monetary policy in order to achieve currency stabilization. For its own part the German government also sought concessions from the Allies: reduction of Reparations payments and access to the international credits which, for the meantime, would eliminate the burden altogether. The German government was in a bargaining situation in the "market-

---

[19] Keynes championed this position in his exchange with Bertil Ohlin on the transfer problem. J. M. Keynes: "The German Transfer Problem", *Economic Journal*, 39 (1929), pp. 1 ff.; reprinted in *The Collected Writings of J. M. Keynes, ed. E. Johnson and D. E. Moggridge, vol. XI* (London, 1983), pp. 451 ff.

[20] Schumpeter drew attention to the moral dimension of the Reparations issue in *Business Cycles. A Theoretical, Historical and Statistical Analysis of the Capitalist Process* (New York, 2 vols. 1939), vol. 2, p. 704, footnote 1. Cp. p. 166, footnote 23, *supra*.

[21] Cp. p. 140 *supra*.

place" of international diplomacy; it (plus the Reichsbank) could make what it had to offer conditional on the delivery of what it sought. Power to concede what Germany sought was not equally distributed among the Allies. The U. S. A., to some extent Britain also, could determine Germany's access to credit, whereas the reduction of Reparations – which the Anglo-Saxon allies also desired after 1921 – depended largely on the attitude of the French – the chief recipient.[22] Interallied debts further complicated the picture: these debts arising out of the war were largely owed by France to the U. K. and U. S. A. and by the U. K. to the U. S. A. Thus the Allies were also in a bargaining situation among themselves.

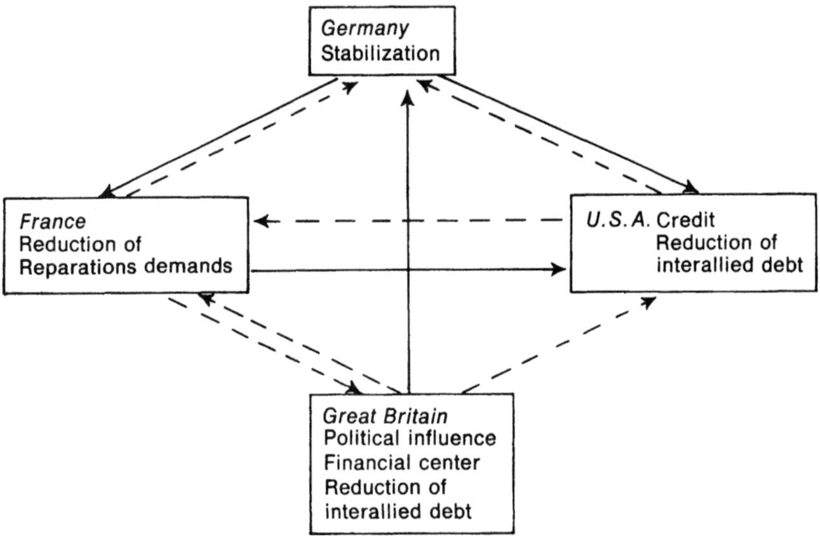

Diagram 9. International financial relationships and diplomatic objectives among the great powers after the First World War
Continuous lines denote major, discontinuous lines subsidiary, objectives. Further explanations in the text.

Diagram 9 summarizes the bargaining relations among the four powers. The boxed key words indicate the demands directed by the other powers at the country whose name is boxed with them, or more generally (in the case of Britain) the properties at its disposal which other countries sought to acquire.

[22] According to the agreement reached at Spa in July 1920 France was to receive 52% of Reparations, the U. K. 22%, Italy 10%, Belgium 8% and all others to share the remaining 8%. Cp. C. Bergmann: *History*, p. 43.

Germany could offer measures to stabilize her currency and demanded reduced Reparations of France and credits of the U.S.A. Great Britain particularly, but France and the U. S. A. as well, had an interest in the stabilization of the mark. The U.S.A. required Reparations reductions of the French before it would sanction credits to Germany. In return for conceding the Reparations reductions desired by the U. S. A. France was energetically seeking the cancellation of interallied debts from the U. S. A. Britain occupied an intermediate role in the interallied debts question, being both debtor and creditor.

In the interplay of forces underlying this bargaining system, the U. S. A. possessed the greatest leverage: her commercial situation did not dictate a strong interest in what France and Germany had to offer, whereas France and Germany had a very strong interest in what the U. S. A. had to offer. The U. K. had a strong interest in German currency stabilization but could offer little in return which was greatly sought after by the other powers. In this situation the key to the reconciliation of the various demands and to the easing of tensions lay with the U. S. A., which possessed the largest political and economic latitude for breaking the bargaining deadlock through moderation of its own position.

The introduction of domestic stabilization measures in Germany was in this sense contingent upon what would happen abroad: either the actual conceding of reduced Reparations and the extending of American credits, or the lively expectation of both. Stabilization had become a question of foreign policy. In the summer of 1922 J. Hirsch and R. Dalberg worked out a plan to stabilize the currency by internal measures alone.[23] But to examine its costs, benefits and technical feasibility in detail would be beside the point. A foreign policy price was demanded in return for domestic stabilization measures; in this situation the actions of the Foreign Ministry were of greater significance than those of the technically better-versed Economics Ministry. Hilferding, then Reich Finance Minister, remarked rightly in my view during a cabinet session in August 1923, that "technical remedies on their own", such as value-maintaining means of payment, would not achieve stabilization; "... in the current situation only action in the field of foreign policy can help."[24]

Among the types of unilateral German action to achieve stabilization being discussed in 1922 and 1923 were a variety of plans for introducing gold-mark

---

[23] Details of the plan are given in Julius Hirsch: *Die deutsche Währungsfrage* (Jena, 1924), pp. 19–21. P. Beusch: *Währungszerfall*, pp. 12–13.

[24] *Akten der Reichskanzlei. Weimarer Republik. Die Kabinette Stresemann I und II*, Dokument Nr. 33, p. 164.

accounting in commercial and credit transactions. To meet public demands for a stable currency basis, banks and savings banks were to permit their clients to open accounts denominated in a value-maintaining unit and the government was to issue similarly denominated treasury paper and bonds. Plans of this type, concerned exclusively with the domestic economy and with the technicalities of currency reform, were also being promoted by the Reich Economics Ministry.[25] They foundered against the opposition of the Reichsbank which feared – rightly in my judgment – that the depreciation of the mark would accelerate if the Reich were to promote "flight" from it by issuing value-maintaining securities.[26] The power of inflation, conceived of as a "tax on real balances", to supply the presumably unchanging fiscal requirements of the Reich would be diminished by this action since the "tax" would fall on a smaller circle of paper-mark users. These in turn would seek to get rid of paper-mark balances ever more quickly; demand for foreign currencies and real assets would further intensify, causing a yet more rapid acceleration of their paper-mark prices. Effective repudiation of the mark would eventuate. "Not only would the Reich itself find the placement of further paper-mark treasury certificates virtually impossible, but treasury paper still in circulation would be disposed of with the greatest rapidity and the Reich's indebtedness at the Reichsbank, and hence inflation, would be much increased."[27] Besides this the Reichsbank repeated the foreign policy price to be exacted in return for stabilization: "The fate of our currency depends... primarily on the outcome of the Reparations issue."[28]

In the early months of 1923 the Reich issued its first dollar treasury certificates to a value of over $ 50 millions (in connection with the conflict in the Ruhr). The foreign exchange thus raised was to be employed by the Reichsbank in an attempt to stabilize the exchange rate. This "stabilization action" succeeded between February and April, but its success could be only temporary because the financing of passive resistance required undiminished, indeed

---

25 P. Beusch: *Währungszerfall*, p. 23. Otto Pfleiderer: "Die Reichsbank in der Zeit der grossen Inflation, die Stabilisierung der Mark und die Aufwertung von Kapitalforderungen", in Deutsche Bundesbank (ed.): *Währung und Wirtschaft in Deutschland 1876–1975* (Frankfurt/M. 1976), p. 177.

26 Willi Prion also argues along these lines. See his "Deutsche Kreditpolitik 1919–1922", *Schmollers Jahrbuch*, 47 (1924), p. 203. The contrary position is not tenable in my view; it is maintained by Julius Hirsch: *Deutsche Währungsfrage*, p. 19, and R. Dalberg: *Deutsche Währungs- und Kreditpolitik*, pp. 21 ff.

27 Letter of the Reichsbank Direktorium to the government of the Reich, dated October 20, 1922, and printed in J. Hirsch: *Deutsche Währungsfrage*, p. 76.

28 *Ibid.*

accelerating, monetary expansion. The Reich's floating debt rose from 2.1 to 6.6 trillion marks[29] between the ends of January and March, tripling thus in the space of two months (cp. Table 20). In the same period the Reichsbank's commercial bill portfolio grew from 0.7 to 2.4 trillion marks.[30] The liquidity lost by the economy through the Reichsbank's selling of foreign exchange (in connection with its "stabilization action") was being speedily replenished by the discounting of treasury and commercial bills, even although the Reichsbank was strictly selective of the clients to whom it extended the latter facility – i.e. was practising a species of credit rationing.[31] As the money market became more liquid, the exchange rate which the Reichsbank was attempting to hold – about twenty thousand marks to the dollar – became untenable. At this rate, market liquidity was causing demand for foreign currency to increase until in April the Reichsbank was losing it at the rate of about sixty million gold marks per day. On April 18 the "action" was abandoned and the dollar rate allowed to climb once more.[32] The Reichsbank had pledged abroad a good part of the one billion gold marks' worth of gold reserves with which it had started 1923, in order to obtain the requisite foreign exchange for the support action. The failure of the action and the procuring of further foreign credits reduced its gold reserves to 467 million gold marks by the end of the inflation.[33] A large part of its silver stocks – which were not explicitly shown in the Bank's Statements – was lost in the same manner during the course of the year: the Reichsbank subsequently put its silver losses in 1923 at 165 thousand kg fine.[34] Schacht valued the total cost of the support action of the early months of the year at more than three hundred million gold marks.[35]

---

29 In this work one trillion = one million million.

30 Statistisches Reichsamt: *Zahlen zur Geldentwertung*, p. 52.

31 H. Schacht: *Stabilization*, p. 64.

32 On this see the "Bericht des 43. Untersuchungsausschusses des Reichstags [i.e. Report of the 43rd Investigative Committee of the Reichstag] zur Prüfung der Wirkung der Massnahmen zur Stützung der Mark", in *Verhandlungen des Reichstags, Bd. 380* (Berlin, 1924), Drucksache Nr. 6591. Willi Prion: "Kreditpolitik und Ruhrkampf (1923)", *Schmollers Jahrbuch*, 49 (1925), pp. 381–405.

33 Statistisches Reichsamt: *Zahlen zur Geldentwertung*, p. 48. The sums expended in the various mark support actions are also given in A. Lansburgh: "Banken", pp. 41–42.

34 *Die Reichsbank 1900–1925* (Berlin, n.d.), p. 139.

35 Schacht: *Stabilization*, p. 64. In his "Die Stabilisierung der Mark 1923/24 unter dem Einfluss der nationalen Interessen Frankreichs, Grossbritanniens und der Vereinigten Staaten von Amerika" (Dissertation, Berlin, 1985) Hans-Otto Schötz recently presented and discussed the hypothesis that Germany initiated her "stabilization action" in early 1923 in order to counteract French plans to introduce a new currency in the Rhineland.

The dollar rate soared once the "action" was abandoned from about twenty-one thousand marks on April 18 to one hundred and sixty thousand marks in early July and 1.1 million marks at the end of July.[36] The realization filtered down through the population that the mark could no longer be saved, and it began to be repudiated, even in retail trade. "From this stage began the so-called repudiation of the mark. Sellers refused to accept marks, first in the occupied territories, later in South Germany, and subsequently throughout the entire country. Retail traders began to close their businesses at particular hours of the day, and even on particular days of the week. The formation of queues... in front of the food shops became once more, as in the war, a regular phenomenon. Plunderings and riots were of daily occurrence; and in the end the Reich, to cope with the social dangers which the collapse of the mark had evoked, declared, on September 27, 1923, a state of siege."[37]

In an endeavor to satisfy the desperate demand for value-maintaining means of payment, the Reich brought out a five hundred million gold mark loan in August 1923. It was issued in notes of small denomination, some as small as one tenth of a dollar, in order that they might serve as means of payment.[38] As backing for, and to the value of, the value-maintaining emergency moneys then in circulation, the Reich also issued exchange-rate linked treasury certificates – i. e. certificates whose value was effectively denominated in dollars, and upon which interest, though paid in marks, was calculated according to the current dollar exchange rate. On the security of these, or of gold-denominated bonds, the Reich permitted provinces, municipalities, chambers of commerce and large business firms to issue emergency money denominated in gold marks. About two hundred million gold marks' worth of such money came into circulation. Besides this the Reich Railroads issued emergency moneys to the value of about one hundred and fifty million gold marks. A few federal states issued gold loans in small notes suitable as means of payment, to a total value of fifty million gold marks, and the Hamburg Bank of 1923 A. G. as well as the Schleswig-Holstein Gold Giro Bank A. G. issued value-maintaining "settlement notes" totaling about thirty-five million gold marks.[39] In all, then, there was about 1.1 billion gold marks' worth of value-maintaining money circulating in Germany before November 15, 1923[40] – the

---

36 Statistisches Reichsamt: *Zahlen zur Geldentwertung*, p. 10.

37 Schacht: *Stabilization*, p. 76.

38 *Deutschlands Wirtschaft, Währung und Finanzen. Im Auftrage der Reichsregierung den von der Reparationskommission eingesetzten Sachverständigenausschüssen übergeben* (Berlin, 1924), p. 71.

39 *Ibid.*, p. 67.

40 A. Lansburgh: "Banken", p. 43, names a figure of about 1 bn. gold marks.

day the rentenmark was introduced. Adding to this the two or three billion gold marks' worth of foreign banknotes thought to have been circulating in Germany, plus the privately issued commodity loans (i.e. denominated in quantities of rye, coal, potash, etc.) also used as means of payment,[41] one obtains a total circulation of value-maintaining paper money in excess of four billion gold marks in the pre-stabilization period. This was not far behind the six billion marks' worth of cash in circulation at the outbreak of war and it dwarfed the value of paper marks and of various non value-maintaining moneys in circulation during the final phase of the inflation. After June 1923 the gold value of these varied between eighty and eight hundred million gold marks.[42]

A comparison of these aggregates makes it abundantly clear that what made the stabilization of the mark imperative was more a crisis of the German state, and less a crisis of the German economy. The economy had already largely turned over to a foreign, hard-currency standard and was able to get by quite adequately on this basis: such a makeshift did not necessarily lead to a slump in production or a breakdown of supply. The crisis arose out of the reluctance of the Reich to permit business to employ foreign means of payment in domestic transactions as desired; indeed the Reich could not permit the practice because of the threat it posed to national sovereignty, especially as long as inflation remained necessary as a "tax" source. This "tax" became progressively less productive to the Reich as foreign currencies became the units of account and means of payment used ever more extensively – even if illegally – by business. The same process made the inflation bear ever more oppressively on that diminishing circle of economic agents which – from choice or from compulsion – still operated in paper marks. Among these were employees paid in paper marks – to the extent that their wages could not be adjusted quickly enough – and farmers who were compelled to deliver fixed quantities of grain against paper-mark payment. In the summer of 1923 employees were increasingly able to secure "indexed wages", thus protecting themselves against the currency collapse.[43] Farmers rebelled about the same time against an "inflation tax" of virtually one hundred percent which the Reich wanted them to accept on the required grain deliveries, by the fact that it insisted on paying in paper marks. Germany was threatening either "to go hungry with its barns full"[44] or

---

[41] Schacht: *Stabilization*, p. 78.

[42] Statistisches Reichsamt: *Zahlen zur Geldentwertung*, p. 47.

[43] *Deutschlands Wirtschaft, Währung und Finanzen*, p. 40.

[44] Hans Luther: *Feste Mark – solide Wirtschaft* (Berlin, 1924), p. 65. P. Beusch: *Währungszerfall*, p. 50: "The issue became reduced to its starkest alternatives in the grim formula:

to conduct "business as usual" but on an illegal basis. Either course was fatal to the authority of the state; "... chaos would be the consequence in both the political and social spheres.[45] From August 1923 there was feverish activity to devise a new currency.

The plans for stabilization, the contemporary debate and the way stabilization was carried out have been discussed many times[46] and no detailed account need be repeated here. Only the broad outlines will be traced.

Beusch divided the plans for stabilizing the currency into three distinct groups.[47]

(i) Plans to use taxation policy, a ban on credit, and regulations regarding foreign-currency holding in order to stabilize the currency. Such plans would seek to generalize the adoption of a value-maintaining unit of account, and by introducing "index linked" assessment of tax liability would seek to halt the collapse of the paper mark; they did not purpose to introduce a new currency in place of or alongside it. This was the line followed by the government initially when in August 1923 it introduced "index-linked" tax assessment, issued value-maintaining loans, sought to aquire foreign-currency holdings and urged the banks and the Reichsbank to offer their clients the facility of gold-mark accounts.

'Currency = food' [Währung – Ernährung]. If the currency question does not receive a speedy solution, famine must soon overtake Germany."

45 P. Beusch: *Währungszerfall*, p. 24.

46 E. g. Beusch: *Währungszerfall*, Schacht: *Stabilization*. Hans Luther: "Die Stabilisierung der deutschen Währung. Aus persönlichen Erinnerungen erzählt", in *Zehn Jahre deutsche Geschichte 1918–1928* (Berlin, 1928). Rolf E. Lüke: *Von der Stabilisierung zur Krise* (Zürich, 1958). Joachim Rehn: "Die Pläne zur Stabilisierung der deutschen Währung 1923. Eine Analyse des ökonomischen Wesens der Stabilisierungspläne der ausschlaggebenden Gruppen der Bourgeoisie und der Junker" (Dissertation, Halle, 1958). Karl Lohnes: "Die deutschen Währungsreformen 1923 bis 1948" (Dissertation, Zürich, 1959). K. B. Netzband and H. P. Widmaier: "Währungsprojekte und Regierungsverhandlungen auf dem Wege zur Rentenmark", in idem: *Währungs- und Finanzpolitik*, pp. 12–34; also in Karl E. Born (ed.): *Moderne deutsche Wirtschaftsgeschichte* (Cologne, 1966), pp. 351–369. Gerd Hardach: *Weltmarktorientierung und relative Stagnation. Währungspolitik in Deutschland 1924–1931* (Berlin, 1976), pp. 10–28. Leland B. Yeager: *Experiences with Stopping Inflation* (Washington, D. C., 1981), pp. 55–67. Thomas J. Sargent: "The Ends of Four Big Inflations", in Robert E. Hall (ed.): *Inflation: Causes and Effects*: (Chicago, 1982), pp. 73–85. Peter M. Garber: "Transition from Inflation to Price Stability", *Carnegie-Rochester Conference Series on Public Policy*, 16 (1982), pp. 11–42. On the political histories of the stabilization plans, cp. *Akten der Reichskanzlei. Weimarer Republik. Die Kabinette Stresemann I and II*, pp. LXXV–LXXXVI and the documents discussed there. On the foreign policy dimension see the recent study by Hans-Otto Schötz: "Die Stabilisierung der Mark 1923/24 unter dem Einfluss der nationalen Interessen Frankreichs, Grossbritanniens und der Vereinigten Staaten von Amerika" (Dissertation, Berlin, 1985).

47 Beusch: *Währungszerfall*, p. 25.

(ii) Plans to return to a gold currency. Under this head come the plans hatched by industry (Krämer) because it needed an internationally acceptable means of payment, and by Schacht, Hilferding,[48] Hirsch and Bernhard.

(iii) Plans to stabilize on the basis of a currency secured against the mortgaging of land or commodities. The plans of Helfferich and Minoux, a long standing colleague of Hugo Stinnes, are the main members of this class.

The plans in groups (ii) and (iii) envisaged the introduction of a wholly new currency alongside the old. In the event it was Helfferich's plan which was implemented, after modifications suggested mainly by Luther and Hilferding who at that time were Reich Food and Finance Ministers respectively. Helfferich's project was presented to the Cuno government at the beginning of August and after modification became the basis of cabinet discussion at the beginning of September. It may be briefly described as follows.[49]

Agriculture, industry and commerce (including transport and banking) – the productive "estates" in society – had retained their credit worthiness, whereas the organs of the state had lost theirs. Acting on this observation, a new and independent Currency Bank was to be established, issuing a new currency – the "rye mark". The basic capital of the bank was to be one billion "rye marks" according to the original plan, 1.25 billion according to the version under discussion in September. A "basic reserve" was also provided for. Half of the capital was to be raised by agriculture and half by industry and commerce, in the form of mortgages representing first charges on their property and amounting to five percent of the valuation placed on it in connection with the wartime assessment of liability under the "Defense Contribution". These mortgage instruments were to be lodged with the Currency Bank itself and interest at five percent per annum was to be paid on them. The Currency Bank would then draw bills on itself to the value of these mortgage assets, but denominated in tons of rye, and designated "rye bills" (*Roggenrentenbriefe*). For every ton-value of rye bills made out, two hundred "rye marks" would be issued; these notes were to be not only fully covered by, but also freely convertible into, "rye bills" and, on a date to be determined by the government, to become legal tender. The Currency Bank was to make 375 million "rye marks" from its basic reserve available to the government for the redemption of its floating debt (i. e. outstanding short-term treasury paper). Beyond this, a

[48] Claus-Dieter Krohn: "Helfferich contra Hilferding. Konservative Geldpolitik und die sozialen Folgen der deutschen Inflation 1918–1923", *Vierteljahrschrift für Sozial- und Wirtschaftsgeschichte*, 62 (1975), pp. 62–92. Idem: *Stabilisierung und ökonomische Interessen. Die Finanzpolitik des Deutschen Reiches 1923–1927* (Düsseldorf, 1974), pp. 22 ff.

[49] Beusch: *Währungszerfall*, pp. 27 ff.

maximum was placed on the amount of credit the Reich was to be entitled to receive from the new bank (2.1 billion "rye marks"); the bank was principally intended to serve the needs of the private sector. The "rye mark" sums that would be received by the Reichsbank from the redemption of Reich treasury paper were to be employed firstly as backing for its own note issue, and later to redeem Reichsbank notes with "rye" notes in a particular fixed ratio. Such a Currency Bank possessing right of issue was devised as a transitional expedient only. Later on, once a currency convertible into gold had been reintroduced, its central bank functions, particularly its right of note issue, would disappear.

Criticism of this plan focused chiefly on its tying of the new currency unit to the price of rye. Since harvests are variable, the exchange relationships between rye and other commodities are variable too. Thus stabilization on a rye basis would secure complete protection against price variation for the suppliers of rye – just as for the suppliers of gold under a gold standard – but expose the suppliers of every other commodity to extreme variability in the prices at which they sold, depending on the state of the harvest. The tail would be wagging the dog. The basis of calculation would be made easy in agriculture, but harder in other sectors because of the (to them) unstable currency standard.

To meet this objection Luther and Hilferding reworked Helfferich's plan, eliminating the dependence of the new currency on the value of rye, and bringing it into a fixed relationship with gold instead. They chose to make the gold value of the new currency identical to that of the prewar mark. Further modifications imposed a credit ceiling of 1.2 billion marks on the new bank's dealings with the private sector – not least in order not to make the Reichsbank wholly redundant – and reduced the ceiling on credit to the Reich to 1.2 billion marks likewise. The "Currency Bank" became the "Rentenbank" and the "rye mark" became the "rentenmark".

The "rentenmark experiment"[50] met with astounding success.[51] On Octo-

---

[50] On the development and the practical working out of the "rentenmark" idea, see, besides the literature already cited, Friedrich Ramhorst: *Die Entstehung der deutschen Rentenbank* (Berlin, 1924). Justus Schoenthal: *Rentenbank und Rentenmark* (Berlin, 1924). Idem: *Papiermark, Rentenmark, Reichsmark. Ein Beitrag zur jüngsten Entwicklungsgeschichte der deutschen Währung* (Leipzig, 1925). F. Wolf: "Rentenbank und Markstabilisierung" (Dissertation, Erlangen, 1925). Wilfried Baumgartner: "Le Rentenmark (15 Octobre 1923 – 11 Octobre 1924)" (Thèse, Paris, 1925). Hans Otto de Boor: *Die deutsche Rentenbank und das Privatrecht. Eine Studie über die Grenzen zwischen bürgerlichem und öffentlichem Recht* (Berlin, 1924). H. Frommer and H. Schlag: *Die Gesetzgebung über die Rentenmark mit ausführlichen Erläuterungen* (Mannheim, 1924). Karl Elster: *Von der Mark zur Reichsmark. Die Geschichte der deutschen Währung in den Jahren 1914 bis 1924* (Jena, 1928),

ber 15 the second Stresemann government, now with Luther as Finance Minister, issued a decree, under the terms of the Enabling Law of October 13, concerning the establishing of the Rentenbank, and this bank came into operation on November 15. Beusch pinpointed the secret of the success in the "return to the accounting basis of the peacetime [i. e. prewar] gold currency. Since the new currency was identical with the former national gold currency as a unit of account, and the government took all manner of steps to ensure that its value remained stable, the German people felt itself liberated from the oppressive burden of astronomical figures and with astonishing rapidity found its way back to reckoning in the old unit of account. The 'miracle of the rentenmark' lay in appreciating the psychological importance of enabling this return to take place. With a 'rye mark' this magic property would have been missed."[52]

The paper-mark currency of the Reichsbank continued to circulate alongside the rentenmark. After issuing the Rentenbank Decree the Reich massively increased its floating debt at the Reichsbank once again and hence the papermark circulation. The full extent of the "destruction of the mark" was reflected in the foreign exchange markets. Even on the controlled Berlin market the dollar rate rocketed from 40.5 billion marks in the second half of October to 2.5 trillion in the first half of November. Abroad and in the occupied territories, where the exchanges were uncontrolled, the exchange rate was even worse. When the rentenmark commenced operation on November 15 the Reichsbank ceased to rediscount treasury paper as had been agreed and "thereby created the precondition for stabilizing the paper mark."[53] A stable paper mark was as important as a stable rentenmark particularly as regards external stabilization, since only the paper mark was traded on the

pp. 215ff. K. A. Prager: "Goldmark, Rentenmark, Reichsmark" (Dissertation, Erlangen, 1926). Edgar Albers: *Die Entstehungsgeschichte und der Streit um den wirtschaftlichen Charakter der deutschen Rentenmarkwährung* (Berlin, 1928). Hans Luther: *Politiker ohne Partei. Erinnerungen* (Stuttgart, 1960), pp. 109–183.

51 The confidence which Germans showed in the rentenmark may to no small degree be attributable to the success with which the so called Rentenbanks financed the redemption of peasant holdings during the 19th century, following peasant emancipation. The Rentenbanks compensated the former landlords in their own bonds (*Rentenbriefe*), interest payments on which were guaranteed by the state. The Rentenbanks for their part were the recipients of the peasants' redemption payments; in this way they financed for the peasants the long-term amortization of their liabilities. *Rentenbriefe* were bearer bonds and were regarded as among the most secure of financial investments during the 19th century; hence a wide class of investors had held them and remembered their good reputation.

52 P. Beusch: *Währungszerfall*, p. 62.

53 G. Hardach: *Weltmarktorientierung*, p. 23.

foreign exchanges; the rentenmark was designed purely for domestic circulation. On November 19 the papermark rate against the dollar rose to 5 trillion in New York and in occupied Cologne 10 trillion was recorded;[54] on November 20 the government resolved to peg it at 4.2 trillion, thus simulating the prewar rate (4.2 marks to the dollar) and forging a simple relationship with the value of the rentenmark. Papermark and rentenmark now stood in a simple one trillion to one ratio[55] and thus the stage was set for amalgamating the two into a unified currency. This eventually took place. Once foreign credits had been sanctioned and after a lengthy process involving the setting up of the "Golddiskontbank" in April 1924,[56] a new gold-exchange-standard currency was introduced in Germany in autumn 1924 in accordance with the recommendations of the Dawes Committee.[57] The new currency was named the "reichsmark".

10.2. Revaluation of Debts

The "revaluation" of fixed money claims[1] whose real value has been reduced by the depreciation of the currency in which they were denominated and perhaps discharged, signifies the acceptance of an obligation to make at least partial reparation to creditors out of the inflationary gains of the debtors. In Germany the legal principle governing the contracting and repayment of debt

---

54 *Ibid.* Also H. Schacht: *Stabilization*, pp. 101 ff. 111.

55 "Billmark" = one million million paper marks.

56 Schacht: *Stabilization*, pp. 121–150. Schacht, more than most, had argued for a rapid tying of the new currency to gold, and achieved a preliminary, partial success with the *Golddiskontbank*.

57 On the basis above all of the Bank Law [*Bankgesetz*] (*Reichsgesetzblatt*, 1924, II, p. 235) and the Law concerning the Liquidation of the Circulation of Rentenbank Notes [*Gesetz über die Liquidierung des Umlaufs an Rentenbankscheinen*] (*Reichsgesetzblatt*, 1924, II, p. 252). Cp. too, Ausschuss zur Untersuchung der Erzeugungs- und Absatzbedingungen der deutschen Wirtschaft: *Die Reichsbank* (Berlin, 1929), pp. 4 ff. Rudolf Dalberg: *Die neue deutsche Währung nach dem Dawes-Plan* (Berlin, 1924). J. Notzke: *Das Bankgesetz von 1924* (Berlin, 1924).

1 For historical precedents compare the debt revaluations following the Thirty Years War. See H. Wunderlich: "Aufwertung", article in the *Handwörterbuch der Staatswissenschaften. Ergänzungsband* (Jena, 1929), p. 25. Cp. also the historical sections of *Referentenentwurf einer Denkschrift über die "Aufwertung", verfasst im Reichsfinanzministerium. Sonderbeilage zur Deutschen Juristen-Zeitung, Heft 4, 1925* (Berlin, 1925); also in R. Michaelis: *Das Aufwertungsrecht* (Leipzig, 1926). Erich Schultze: *Die volkswirtschaftlichen Gesichtspunkte unserer Aufwertung* (Frankfurt, n. d.).

laid down that "mark equals mark"; naturally this principle dated from days of currency stability, and in such times embodied both normal commercial practice and the requirement, laid down in § 242 of the *Bürgerliches Gesetzbuch*, that "good faith" (*Treu und Glauben*) be observed in business dealings. In inflationary conditions however this formal legal principle ("mark equals mark") came into conflict with the material right of the parties to a debt transaction to expect that, even though there was a temporal displacement between the two sides of the exchange in which they were engaged, reasonable equivalence would be observed between them.

Such a conflict was already surfacing in Germany during the second half of the war as prices rose. After the end of the war the Supreme Court of Justice (*Reichsgericht*) upheld the opinion that in commodity transactions "every contract remains valid only under the proviso that circumstances do not alter" (the "rebus sic stantibus" clause). This was the basis on which business was conducted, in the Court's view. "Unforseeable and fundamental" changes such as the currency depreciation of 1918–1919 brought about the "absence or disappearance of this basis for business" and justified "accommodation to an altered" legal situation (in which, for example, greater attention must be paid to the matter of equivalence of performance on both sides of the transaction, and the parties would have to fall back on the principle of "good faith").[2] When hyperinflation commenced in July 1922 these considerations became more applicable than ever. A number of legal judgments were handed down in 1923 which, taking their stand on the principle of "good faith", embodied the view that even in purely financial transactions such as mortgage contracts the basis for business had been destroyed by the depreciation of the currency. Their viewpoint was also acknowledged in the celebrated Supreme Court Judgment of November 28, 1923 by which, under reference to the rapid currency depreciation, departure from the principle "mark equals mark" was sanctioned in mortgage contracts, and revaluation was declared fundamentally justifiable.

Mortgage contracts afford the greatest possibilities of loss during an inflation. Their term is longer than that of most other debt contracts and usually the debtor only, not the creditor, has the right to terminate them prematurely. Shorter term and more highly fungible debts do not create such possibilities of injustice. During the second half of 1922 mortgage debtors had made increased use of their right to discharge their obligations prematurely, paying off their mortgages in paper marks. Between November 1922 and May 1923 the

[2] Court decision of September 21, 1920. Cp. Otto Pirlet: "Der politische Kampf um die Aufwertungsgesetzgebung nach dem Ersten Weltkriege" (Dissertation, Cologne, 1959), p. 22.

problem was variously taken up by the Reich Ministry of Justice, the Reich Economic Council, and the Reichstag. A bill was introduced into the Reichstag on March 1, 1923, by Reichstag Deputy Düringer together with representatives of all the parties, prohibiting until January 1, 1927 the repayment of mortgages, on buildings or land, contracted before January 1, 1922, except by agreement of the creditor. This bill and others like if foundered in Reichstag committees however against the argument that it was necessary to legislate uniformly for all debts and undesirable to deal with mortgages in isolation.

The decision by the State Supreme Court in Darmstadt – whose President was Georg Best, organizer of the Association for the Protection of Mortgage Creditors and Savers, a revaluation pressure group[3] – on May 18, 1923 to grant a mortgage creditor a revaluation, put the legislators on the spot again. On July 4 Düringer's bill was once more sent by the Reichstag to its legal committee for examination. More urgent business connected with stabilizing the currency prevented any further action however. But the basis of stabilization – involving a rentenmark whose value was declared to be one trillion paper marks, and the Supreme Court's Judgment of November 28, 1923 which "hit the politicians like a bombshell"[4] – made some legislative action unavoidable.

The Reich Finance Ministry, with Luther at the helm, was at that time opposed to any form of revaluation, for fiscal reasons. This was understandable, for the Reich was the largest paper-mark debtor of all and a revaluation of "old debts" (*Altschulden*), as they came to be called, would impose a great financial burden which the Reich's ordinary revenues would be able to bear only with difficulty. Since, even in the absence of revaluation, budgetary balance was by no means assured at this time, the imposition of additional expenditure might jeopardize the currency stabilization itself. But the Justice Ministry under Erich Emminger, modeling its viewpoint on the courts' rulings and opinions, persuaded the cabinet to attend to the revaluation issue,[5] particularly once the Association of High Court Judges had on January 8, 1924 submitted a statement to the chancellor[6] warning of the devastation

---

3 From December 1924 Best was a German National Peoples' Party member of the Reichstag; from May 1925 his links with the National Socialist group in the Reichstag became closer.

4 Hans Luther: *Politiker ohne Partei. Erinnerungen* (Stuttgart, 1960), p. 230.

5 Claus-Dieter Krohn: *Stabilisierung und ökonomische Interessen. Die Finanzpolitik des Deutschen Reiches 1923–1927* (Düsseldorf, 1974), p. 46.

6 Printed in *Akten der Reichskanzlei. Weimarer Repbulik. Das Kabinett Marx I*, Nr. 49, pp. 200–201. Cp. too Otto Pfleiderer: "Die Reichsbank in der Zeit der grossen Inflation, die Stabilisierung der Mark und die Aufwertung von Kapitalforderungen", in Deutsche Bundesbank (ed.): *Währung und Wirtschaft in Deutschland 1876–1975* (Frankfurt/M. 1976), pp. 197–198.

which disregard of the Supreme Court ruling would wreak in the public's attitude to the law. Eventually, using its powers under the Enabling Law of December 8, 1923, the government promulgated the so-called Third Emergency Tax Decree on February 14, 1924. Under the terms of the Enabling Law this Decree did not need the assent of the Reichstag or the relevant Reichstag committees; neither did it obtain it. Controversy about revaluation was to occupy the Reichstag repeatedly during the years to come.[7]

The Third Emergency Tax Decree constituted the first public legislative acknowledgment of the justifiability of revaluation. Progress had been made on the matter of principle, and from then on controversy confined itself to the rate of revaluation and the terms governing payment of interest and repayment of the principal. The Decree regulated these specific details as well, but not to everyone's satisfaction. Fierce opposition immediately broke out on the floor of the Reichstag to its – allegedly – niggardly rates of revaluation, and in the second half of February motions were introduced demanding the amendment or even the entire abrogation of the Decree. This vehement opposition was one of the factors inducing the government to dissolve the Reichstag in mid-March, but the May elections yielded a new Reichstag even more sympathetic to revaluation than the old.

The Third Emergency Tax Decree[8] proposed a revaluation of the principals

---

[7] Otto Pirlet: "Der politische Kampf". Hugo Heimann: *Der Kampf um die Aufwertung, von Helfferich bis Hindenburg. Wie ihn die Deutschnationalen und wie ihn die Sozialdemokraten führten* (Berlin, 1925). Ignatz Jastrow: *Die Prinzipienfragen in den Aufwertungsdebatten* (Brünn, 1937). On the effects of the inflamed political debate about revaluation, see Larry E. Jones: "Inflation, Revaluation and the Crisis of Middle Class Politics. A Study in the Dissolution of the German Party System 1923–1928", *Central European History*, 12 (1979), pp. 143–188. David B. Southern: "The Revaluation Question", *Journal of Modern History*, 51 (1979). D. B. Southern: "The Impact of the Inflation: Inflation, the Courts and Revaluation", in Richard Bessel and E. J. Feuchtwanger (eds.): *Social Change and Political Development in Weimar Germany* (Totowa, N. J., 1981), pp. 55–76.

[8] *Die dritte Steuernotverordnung vom 14. Februar 1924. Textausgabe* (Berlin, 1924). Gustav Wagemann: *Aufwertung und Geldentwertungsausgleich nach der dritten Steuernotverordnung vom 14. Febr. 1924* (Berlin, 1924). John Wolfsohn: *Die Aufwertung der Hypotheken und Wertpapiere nach der dritten Steuernotverordnung. Eine rechtliche und volkswirtschaftliche Darstellung* (Berlin, 1924). A. Wehinger: "Die praktischen Regelungsversuche der Aufwertungsfrage, insbes. in der Zeit nach der Markstabilisierung" (Dissertation, Heidelberg, 1927). On the pre-history of the Decree, see the memoranda of December 31, 1923, "Revalorisation des dettes d'avant-guerre en Allemagne et particulièrement des dettes hypothécaires" and that of February 5, 1924, "La revalorisation des créances en Allemagne et la 3ᵉ ordonnance fiscale d'exception", Archives Générale du Royaume, Brussels, Papiers de Maurice Frère, No. 255, 260; these overlap partially with: Commission de Réparations, Comité de Garantie, Service d'Information, Document Berlin 2973, also Document Paris 3030 – both in Archives Nationales, Paris, Fond AJ 6, 563.

of private prewar debts – i. e. mortgages, business firms' bonds (debentures), etc. – to fifteen percent of their gold mark value. The revaluation of public debts – those owed by the Reich, federal states and communes, but not including bonds of public enterprises with corporate legal form – would not proceed until after the discharge of Germany's Reparations liabilities, in view of the precarious state of the public finances. Private debts contracted after the outbreak of war, that is, after the suspension of the gold currency and commencement of depreciation, were to be revalued as follows: contracts entered upon prior to January 1, 1918 were to be treated identically to prewar debts and subject to a fifteen percent revaluation. Contracts entered after January 1, 1918 were to be converted to gold marks at the dollar rate ruling on the day they were contracted and this sum was to be revalued at fifteen percent.[9] The effective burden – and benefit – of revaluation was equally sensitive to the detailed regulation of payment of interest and repayment of principal. Should the revalued claims be immediately repayable? Should there be a retrospective revaluation of interest payments too? If a moratorium was to be placed on immediate repayment, what arrangements should be reached about future interest payment on the revalued debt? The manner in which these questions were regulated in the Third Emergency Tax Decree implied a revaluation of net present values at a rate much lower than that implied by the fifteen percent revaluation of principals. No retrospective revaluation of interest charges was required. In the future, payment of interest was not to commence until January 1, 1925, was to amount to two percent in the first year, and to rise by one percent every year thereafter until January 1, 1928, after which a constant rate of five percent was to be paid. Amortization could begin on this last date on an installment basis. If gradual repayment was neither desired nor demanded, lump sum repayment could not be made before January 1, 1932.

Private claims held against financial institutions (mortgage banks, savings banks, insurance companies) were to be revalued in a ratio corresponding to the overall ratio of revaluation of the assets of the institution in question. But

On the effects of revaluation terms on holders of mark bonds in the U. S. A. cp. the memorandum of the U. S. Department of Commerce dated September 15, 1925 in the Archives of the Hoover Institution, Stanford, California, Arthur N. Young Papers, Box 3: "A distinction is made, however, between 'old' owners, or those who purchased before July 1, 1920, and later purchasers. The latter... will receive neither interest nor amortization payments until the reparations obligations have been discharged. This means that American speculative purchases, most of which were made after this date, are in effect a total loss."

[9] André Fourgeaud: "La Dépréciation et la Revalorisation du Mark Allemand et les Enseignements de l'Expérience Monétaire Allemande" (Thèse, Paris, 1926), p. 224.

claims, of whatever sort, extinguished prior to the promulgation of the decree, were not to be eligible for revaluation.

The section of the Decree relating to taxation announced the introduction of three special and non-recurrent taxes designed to cream off some of the windfall gains of the debtors for the Reich.[10] The first of these was the so-called Debenture Tax (*Obligationssteuer*). Applying equally to private bonds (debentures) still in force and already extinguished, it levied on the debtor a two percent tax on the difference between the full original gold mark value of the principal and the fifteen percent revaluation sum. If for example a firm had issued bonds before 1918 to a value of one million marks, then under the Decree only those private creditors still holding the bond stock after February 14, 1924 were to be credited with the fifteen percent revaluation of their holdings. The Reich received seventeen thousand gold marks/reichsmarks [= 2% of (100 − 15)% of one million] under all circumstances. But if part of the bond had already been redeemed in paper marks whose gold mark equivalent was less than that implied by the fifteen percent revaluation rate, the difference was payable to the Reich in full. Suppose that in the above case the firm had already redeemed the bond in paper marks equivalent in value to fifty thousand gold marks, then this firm had, additionally, to forfeit one hundred thousand gold marks/reichsmarks (= 15% of one million, minus fifty thousand) to the Reich.

The rate of revaluation imposed on debtors was thus uniform, irrespective of whether the debt had been redeemed prior to the issuing of the Decree. Creditors however were treated far from uniformly. Those who had been repaid prior to the date of the Decree got nothing more; the gold mark difference between what they had received and what they would have received had their claim still been outstanding was appropriated by the exchequer. And the benefits received even by creditors whose claims were still in force on February 14, 1924 were modest. All in all the provisions of the Decree were less of a recognition of creditors' claims to revaluation than a basis for taxing debtors' gains, thus opening up new revenue sources to the Reich. The settlement it effected between debtor and creditor bore a lesser relation to the principle of "good faith" than the legal rulings had had in mind. The terms of the Decree may have been the inevitable corollary of the need to balance the budget and secure the stability of the rentenmark, but they explain the bitterness and disillusionment of those who had had hopes of more generous compensation for their creditor losses. In no way had they been responsible for the

[10] Karl-Bernhard Netzband and Hans Peter Widmaier: *Währungs- und Finanzpolitik der Ära Luther 1923–1925* (Basel, 1964), pp. 190ff.

inflation, yet the Decree sent them almost empty away, whereas the state which had relentlessly pursued inflationary policies was even devising new revenue sources for itself out of their losses. Underneath the legal and political arguments over revaluation there lay moral outrage. The government had paid good attention to fiscal necessities by this Decree, but at the cost of creating a sense of injury and unfairness among large sections of the governed. Now these felt further alienated from the state and proceeded to campaign for a revision of the terms with which the government had dismissed them – just as the government itself had campaigned in the international arena for the revision of its Reparations liabilities.

The other two non-recurrent taxes announced in the Third Emergency Decree should be briefly mentioned. Like the first, both were designed to appropriate debtors' windfall gains. One of them, designated a "Credit Acceptance Tax", was to be levied on the debtors of banks and other credit institutions while the other, the "Emergency Currency Tax" was to be levied on the seignorage realized during 1923 by the issuers of emergency moneys. Neither tax actually came into force.[11] The most productive of all the taxes announced in the Decree remains to be described. Called the *Hauszinssteuer* or *Mietzinssteuer* it was, unlike the three already mentioned, designed as a recurrent tax and was payable to the federal states, not to the Reich.[12] This was a tax on the windfall gains accruing to house owners out of the complete or partial repayment of mortgages during the inflation. At the same time, the ceiling on rents of dwellings was to be raised to eighty percent of the prewar rent.

Debate on the revaluation issue, both in the Reichstag and outside it, was inflamed more than ever by the Decree. It was a dominant issue in the two Reichstag elections of May and December 1924. Opponents of revaluation emphasized the fiscal burden of revaluing public debts, alleging that it would jeopardize budgetary stability, in any case precarious, and hence currency stability. Revaluation of private debt would burden industry and agriculture, and these in any case were suffering from lack of capital and were being forced into new debt. It would jeopardize the reconstruction of the productive base.[13] Advocates of revaluation emphasized the general public's sense of what was fair, the immiserization of the creditor class, and the repercussions

11 *Ibid.*, pp. 194 ff.

12 *Ibid.*, pp. 196 ff. Peter-Christian Witt: "Inflation, Wohnungszwangswirtschaft und Hauszinssteuer", in Lutz Niethammer (ed.): *Wohnen im Wandel* (Wuppertal, 1979), pp. 385–407.

13 Ferdinand Anders: *Der Stand der Aufwertung. Eine unparteiische Untersuchung ihrer volkswirtschaftlichen Grundlagen und ihrer Voraussetzungen* (Berlin, 1924). P. Oertmann: *Die Aufwertungsfrage bei Geldforderungen, Hypotheken und Anleihen* (Berlin, 1924).

on the Reparations issue: the greed of Germany's Reparations creditors would be excited if the Reich remained entirely unencumbered by domestic debt.[14]

After numerous court rulings conflicting with the legislation[15] and a protracted political tug-of-war, both in public[16] and behind the scenes in the cabinet,[17] the revaluation issue was at length settled in two Laws passed by the Reichstag on July 14, 1925, and coming into force two days later upon receiving President Hindenburg's signature. One regulated the "Revaluation of Mortgages and Other Claims", that is, private debts; the other regulated the "Redemption of Public Loans."[18] Jointly they superseded the revaluation provisions of the Third Emergency Tax Decree.

The former of the two Laws raised the rate of revaluation of mortgages, from the fifteen percent laid down in the Decree, to twenty-five percent, but it left the rate of revaluation of the bonds of business firms (debentures) at fifteen percent. Debtors who believed that they suffered hardship unfairly on account of these rulings could appeal to have the rate lowered. Certificates (*Genussscheine*) to a maximum of ten percent of the gold value of the debenture were to be distributed to "old holders" – defined as those who had bought the stock prior to July 1, 1920 and held it continuously since that day; these certificates

[14] C.-D. Krohn: *Stabilisierung*, p. 48.

[15] H. Wunderlich: "Aufwertung", p. 27.

[16] Cp. the polemical pamphlet of Ernst Sontag: *Hypothekengläubiger und Anleihebesitzer im Kampf um ihr Recht. Eine Kritik des Entwurfs eines Gesetzes über die Aufwertung von Hypotheken und anderen privatrechtlichen Ansprüchen sowie des Entwurfs eines Gesetzes über die Ablösung öffentlicher Anleihen* (Berlin, 1925).

[17] Krohn: *Stabilisierung*, pp. 164–173.

[18] Summarizing report – dated June 6, 1926, "La Législation Allemande sur la Revalorisation", Archives Générales du Royaume, Brussels, Papiers de Maurice Frère, No. 291. Cp. Paul Moldenhauer: *Die Regelung der Aufwertungsfrage* (Cologne, 1925). Fritz Koppe: *In welchen Fällen und wie hoch wird aufgewertet? Ein gemeinverständlicher Führer durch das neue Aufwertungsrecht* (Berlin, 1925). Franz Schlegelberger and Rudolf Harmening: *Das Gesetz über die Aufwertung von Hypotheken und anderen Ansprüchen vom 16. Juli 1925* (Berlin, 1925). Hermann Stenger: *Die Aufwertung von Hypotheken und anderen Ansprüchen und die Ablösung öffentlicher Anleihen* (Munich, 3 Bde. 1925–6). Oskar Mügel: *Die Aufwertung. Überblick über die Entwicklung* (Berlin, 1926). Hans Riss: *Leitfaden durch das Aufwertungsrecht* (Gladbach, 1926). Hans Ulrich: "Der Währungszerfall, die Aufwertung und der Wiederaufbau bei den privaten deutschen Lebensversicherungsgesellschaften", *Jahrbücher für Nationalökonomie und Statistik*, 125 II (1926). Georg Winnewisser: *Die Aufwertung der Industrieobligationen. Eine wirtschaftliche Untersuchung* (Karlsruhe, 1927). Manfred Simon: "La valorisation des obligations en Allemagne comme conséquence de la chute du mark papier" (Thèse, Paris, 1927). René Huas: *La valorisation des obligations industrielles en Allemagne. Ses rapports avec la réforme monétaire* (Paris, 1928). Arthur Nussbaum: *Die Bilanz der Aufwertungstheorie* (Tübingen, 1929). Cp. also: *Nachtrag vom 1.9.25 zur Goldwerttabelle für Papiermark 1914–1924 mit den durch das Aufwertungsgesetz und das Gesetz zur Ablösung öffentlicher Anleihen verursachten Änderungen* (Stuttgart, 1925).

entitled them to participation in the distributed profits of the debtor company along with the shareholders.

As in the February 1924 Decree, debt contracts concluded before January 1, 1918 received the same treatment as prewar debts, i. e. the prescribed revaluation rate applied to the nominal principal of the claim. However the Law revised the deflation factor which was to be used to ascertain the gold mark values of the principals of debts contracted after that date, to which the revaluation rate would then be applied. Whereas the Decree had specified the dollar exchange rate, the Law now specified a deflation factor corresponding roughly to the average between the dollar rate and the wholesale price index.[19] By this concession the government went some way towards meeting the creditors' objection that the dollar rate had depreciated more rapidly than the domestic price level had risen. Many creditors had hoped for more: the substitution of the cost-of-living index whose rate of depreciation had been still lower; nevertheless the deflation factor actually specified did enhance the terms for creditors.

As far as the lump-sum repayment of private debts was concerned, the general moratorium till January 1, 1932 was upheld as in the Decree. Debtors gained the right however to discharge their revalued liabilities, inclusive of interest due, before that date, if they gave three months notice of their intention. Upon application of either party, those ordinary courts specified as "Revaluation Tribunals" for resolving (subject to appeal) disputes arising out of the Law's provisions, could order that the debtor amortize his debt with annual payments amounting to ten percent of the principal, beginning from January 1, 1926. Mortgage repayments could likewise be rescheduled from a lump sum to an installment basis: the repayments in this case being spread over the period 1930–37.

As far as interest charges were concerned, liability in respect of interest due before December 31, 1924 was regarded as discharged. Interest was due thereafter at the following rates: from January 1, 1925 at 1.2%, from July 1, 1925 at 2.5%, from January 1, 1926 at 3% and from January 1, 1928 at 5%. Interest rates on newly contracted debt were far higher than this on the German capital market in the later 1920s; in reality then the net present value of the sums not repayable before 1932 was considerably lower than the rate of revaluation of the principals would at first sight suggest. Appearance and reality differed in the regulation of these domestic liabilities, just as they differed in the case of Germany's external liability – Reparations. The net present value of this latter

[19] The actual conversion factors derived from this deflation index are printed in a Table in the last-mentioned item in the preceding footnote, pp. 88–89.

liability was also a good deal less than the 132 billion gold marks, laid down in the London Ultimatum, suggested – since more than half of this sum (the so-called "C" bonds) bore neither interest nor amortization for the time being.

Unlike the Third Emergency Decree the Revaluation Law did provide for a resuscitation of claims on private debtors extinguished between June 14, 1922 and February 14, 1924 – the latter date being that of the Decree's promulgation. Such claims were subject to the provisions of the Act. This, too, improved the treatment of creditors by comparison with the Decree: however there was a "hardship clause" in respect of this provision also, and where debtors appealed to it the rate of revaluation was to be decided by the "Revaluation Tribunal" individually in each case.

Mortgage bonds, savings bank deposits and insurance claims were subject to a rate of revaluation consonant with the rate of revaluation of the assets of the institution against which they were held. However the minimum rate of revaluation of savings deposits was to be 12½%, and if the savings bank's assets were insufficient for this, its public (usually municipal) owners had to provide a subsidy.

So much for private claims. Under the Loan Redemption Act, coming into force on the same day (July 16, 1925) as the Revaluation Act, the holders (or, rather, certain holders) of public bonds gained a revaluation, as they had not done under the Third Emergency Tax Decree. The fiscal implications of taking this matter up were large, as a statement of the dimensions of the debt will show. It comprised the prewar public bond stock (4.8 billion marks for the Reich, 17 billions for the federal states, 10–12 billions for the communes) plus about 98 billion marks worth of War Loan stock. Interest payments on these at 5% would alone come to about five billion marks per annum – about twice the annual expenditure of the Reich before the war.[20] After the war the Reich had assumed responsibility for the Loan stock of the federal states, but it had also been reducing its total funded debt, partly by accepting it in discharge of tax liabilities and partly by open market purchases. The liquidity-enhancing and inflation-stimulating properties of these actions need not be discussed here. They did however mean that by the time the Loan Redemption Law came into effect the funded debt of the Reich had been reduced to 72 billion marks, of the federal states to 1.5 billion and of the communes to 8–9 billions.[21] These sums must be judged against the fact that in fiscal year 1924/25 the ordinary revenue

---

20 Peter-Christian Witt, in his *Die Finanzpolitik des Deutschen Reiches von 1903 bis 1913. Eine Studie zur Innenpolitik des Wilhelminischen Deutschland* (Lübeck, 1970), p. 379, gives the value of the Reich's revenues in 1913 as 2.2 bn. marks.

21 H. Wunderlich: "Aufwertung", p. 32.

of the Reich amounted to 7.8 billion marks[22] – i.e. about one tenth of the above funded liability. There were thus narrow limits to the generosity of the revaluation. The modest revaluation actually effected did not deal with creditors according to uniform criteria, but in a manner graduated according to social considerations, awarding the more needy creditors a higher rate of revaluation. The details of the revaluation of Reich debt were as follows.[23]

(i) All funded mark loans of the Reich were consolidated into a single "Redemption Debt", their face values being reduced in the ratio 40 : 1. Thus, out of bonds whose capital value had totaled about 70 billion marks there emerged a "Redemption Debt" of about 1.75 billion reichsmarks. Except for "old holders" (defined in this case as those who had bought stock before July 1, 1920 and held it continuously since that date) no interest was payable on this principal until the extinction of the Reparations liability. Nor was amortization prescribed – except in the case of "old holders".

(ii) "Old holders" as just defined participated in a lottery. A draw each year selected the holders of 3⅓% of the aggregate held by "old holders" and this was repaid. The repaid sum amounted to five times the face value of the Redemption Debt stock held (i.e. one eighth of the nominal paper mark value of the Loan stock originally held). In this way, the claims of all "old holders" would be redeemed over thirty years. The possessor of an "old holding" of War Loan with original face value of one thousand marks would for example receive a "Redemption Debt" holding worth only twenty-five marks. But when this was drawn in the lottery, he would receive 125 marks – 12½% of the nominal value of his original holding. "Old holdings" were to attract interest at 4½% from January 1926; this would not actually be paid however until the redemption of the holding.

Sixty percent of the entire funded debt of the Reich was in the hands of "old holders". This represented one billion reichsmarks of the capital value of the Redemption Debt but five billion reichsmarks in actual redemption payments, plus accumulated interest charges, over thirty years.[24] The reason why July 1, 1920 had been selected as the date dividing "old" from "new" holders was that by that date the registration of security holdings had been completed,

---

[22] C.-D. Krohn: *Stabilisierung*, p. 133.

[23] Wunderlich: "Aufwertung", pp. 32–33.

[24] At the end of March 1928, that is, after all revaluation claims had been registered but also after some repayment of principal had occurred, the value of the consolidated pre-stabilization "Redemption Debt" in the hands of "old holders" was stated to be 4.55 bn. reichsmarks, and in the hands of "new holders", 0.70 bn. reichsmarks. See *Deutschlands wirtschaftliche Lage. Die Entwicklung nach dem Kriege. Eine Materialsammlung* (Berlin, 3rd edn. 1926. Vierte Ergänzung, Berlin, 1928), p. 119b.

which the Reich had undertaken in connection with its measures against the flight of capital announced on October 24, 1919. The registration afforded the holders proof of their claims.

(iii) Needy "old holders" (Germans only) – those whose annual income was less than one thousand reichsmarks per annum – received a preferential annuity to the value of eighty percent of their Redemption Debt holding; this was in addition to their participation in the lottery. If for example the original nominal value of their holding had been one thousand marks, so that they now held twenty-five reichsmarks of Redemption Debt, their annuity would amount to twenty marks. If they renounced their rights in the lottery, this annuity would increase by one quarter; if at the time of his renunciation the debtor was more than sixty years old it would rise by one half. In no case however could the annuity to which an individual was entitled exceed eight hundred marks.

(iv) The smallest holdings – those whose original nominal values had not exceeded five hundred marks – were not eligible for redemption except where the holder had a low income. In such cases a cash settlement of between eight and fifteen percent was made.

Redemption of the funded debt of the states and communes was regulated in a similar manner. The passing of this legislation did not still the public agitation. Many considered it inadequate, and two plebiscites favoring its revision were interdicted by decisions of the Reich Interior Ministry. But all in all one can hardly fail to conclude that creditors received reasonably equitable treatment. A domestic citizen who had wished in June 1920 to convert a money holding of "hard" foreign currency – e. g. U. S. dollars – into a holding of five percent War Loan stock with a par value of one thousand marks, would have needed only $20.40 to do so. In that month five percent War Loan was standing at about eighty percent of par[25] and the dollar exchange rate was averaging 2.55 cents to the mark.[26] After the passing of the Loan Redemption Act he would have been entitled to a capital repayment of 125 reichsmarks, disregarding interest payments and possible entitlement to the preferential annuity. At the post-stabilization exchange rate of 4.20 reichsmarks to the dollar this represented $30.00. The rate of revaluation was thus not unattractive to Germans who before July 1, 1920 had invested foreign exchange or the proceeds of sale of real assets in Reich bonds. Because of the low market standing of public bonds after the war the effective rate of revaluation was

[25] *Statistisches Jahrbuch f. d. Deutsche Reich*, 42 (1921/22), p. 271. See also p. 127 *supra*.

[26] Statistisches Reichsamt: *Zahlen zur Geldentwertung in Deutschland 1914–1923* (Berlin, 1925), p. 6.

greater than 12½% – it was 16% for example for those who purchased at eighty percent of par. "Old holders" who had bought Reich bonds before the war or during its early stages and held on to them ever since came off worst; they had to make do with a 12½% revaluation of their principal and a considerably smaller revaluation of the net present value of their investment. Still, bondholders in France and Belgium had fared little better. These countries had experienced neither hyperinflation nor revaluation, but instead moderate rates of inflation that reduced their currencies to one fifth and one seventh, respectively, of their prewar values,[27] implying a corresponding depreciation in the value of fixed money claims. It is against this standard that the treatment of "old holders" in Germany should also be judged.[28]

27 Ragnar Nurkse: *The Course and Control of Inflation. A Review of Monetary Experience in Europe after World War I. League of Nations Publication 1946 II A 6* (Geneva, 1946), p. 93. Derek H. Aldcroft: *From Versailles to Wall Street 1919–1929* (London, 1977), pp. 148–9.

28 Statistical information on financial results of the revaluation of Reich bonds, on the social composition of the bondholders, on the share of foreign holdings etc. is presented in "Denkschrift über die Ablösung der Markanleihen des Reichs", in *Verhandlungen des Reichstags, Bd. 423* (Berlin, 1928), Drucksache Nr. 474.

Summary and Conclusions

The main conclusions of the present work may be summed up as follows:

1. The process of inflation in Germany commenced during the First World War; particularly from 1916 it was clearly at work. However wartime economic controls prevented prices and the exchange rate from fully registering its impact; to this extent wartime inflation was of the "suppressed" variety. "Open" inflation developed in 1919–20 as controls were removed.
2. In the long term the growth of the money supply was at least a permissive factor in the process of currency depreciation, though not perhaps its direct determinant. In the short term changes in the value of the mark, external and domestic, were determined rather by variations in the demand for money (or the velocity of circulation) and in the rate of productive activity. Variations in the demand for money reflected changing confidence in the currency.
3. However an adequate account of the process of depreciation will be gained only by pursuing the analysis beyond the proximate determinants just described, to uncover the political forces governing their behavior. Thus the constitutional weakness in the fiscal basis of the Reich vis-a-vis that of the federal states, before 1918, was the chief reason why so much smaller a proportion of war expenditure was financed out of taxation in Germany than in Great Britain. The continuing deficitary financing of Reich expenditure during the postwar years was a consequence of the domestic political instability flowing from military defeat and revolution. This brought weak governments to power at a time when strong governments would have been needed to cope, in a manner not injurious to the currency, with the fiscal legacy of the imperial state, with the burden of Reparations, and with the "quantum leap" in the social programs which the state had to finance. However in 1919, not only would stabilization have been difficult to achieve for political reasons; one must also question whether it would have been desirable. Given the vast increase in monetary assets brought about by wartime borrowing, a currency stabilization in 1919 would have benefited the rentier class by burdening business and labor income – i.e. the income of the productive classes – with oppressive taxation. In 1919 the economy needed to be rapidly reconverted to civilian production and the demobilized servicemen needed to be reintegrated

into productive jobs; in such circumstances the appropriate policy was one that stimulated production, not one that would have retarded it.

External relations also contributed to the destabilization of the Reich's budget and hence to the postwar monetary expansion: Reparations. Besides the size of the sums paid or demanded for payment in the immediate future, the failure to fix the aggregate liability also played an important part in the inflationary process. It made it appear that attempts at domestic fiscal discipline would benefit only foreigners and not Germany. The actual Reparations demands increased the Reich's fiscal deficit and hence the fiscal problem requiring solution; uncertainty as to how far future Reparations demands would rise destroyed the incentive to try to solve it.

So much for the political forces at work to sustain long-term monetary expansion. Behind the short-term proximate determinants of price change – the demand for money and the rate of production – political forces were also at work. The political conflicts and strikes in Germany in 1919 caused production to sink to a record low in that year; the foreign-policy tensions of 1923 that led to the occupation of the Ruhr severely affected production too. Low levels of production may well have accelerated the rate of inflation in both years.

The demand for money depended largely on confidence in the future value of the currency and this exhibited sharp sensitivity to political events. Among such events was the stabilization of domestic political conditions in 1920/21 – with the result that, despite continuing Reich deficits, prices tended to stabilize too at that time. Another such event was the coming to a head of the tensions over Reparations in 1922; this precipitated the collapse into hyperinflation.

4. The inflation eased the conversion of the productive economy to a war basis in 1914 and its reconversion to a civilian basis in 1918/19. It stimulated growth and full employment in postwar Germany; and in particular it insulated Germany from the influences of the world slump of 1920/21.
5. Further than this, inflation in Germany may have made a significant contribution toward the rapid recovery of the *world* economy from the 1920/21 slump, particularly when we recollect that it caused German imports from the U.S.A. to double by volume between these two years and stimulated German imports from other leading economies likewise. To this extent the German economy, animated by inflationary forces, acted as the only "agent of expansion" among the world's industrial nations at the time. Thus the inflationary policy then being followed in Germany may have been the reason why the world economy was already pulling out of depression in 1922, in spite of the sharpness and severity of the preceding

slump, whereas after 1929 the world slump, despite its far less virulent onset, lasted for years and brought political destabilization in its train.

6. If we compare real wages between 1919 and 1922 with those of 1913 we find that they had fallen far less than real national income as a whole; that is, the relative position of the worker had improved, particularly if we take the reduction of working hours into account. This relative improvement was not experienced however by higher-paid employees such as civil servants or salary earners for example, nor even by all skilled wage earners. Profits from business enterprise were also good during the postwar inflation; and so owners of monetary assets were the main victims of inflation – in respect both of their income and their capital. As to financial asset-holding a violent redistribution of wealth took place between 1919 and 1923, undoing in this sphere the wealth-concentrating effects of German industrialization during the second half of the nineteenth century. Since the distribution of wealth is the chief determinant of the degree of inequality in the distribution of income, this process explains why the distribution of income was so much more equal after the inflation than in 1913; the inflation destroyed large incomes, but not medium-sized or small ones. Wage differentials and the differential between wages and salaries were also compressed by the inflation. Thus, by a different route, the inflation achieved the very aims of the Erzberger tax reforms which, in a direct sense, it had frustrated.
7. A significant proportion of creditors' losses arising out of the inflation was borne by foreigners who had taken up creditor positions in marks. The losses these suffered were of at least the same order of magnitude as German Reparations payments between 1919 and 1923. "Inflation tax" was the only type of taxation which could involve foreigners in the financing of German public expenditure and German investment. Germany was able to run import surpluses – to enlarge her imports of raw materials and foodstuffs – in the measure that foreigners were willing to accumulate mark claims; this facilitated speedy economic reconstruction. The hyperinflation began, however, when foreigners lost confidence in the future external value of the mark, because of the diplomatic crisis over Reparations. Capital imports ceased and the "cake" for distribution among Germans grew smaller. This is the real background to the distress experienced in Germany in the final phase of the inflation – resembling that experienced between 1917 and 1919. This distress was exacerbated of course by the disruption of production and of distributive networks that accompanied the occupation of the Ruhr; but it was not properly overcome until capital began to flow into Germany again in the summer of 1924.

8. For a large sector of the German economy currency stabilization had already taken place in practice long before the official stabilization measures were put into effect in November 1923. Large quantities of foreign and domestic value-maintaining currencies were in circulation before that date: their total value was not far short of the value of money in circulation before the war. As the incidence of "inflation tax" became confined to an ever shrinking class of papermark users – chiefly wage and salary earners paid in papermarks – its burden on them weighed ever more oppressively, but by the same token its "yield" to the state diminished. Revolutionary potential built up that threatened domestic public order and the integrity of the Reich. Currency stabilization thus became a necessity of the political system, if the Reich were to survive; to a far lesser degree was it a necessity for the continued functioning of the economic system.

   In the field of foreign relations stabilization paved the way for the revision of Reparations arrangements under the "Dawes Plan".
9. The "revaluation" brought some adjustment of creditors' losses. After a certain delay the German rentier recovered a proportion of his original claims that was not too far behind the proportion to which the money claims of citizens of countries which had experienced more moderate inflations – Belgium, France, Italy – were reduced.
10. In terms of foreign policy inflation served the German national interest in the short run by providing foreign resources for financing imports and Reparations over a finite period. Exchange rate depreciation promoted German recovery of export markets lost during the war. Inflation may well have helped to induce the Allied governments to moderate their Reparations demands.

    In the sphere of domestic politics the inflation effected a massive redistribution of income and wealth – in an egalitarian direction; after 1924 the tendency to inequality reasserted itself. Which tendency is preferable, and whether those who control economic policy may legitimately employ inflation as a means of effecting such a redistribution, are questions to which every individual must find his or her own answers.

Bibliography

1. Unpublished Sources

Archives of the Hoover Institution, Stanford, California: Arthur N. Young Papers, Henry M. Robinson Papers, James A. Logan Papers.

Archives Générales du Royaume, Brussels: Papiers de Maurice Frère.

Archives Nationales, Paris, Fond AJ 6: Commission de Réparation.

Bundesarchiv, Koblenz: Akten der Reichskanzlei (R 43 I), Akten des Reichsfinanzministeriums (R 2).

Harvard University, Cambridge, Mass.: Frank W. Taussig Papers, Thomas W. Lamont Papers.

Hoover Institution on War, Revolution and Peace, Stanford, California: Allied Powers (1919-) Reparation Commission: Documents Collected by the Second Committee of Experts, 1924.

Library of Congress, Manuscript Division, Washington D.C.: Leonard P. Ayres Papers.

National Archives, Washington, D.C.: Records of the Department of State.

Politisches Archiv des Auswärtigen Amts, Bonn: Akten der Abt. Wirtschafts-Reparationen.

Public Record Office, London (i.e. Kew, Surrey): Treasury Papers, Foreign Office Papers.

Zentrales Staatsarchiv, Potsdam: Akten der Reichsbank (25.01).

2. Official Statistical Publications

Ausschuss zur Untersuchung der Erzeugungs- und Absatzbedingungen der deutschen Wirtschaft: *Der Bankkredit* (Berlin, 1930).

– *Die deutsche Zahlungsbilanz* (Berlin, 1930).

– *Die Reichsbank* (Berlin, 1929).

– IV Unterausschuss: *Die Arbeitsleistung* (Berlin, 9 Bde. 1927–30).

Board of Governors of the Federal Reserve System: *Banking and Monetary Statistics* (Washington, D.C., 1943).

British Labour Statistics. Historical Abstract 1886–1968. Issued by Department of Employment and Productivity (London, 1971).

Deutsche Bundesbank: *Deutsches Geld- und Bankwesen in Zahlen 1876–1975* (Frankfurt/M., 1976).

Deutschlands Wirtschaft, Währung und Finanzen. Im Auftrage der Reichsregierung den von der Reparationskommission eingesetzten Sachverständigenausschüssen übergeben (Berlin, 1924).

Einzelschriften zur Statistik des Deutschen Reichs, Nr. 1ff. (1927ff.): see Statistisches Reichsamt.

International Labor Office: *Enquête sur la Production. Rapport Général, Tome II, 2* (Paris, 1924).

– *Fluctuations des salaires dans différents pays de 1914 à 1921* (Geneva, 1922).

– *Wage Changes in Various Countries 1914 to 1925* (Geneva, 1926).

– *Workers' Standard of Life in Countries with Depreciated Currency* (Geneva, 1925).

International Abstracts of Economic Statistics 1919–1930. Issued by the International Conference of Economic Services (London, 1934).

Die Kosten des Ernährungsbedarfs. Monatliche Ermittlungen hrsg. vom Statistischen Amt der Stadt Berlin 1 (1920), and subsequent vols.

Kuczynski, Robert R.: *Postwar Labor Conditions in Germany. Bulletin of the U.S. Bureau of Labor Statistics No. 380* (Washington, D.C., 1925).

Statistical Abstract for the United Kingdom 1913–1929. Prepared by the Board of Trade Statistical Office (London, 1931).

Statistik des Deutschen Reichs: see Statistisches Reichsamt.

Statistisches Bundesamt: *Bevölkerung und Wirtschaft 1872–1972* (Stuttgart, 1972).

Statistisches Handbuch von Deutschland 1928–1944. Issued by the Länderrat des Amerikanischen Besatzungsgebiets (Munich, 1949).

Statistisches Jahrbuch für das Deutsche Reich 40 (1919) and subsequent vols.

Statistisches Reichsamt: *Der Auswärtige Handel Deutschlands in den Jahren 1920, 1921, und 1922 verglichen mit dem Jahre 1913 nach Warengruppen, Warengattungen und Ländern. Statistik des Deutschen Reichs, Bd. 310* (Berlin, 1924).

– *Die deutsche Finanzwirtschaft vor und nach dem Kriege. Einzelschriften zur Statistik des Deutschen Reichs, Nr. 14* (Berlin, 1930).

– *Die deutsche Vermögensbesteuerung vor und nach dem Kriege. Statistik des Deutschen Reichs, Bd. 337* (Berlin, 1927)

– *Das deutsche Volkseinkommen vor und nach dem Kriege. Einzelschriften zur Statistik des Deutschen Reichs, Nr. 24* (Berlin, 1932).

– *Die deutsche Zahlungsbilanz der Jahre 1924–1933. Sonderheft 14 zu Wirtschaft und Statistik* (Berlin, 1934).

– *Die deutschen Banken 1924–1926. Einzelschriften zur Statistik des Deutschen Reichs, Nr. 3* (Berlin, 1927).

– *Deutschlands Wirtschaftslage unter den Nachwirkungen des Weltkrieges* (Berlin, 1923).

– *Die interalliierten Schulden. Ihre Entstehung und ihre Bedeutung im Young Plan. Einzelschriften zur Statistik des Deutschen Reichs, Nr. 11* (Berlin, 1930).

– *Die Lohn- und Gehaltserhebung von 1920. Statistik des Deutschen Reichs, Bd. 293* (Berlin, 1921).

– *Die Staatsausgaben von Grossbritannien, Frankreich, Belgien und Italien in der Vor- und Nachkriegszeit. Einzelschriften zur Statistik des Deutschen Reichs, Nr. 2* (Berlin, 1927).

– *Die Wirtschaft des Auslandes 1900–1927. Einzelschriften zur Statistik des Deutschen Reichs, Nr.* 5 (Berlin, 1928).

– *Zahlen zur Geldentwertung in Deutschland 1914 bis 1923. Sonderheft 1 zu Wirtschaft und Statistik* (Berlin, 1925).

Untersuchung des Bankwesens 1933. Issued by the Untersuchungsausschuss für das Bankwesen, 1933 (Berlin, 2 Teile [i.e. Parts], 1933).

Vierteljahrshefte zur Statistik des Deutschen Reichs 29 (1920) and subsequent vols.

Wattenberg Ben. J.: *The Statistical History of the United States. From Colonial Times to the Present* (New York, 1976).

Wirtschaft und Statistik 1 (1921) and subsequent vols.
Young, John P.: *European Currency and Finance. Commission of Gold and Silver Inquiry. United States Senate, Foreign Currency and Exchange Investigation, Serial 9* (Washington, D.C., 2 vols., 1925).
Zeitschrift des Preussischen Statistischen Landesamts, 49 (1909) and subsequent vols.

3. Books, Dissertations, Articles and Other Works

Abel, Andrew, Rudiger Dornbusch, John Huizinga and Alan Marcus; "Money Demand during Hyperinflation", *Journal of Monetary Economics*, 5 (1979) pp. 97–104.
Abelshauser, Werner: "Inflation und Stabilisierung. Zum Problem ihrer makroökonomischen Auswirkungen auf die Rekonstruktion der deutschen Wirtschaft nach dem Ersten Weltkrieg", in Otto Büsch and G.D. Feldman (eds.): *Historische Prozesse*, pp. 161–174.
– "Verelendung der Handarbeiter? Zur sozialen Lage der deutschen Arbeiter in der grossen Inflation der frühen zwanziger Jahre", in Hans Mommsen and Winfried Schulze (eds.): *Vom Elend der Handarbeit. Probleme historischer Unterschichtenforschung* (Stuttgart, 1981), p. 445–476.
Abelshauser, Werner and Dietmar Petzina: "Krise und Rekonstruktion. Zur Interpretation der gesamtwirtschaftlichen Entwicklung Deutschlands im 20. Jahrhundert", in W. Abelshauser and D. Petzina (eds.): *Deutsche Wirtschaftsgeschichte im Industriezeitalter. Konjunktur, Krise, Wachstum* (Königstein/Ts., 1981), pp. 47–93.
Aereboe, Friedrich: *Der Einfluss des Krieges auf die landwirtschaftliche Produktion in Deutschland* (Stuttgart, 1927).
Aereboe, Friedrich, H. Warmbold and A. Hesse: *Preisverhältnisse landwirtschaftlicher Erzeugnisse im Kriege. Beiträge zur Kriegswirtschaft, Heft 6* (Berlin, 1917).
Aghte, A.: "Lohnsteigerungen 1913 bis 1920", *Wirtschaft und Statistik*, 1 (1921), pp. 81–84.
Akten der Reichskanzlei. Weimarer Republik: see Erdmann, K.D. and W. Mommsen.
Albers, Edgar: *Die Entstehungsgeschichte und der Streit um den wirtschaftlichen Charakter der deutschen Rentenmarkwährung* (Berlin, 1928).
Albrecht, Gerhard: *Zur Krisis der Landwirtschaft* (Jena, 1924).
Aldcroft, Derek H.: *From Versailles to Wall Street 1919–1929* (London, 1977).
– *The Inter-War Economy: Britain 1919–1939* (London, 1970).
Allen, Roy G.D.: *Index Numbers in Theory and Practice* (London, 1975).
Die den Alliierten seit Waffenstillstand übermittelten deutschen Angebote und Vorschläge zur Lösung der Reparations- und Wiederaufbaufrage (Berlin, 1923).
"Die amtliche Höchstpreispolitik", *Zeitschrift des Preussischen Statistischen Landesamts*, 61 (1921), pp. 26^{+}–28^{+}.
Anders, Ferdinand: *Der Stand der Aufwertung. Eine unparteiische Untersuchung ihrer volkswirtschaftlichen Grundlagen und ihrer Voraussetzungen* (Berlin, 1924).
Anderson, Oskar: "Indexzahlen", in *Handwörterbuch der Wirtschaftswissenschaften*, Bd. 4 (1978), pp. 98–108.
Angell, James: *The Theory of International Prices* (Cambridge, Mass., 1926).
Angelopoulos, Angelos: *Die Einkommensverteilung im Lichte der Einkommensteuerstatistik (Leipzig, 1931).*

Arbeitszeit, Lohn und Verdienst in den Nürnberger Gewerben 1904–1919. Beilage zu den statistischen Monatsberichten der Stadt Nürnberg vom Mai 1920 (Nuremberg, 1920).

Aubin, Hermann and Wolfgang Zorn (eds.): *Handbuch der deutschen Wirtschafts- und Sozialgeschichte* (Stuttgart, 2 Bde. 1971–76).

Bach, W.: *Untersuchungen über die Lebensmittelrationierung im Kriege und ihre physiologisch-hygienische Bedeutung auf Grund der Lebensmittelversorgung in Bonn während der Zeit vom 1. Juli 1916 bis 28. Dezember 1918* (Munich, n.d.).

Bagehot, Walter: *Lombard Street. A Description of the Money Market* (London, 1873).

Bain, Andrew D.: *The Control of the Money Supply* (Harmondsworth, 3rd. edn. 1980).

Balabkins, Nicholas: *Germany under Direct Controls. Economic Aspects of Industrial Disarmament 1945–1948* (New Brunswik, N. J., 1964).

Bane, Suda L. and Ralph H. Lutz (eds.): *The Blockade of Germany after the Armistice. 1918–1919. Selected Documents of the Supreme Economic Council, American Relief Administration, and Other Wartime Organizations* (London, 1942).

Bang, Paul: *Staatsbankerott oder -erneuerung?* (Munich, 1920).

Bankenquete 1908–1909: Stenographische Berichte nebst Materialien, Heft 1–3 (Berlin, 1909–1910).

Bariety, Jacques: *Les Relations Franco-Allemandes après la Première Guerre Mondiale. 10. Nov. 1918–10. Jan. 1925: De l'Exécution à la Négociation* (Paris, 1977).

Baruch, Bernard M.: *The Making of the Reparation and Economic Sections of the Treaty* (New York, 1920).

Baudis, Dieter and Helga Nussbaum: *Wirtschaft und Staat in Deutschland vom Ende des 19. Jahrhunderts bis 1918/19* (Berlin-East, 1978).

Baumgartner, Wilfried: "Le Rentenmark (15. Octobre 1923–11. Octobre 1924)" (Thèse, Paris, 1925).

Beckermann, Wilfred: *An Introduction to National Income Analysis* (London, 2nd. edn. 1976).

Beckmann, Fritz: *Die weltwirtschaftlichen Beziehungen der deutschen Landwirtschaft und ihre wirtschaftliche Lage 1919–1924* (Bonn, 1924).

Bell, A. C.: *The Blockade of Germany 1914–1918* (London, 1961).

Bendixen, Friedrich: "Devalvation. Eine Richtigstellung", *Bank-Archiv*, 19 (1919/20) pp. 163–169.

– "Die Inflation als Rettungsmittel", *Bank-Archiv*, 19 (1919/20) pp. 53–56.

– *Das Inflationsproblem* (Stuttgart, 1917).

– *Kriegsanleihen und Finanznot. Zwei finanzpolitische Vorschläge* (Jena, 1919).

– "Die Parität und ihre Wiederherstellung", *Bank-Archiv*, 18 (1918/19) pp. 9–13.

– *Währungspolitik und Geldtheorie im Lichte des Weltkrieges* (Munich, 1915, 2nd. edn. 1919).

Bente, Hermann: "Die deutsche Währungspolitik von 1914–1924", *Weltwirtschaftliches Archiv*, 23 (1926) pp. 117*–191*.

Bergmann, Carl: *The History of Reparations* (London, 1927). German original, 1926.

"Bericht des 43. Untersuchungsausschusses zur Prüfung der Wirkung der Maßnahmen zur Stützung der Mark", in *Verhandlungen des Reichstags, Bd. 380* (Berlin, 1924), Drucksache Nr. 6591.

Berthold, Rudolf: "Zur Entwicklung der deutschen Agrarproduktion und Ernährungswirtschaft zwischen 1907 und 1925", *Jahrbuch für Wirtschaftsgeschichte* (1974) II, pp. 83–111.

Beusch, Paul: *Währungszerfall und Währungsstabilisierung* (Berlin, 1928).

Biermer, Magnus: *Die finanzielle Mobilmachung* (Gießen, 1913).

Blaich, Fritz: *Die Wirtschaftskrise 1925/26 und die Reichsregierung: von der Erwerbslosenfürsorge zur Konjunkturpolitik* (Kallmünz, 1977).

Bloomfield, Arthur J.: *Short-term Capital Movements Under the Pre-1914 Gold Standard. Princeton*

Studies in International Finance, No. 11 (Princeton, 1963).
Bonn, Moritz Julius: *Die Stabilisierung der Mark* (Berlin, 1922); transl. as *The Stabilization of the Mark. Authorized Translation issued by the First National Bank of Chicago* (Chicago, 1922).
– *Wandering Scholar* (New York, 1948).
Borchardt, Knut: "Die Erfahrung mit Inflationen in Deutschland", in J. Schlemmer (ed.): *Enteignung durch Inflation? Fragen der Geldwertstabilität* (Munich, 1972), pp. 9–22; reprinted in K. Borchardt: *Wachstum, Krisen*, pp. 151–161.
– *Wachstum, Krisen, Handlungsspielräume der Wirtschaftspolitik. Studien zur Wirtschaftsgeschichte des 19. und 20. Jahrhunderts* (Göttingen, 1982).
– "Wachstum und Wechsellagen 1914–1970", in H. Aubin and W. Zorn (eds.): *Handbuch*, Bd. 2, pp. 685–740.
– "Zwangslagen und Handlungsspielräume in der grossen Wirtschaftskrise der frühen dreissiger Jahre: Zur Revision des überlieferten Geschichtsbildes", *Jahrbuch der Bayerischen Akademie der Wissenschaften*, 1979, pp. 1–47: reprinted in Borchardt: *Wachstum, Krisen*, pp. 165–182.
Born, Karl Erich: *Die deutsche Bankenkrise 1931. Finanzen und Politik* (Munich, 1967).
– "Vom Beginn des Ersten Weltkrieges bis zum Ende der Weimarer Republik (1914–1933)", in Institut für bankhistorische Forschung (ed.): *Deutsche Bankengeschichte, Bd. 3: Vom Ersten Weltkrieg bis zur Gegenwart* (Frankfurt/M., 1983), pp. 17–146.
Bowley, A. L. and J. Stamp: *The National Income 1924. A Comparative Study of the Income of the United Kingdom in 1911 and 1924* (Oxford, 1927).
Bräuer, Karl: *Die Neuordnung der deutschen Finanzwirtschaft und das neue Reichssteuersystem* (Stuttgart, 1920).
– *Die Anpassung der Löhne und Gehälter an die Lebenshaltungskosten mit besonderer Rücksicht auf die deutschen und englischen Verhältnisse* (Dresden, 1922).
Bresciani-Turroni, Costantino: *The Economics of Inflation. A Study of Currency Depreciation in Post-War Germany*. (London, 1937; reprinted 1968). Original Italian edn. 1931.
– "The Movements of Wages in Germany during the Depreciation of the Mark and after Stabilization", *Journal of the Royal Statistical Society*, 92 (1929), pp. 374–414.
Briefs, Götz: "Kriegswirtschaftslehre und Kriegswirtschaftspolitik", article in the *Handwörterbuch der Staatswissenschaften, Bd. 5* (1923), pp. 984–1022.
Briefs, Götz *et al.*: *Die Hauswirtschaft im Kriege* (Berlin, 1917).
Bronfenbrenner, Martin: *Income Distribution Theory* (New York, 1971).
Brown, William A: *The International Gold Standard Reinterpreted, 1914–1934* (New York, 2 vols. 1940).
Bry, Gerhard: *Wages in Germany 1871–1945* (Princeton, 1960).
Büsch, Otto and Gerald Feldman (eds.): *Historische Prozesse der deutschen Inflation 1914 bis 1924. Ein Tagungsbericht* (Berlin, 1978).
Büscher, Gustav: *Die Inflation und ihre Lehren* (Zürich, 1926).
Bumm, Franz (ed.): *Deutschlands Gesundheitsverhältnisse unter dem Einfluss des Weltkrieges* (Stuttgart, 1928).
Burchardt, Lothar: *Friedenswirtschaft und Kriegsvorsorge. Deutschlands wirtschaftliche Rüstungsbestrebungen vor 1914* (Boppard am Rhein, 1968).
Burnett, Philip M.: *Reparation at the Peace Conference. From the Standpoint of the American Delegation* (New York, 2 vols. 1940).
Cagan, Phillip: "The Monetary Dynamics of Hyperinflation", in M. Friedman (ed.): *Studies in the Quantity Theory of Money* (Chicago, 1956), pp. 25–117.
Calwer, Richard: *Monatliche Übersichten über Lebensmittelpreise* (Berlin), 1914 and subsequent years.

Cassel, [Karl] Gustav: *Deutschlands wirtschaftliche Widerstandskraft* (Berlin, 1916). English edn.: *Germany's Economic Power of Resistance* (Stockholm/New York, 1916).

– *Money and Foreign Exchange after 1914* (London, 1922).

– *The Theory of Social Economy* (London, 2 vols. 1923). First German edn. 1918.

Caves, Richard E. and Ronald W. Jones: *World Trade and Payments. An Introduction* (Boston, 1973).

Clausing, Gustav: *Die wirtschaftlichen Wechsellagen von 1919 bis 1932* (Jena, 1933).

Cohnstaedt, L.: *Ergebnisse der Bankenquete* (Frankfurt/M., 1908).

Colm, Gerhard: "War Finance", article in the *Encyclopaedia of the Social Sciences ed. E.R.A. Seligman* (New York, 15 vols. 1930–35), vol. 15, pp. 347–352.

Committee on Currency and Foreign Exchange after the War (i.e. Cunliffe Committee), *First Interim Report* (London, 1919).

Czada, Peter: *Die Berliner Elektroindustrie in der Weimarer Zeit. Eine regionalstatistisch-wirtschaftshistorische Untersuchung* (Berlin, 1969).

– "Grosse Inflation und Wirtschaftswachstum", in H. Mommsen *et al.* (eds.): *Industrielles System*, pp. 386–395.

– "Ursachen und Folgen der grossen Inflation", in Harald Winkel (ed.): *Finanz- und wirtschaftspolitische Fragen der Zwischenkriegszeit. Schriften des Vereins für Socialpolitik, N.F. Bd. 73* (Berlin, 1973), pp. 11–43.

D'Abernon, Viscount: *An Ambassador of Peace: Pages from the Diary of Viscount D'Abernon, Berlin 1920–26* (London, 3 vols. 1929–30). U.S. edn. *The Diary of an Ambassador* (New York, 3 vols. 1929–30).

– "German Currency. Its Collapse and Recovery 1920–1926", *Journal of the Royal Statistical Society*, 90 (1927), pp. 1–40.

Dalberg, Rudolf: *Deutsche Währungs- und Kreditpolitik 1923–1926* (Berlin, 1926).

– *Die neue deutsche Währung nach dem Dawes-Plan* (Berlin, 1924).

De Boor, Hans Otto: *Die deutsche Rentenbank und das Privatrecht. Eine Studie über die Grenzen zwischen bürgerlichem und öffentlichem Recht* (Berlin, 1924).

Deane, Phyllis and W. A. Cole: *British Economic Growth 1688–1959. Trends and Structure* (Cambridge, UK, 1964).

"Denkschrift über die seit dem 9. November 1918 auf dem Gebiete der Sozialpolitik getroffenen Massnahmen", in *Verhandlungen der Verfassungsgebenden Deutschen Nationalversammlung, Bd. 335* (Berlin, 1920), Drucksache Nr. 215.

"Denkschrift über die Finanzen des Deutschen Reichs in den Rechnungsjahren 1914 bis 1918", in *Verhandlungen der Verfassungsgebenden Deutschen Nationalversammlung, Bd. 335* (Berlin, 1920), Drucksache Nr. 158.

"Denkschrift über den künftigen finanziellen Bedarf des Reichs und seine Deckung", in *Verhandlungen der Verfassungsgebenden Deutschen Nationalversammlung, Bd. 338* (Berlin, 1920), Drucksache Nr. 760.

"Denkschrift über die finanzielle Lage des Reichs", in *Verhandlungen des Reichstags, Bd. 363* (Berlin, 1924), Drucksache Nr. 254.

"Denkschrift über die Ablösung der Markanleihen des Reichs", in *Verhandlungen des Reichstags, Bd. 423* (Berlin, 1928), Drucksache Nr. 474.

Denkschrift über die Zahlungsfähigkeit Deutschlands für die Wiedergutmachung (Berlin, 1920).

Department of Commerce, Bureau of Foreign and Domestic Commerce, *Trade of the United States with the World 1918–1919* (Washington, D.C., 1920).

Deutsche Bundesbank: *Währung und Wirtschaft in Deutschland 1876–1975* (Frankfurt/M., 1976).

Deutscher Metallarbeiterverband, Vorstand: *320 Haushaltsrechnungen von Metallarbeitern* (Stuttgart, 1909).

Die deutsche Steuernotverordnung vom 14. Februar 1924. Textausgabe (Berlin, 1924).
Deutschlands wirtschaftliche Lage. Die Entwicklung nach dem Kriege. Eine Materialsammlung (Berlin, 3rd edn. 1926). Vierte Ergänzung, 1928.
Deutschlands wirtschaftliche Leistungsfähigkeit (Berlin, 1920).
Diehl, Karl: "David Ricardo und der finanzielle Wiederaufbau Englands nach den napoleonischen Kriegen", *Bank-Archiv*, 19 (1919/20), pp. 106–109, 122–127.
Dietzel, Carl: *Das System der Staatsanleihen im Zusammenhang der Volkswirtschaft betrachtet* (Heidelberg, 1855).
Dietzel, Heinrich: "Abbürdung der Kriegsschuld", in H. Herkner (ed.): *Die Neuordnung der deutschen Finanzwirtschaft. Schriften des Vereins für Socialpolitik, Bd. 156 I* (Berlin, 1918).
– *Kriegssteuer oder Kriegsanleihe?* (Tübingen, 1912).
Dornbusch, Rudiger and S. Fischer: *Macroeconomics* (New York, 1978).
Duwendag, Dieter *et al.*: *Geldtheorie und Geldpolitik. Eine problemorientierte Einführung* (Cologne, 1974).
Eheberg, Karl Theodor: "Finanzen im Weltkrieg", article in the *Handwörterbuch der Staatswissenschaften*, Bd. 4 (1927), pp. 75–86.
Ehlert, Hans Gotthard: *Die wirtschaftliche Zentralbehörde des Deutschen Reiches 1914 bis 1919. Das Problem der "Gemeinwirtschaft" in Krieg und Frieden* (Wiesbaden, 1982).
Eichhorn, Robert: *Die einmaligen Vermögensabgaben im Deutschen Reiche* (Jena, 1925).
Einzig, Paul: *The Theory of Forward Exchange* (London, 1937).
Ellis, Howard S: *German Monetary Theory 1905–1933* (Cambridge, Mass., 1937).
Elsas, Moritz: *Der Stand der Kosten der Lebenshaltung. Indexziffern zur Förderung gleitender Entlohnung* (Frankfurt/M., 1920).
Elster, Karl: "Kriegsanleihen und Finanznot", *Bank-Archiv*, 18 (1918/19), pp. 212–216.
– *Von der Mark zur Reichsmark. Die Geschichte der deutschen Währung in den Jahren 1914 bis 1924* (Jena, 1928).
– (ed.): *Wörterbuch der Volkswirtschaft* (Jena, 4. Auflage [i.e. 4th edn.] 3 Bde. 1932–3).
Epstein, Klaus: *Matthias Erzberger and the Dilemma of German Democracy* (Princeton, 1959).
Erdmann, Karl D. and Wolfgang Mommsen (eds.): *Akten der Reichskanzlei. Weimarer Republik* (Boppard am Rhein, 9 Bde. 1968–78).
Erhebungen von Wirtschaftsrechnungen minderbemittelter Familien im Deutschen Reich. 2. Sonderheft zum Reichsarbeitsblatt (Berlin, 1909).
Eucken, Walter: *Kritische Betrachtungen zum deutschen Geldproblem* (Jena, 1923).
Eulenburg, Franz: "Die sozialen Wirkungen der Währungsverhältnisse," *Jahrbücher für Nationalökonomie und Statistik*, 122 (1924), pp. 748–794.
Eyck, Erich: *A History of the Weimar Republic* (Cambridge, 2 vols. 1962–4). Swiss original 1954–62.
Eynern, Gert von: *Die Reichsbank. Probleme des deutschen Zentralnoteninstituts in geschichtlicher Darstellung* (Jena, 1928).
Feavearyear, Albert: *The Pound Sterling. A History of English Money* (Oxford, 1931; 2nd edn. 1963).
Feierabend, Hans: *Die volkswirtschaftlichen Bedingungen und die Entwicklung des Fleischverbrauchs in Deutschland seit Beginn des Weltkrieges* (Berlin, 1928).
Feldman, Gerald D.: *Army, Industry, and Labor in Germany 1914–1918* (Princeton, 1966).
– "Gegenwärtiger Forschungsstand und künftige Forschungsprobleme zur deutschen Inflation", in O. Büsch and G. Feldman (eds.): *Historische Prozesse*, pp. 3–21.
– "German Business between War and Revolution: The Origins of the Stinnes-Legien Agreement", in Gerhard A. Ritter (ed.): *Entstehung und Wandel*, pp. 312–341.
– *Iron and Steel in the German Inflation 1916–1923* (Princeton, 1977).

– "The Political Economy of Germany's Relative Stabilization During the 1920/21 World Depression", in G. D. Feldman *et al.* (eds.): *The German Inflation Reconsidered. A Preliminary Balance* (Berlin/New York, 1982), pp. 180–206.

– "Wirtschafts- und sozialpolitische Probleme der deutschen Demobilmachung 1918/19", in H. Mommsen *et al.* (eds.): *Industrielles System*, pp. 618–636.

Feldman, Gerald D., Carl-Ludwig Holtfrerich, Gerhard A. Ritter and Peter-Christian Witt (eds.): *The German Inflation Reconsidered. A Preliminary Balance* (Berlin/New York, 1982).

– *The Experience of Inflation. International and Comparative Studies* (Berlin/New York, 1984).

Feldman, Gerald D. and Heidrun Homburg: *Industrie und Inflation. Studien und Dokumente zur Politik der deutschen Unternehmer 1916–1923* (Hamburg, 1977).

Ferguson, Adam: *When Money Dies. The Nightmare of the Weimar Collapse* (London, 1975).

Ferguson, C. E.: *The Neo-classical Theory of Production and Distribution* (Cambridge, U.K. 1969).

Fetter, Frank W.: *The Development of British Monetary Orthodoxy 1797–1875* (Cambridge, Mass., 1965).

Feuchtwanger, Leo: *Die Darlehenskassen des deutschen Reiches* (Stuttgart, 1918).

Finck von Finckenstein, Hans Wolfram: *Die Entwicklung der Landwirtschaft in Preussen und Deutschland 1800–1930* (Würzburg, 1960).

Fischer, Wolfram: "Bergbau, Industrie und Handwerk 1914–1970", in H. Aubin and W. Zorn (eds.): *Handbuch*, Bd. 2, pp. 796–844.

– *Deutsche Wirtschaftspolitik 1918–1945* (Opladen, 3rd edn. 1968).

Fischer, Wolfram and Peter Czada: "Wandlungen in der deutschen Industriestruktur im 20. Jahrhundert. Ein statistisch-deskriptiver Ansatz", in Gerhard A. Ritter (eds.): *Entstehung und Wandel*, pp. 116–165.

Fisher, Irving: *The Making of Index Numbers. A Study of their Varieties, Tests and Reliability* (Boston, 1922).

Flaskämper, Paul: "Indexzahlen", article in the *Handwörterbuch der Sozialwissenschaften*, Bd. 5 (1956), pp. 191–195.

Flemming, Jens: *Landwirtschaftliche Interessen und Demokratie. Ländliche Gesellschaft, Agrarverbände und Staat 1890–1925* (Bonn, 1978).

Flemming, Jens *et al.*: "Sozialverhalten und politische Reaktionen von Gruppen und Institutionen im Inflationsprozess. Anmerkungen zum Forschungsstand", in O. Büsch and G. Feldman (eds.): *Historische Prozesse*, pp. 239–263.

Flemming, John S.: *Inflation*, (Oxford, 1976).

Flink, Salomon: *The Reichsbank and Economic Germany. A Study of the Policies of the Reichsbank in their Relation to the Economic Development of Germany with Special Reference to the Period after 1923* (New York, 1929).

Flora, Peter: *Indikatoren der Modernisierung. Ein historisches Datenhandbuch* (Opladen, 1975).

Forstmann, Albrecht: *Die Grundlagen der Aussenwirtschaftstheorie* (Berlin, 1956).

Fourgeaud, André: "La Dépréciation et la Revalorisation du Mark Allemand et les Enseignements de l'Expérience Monétaire Allemande" (Thèse, Paris, 1926).

Frenkel, Jacob A.: "The Forward Exchange Rate, Expectations, and the Demand for Money: The German Hyperinflation", *American Economic Review*, 67 (1977), pp. 653–670.

– "Further Evidence on Expectations and the Demand for Money during the German Hyperinflation", *Journal of Monetary Economics*, 5 (1979), pp. 81–96.

Frenkel, Johannes: "Zur Preisentwicklung der Nachkriegszeit", *Zeitschrift des Preussischen Statistischen Landesamts*, 61 (1921), pp. 196–199.

Frey, Bruno S.: "Theorie und Empirie 'Politischer Konjunkturzyklen'", *Zeitschrift für Nationalökonomie*, 36 (1976), pp. 95–120.

Frey, Hans-Dieter: *Auswirkungen von Preissteigerungen auf die Verteilung des Einkommens und des Vermögens* (Tübingen, 1975).

Friedman, Milton: "The Quantity Theory of Money – A Restatement", in M. Friedman (ed.): *Studies in the Quantity Theory of Money* (Chicago, 1956), pp. 3–21.

Friedman, Milton and Anna J. Schwartz: *A Monetary History of the United States 1867–1960* (Princeton, 1963).

Friedrich, Karl: "Kreditnot und ihre Bekämpfung", *Bank-Archiv*, 21 (1921/22), pp. 319–323.

– "Vom alten zum neuen Bankgesetz", *Bank-Archiv*, 23 (1923/24), pp. 341–344.

Frommer, H. and H. Schlag: *Die Gesetzgebung über die Rentenmark mit ausführlichen Erläuterungen* (Mannheim, 1924).

Fuchs, Carl J.: *Deutsche Agrarpolitik vor und nach dem Kriege* (Stuttgart, 1927).

Fürth, Henriette: *Der Haushalt vor und nach dem Krieg. Dargestellt an Hand eines mittelbürgerlichen Budgets* (Jena, 1922).

Fux, Boleslav: "Die Vermögenssteuer", in *Handbuch der Finanzwissenschaft*, 1st edn., Bd. 2 (1927), pp. 133–158.

Garber, Peter M.: "Transition from Inflation to Price Stability", *Carnegie-Rochester Conference on Public Policy*, 16 (1982), pp. 11–42.

Gehrig, Gerhard: "Eine Zeitreihe für den Sachkapitalbestand 1925 bis 1938 und 1950 bis 1957" *IFO-Studien*, 7 (1961), pp. 7–60.

Geiger, Theodor: *Die soziale Schichtung des deutschen Volkes. Soziographischer Versuch auf statistischer Grundlage* (Darmstadt, 1967). Original edn. 1932.

Gemtos, Petros A: *Die Neubegründung der Quantitätstheorie durch Milton Friedman* (Tübingen, 1975).

Gerloff, Wilhelm: "Der Staatshaushalt und das Finanzsystem Deutschlands", in *Handbuch der Finanzwissenschaft*, 1st edn., Bd. 3 (1929).

Gerloff, Wilhelm and Franz Meisel (eds.): *Handbuch der Finanzwissenschaft*, 1. Auflage [i.e. 1st edn.], (Tübingen, 3 Bde. 1925–8).

Gerloff, Wilhelm and Fritz Neumark (eds.): *Handbuch der Finanzwissenschaft*, 2. Auflage [i.e. 2nd edn.], (Tübingen, 3 Bde. 1952–8).

Giersch, Herbert: "Inflation", article in the *Handwörterbuch der Sozialwissenschaften*, Bd. 5 (1956), pp. 281–293.

Glasenapp, Otto von: "Germany's Balance of Payments with Other Countries", in *Manchester Guardian Commercial Supplement: Reconstruction in Europe* (April 20, 1922), pp. 28–29.

Goebel, Otto: *Die deutsche Rohstoffwirtschaft im Weltkrieg* (Stuttgart, 1930).

Goerzig, Bernd: *Die Verteilungswirkungen der Inflation auf den privaten und öffentlichen Sektor. Ermittlung von Inflationswirkungen nach alternativen Berechnungsansätzen* (Göttingen, 1975).

Gordon, Robert A.: "Cyclical Experience in the Inter-War Period. The Investment Boom of the Twenties", in National Bureau of Economic Research: *Conference on Business Cycles* (New York, 1951).

Gossweiler, Kurt: *Grossbanken, Industriemonopole, Staat. Ökonomie und Politik des staatsmonopolistischen Kapitalismus in Deutschland 1914–1932* (Berlin-East, 1971).

Gradnauer, Georg and Robert Schmidt: *Die deutsche Volkswirtschaft. Eine Einführung* (Berlin, 1921).

Graham, Frank D.: *Exchange, Prices, and Production in Hyper-Inflation: Germany, 1920–1923.* (Princeton, 1930), reprinted 1967.

Grubel, Herbert G: *Forward Exchange, Speculation, and International Flow of Capital* (Stanford, 1966).

Grumbach, Franz: "Statistische Untersuchungen über die Entwicklung der Einkommensverteilung in Deutschland" (Diss., Münster, 1957).

Guderjahn, Walter: "Ursachen und Wirkungen der Inflation in Deutschland unter besonderer Berücksichtigung des Zinsfusses" (Diss., Frankfurt, 1926).

Gündell, Gisela: *Die Organisation der deutschen Ernährungswirtschaft im Weltkriege* (Leipzig, 1939).

Günther, Adolf: "Die Folgen des Krieges für Einkommen und Lebenshaltung der mittleren Volksschichten Deutschlands", in R. Meerwarth *et al.*: *Die Einwirkung des Krieges*, pp. 99–279.

– *Die gesunkene Kaufkraft des Lohnes und ihre Wiederherstellung, Teil II: Kriegslöhne und -preise und ihr Einfluss auf Kaufkraft und Lebenskosten. Schriften der Gesellschaft für soziale Reform, Bd. 66* (Jena, 1919).

"Das Gutachten der deutschen Finanzkommission zu den gegnerischen Friedensbedingungen", *Bank-Archiv*, 18 (1918/19), pp. 185–192.

Das Gutachten der internationalen Sachverständigen über die Stabilisierung (Berlin, 1922).

Guttmann, William and Patricia Meehan: *The Great Inflation. Germany 1919–1923* (London, 1975).

Habedank, Heinz: *Die Reichsbank in der Weimarer Republik. Zur Rolle der Zentralbank in der Politik des deutschen Imperialismus 1919–1933* (Berlin-East, 1981).

Haberland, Günther: *Elf Jahre staatlicher Regelung der Ein- und Ausfuhr. Eine systematische Darstellung der deutschen Aussenhandelsregelung in den Jahren 1914–1925* (Leipzig, 1927).

Haberler, Gottfried: *Prosperity and Depression. A Theoretical Analysis of Cyclical Movements* (London, 5th edn. 1964).

– *Der Sinn der Indexzahlen* (Tübingen, 1927).

– *The Theory of International Trade with its Applications to Commercial Policy* (London, 1936). German original, 1933.

Haensel, Paul: "Der Staatshaushalt und das Finanzsystem Grossbritanniens", in *Handbuch der Finanzwissenschaft*, 1st edn. Bd. 3 (1929), pp. 70–102.

Haefner-Hainen, Waldemar: *Der Staatsbankrott in Deutschland unvermeidlich. Ein ernster Mahnruf an die Nationalversammlung in Weimar* (Leipzig, 1919).

Hahn, L. Albert: "Die Frage des sog. Vertrauens in die Währung", *Archiv für Sozialwissenschaft und Sozialpolitik*, 52 (1924), Heft 2.

– *Fünfzig Jahre zwischen Inflation und Deflation* (Tübingen, 1963).

– *Geld und Kredit* (Tübingen, 1924).

– "Handelsbilanz, Zahlungsbilanz, Valuta, Güterpreise", *Archiv für Sozialwissenschaft und Sozialpolitik*, 48 (1920/21), pp. 596–614.

Haller, Heinz: *Finanzpolitik, Grundlagen und Hauptprobleme* (Tübingen, 5th edn. 1972).

– "Die Rolle der Staatsfinanzen für den Inflationsprozess", in Deutsche Bundesbank: *Währung und Wirtschaft*, pp. 115–155.

Handbuch der Finanzwissenschaft: see Gerloff, W. and F. Meisel, and Gerloff, W. and F. Neumark.

Handwörterbuch der Sozialwissenschaften, ed. E. von Beckerath et al. (Stuttgart/Tübingen/Göttingen, 12 Bde. 1956–65).

Handwörterbuch der Staatswissenschaften, ed. L. Elster et al. (Jena 8 Bde. + Ergänzungsbände, 1921–9).

Handwörterbuch der Wirtschaftswissenschaften, ed. W. Albers et al. (Göttingen 9 Bde. + Registerband 1977–83).

Hansmeyer, Karl-Heinrich and Rolf Caesar: "Kriegswirtschaft und Inflation (1936–48)", in Deutsche Bundesbank: *Währung und Wirtschaft*, pp. 367–429.

Hardach, Gerd: *The First World War* (London, 1977). German original, 1973.

– *Weltmarktorientierung und relative Stagnation. Währungspolitik in Deutschland 1924–1931* (Berlin, 1976).

Hardach, Karl: "Zur zeitgenössischen Debatte der Nationalökonomen über die Ursachen der deutschen Nachkriegsinflation", in Hans Mommsen *et al.* (eds.): *Industrielles System*, pp. 368–375.

Harms, Bernhard (ed.): *Strukturwandlungen der deutschen Volkswirtschaft* (Berlin, 1928; 2nd edn. 1929).

Harrod, Roy F.: *The Life of John Maynard Keynes* (London, 1951).

Hartwich, Hans-Hermann: *Arbeitsmarkt, Verbände und Staat 1918–1933. Die öffentliche Bindung unternehmerischer Funktionen in der Weimarer Republik* (Berlin, 1967).

Haupts, Leo: *Deutsche Friedenspolitik 1918–1919. Eine Alternative zur Machtpolitik des Ersten Weltkrieges?* (Düsseldorf, 1977).

Hauschild, Harry: *Der vorläufige Reichswirtschaftsrat 1920–1926. Denkschrift* (Berlin, 1926).

Hauser, Richard: "Unsere Währung nach dem Kriege", *Bank-Archiv*, 17 (1917/18), pp. 2–6.
– "Zur Währungsfrage", *Bank-Archiv*, 18 (1918/19), pp. 197–199.

Haushofer, Heinz: *Die deutsche Landwirtschaft im technischen Zeitalter* (Stuttgart, 1963).

Hawtrey, Ralph G.: *The Art of Central Banking* (London, 1932).

Heiber, Helmut: *Die Republik von Weimar* (Munich, 4th edn. 1969).

Heilperin, Michael A.: "Postwar European Inflations, World War I. A Study of Selected Cases" (New York: National Bureau of Economic Research, unpublished manuscript, 1945).

Heimann, Hugo: *Der Kampf um die Aufwertung, von Helfferich bis Hindenburg. Wie ihn die Deutschnationalen und wie ihn die Sozialdemokraten führten* (Berlin, 1925).

Helfferich, Karl: "Die Autonomie der Reichsbank", *Bank-Archiv*, 21 (1921/22), pp. 215–217.
– "Aussenhandel und Valutaschwankungen", *Schmollers Jahrbuch*, 21 (1897), pp. 353–409.
– *Deutschlands Volkswohlstand 1888–1913* (Berlin, 6th edn. 1915).
– *Das Geld* (Leipzig, 6th edn. 1923).
– "Volksvermögen, Volkseinkommen und Steuerlast einst und jetzt", in *Weltpolitik und Weltwirtschaft, Bd. 1* (1925), Heft 1, S. 11 ff.
– *Der Weltkrieg* (Berlin, 3 Bde. 1919).

Helmstätter, Ernst: *Wirtschaftstheorie, Bd. 2: Kreislaufgleichgewicht* (Munich, 1976).

Henke, Carl: "Das deutsche Geldwesen im Kriege", *Vierteljahreshefte für Truppenführung und Heereskunde*, 10 (1913), pp. 260–279.

Henning, Friedrich-Wilhelm: *Das industrialisierte Deutschland 1914–1972* (Paderborn, 1974).

Herkner, Heinrich (ed.): *Die Neuordnung der deutschen Finanzwirtschaft. Schriften des Vereins für Socialpolitik, Bd. 156 I–III* (Munich, 1918).

Hertz-Eichenrode, Dieter: *Wirtschaftskrise und Arbeitsbeschaffung. Konjunkturpolitik 1925/26 und die Grundlagen der Krisenpolitik Brünings* (Frankfurt/M., 1982).

Hesse, Friedrich: *Die deutsche Wirtschaftslage von 1914 bis 1923. Krieg, Geldblähe und Wechsellagen* (Jena, 1938).

Heuer, Hildegard: "Die Entwicklung der Metallarbeiterreallöhne auf den Kieler Werften in der Zeit vom 1.4.1920 bis 30.10.1923" (Diss., Kiel, 1929).

Heyn, Otto: "Die Geldentwertung, ihre Ursache und die Mittel zu ihrer Beseitigung", *Bank-Archiv*, 18 (1918/19), pp. 71–72.

Hicks, Ursula K.: *The Finance of British Government 1920–36* (Oxford, 1938).
– "Die öffentliche Finanzwirtschaft Grossbritanniens 1799–1949", in *Handbuch der Finanzwissenschaft*, 2nd edn. Bd. 1 (1952), pp. 327–339.

Hirsch, Fred und John Goldthorpe (eds.): *The Political Economy of Inflation* (London, 1978).

Hirsch, Julius: *Die deutsche Währungsfrage* (Jena, 1924).
– "Wandlungen im Aufbau der deutschen Industrie", in B. Harms (ed.): *Strukturwandlungen*, Bd. 1, pp. 191–226.

Höchstpreise. Alphabetisches Verzeichnis der Gegenstände, für welche Preisbindungen irgendwelcher Art, insbesondere Höchstpreise, seit Kriegsbeginn vorgeschrieben und im Reichs-Gesetzblatt oder im Zentralblatt für das Deutsche Reich veröffentlicht worden sind, hrsg. v.d. Volkswirtschaftlichen Abteilung des Kriegsernährungsamts (Berlin, 1917).

Hoelzer, Heinrich and Josef van Almsick: "Der Einfluss der Inflation auf die Verteilung von Einkommen und Vermögen", *Wirtschaftswissenschaftliches Studium*, 5 (1976), pp. 351–356.

Hoffmann, Friedrich: *Kritische Dogmengeschichte der Geldwerttheorien* (Leipzig, 1907).

Hoffmann, Walther G., F. Grumbach and H. Hesse: *Das Wachstum der deutschen Wirtschaft seit der Mitte des 19. Jahrhunderts* (Berlin, 1965).

Hoffmann, Walther G. and J.H. Müller: *Das deutsche Volkseinkommen 1851–1957* (Tübingen, 1959).

Holtfrerich, Carl-Ludwig: "Alternativen zu Brünings Wirtschaftspolitik in der Weltwirtschaftskrise?" *Historische Zeitschrift*, 235 (1982), pp. 605–631.

– "Amerikanischer Kapitalexport und Wiederaufbau der deutschen Wirtschaft 1919–1923 im Vergleich zu 1924–1929", *Vierteljahrschrift für Sozial- und Wirtschaftsgeschichte*, 64 (1977), pp. 497–529.

– "Die konjunkturanregenden Wirkungen der deutschen Inflation auf die US-Wirtschaft in der Weltwirtschaftskrise 1920/21", in G.D. Feldman *et al.* (eds.): *The German Inflation Reconsidered. A Preliminary Balance* (Berlin/New York, 1982), pp. 207–234.

– "Zu hohe Löhne in der Weimarer Republik? Bemerkungen zur Borchardt-These", *Geschichte und Gesellschaft*, 10 (1984), pp. 122–141.

Hoppe, Ernst: *Der Krieg und die deutsche Geldwirtschaft* (Essen, 1919).

House, Edward M. and Charles Seymour (eds.): *What Really Happened at Paris. The Story of the Peace Conference by the American Delegates, 1918–1919* (New York, 1921).

Huas, René: *La Valorisation des Obligations Industrielles en Allemagne. Ses Rapports avec la Réforme Monétaire* (Paris, 1928).

Internationaler Gewerkschaftsbund [i.e. International Federation of Trade Unions], Amsterdam: *Die Lage der Arbeiterschaft in Deutschland* (Berlin, 1923).

Issing, Otmar: *Einführung in die Geldtheorie* (Munich, 3rd edn. 1977).

Jacobs, Rodney L: "A Difficulty With Monetarist Models of Hyperinflation", *Economic Inquiry*, 13 (1975), pp. 337–360.

Jacobsen, Eugen: "Die Wiedereinführung des Terminhandels und das Börsengesetz", *Bank-Archiv*, 20 (1920/21), pp. 129–130.

Jastrow, Ignatz: *Die Prinzipienfragen in den Aufwertungsdebatten* (Brünn, 1937).

Jecht, Horst: *Kriegsfinanzen* (Jena, 1938).

Jeck, Albert: *Wachstum und Verteilung des Volkseinkommens. Untersuchungen und Materialien zur Einkommensverteilung in Deutschland 1870–1913* (Tübingen, 1970).

Jessen, Arnd: *Finanzen, Defizit und Notenpresse 1914–1922* (Berlin, 1923).

Jessen, Jens: "Kriegsfinanzen", article in L. Elster (ed.): *Wörterbuch*, Bd. 3, pp. 674–682.

– "Reparationen", article in L. Elster (ed.): *Wörterbuch*, Bd. 2 pp. 35–95.

Jèze, Gaston: *Les finances de guerre de l'Angleterre 1915–1918* (Paris, 1919).

Johnson, Harry G.: *Macroeconomics and Monetary Theory* (London, 1971).

Jordan, William M.: *Great Britain, France and the German Problem, 1918–1939* (London, 1943).

Jones, Larry E.: "Inflation, Revaluation, and the Crisis of Middleclass Politics: A Study in the Dissolution of the German Party System 1923–1928", *Central European History*, 12 (1979), pp. 143–168.

Kalt, Robert: "Rationierung der Nahrungsmittel und schwarzer Markt in der Kriegswirtschaft" (Diss., Freiburg, 1949).

Kessler, Gerhard: "Die Lage der deutschen Arbeiterschaft seit 1914", in B. Harms (ed.): *Strukturwandlungen*, Bd. 1, pp. 455–489.

Keynes, John Maynard: *The Collected Writings of J. M. Keynes, ed. E. Johnson and D. E. Moggridge* (London, 1971–).

– *The Economic Consequences of the Peace* (London, 1919); reprinted as *Collected Writings*, vol. II.

– "The Forward Market in Foreign Exchange", in *Manchester Guardian Commercial Supplement: Reconstruction in Europe* (April 20, 1922), substantially reprinted in *Collected Writings*, vol. IV, pp. 94–95.

– "The German Transfer Problem", *Economic Journal*, 39 (1929), pp. 1 ff.; reprinted in *Collected Writings*, vol. IX, pp. 451–9.

– *Indian Currency and Finance* (London, 1913); reprinted as *Collected Writings*, vol. I.

– "Inflation as a Method of Taxation", in *Manchester Guardian Commercial Supplement: Reconstruction in Europe* (July 27, 1922), pp. 268–9; substantially reprinted in *Collected Writings*, vol. IV, pp. 37–38.

– *The Revision of the Treaty* (London, 1923); reprinted as *Collected Writings* , vol. III.

– "Speculation in the Mark and Germany's Balances Abroad", in *Manchester Guardian Commercial Supplement: Reconstruction in Europe* (September 28, 1922), pp. 480–482.

– *A Tract on Monetary Reform* (London, 1923); reprinted as *Collected Writings*, vol. IV.

Kindleberger, Charles P.: *Manias, Panics, and Crashes. A History of Financial Crises* (New York, 1978).

– "Speculation and Forward Exchange", in C. P. Kindleberger: *Europe and the Dollar* (Cambridge, Mass., 1966), pp. 271–289.

– "A Structural View of the German Inflation", in G. D. Feldman *et al.* (eds.): *The Experience of Inflation. International and Comparative Studies* (Berlin/New York, 1984), pp. 10–33.

– *The World in Depression* (London, 1973).

Kindleberger, Charles P. and P. H. Lindert: *International Economics* (Homewood, 6th edn. 1978).

Kirkaldy, A. W. (ed.): *British Finance 1914–21* (London, 1921).

Klebba, Walter: *Börse und Effektenhandel im Kriege* (Berlin, 1920).

Kleine-Natrop, Heinrich: *Devisenpolitik in Deutschland vor dem Kriege und in der Kriegs- und Nachkriegszeit* (Berlin, 1922).

Knauss, Robert: *Die deutsche, englische und französische Kriegsfinanzierung* (Berlin, 1923).

Knecht, Hermann: "Die Entwicklung der Löhne und Gehälter der Münchener Arbeiter- und Beamtenschaft in der Kriegs- und Nachkriegszeit bis Ende 1923 mit besonderer Berücksichtigung der Frage des Reallohnes in der Zeit der Geldentwertung (Inflation)" (Diss., Erlangen, 1925).

Koblitz, Horst Georg: *Einkommensverteilung und Inflation in kurzfristiger Analyse* (Berlin, 1971).

Kocka, Jürgen: *Klassengesellschaft im Krieg 1914–1918* (Göttingen, 1973).

Köhler, Claus: *Geldwirtschaft, Bd. 1: Geldversorgung und Kreditpolitik* (Berlin, 2nd edn. 1977).

Koppe, Fritz: *In welchen Fällen und wie hoch wird aufgewertet? Ein gemeinverständlicher Führer durch das neue Aufwertungsrecht* (Berlin, 1925).

Krohn, Claus-Dieter: *Die grosse Inflation in Deutschland, 1918–1923* (Cologne, 1977).

– "Helfferich contra Hilferding. Konservative Geldpolitik und die sozialen Folgen der deutschen Inflation 1918–1923", *Vierteljahrschrift für Sozial- und Wirtschaftsgeschichte*, 62 (1975), pp. 62–92.

– *Stabilisierung und ökonomische Interessen. Die Finanzpolitik des Deutschen Reiches 1923–1927* (Düsseldorf, 1974).

Krüger, Peter: *Deutschland und die Reparationen 1918/19. Die Genesis des Reparationsproblems in Deutschland zwischen Waffenstillstand und Versailler Friedenschluss* (Stuttgart, 1973).

Kuczynski, Jürgen: *Die Geschichte der Lage der Arbeiter unter dem Kapitalismus. Bd. 4: Darstellung der Lage der Arbeiter in Deutschland von 1900 bis 1917/18* (Berlin-East, 1967).

– *Geschichte der Lage... Bd. 5: Darstellung der Lage der Arbeiter in Deutschland von 1917/18 bis 1932/33* (Berlin-East, 1966).

Kuczynski, Robert R. (ed.): *Finanzpolitische Korrespondenz* (Berlin, 1920 and subsequent years).

Kühne, Rudolf: *Die Devisenzwangswirtschaft im Deutschen Reich während der Jahre 1916 bis 1926. Eine währungspolitische Reminiszenz* (Frankfurt, 1970).

Kuhn, Thomas S.: *The Structure of Scientific Revolutions* (Chicago, 2nd edn. 1970).

Kunz, Andreas: "Verteilungskampf oder Interessenkonsensus? Einkommensverteilung und Sozialverhalten von Arbeitnehmergruppen in der Inflationszeit 1914 bis 1924", in G. D. Feldman *et al.*: *The German Inflation Reconsidered. A Preliminary Balance* (Berlin/New York, 1982), pp. 347–384.

Lansburgh, Alfred: "Banken. Die Notenbanken in der Zeit des wirtschaftlichen Aufbaues", article in *Handwörterbuch der Staatswissenschaften, Ergänzungsband* (1929), pp. 35–62.

– *Die Massnahmen der Reichsbank zur Erhöhung der Liquidität der deutschen Kreditwirtschaft* (Stuttgart, 1914).

– *Die Politik der Reichsbank und die Reichsschatzanweisungen nach dem Kriege. Schriften des Vereins für Socialpolitik, Bd. 166 II* (Munich, 1924), pp. 1–54.

Lanter, Max: *Die Finanzen des Krieges. Quellen, Methoden und Lösungen seit dem Mittelalter bis Ende des Zweiten Weltkrieges 1939–1945* (Lucerne, 1950).

– "Kriegsfinanzen", article in *Handwörterbuch der Sozialwissenschaften*, Bd. 6 (1959), pp. 357–365.

Lary, Hal B.: *The United States in the World Economy* (Washington, D. C., 1943).

Laursen, Karsten und Jørgen Pedersen: *The German Inflation 1918–1923* (Amsterdam, 1964).

League of Nations: *Currencies after the War. A Survey of Conditions in Various Countries* (London, 1920).

– *Economic Fluctuations in the United States and the United Kingdom 1918–1922* (Geneva, 1942).

– *Economic Stability in the Post-War World. The Conditions of Prosperity after the Transition from War to Peace* (Geneva, 1945).

– *Report of the International Financial Conference of Brussels, 1920* (1920).

Le Coutre, Walter: *Die Grundgedanken der deutschen Preispolitik im Weltkriege 1914–1918* (Berlin, 1919).

Lederer, Emil: "Umschichtung der Einkommen und des Bedarfs", in B. Harms (ed.): *Strukturwandlungen*, Bd. 1, pp. 33–56.

Lenz, Rudolf: *Kosten und Finanzierung des deutsch-französischen Krieges 1870/71* (Boppard am Rhein, 1971).

Lewis, W. Arthur: *Economic Survey 1919–1939* (London 1949, reprinted 1969).

Liefmann, Robert: *Die Geldvermehrung im Weltkriege und die Beseitigung ihrer Folgen* (Berlin, 1918).

Lindenlaub, Dieter: "Maschinenbauunternehmen in der Inflation 1919 bis 1923: Unternehmenshistorische Überlegungen zu einigen Inflationstheorien", in G. D. Feldman *et al.* (eds.): *The German Inflation Reconsidered. A Preliminary Balance* (Berlin/New York, 1982). pp. 49–106. More extensively also as a monograph with the same title (Berlin/New York, 1985).

Link, Werner: *Die amerikanische Stabilisierungspolitik in Deutschland 1921–1932* (Düsseldorf, 1970).

Lloyd George, David: *The Truth about War Debts and Reparations* (London, 1932).

Loeb, Ernst: *Wirtschaftliche Vorgänge, Erfahrungen und Lehren im Europäischen Krieg* (Jena, 1915).

Lohnes, Karl: "Die deutschen Währungsreformen 1923 bis 1948" (Diss., Zürich, 1959).

Lotz, Walter: "Darlehnskassen", article in *Handwörterbuch der Staatswissenschaften*, Bd. 3 (1926), pp. 209–215.

– *Die deutsche Staatsfinanzwirtschaft im Kriege* (Stuttgart, 1927).

Lüke, Rolf: *Von der Stabilisierung zur Krise* (Zürich, 1958).
Luther, Hans: *Feste Mark – solide Wirtschaft* (Berlin, 1924).
– *Politiker ohne Partei. Erinnerungen* (Stuttgart, 1960).
– "Die Stabilisierung der deutschen Währung. Aus persönlichen Erinnerungen erzählt", in *Zehn Jahre deutsche Geschichte 1918–1928* (Berlin, 1928), pp. 159–178.
MacFadyean, Andrew: *Reparation Reviewed* (London, 1930).
Machlup, Fritz: *International Payments, Debts and Gold* (New York, 1964; 2nd edn. 1976). The London, 1966 edn. was entitled *International Monetary Economics*.
– *International Trade and the National Income Multiplier* (Philadelphia, 1943).
– "Die Theorie der Kapitalflucht", *Weltwirtschaftliches Archiv*, 36 (1932), pp. 512–529.
– "The Transfer Problem. Theme and Four Variations", in idem: *International Payments*, pp. 374 ff. German original 1963.
Maddison, Angus: *Economic Growth in the West. Comparative Experience in Europe and North America* (New York, 1964).
Maier, Charles S.: *Recasting Bourgeois Europe. Stabilization in France, Germany, and Italy in the Decade After World War I* (Princeton, 1975).
Manes, Alfred: *Staatsbankrotte. Wirtschaftliche und rechtliche Betrachtungen* (Berlin, 1918).
Mantoux, Etienne: *The Carthaginian Peace or the Economic Consequences of Mr. Keynes* (London, 1946).
Marks, Sally: "Reparations Reconsidered: A Reminder", *Central European History*, 2 (1969), pp. 356–365.
– "The Myths of Reparations", *Central European History*, 11 (1978), pp. 231–255.
Marshall, Robert H. and R. B. Swanson: *The Monetary Process. Essentials of Money and Banking* (Boston, 2nd edn. 1980).
May, R. E.: "Die deutsche Volksernährung gemessen am tatsächlichen Konsum grosser Konsumentenkreise", *Schmollers Jahrbuch*, 41 (1917), pp. 153–232.
Mayer, Arno J.: *Politics and the Diplomacy of Peacemaking. Containment and Counterrevolution at Versailles 1918–1919* (New York, 1967).
Meerwarth, Rudolf: "Über die Bedeutung der Teuerungsziffern", *Schmollers Jahrbuch*, 45 (1921), pp. 739–772.
– "Zur neuesten Entwicklung der Löhne", *Zeitschrift des Preussischen Statistischen Landesamts*, 62 (1922), pp. 327–340.
Meerwarth, Rudolf, Adolf Günther and Waldemar Zimmermann: *Die Einwirkung des Krieges auf Bevölkerungsbewegung, Einkommen und Lebenshaltung in Deutschland* (Stuttgart, 1932).
Meier, Ernst: *Handbuch der deutschen Reparationen* (Leipzig, 1927).
Mendershausen, Horst: *Two Postwar Recoveries of the German Economy* (Amsterdam, 1955).
Menges, Franz: *Reichsreform und Finanzpolitik. Die Aushöhlung der Eigenstaatlichkeit Bayerns auf finanzpolitischem Wege in der Zeit der Weimarer Republik* (Berlin, 1971).
Metschies, Kurt: "Der Bestand 'Deutsche Reichsbank', Volkswirtschaftliche und Statistische Abteilung, im Deutschen Zentralarchiv Potsdam, Historische Abteilung I", *Jahrbuch für Wirtschaftsgeschichte* 1968 III, pp. 387–391.
Meyer, Lothar: *Die deutsche Landwirtschaft während der Inflation und zu Beginn der Deflation 1919–1923* (Tübingen, 1924).
Michaelis, Herbert and Ernst Schraepler (eds.): *Ursachen und Folgen. Vom deutschen Zusammenbruch 1918 und 1945 bis zur staatlichen Neuordnung Deutschlands in der Gegenwart, Bd. 5* (Berlin, 1960).
Michaelis, R.: *Das Aufwertungsrecht* (Leipzig, 1926).
Mill, John Stuart. *Principles of Political Economy with Some of their Applications to Social Philosophy* (London, 1848); reprinted as *Collected Works of J. S. Mill*, vol. II (Toronto, 1965).

Mises, Ludwig von: *Die geldtheoretische Seite des Stabilisierungsproblems. Schriften des Vereins für Socialpolitik, Bd. 164 II* (Munich, 1923).
– *Theorie des Geldes und der Umlaufmittel* (Munich, 1912).
Mitchell, Brian R.: *European Historical Statistics 1750–1970* (London, 1975).
Mitchell, Brian R. and Phyllis Deane: *Abstract of British Historical Statistics* (Cambridge, UK, 1962).
Moeller, Robert G.: "Peasants, Politics and Pressure Groups in War and Inflation: A Study of the Rhineland and Westphalia, 1914–1924" (Ph. D. Dissertation, Univ. of California, Berkeley, 1980).
– "Winners as Losers in the German Inflation: Peasant Protest over the Controlled Economy, 1920–1923", in G.D. Feldman *et al.* (eds.): *The German Inflation Reconsidered. A Preliminary Balance* (Berlin, 1982), pp. 256–288.
Moggridge, Donald E.: *British Monetary Policy 1924–1931. The Norman Conquest of* $ 4.86 (Cambridge, UK, 1972).
Moldenhauer, Paul: *Die Regelung der Aufwertungsfrage* (Cologne, 1925).
Mommsen, Hans, Dietmar Petzina and Bernd Weisbrod (eds.): *Industrielles System und politische Entwicklung in der Weimarer Republik* (Düsseldorf, 1974; reprinted 1977).
Mommsen, Wolfgang J.: "Die deutsche Revolution 1918–1920. Politische Revolution und soziale Protestbewegung", *Geschichte und Gesellschaft*, 4 (1978), pp. 362–391.
Morgan, E. Victor: *Studies in British Financial Policy* 1914–1925 (London, 1952).
Morgenroth, Wilhelm: "Indexziffern", article in *Handwörterbuch der Staatswissenschaften*, Bd. 5 (1923), pp. 392–408.
Morgenthau, Hans J.: *Politics among Nations. The Struggle for Power and Peace* (New York, 3rd edn. 1960).
Mottek, Hans, *et al.*: *Wirtschaftsgeschichte Deutschlands. Ein Grundriss. Bd. III* (Berlin-East, 2nd edn. 1975).
Moulton, Harold G.: *The Reparation Plan. An Interpretation of the Expert Committees appointed by the Reparation Commission, November 30, 1923* (New York, 1924).
Moulton, Harold G. and C.E. McGuire: *Germany's Capacity to Pay. A Study of the Reparation Problem* (New York, 1923).
Moulton, Harold G. and L. Pavlovsky: *War Debts and World Prosperity* (Washington, D.C., 1932).
Mückl, Wolfgang J. and Richard Hauser: *Die Wirkungen der Inflation auf die Einkommens- und Vermögensverteilung. Zwei Literaturstudien* (Göttingen, 1975).
Mügel, Oskar: *Die Aufwertung. Überblick über die Entwicklung* (Berlin, 1926).
Müller, Alfred: *Die Kriegsrohstoffbewirtschaftung 1914–1918 im Dienste des deutschen Monopolkapitals* (Berlin-East, 1955).
Müller, J. Heinz and Siegried Geisenberger: *Die Einkommensstruktur in verschiedenen deutschen Ländern 1874–1913* (Berlin, 1972).
Nachtrag vom 1.9.1925 zur Goldwerttabelle für Papiermark 1914–1924 mit den durch das Aufwertungsgesetz und das Gesetz zur Ablösung öffentlicher Anleihen verursachten Änderungen (Stuttgart, 1925).
Néré, Jacques: *La Crise de 1929* (Paris, 1967).
Netzband, Karl-Bernhard and Hans Peter Widmaier: *Währungs- und Finanzpolitik der Ära Luther 1923–1925* (Basel, 1964).
– "Währungsprojekte und Regierungsverhandlungen auf dem Wege zur Rentenbank", in idem: *Währungs- und Finanzpolitk*, pp. 12–34; also in K.E. Born (ed.): *Moderne deutsche Wirtschaftsgeschichte* (Cologne, 1966), pp. 351–369.
Neubürger, Fritz: *Die Kriegsbereitschaft des deutschen Geld- und Kapitalmarktes* (Berlin, 1913).
Neumark, Fritz: *Begriff und Wesen der Inflation* (Jena, 1922).

– "Die Finanzpolitik in der Zeit vor dem Ersten Weltkrieg", in Deutsche Bundesbank: *Währung und Wirtschaft*, pp. 57–111.

Newlyn, W. T.: *The Theory of Money* (Oxford, 2nd edn. 1971).

Niehuss, Merith: *Arbeiterschaft in Krieg und Inflation. Soziale Schichtung und Lage der Arbeiter in Augsburg und Linz 1910 bis 1925* (Berlin/New York, 1985).

Nöll von der Nahmer, Robert: *Lehrbuch der Finanzwissenschaft, Bd. 2: Spezielle Steuerlehre* (Cologne, 1964).

Nordhaus, William D.: "The Political Business Cycle", *Review of Economic Studies*, 42 (1975), pp. 169–190.

Nordhoff, Karl: "Die Massnahmen der Reichsbank zur Verbesserung der Publizität, Liquidität und Solidarität der Banken", in *Untersuchung des Bankwesens 1933, I. Teil, Bd. 2* (Berlin, 1933), pp. 243–268.

Notzke, Johann (ed.): *Das Bankgesetz von 1924 nebst Satzung der Reichsbank, Privatnotenbankgesetz, Liquidierung des Umlaufs an Rentenbankscheinen, Münzgesetz*... (Berlin, 1924).

Nurkse, Ragnar: *The Course and Control of Inflation. A Review of Monetary Experience in Europe After World War I* (LoN Publication 1946 II A. 6) (Geneva, 1946).

Nussbaum, Arthur: *Die Bilanz der Aufwertungstheorie* (Tübingen, 1929).

Oberhauser, Alois: "Geld- und Kreditpolitik bei weitgehender Vollbeschäftigung und mässigem Preisanstieg", in Deutsche Bundesbank: *Währung und Wirtschaft*, pp. 609–642.

Oertmann, P.: *Die Aufwertungsfrage bei Geldforderungen, Hypotheken und Anleihen* (Berlin, 1924).

Papers Relating to the Foreign Relations of the United States 1922 (Washington, D. C., 1938).

Patschan, Herbert: "Die Entwicklung der Bankingtheorie in Deutschland. Ein dogmenkritischer Beitrag" (Diss., Freiburg, 1929).

Pedersen, Jørgen: "Some Notes on the Economic Policy of the United States during the Period 1919–1932", in H. Hegeland (ed.): *Money, Growth and Methodology. Essays in Honour of Johan Akerman* (Lund, 1961), pp. 473–494.

Petzina, Dietmar: *Die deutsche Wirtschaft in der Zwischenkriegszeit* (Wiesbaden, 1977).

Petzina, Dietmar and Werner Abelshauser: "Zum Problem der relativen Stagnation der deutschen Wirtschaft in den zwanziger Jahren", in H. Mommsen *et al.* (eds.): *Industrielles System*, pp. 57–76.

Pfleiderer, Otto: "Die Reichsbank in der Zeit der grossen Inflation, die Stabilisierung der Mark und die Aufwertung von Kapitalforderungen", in Deutsche Bundesbank: *Währung und Wirtschaft*, pp. 157–201.

Pieper, Werner: "Die Versorgung Deutschlands mit Brotgetreide während des Weltkrieges 1914/18 und der Übergang zur freien Wirtschaft in den folgenden Jahren" (Diss., Berlin, 1927).

Pilgrim, John D: "The Upper Turning Point of 1920: A Reappraisal", *Explorations in Economic History*, 11 (1973/74), pp. 271–298.

Pirlet, Otto: "Der politische Kampf um die Aufwertungsgesetzgebung nach dem Ersten Weltkrieg" (Diss., Cologne, 1959).

Plachetka, Günther: "Die Getreide-Autarkiepolitik Bismarcks und seiner Nachfolger im Reichskanzleramt. Darstellung mit Auswirkungen insbesondere während des ersten Weltkrieges" (Diss., Bonn, 1969).

Plenge, Johann: "Zur Diagnose der Reichsfinanzreform", *Zeitschrift für die Gesamte Staatswissenschaft*, 65 (1909), pp. 288–337.

– *Von der Diskontpolitik zur Herrschaft über den Geldmarkt* (Berlin, 1913).

Pohle, Ludwig: *Geldentwertung, Valutafrage und Währungsreform* (Leipzig, 1920).

– *Das Problem der Valutaentwertung* (Dresden, 1919).

Popitz, Johannes: "Die deutschen Finanzen 1918–1928", in *Zehn Jahre deutsche Geschichte 1918–1928* (Berlin, 1928), pp. 179–202.

Potthoff, Heinrich: *Gewerkschaften und Politik zwischen Revolution und Inflation* (Düsseldorf, 1979).

Prager, K. A.: "Goldmark, Rentenmark, Reichsmark" (Diss., Erlangen, 1926).

Preiser, Erich: *Nationalökonomie heute. Eine Einführung in die Volkswirtschaftslehre* (Munich, 8th edn. 1969).

Preller, Ludwig: *Sozialpolitik in der Weimarer Republik* (Stuttgart, 1949).

Preyer, W. D.: *Roggenpapiere und Roggensteuern* (Jena, 1923).

Prion, Willi: "Deutsche Kreditpolitik 1919–1922", *Schmollers Jahrbuch*, 47 (1924), pp. 163–205.

– *Die deutschen Kreditbanken im Kriege und nachher* (Stuttgart, 1917).

– *Inflation und Geldentwertung. Finanzielle Massnahmen zum Abbau der Preise. Gutachten erstattet dem Reichsfinanzministerium* (Berlin, 1919).

– "Kreditpolitik und Ruhrkampf (1923)", *Schmollers Jahrbuch*, 49 (1925), pp. 381–405.

– *Steuer- und Anleihepolitik in England während des Krieges* (Berlin, 1918).

Quante, Peter: "Lohnpolitik und Lohnentwicklung im Kriege", *Zeitschrift des Preussischen Statistischen Landesamts*, 59 (1919), pp. 323–384.

Ramhorst, Friedrich: *Die Entstehung der deutschen Rentenbank* (Berlin, 1924).

Rathenau, Walther: *Cannes und Genua. Vier Reden zum Reparationsproblem* (Berlin, 1922).

Referentenentwurf einer Denkschrift über die "Aufwertung", verfasst im Reichsfinanzministerium. Sonderbeilage zur deutschen Juristenzeitung, 1925, Heft 4 (Berlin, 1925).

"Die Reform der Reichsindexziffer für die Lebenshaltungskosten", *Wirtschaft und Statistik*, 5 (1925), pp. 159–163.

Rehn, Johannes: "Die Pläne zur Stabilisierung der deutschen Währung 1923. Eine Analyse des ökonomischen Wesens der Stabilisierungspläne der ausschlaggebenden Gruppen der Bourgeoisie und der Junker" (Diss., Halle, 1958).

Reichsarchiv: *Der Weltkrieg 1914–1918. Kriegsrüstung und Kriegswirtschaft. Bd. 1: Die militärische, wirtschaftliche und finanzielle Rüstung Deutschlands von der Reichsgründung bis zum Ausbruch des Weltkrieges* (Berlin, 1930).

Die Reichsbank 1901–1925 (Berlin, n. d.; 1925)

Renauld, Josef von: "Finanzielle Mobilmachung", *Bank-Archiv*, 4 (1904/05).

Renell, Erich: "Der Warenwechsel in Deutschland in der Geldentwertungszeit 1919–1923" (Diss., Berlin, 1926).

Reports of the Expert Committees appointed by the Reparation Commission. English Edition. Cmnd. 2105 (London, 1924). Reprinted as appendixes to H. G. Moulton, *The Reparation Plan.*

Respondek, Erwin: *Die Reichsfinanzen auf Grund der Reform von 1919/20* (Berlin, 1921).

Reulecke, Jürgen: *Die wirtschaftliche Entwicklung der Stadt Barmen von 1910 bis 1925* (Neustadt an der Aisch, 1973).

Ricardo, David: *On the Principles of Political Economy and Taxation. The Works and Correspondence of D. Ricardo ed. P. Sraffa, vol. I* (London, 1951). Original edn. 1817.

Richardson, J. H.: "Some Aspects of Recent Wage Movements and Tendencies in Various Countries", *International Labour Review*, 17 (1928), pp. 179–203.

Riensberg, Wilhelm: "Die preussischen Sparkassen im Kriegs- und Revolutionsjahre 1918", *Zeitschrift des Preussischen Statistischen Landesamts*, 60 (1920), pp. 139–140.

Riesser, Jakob: *Finanzielle Kriegsbereitschaft und Kriegsführung* (Jena, 1909; 2nd edn. 1913).

– *The German Great Banks and their Concentration in Connection with the Economic Development of Germany* (Washington, D. C., 3rd edn. 1911).

Ringer, Fritz K.: *The Decline of the German Mandarins. The German Academic Community 1890–1933* (Cambridge, Mass., 1969).

– (ed.): *The German Inflation of 1923* (New York, 1969).

Riss, Hans: *Leitfaden durch das Aufwertungsrecht* (Gladbach, 1926).
Rist, Charles: *History of Monetary and Credit Theory from John Law to the Present Day* (New York, 1940).
Ritter, Gerhard A. (ed.): *Entstehung und Wandel der modernen Gesellschaft. Festschrift für Hans Rosenberg zum 65. Geburtstag* (Berlin, 1970).
Robertson, D. H.: "C. Bresciani-Turroni, The Economics of Inflation...", book review in *Economica*, 5 (1938), pp. 233–235.
Roesler, Konrad: *Die Finanzpolitik des Deutschen Reiches im Ersten Weltkrieg* (Berlin, 1967).
Ruedorffer, Robert Axel v.: "Reichsbank und Darlehnskassen in der Kriegsfinanzierung 1914–1918" (Diss., Cologne, 1968).
Rupieper, Hermann J.: "Industrie und Reparationen. Einige Aspekte des Reparationsproblems 1922–1924", in H. Mommsen *et al.* (eds.): *Industrielles System*, pp. 582–592.
– *The Cuno Government and Reparations 1922–1923. Politics and Economics* (The Hague, 1979).
Sachverständigenrat zur Begutachtung der gesamtwirtschaftlichen Entwicklung: Jahresgutachten, various issues.
Salemi, Michael K.: "Adaptive Expectations, Rational Expectations, and Money Demand in Hyperinflation Germany", *Journal of Monetary Economics*, 5 (1979), pp. 593–604.
Sammlung von Aktenstücken über die Verhandlungen auf der Sachverständigenkonferenz zu Brüssel von 16. bis 22. Dezember 1920 (Berlin, 1921).
Sargent, Thomas J.: "The Ends of Four Big Inflations", in Robert E. Hall (ed.): *Inflation: Causes and Effects* (Chicago, 1982), pp. 41–97.
Sayers, Richard S.: *The Bank of England 1891–1944, vol. 1* (Cambridge, UK, 1976).
– *Central Banking After Bagehot* (Oxford, 1957).
Schacht, Hjalmar: *Die Reichsgesetzgebung über Münz- und Notenbankwesen* (Berlin, 1926).
– *The Stabilization of the Mark* (London, 1927). German original 1927.
Schaeffer, Luise: "Die Zweimonatsbilanzen der Grossbanken", *Zeitschrift für handelswissenschaftliche Forschung*, 13 (1919), pp. 102–123.
Schär, A.: "Aufwand- und Deckungsgrundsätze im schweizerischen Bundeshaushalt, insbesondere in der Kriegs- und Nachkriegszeit" (Diss., Zürich, 1930).
Scherf, Harald: "Inflation", article in *Handwörterbuch der Wirtschaftswissenschaften*, Bd. 4 (1978), pp. 159–184.
Schieck, Hans: "Der Kampf um die deutsche Wirtschaftspolitik nach dem Novemberumsturz 1918" (Diss., Heidelberg, 1958).
Schiffer, Eugen: *Deutschlands Finanzlage nach dem Kriege. Rede [des Reichsfinanzministers], gehalten in der Deutschen Nationalversammlung am 15. Februar 1919* (Berlin, 1919).
Schlegelberger, Franz and Rudolf Harmening: *Das Gesetz über die Aufwertung von Hypotheken und anderen Ansprüchen vom 16. Juli 1925* (Berlin, 1925).
Schlesinger, Karl: *Die Veränderungen des Geldwertes im Kriege* (Vienna, 1916).
Schmidt, Carl T.: *German Business Cycles 1924–33* (New York, 1934).
Schmidt, Fritz: *Internationaler Zahlungsverkehr und Wechselkurse* (Leipzig, 1922).
Schmitt, Wilhelm: "Die Diskontpolitik der Reichsbank während der Inflation" (Diss., Freiburg, 1926).
Schmölders, Günter: *Psychologie des Geldes* (Reinbek, 1966).
Schmoller, Gustav: *Umrisse und Untersuchungen zur Verfassungs-, Verwaltungs- und Wirtschaftsgeschichte bes. des Preussischen Staates im 17. und 18. Jahrhundert* (Leipzig, 1898; reprinted 1974).
Schneider, Erich: *Einführung in die Wirtschaftstheorie, Teil III: Geld, Kredit, Volkseinkommen und Beschäftigung* (Tübingen, 9th edn. 1965).

Schoenthal, Justus: *Papiermark, Rentenmark, Reichsmark. Ein Beitrag zur jüngsten Entwicklungsgeschichte der deutschen Währung* (Leipzig, 1925).
– *Rentenbank und Rentenmark* (Berlin, 1924).
Schötz, Hans-Otto: "Die Stabilisierung der Mark 1923/24 unter dem Einfluss der nationalen Interessen Frankreichs, Grossbritanniens und der Vereinigten Staaten von Amerika" (Diss., Berlin, 1985)
Schrage, Ulrich: *Einkommensverteilung und Inflation* (Bamberg, 1973).
Schreiber, Georg: *Die Not der deutschen Wissenschaft und der geistigen Arbeiter* (Leipzig, 1923).
Schröter, Alfred: *Krieg–Staat–Monopol 1914–1918. Die Zusammenhänge von imperialistischer Kriegswirtschaft, Militarisierung der Volkswirtschaft und staatsmonopolistischem Kapitalismus in Deutschland während des ersten Weltkrieges* (Berlin-East, 1965).
Schuker, Stephen A.: *The End of French Predominance in Europe. The Financial Crisis of 1924 and the Adoption of the Dawes Plan* (Chapel Hill, 1976).
– "Finance and Foreign Policy in the Era of the German Inflation. British, French, and German Strategies for Economic Reconstruction after the First World War," in O. Büsch and G. D. Feldman (eds.): *Historische Prozesse*, pp. 343–361.
– "Frankreich und die Weimarer Republik", in M. Stürmer (ed.): *Die Weimarer Republik. Belagerte Civitas* (Königstein/Ts., 1980), pp. 93–112.
Schultze, Erich: *Die volkswirtschaftlichen Gesichtspunkte unserer Aufwertung* (Frankfurt, n. d.).
Schumpeter, Joseph A.: *Business Cycles. A Theoretical, Historical and Statistical Analysis of the Capitalist Process* (New York, 2 vols. 1939).
– *A History of Economic Analysis. Edited from Manuscript by E. B. Schumpeter* (New York, 1954).
Schwabe, Klaus: *Deutsche Revolution und Wilson-Frieden. Die amerikanische und deutsche Friedensstrategie zwischen Ideologie und Machtpolitik 1918/19* (Düsseldorf, 1971).
Sering, Max: *Agrarkrisen und Agrarzölle* (Berlin, 1925).
Simon, Manfred: "La Valorisation des Obligations en Allemagne comme Conséquence de la Chute du Mark Papier" (Thèse, Paris, 1927).
Singer, Kurt: "Die deutsche Auslandsverschuldung", *Wirtschaftsdienst*, 7 (1922), pp. 660–661.
– "Die Autonomie der Reichsbank", *Wirtschaftsdienst*, 7 (1922), pp. 734–735.
– "Inflation", article in *Handwörterbuch der Staatswissenschaften*, Bd. 5 (1923), pp. 444–446.
Skalweit, August: *Die deutsche Kriegsernährungswirtschaft* (Stuttgart, 1927).
Skalweit, August und Hans Krieger: *Die Nahrungsmittelwirtschaft grosser Städte im Kriege. Beiträge zur Kriegswirtschaft, Heft 7/8* (Berlin, 1917).
Sköllin, Helmut: *Der Wert der Gehälter und Löhne in Hamburg. Statistische Mitteilungen über den Hamburgischen Staat, Nr. 13* (Hamburg, 1922).
Soecknick, Margarete: *Die Entwicklung der Reallöhne in der Nachkriegszeit, dargestellt an typischen Thüringer Industrien* (Jena, 1927).
Sommer, Friedrich: "Die Inflationssteuer" (Diss., Frankfurt/M., 1924).
Sontag, Ernst: *Hypothekengläubiger und Anleihebesitzer im Kampf um ihr Recht. Eine Kritik des Entwurfs eines Gesetzes über die Aufwertung von Hypotheken und anderen privatrechtlichen Ansprüchen sowie des Entwurfs eines Gesetzes über die Ablösung öffentlicher Anleihen* (Berlin, 1925).
Southern, David B.: "The Revaluation Question", *Journal of Modern History*, 51 (1979).
– "The Impact of the Inflation: Inflation, the Courts and Revaluation", in Richard Bessel and E. J. Feuchtwanger (eds.): *Social Change and Political Development in Weimar Germany* (Totowa, N. J., 1981), pp. 55–76.
Specht, Agnete von: *Politische und wirtschaftliche Hintergründe der deutschen Inflation 1918–1923* (Frankfurt/M., 1982).

Spiethoff, Arthur: *Die wirtschaftlichen Wechsellagen. Aufschwung, Krise, Stockung* (Tübingen, 2 Bde. 1955).
Spree, Reinhard: *Wachstumstrends und Konjunkturzyklen in der deutschen Wirtschaft von 1820 bis 1913* (Göttingen, 1978).
Stadthagen, Hans and Götz Briefs: *Die Preisprüfungsstellen. Beiträge zur Kriegswirtschaft, Heft 22/23* (Berlin, 1917).
Stenger, Hermann: *Die Aufwertung von Hypotheken und anderen Ansprüchen und die Ablösung öffentlicher Anleihen* (Munich, 3 Bde. 1925/6).
Stern, E.: *Der Höchstpreis. Eine systematische Untersuchung auf Grund der Erfahrungen der deutschen Kriegswirtschaft* (Munich, 1923).
Stern, Leo (ed.): *Die Auswirkungen der grossen sozialistischen Oktoberrevolution auf Deutschland, Bd. 4* (Berlin-East, 1959).
Sternberg, Fritz: *Der Niedergang des deutschen Kapitalismus* (Berlin, 1932).
Stobbe, Alfred: *Volkswirtschaftslehre I. Volkswirtschaftliches Rechnungswesen* (Berlin, 4th edn. 1976).
Stolper, Gustav, Karl Häuser and Knut Borchardt: *The German Economy: 1879 to the Present* (London, 1967); original edn. 1940.
Ströll, Moritz: "Über das deutsche Geldwesen im Kriegsfall", *Schmollers Jahrbuch*, 23 (1899).
Strutz, G.: "Die Reichssteuerpolitik der Nachkriegszeit", *Zeitschrift für die Gesamte Staatswissenschaft*, 78 (1924), pp. 631 ff.
Stucken, Rudolf: *Deutsche Geld- und Kreditpolitik 1914–1963* (Tübingen, 3rd edn. 1963).
Svennilson, Ingvar: *Growth and Stagnation in the European Economy* [United Nations Economic Commisssion for Europe] (Geneva, 1954).
Tardieu, André: *La Paix* (Paris, 1921).
Die Tarifverträge im Deutschen Reich am 1.1.27. Reichsarbeitsblatt, Sonderheft 43 (Berlin, 1928).
Temin, Peter: *Did Monetary Forces Cause the Great Depression?* (New York, 1976).
Temperley, H. W. V. (ed.): *A History of the Peace Conference of Paris*, 6 vols. (London, 1920–24).
Terhalle, Fritz: "Geschichte der deutschen öffentlichen Finanzwirtschaft vom Beginn des 19. Jahrhunderts bis zum Schlusse des zweiten Weltkrieges", in *Handbuch der Finanzwissenschaft*, 2nd. edn., Bd. 1 (1952), pp. 273–326.
– "Zum Inflationsproblem der Übergangswirtschaft", *Bank-Archiv*, 18 (1918/19), pp. 91–95.
Die Teuerung in Hamburg. Untersuchungen über die Lebenshaltung der hamburgischen Bevölkerung nach dem Kriege. Statistische Mitteilungen über den hamburgischen Staat, Nr. 12 (Hamburg, 1921).
"Die Teuerungsstatistik im Reich", *Vierteljahrshefte zur Statistik des Deutschen Reichs*, 29 (1920), Heft 3, pp. 65–84.
"Teuerungsstatistik und Reichsindexziffer", *Vierteljahrshefte zur Statistik des Deutschen Reichs*, 32 (1923), Heft 1, pp. 33–41.
Thelwall, J. W. F. and C. J. Kavanagh: *Report on the Economic and Financial Conditions in Germany to March 1922* (London, 1922).
Thieme, H. Jörg: "Inflation in den westlichen Marktwirtschaften und östlichen Planwirtschaften", *List Forum*, 9 (1977/78), pp. 290–309.
Thieß, Karl: *Höchstpreispolitik. Beiträge zur Kriegswirtschaft, Heft 1* (Berlin, 1916).
Trachtenberg, Marc: "Reparation at the Paris Peace Conference", *Journal of Modern History*, 51 (1979), pp. 24–55.
– *Reparation in World Politics. France and European Economic Diplomacy, 1916–1923* (New York, 1980).
Trevithick, James A. and Charles Mulvey: *The Economics of Inflation* (London, 1975).
Ulrich, Hans: "Der Währungszerfall, die Aufwertung und der Wiederaufbau bei den privaten

deutschen Lebensversicherungsgesellschaften", *Jahrbücher für Nationalökonomie und Statistik*, 125 II (1926).
Veit, Otto: *Grundriss der Währungspolitik* (Frankfurt, 3rd edn. 1969).
Verhandlungen des 5. Allgemeinen Deutschen Bankiertages (Berlin, 1920).
Verhandlungen der Sozialisierungskommission über die Reparationsfragen (Berlin, 3 Bde. 1921/22).
Verwaltungsbericht der Reichsbank (Berlin, 1916 and subsequent years).
Viner, Jacob: *Studies in the Theory of International Trade* (New York, 1937).
Vogel, Joachim: *Das Devisentermingeschäft* (Berlin, 1924).
Wagemann, Ernst: *Die Nahrungswirtschaft des Auslandes. Beiträge zur Kriegswirtschaft, Heft 9* (Berlin, 1917).
Wagemann, Gustav; *Aufwertung und Geldentwertungsausgleich nach der dritten Steuernotverordnung vom 14. Februar 1924* (Berlin, 1924).
Wagenführ, Rolf: *Die Industriewirtschaft. Entwicklungstendenzen der deutschen und internationalen Industrieproduktion 1860–1932. Vierteljahreshefte zur Konjunkturforschung, Sonderheft 31* (Berlin, 1933).
Wagner, Adolph: *Die Ordnung des österreichischen Staatshaushalts* (Vienna, 1863).
Wagner, Kurt: *Stationen deutscher Bankgeschichte. 75 Jahre Bankenverband* (Cologne, 1976).
Wallich, Paul: "Der Bedarf an fremden Devisen per spätere Termine", *Bank-Archiv*, 22 (1922/23), pp. 1–2.
Webb, Steven B.: "Government Revenue and Spending in Germany, 1919 to 1923", in G. D. Feldman *at al.* (eds.): *The Adaption to Inflation* (Berlin/New York, 1986).
Weber, Alfred: "Die Not der geistigen Arbeiter", in *Die Zukunft der Sozialpolitik, mit Beiträgen von L. Brentano u.a. Schriften des Vereins für Socialpolitik, Bd. 163* (Munich, 1923), pp. 165–184.
Weber Wilhelm: "Chronik der deutschen Agrarpolitik 1914–1932", in Fritz Beckmann *et al.* (eds.): *Deutsche Agrarpolitik im Rahmen der inneren und äußeren Wirtschaftspolitik, Teil II* (Berlin, 1932).
Wehinger, A.: "Die praktischen Regelungsversuche der Aufwertungsfrage, insbes. in der Zeit nach der Markstabilisierung" (Diss., Heidelberg, 1927).
Weill, Carl: "Betrachtungen zum Devalvationsproblem", *Bank-Archiv*, 19 (1919/20), pp. 183–185.
Weill-Raynal, Etienne: *Les Réparations Allemandes et la France* (Paris, 3 vols. 1947).
Whale, P. Barret: *Joint Stock Banking in Germany. A Study of German Credit Banks before and after the War* (London, 1930).
Wheeler-Bennett, John W. and Hugh Latimer: *Information on the Reparation Settlement. Being the Background and History of the Young Plan and the Hague Agreements 1929–1930* (London, 1930).
Wicker, Elmus R.: *Federal Reserve Monetary Policy 1917–1933* (New York, 1966).
Wiedenfeld, Kurt: *Die Organisation der Kriegsrohstoffbewirtschaftung im Weltkrieg* (Hamburg, 1936).
Wiedfeldt, Otto: *Die Bewirtschaftung von Korn, Mehl und Brot im Deutschen Reiche, ihre Entstehung und ihre Grundzüge. Beiträge zur Kriegswirtschaft, Heft 50/53* (Berlin, 1919).
Will, Rudolf: *Die schwebenden Schulden der europäischen Grosstaaten* (Tübingen, 1921).
Williams, John M.: "German Foreign Trade and the Reparation Payments", *Quarterly Journal of Economics*, 36 (1922), pp. 488 ff.
Williamson, John G.: *Karl Helfferich 1872–1924. Economist, Financier, Politician* (Princeton, 1971).
Winkler, Heinrich August: *Mittelstand, Demokratie und Nationalsozialismus. Die politische Entwicklung von Handwerk und Kleinhandel in der Weimarer Republik* (Cologne, 1972).
– *Von der Revolution zur Stabilisierung. Arbeiter und Arbeiterbewegung in der Weimarer Republik 1918 bis 1924* (Berlin, 1984).
Winkler, Wilhelm: "Volksvermögen", article in *Handwörterbuch der Staatswissenschaften*, Bd. 8 (1928), pp. 770–786.

Winnewisser, Georg: *Die Aufwertung der Industrieobligationen. Eine wirtschaftliche Untersuchung* (Karlsruhe, 1927).

"Die Wirkungen der Geldentwertung auf die Gehälter der Beamten und Staatsangestellten in den Jahren 1919 bis 1923", *Hamburger Statistische Monatsberichte* (1924), pp. 77–80.

Wissell, Rudolf: "Die Lebenshaltung der deutschen Arbeiterschaft seit dem Kriege", in *Deutschland. Jahrbuch für das deutsche Volk, hrsg. v. W. Külz, Bd. 1* (Leipzig, 1927), pp. 164–172.

Witt, Peter-Christian: *Die Finanzpolitik des Deutschen Reiches von 1903 bis 1913* (Lübeck, 1970).

– "Finanzpolitik und sozialer Wandel in Krieg und Inflation 1918–1924", in H. Mommsen *et al.* (eds.): *Industrielles System*, pp. 395–425.

– *Die Finanz- und Wirtschaftspolitik des Deutschen Reiches 1918–1924. Wohlfahrtsstaat und Demokratie am Anfang der Weimarer Republik.* Forthcoming.

– "Inflation, Wohnungszwangswirtschaft und Hauszinssteuer", in Lutz Niethammer (ed.): *Wohnen im Wandel* (Wuppertal, 1979), pp. 385–407.

– "Tax Policies, Tax Assessment and Inflation: Toward a Sociology of Public Finances in the German Inflation 1914–1923", in Nathan Schmukler and Edward Marcus (eds.): *Inflation Through the Ages: Economic, Social, Psychological and Historical Aspects* (New York, 1983), pp. 450–472.

Wörterbuch der Volkswirtschaft: see Elster, L. (ed.).

Wolf, F.: "Rentenbank und Markstabilisierung" (Diss., Erlangen, 1925).

Wolf, Hans: "Inflationswirtschaft und Kreditmarkt. Dargestellt an der Entwicklung der deutschen Kreditkrise der Jahre 1922–1923" (Diss., Frankfurt, 1925).

Wolf, Julius: *Die Steuerreserven in England und Deutschland* (Stuttgart, 1914).

Wolfsohn, John: *Die Aufwertung der Hypotheken und Wertpapiere nach der dritten Steuernotverordnung. Eine rechtliche und volkswirtschaftliche Darstellung* (Berlin, 1924).

Woll, Artur: *Allgemeine Volkswirtschaftslehre* (Munich, 5th edn. 1976).

Woytinsky, Wladimir: *Die Welt in Zahlen. 3. Buch: Die Landwirtschaft; 4. Buch: Das Gewerbe* (Berlin, 1926).

Wu, Chi-Yuen: *An Outline of International Price Theories* (London, 1939).

Wuest, Erich: *Der Vertrag von Versailles im Licht und Schatten der Kritik. Die Kontroverse um seine wirtschaftlichen Auswirkungen* (Zürich, 1962).

Wulf, Peter: *Hugo Stinnes: Wirtschaft und Politik 1918–1924* (Stuttgart, 1979).

Wulfsohn, L. und G. Wernlé: *L'Évasion des Capitaux Allemands* (Paris, 1923).

Wunderlich, H.: "Aufwertung", article in *Handwörterbuch der Staatswissenschaften*, Ergänzungsband (1929), pp. 24–34.

Wygodzinski, Willi: "Agrarpolitik", article in *Handwörterbuch der Staatswissenschaften,* Bd. 1 (1923), pp. 76–81.

Yeager, Leland B.: *Experiences with Stopping Inflation* (Washington, D.C., 1981).

Zehn Jahre deutsche Geschichte 1918–1928 (Berlin, 1928).

Ziercke, Manfred: *Die redistributiven Wirkungen von Inflationen* (Göttingen, 1970).

Zilch, Reinhold: "Reichsbank und finanzielle Kriegsvorbereitung des deutschen Imperialismus 1907–1914" (Diss., Berlin-East, 1976).

Zimmermann, Ludwig: *Frankreichs Ruhrpolitik von Versailles bis zum Dawes-Plan* (Göttingen, 1971).

Zimmermann, Waldemar: "Die Veränderung der Einkommens- und Lebensverhältnisse der deutschen Arbeiter durch den Krieg", in Rudolf Meerwarth *et al.*: *Die Einwirkung des Krieges,* pp. 281–474.

Zunkel, Friedrich: *Industrie und Staatssozialismus. Der Kampf um die Wirtschaftsordnung in Deutschland 1914–1918* (Düsseldorf, 1974).

"Zusammensetzung und Löhne der Arbeiterschaft sowie die Arbeitszeit während des Krieges", *Reichsarbeitsblatt*, 17 (1919), pp. 618–623.

Zwiedineck-Südenhorst, Otto von: "Lohnstatistik", article in *Handwörterbuch der Staatswissenschaften*, Bd. 6 (1925), pp. 375–396.

4. Periodicals

Der Arbeitsmarkt 2 (1898).

Auszüge aus Presseartikeln [i.e. Excerpts from Articles in the Press], hrsg. von der Deutschen Bundesbank, 1978.

Die Bank. Wochenheft für Finanz-, Kredit- und Versicherungswesen, 12 (1919) and subsequent vols.

Bank-Archiv, 1 (1901/02) and subsequent vols.

Finanz-Archiv, 31 (1914) and subsequent vols.

Monatsberichte der Deutschen Bundesbank, 31, Nr. 4 (April, 1979).

Reichsarbeitsblatt, 11 (1913–14) and subsequent vols.

Die Sparkasse (1919) and subsequent vols.

Die Wirtschaftskurve mit Indexzahlen der Frankfurter Zeitung, 1 (1921) and subsequent vols.

Zentralblatt für die gesamte Unterrichtsverwaltung in Preussen (1913) and subsequent vols.

Index of Subjects

Index of Persons